THE
INTERNATIONAL
PROCUREMENT
SYSTEM

Published by Dalston Press
204 11th Street SE
Washington, District of Colombia 20003

LIBRARY OF CONGRESS CATALOGING-IN-PUBLICATION DATA
Library of Congress Control Number: 2022918775
Jean Heilman Grier, 1947 Jan. 29-
The International Procurement System/Jean Heilman Grier
p. cm
Includes bibliographical references

ISBN: 979-8-9870892-2-4   *Paperback*
        979-8-9870892-0-0   *eBook*
        979-8-9870892-1-7   *Kindle eBook*

www.dalstonpress.com

Printed in the United States of America
10 9 8 7 6 5 4 3 2 1

THE INTERNATIONAL PROCUREMENT SYSTEM

SYSTEM

Liberalization & Protectionism

JEAN HEILMAN GRIER

DALSTON PRESS

For David

CONTENTS

PART ONE
GOVERNMENT PROCUREMENT IN
THE MULTILATERAL ARENA

PART TWO
US PROCUREMENT: BALANCING LIBERALIZATION AND PROTECTIONISM

PART FOUR
PROSPECTS FOR GOVERNMENT PROCUREMENT IN THE INTERNATIONAL ARENA

LIST OF TABLES

INTRODUCTION

Government procurement is both a highly important and a highly problematic element of the international trading system. It is important because governments purchase enormous amounts of goods and services, which generally account for 10% to 20% of a nation's gross domestic product (GDP).[1] Simultaneously, it is problematic because it is uniquely sensitive to the twin forces that shape international trade: liberalization and protectionism. Liberalization strives to open international markets for firms and other economic actors. Protectionism moves in the opposite direction and attempts to protect domestic markets from foreign competition. As governments purchase goods and services with their taxpayers' funds, they face strong protectionist pressure to spend that money on domestic goods and services. The international procurement system has developed a sophisticated set of agreements that open foreign procurement markets while allowing countries to balance these antithetical forces of liberalization and protectionism.

A country can choose to 'buy local' when it purchases domestic goods and services. A decision to keep purchases at home will be supported by domestic producers of goods and suppliers of

1. US Library of Congress, Congressional Research Service, *U.S. Government Procurement and International Trade*, by Andres B. Schwarzenberg, R47243 (2022), Figure 1, https://crsreports.congress.gov/product/pdf/R/R47243.

services. That decision will come under challenge if a country has producers and suppliers that seek market opportunities in other countries' government procurement markets and encounter 'buy local' obstacles there. If both countries maintain their protectionist measures, they enter in effect a standoff with each party asking the question, "why should I open my markets to your suppliers if you lock mine out of your procurement?".

One of the means for resolving such dilemmas is negotiations of agreements between countries. In such agreements, each party agrees to allow suppliers from the other country to participate in some portion of its government procurement, based on reciprocity and under an agreed set of principles and procedures.

There are three potential types of such agreements that could be negotiated: multilateral, plurilateral, and bilateral. Multilateral agreements cover all the participants in the international trading system. Plurilateral agreements involve only a subset of those participants, namely those willing to open their procurement to their counterparts. Bilateral agreements are entered between two countries or economies. An alternative to such agreements is unilateral action, which are measures taken by individual countries or economies to address domestic concerns relating to procurement issues that have not or cannot be addressed by international agreements.

Because of its political sensitivities, government procurement has never been embraced at the multilateral level. There has never been a multilateral consensus to treat procurement like other areas of trade. The only agreements reached at the multilateral level were to exclude procurement from the trading rules. The parties to the first international trade agreement covering trade in goods, the General Agreement on Tariffs and Trade (GATT), excluded procurement from its rules. Fifty years later, when multilateral rules on trade in services were established under the World Trade Organization (WTO), the government procurement of services was excluded from trade in services rules.

Unable to utilize multilateral agreements to expand the international procurement market, nations have turned to plurilateral agreements to accomplish this goal. These agreements are not imposed upon all nations but are limited to those willing to accept disciplines on their procurement in exchange for access to foreign procurement markets. Two plurilateral procurement agreements have been negotiated: first, the GATT Code on Government Procurement, and then the Agreement on Government Procurement (GPA).

The parties to those plurilateral agreements specified the procurement that they would open to one another. Opening procurement involved adhering to certain principles, with non-discrimination as the most prominent principle. Non-discrimination required the parties to treat the goods, services, and suppliers from the other parties in the same manner as domestic ones. They could not apply 'buy local' requirements or other domestic preferences in such procurement. Nor could they favor one party over another.

The international procurement system has also been shaped by both bilateral and regional free trade agreements (FTAs). These agreements often build upon the plurilateral procurement agreements by expanding procurement among select partners. In addition, they place procurement in the larger context of international trade. Unlike the plurilateral agreements, the FTAs are multi-issue agreements. Some FTAs have few, if any, procurement provisions. For those that do, the market access terms may be negotiated in the context of the full agreement. A procurement offer to one signatory may be matched by a concession in some other part of the trade agreement rather than a concession on procurement. FTAs have been negotiated throughout much of the world. At different times, both the European Union (EU) and the United States (US) have been heavily engaged in FTA negotiations. The 11-member Comprehensive and Progressive Trans-Pacific Partnership (CPTPP) is the most significant FTA with procurement commitments comparable to the GPA.

In addition to FTAs, specialized agreements have also been used to expand the global procurement market. The US has negotiated bilateral procurement agreements with Canada and the EU. It also negotiated a series of agreements with Japan, which were intended to address inequities that American companies and Congress saw in Japanese procurement markets.

Unilateralism characterizes government procurement measures in which countries or economies adopt measures focused on promoting or preserving domestic interests or protecting domestic markets. It plays a prominent role in the US approach to procurement and is seen in a broad array of 'Buy American' laws and policies. Other GPA parties, most notably the EU and Canada have adopted, or are considering adoption of, their own unilateral measures. While the unilateral measures have been constrained by GPA and FTA obligations, they may nonetheless have ramifications for the international procurement system.

Unilateral action is central to China's approach to international procurement. As a relative newcomer to the international procurement arena, China has yet to accept any international procurement disciplines that would curb its 'buy local' measures.

This book examines the multifaceted nature of the international procurement system, primarily but not exclusively, through the approach of the US. It presents its assessment in four parts. Part One begins by considering multilateralism and probing the reasons why such an approach has never been successfully applied to procurement. It then surveys the plurilateral procurement agreements.

Part Two provides a comprehensive look at the interrelationship of trade and government procurement in the US over 40 years, beginning with the implementation of the first international procurement agreement in 1981 and continuing through the procurement policies of 2020. It examines the FTAs that the US negotiated and implemented during this period from the perspective of their government procurement commitments. It also considers how the US balanced its market-opening objectives and the legal constraints aimed at protecting domestic procurement. It then turns to how the country began to pivot away from liberalization to protectionism under President Trump's 'America First' policy. Finally, this part explores how the US threat of unilateral action has, at times, shaped procurement negotiations. Specifically, it considers a series of negotiations between the US and Japan that sought to remove perceived barriers to Japan's procurement market.

Part Three explores the US retreat from FTAs. It contrasts the US strategy with the EU's ambitious FTA agenda. The EU has outpaced the US in the negotiation of FTAs. Since 2012, it has used FTAs to expand its access to the procurement markets of GPA countries. It has also negotiated broad procurement commitments with developing countries, an aim that has proven to be difficult for the GPA. This part also examines the CPTPP, including the US withdrawal from that agreement's predecessor, and its conclusion and implementation without the US. The CPTPP, a comprehensive regional trade agreement, may offer the most promise for the advancement of the international procurement system as it draws in GPA parties along with countries that are not parties to the GPA both within and outside Asia.

Part Four considers the prospects for the growth and development of the international procurement system. It examines the increasing use of unilateral measures by three original members of the plurilateral agreements: Canada, the EU, and the US, and considers the ramifications of those measures. Second, it explores the prospect for engaging the large and expanding procurement market of China in the international system. Finally, it reviews the prospects for the GPA, both in terms of expansion of its membership and maintaining its relevancy.

Together, these four parts give a detailed portrait of the international procurement system, the US role in that system, and the possible ways that this system may grow and develop.

A NOTE ON TERMS

This note explains several of the terms used in this book.

This is not a history but a book about the present state of the international procurement regime. However, it describes negotiations of trade agreements and other activities that happened in the past. In these sections, the book uses the past tense to convey the give and take of negotiations. In the remainder of the book, the present test is generally used to indicate that the provisions of agreements remain in force.

The name of several institutions changed names over the time period covered by this book. Most notably, the European Economic Community or the European Community became the European Union. This book uses the present name–European Union or EU– throughout to avoid confusion.

This book applies the term 'buy national' to laws, regulations, and policies that require or encourage government entities to give preferences to domestic goods and services in their procurement, discriminate against foreign goods, services, or suppliers, or acquire only locally made goods or locally provided services.

US domestic preference laws or domestic source restrictions are often referred to interchangeably as 'Buy America' or 'Buy American' laws or restrictions (or 'Made in America' under the Biden administration). 'Buy American' generally refers to restrictions, especially the

Buy American Act of 1933, that require federal agencies to purchase from domestic sources, while 'Buy America' often refers to similar statutes and regulations that apply to federal funds provided to nonfederal entities for infrastructure projects. In this book, 'Buy American' is generally used to refer to any domestic purchasing requirements, whether they apply to federal agencies or nonfederal entities.

The book generally refers to the WTO Agreement on Government Procurement or GPA and does not distinguish between the GPA 1994, which was established in 1994, and the GPA 2012, which amended the earlier agreement.

LIST OF FREQUENTLY USED ABBREVIATIONS

BAA	Buy American Act of 1933
BOT	build-operate-transfer contracts
Committee	WTO Committee on Government Procurement
CPTPP	Comprehensive and Progressive Trans-Pacific Partnership
DFARS	Defense Acquisition Regulation Supplement
DHS	US Department of Homeland Security
DoD	US Department of Defense
DoT	US Department of Transportation
EU	European Union
FAR	Federal Acquisition Regulation
FTA	Free Trade Agreement
FY	Fiscal Year
GAO	US Government Accountability Office
GATS	General Agreement on Trade in Services
GATT	General Agreement on Tariffs and Trade
GPA	WTO Agreement on Government Procurement
MFN	most-favored-nation
NAFTA	North American Free Trade Agreement
NTE	National Trade Estimate Report on Foreign Trade Barriers
NUTS	nomenclature of territorial units for statistics

PPPs	public-private partnerships
R&D	research and development
SDRs	Special Drawing Rights
SMEs	small and medium-sized enterprises
TAA	Trade Agreements Act of 1979
TPP	Trans-Pacific Partnership
UK	United Kingdom
US	United States
USMCA	US-Mexico-Canada Agreement
USTR	Office of the US Trade Representative
WTO	World Trade Organization

PART ONE

GOVERNMENT PROCUREMENT IN THE MULTILATERAL ARENA

INTRODUCTION

Any understanding of the international government procurement system must begin with the agreement now known as the WTO GPA.[1] Over its 40-year history, this agreement has become the preeminent procurement agreement, providing the foundation for bilateral and regional agreements that open procurement markets across the globe.

The primary purpose of the GPA is to open government procurement to participation by foreign suppliers under rules tailored to such procurement and designed to ensure it will be conducted in a non-discriminatory, transparent, and fair manner. It requires its parties to treat the goods, services, and suppliers of the other parties in the same manner as they treat their domestic counterparts and accord equal treatment to all parties.

The GPA, like its predecessor, the 1979 GATT Code, is an agreement based on accommodations that reflect the challenges of bringing government procurement into the international trading system. The first, and perhaps most important, accommodation is that the GPA is a plurilateral–not a multilateral–agreement. It only provides benefits to–and imposes obligations on–its signatories. It does not extend to all WTO members. Second, the GPA does not

---

1. WTO, GPA, accessed May 18, 2022, https://www.wto.org/english/tratop_e/gproc_e/gp_gpa_e.htm.

apply to all the procurement of its signatories. It only covers the procurement that each party specifies in the schedules to the agreement, and even that procurement is not open to all parties. With the application of the concept of mutual reciprocity, parties withhold specific procurement from other parties that do not offer comparable procurement. Hence, the GPA market access commitments are an accumulation of bilateral agreements between its parties incorporated into the agreement's framework.

CHAPTER 1

DEVELOPMENT OF PLURILATERAL PROCUREMENT AGREEMENTS

1. INTRODUCTION

In 1946, as the post-World War II international trading regime was starting to take shape, the US proposed that government procurement be treated as any other measure relating to trade in goods in the GATT. The idea was roundly rejected, as few countries were willing to take the politically difficult step of opening their procurement markets to non-domestic suppliers. Hence, government procurement was excluded from the GATT for more than 30 years.

The idea of bringing government procurement into the international trading system was revived in the 1960s. After negotiations that extended through the 1970s, several like-minded trading partners developed an agreement on government procurement. When not all GATT contracting parties were willing to sign the agreement, it was established as a plurilateral agreement with its benefits and obligations limited to its signatories. Rather than cover all the procurement of its signatories, the agreement covered only the purchase of goods by central governments. It required this procurement to be conducted in accordance with rules tailored to government procurement. The resulting agreement was the GATT Code, which came into force in 1981.

The GATT Code was renegotiated in the 1990s as part of the Uruguay Round of multilateral trade negotiations that established the WTO. The new agreement was designed to open more procurement and remove some of the limitations of the GATT Code. Its coverage expanded to include procurement by regional and local governments as well as by other entities. Furthermore, it extended to services and public works. Finally, it allowed individual parties to tailor their market access commitments to those of the other signatories based on reciprocity.

The GPA was renegotiated again in 2012. Its substantially revised text changed little of the operation of the agreement, but it reorganized and rationalized the text to facilitate the understanding and application of the agreement. It remained a plurilateral agreement under the WTO umbrella, as a fully mature document that has stood the test of time.

2. ESTABLISHMENT OF THE GATT AND EXCLUSION OF GOVERNMENT PROCUREMENT

The post-World War II effort to build an open, stable, and long-standing international economic framework resulted in the negotiations of the GATT, signed by 23 contracting parties at the end of October 1947 and implemented at the beginning of 1948. The GATT was an international trade agreement, not a formal international organization. It constituted the principal set of rules that governed the international trade of its contracting parties for 47 years until the creation of the WTO in 1995.

During the negotiations that established the GATT, the US proposed bringing the government procurement of goods under the same rules, including non-discrimination, as other trade measures, a proposal "which today would still be considered revolutionary."[1] Other delegations rejected it because it would have required them to alter or eliminate national laws that contained many 'buy national' preferences. Consequently, the GATT excluded the government procurement of goods from its national treatment obligations.[2] A similar exclusion was extended to services when multilateral trade rules were negotiated for trade in services.[3] Thus, government procurement remained outside international trading rules until the first international procurement agreement was implemented in 1981.

3. NEGOTIATIONS OF THE 1979 GATT CODE

3.1 Beginning Negotiations in the OECD

Soon after the Organisation for Economic Cooperation and Development (OECD) was formed in 1961, an OECD member's complaint about a US procurement practice began a process that eventually led to negotiations of a procurement agreement. In 1962, Belgium, joined by the United Kingdom (UK), brought a complaint against the US Buy American Act of 1933. It related to an increase of the Act's basic 6% preference to 50% for procurement by the

---

1. Annet Blank and Gabrielle Zoe Marceau, "History of the Government Procurement Negotiations Since 1945," *Public Procurement Law Review* 4 (1996): 77.

2. GATT, art. III:8(a). That article (National Treatment and Internal Taxation and Regulation) does "not apply to laws, regulations or requirements governing the procurement by governmental agencies of products purchased for governmental purposes and not with a view to commercial resale or with a view to use in the production of goods for commercial sale."

3. The 1995 WTO General Agreement on Trade in Services (GATS) excluded the government procurement of services from its national treatment, most-favored-nation treatment, and market access obligations. GATS, art. XIII:1.

US Department of Defense as a balance of payments measure. Belgium and the UK requested consultations with the US in the OECD Trade Committee, contending that it discriminated against purchases of foreign goods, even though there were no international rules on procurement. When the OECD Trade Committee met in 1964 to consider a working party's report on the complaint against the US, the US delegate agreed to the OECD's further study of the complaint and shifted "the focus of the investigation to a general review of government procurement procedures in all of the member countries."[4] Thus began the development of a government procurement code.[5]

The OECD Committee examining government procurement procedures found that practically all countries either maintained price preferences or discriminated against foreign suppliers or products in their procurement process.[6] While the US's application of price preferences under the Buy American Act was transparent, "most other countries used invisible administrative procurement practices and procedures" to award contracts to domestic suppliers.[7] Such practices illustrated the need to require both transparency of formal domestic preferences and procurement procedures or minimum standards that opened the window on the procurement process. Thus, the OECD Committee focused on establishing a framework (or code) in which the procedural steps of the

4. Morton Pomeranz, "Toward a New International Order in Government Procurement," *Public Contract Law Journal* 12, no. 2 (1982): 137.

5. For a detailed discussion of the negotiations on government procurement from 1946 through the Uruguay Round of multilateral negotiations, see Blank and Marceau, "The History of the Government Procurement;" Gerard De Graaf and Matthew King, "Towards a More Global Government Procurement Market: The Expansion of the GATT Government Procurement Agreement in the Context of the Uruguay Round," *The International Lawyer* 29, no. 2 (1995): 435–52; Pomeranz, "Toward a New International Order," 129–61.

6. Blank and Marceau, "History of the Government Procurement," 88–89.

7. Pomeranz, "Toward a New International Order," 137.

tendering process and the government's purchases would reflect the non-discrimination principle.[8]

In late 1967, the OECD Secretariat prepared draft guidelines. The US considered them inadequate because they would have required the elimination of specifically stated preferences, such as those in the US system, but would not have ensured open bidding and award procedures by other countries.[9] As a consequence, in 1969, the US proposed more binding procurement guidelines. It suggested that they be applied initially to the heavy electrical equipment sector because of its trade importance and later to other sectors. However, limiting disciplines to the electrical sector "proved impossible because of the difference in the degree of governmental ownership in that sector between the member countries."[10] Indeed, any sectoral approach was regarded as too narrow to allow for reciprocal trade advantages. That led to the conclusion that a list of entities would be needed.[11]

After the US submitted the draft guidelines, negotiations continued in the OECD for eight years until they were transferred–in December 1976–to the broader forum of the Tokyo Round of multilateral trade negotiations.[12] That transfer "was the only way to save years of efforts and negotiations because a wider base of negotiations was needed for countries to trade-off concessions."[13] In addition, because no government was prepared to open its procurement market unless other major trading partners did so, any

---

8. Blank and Marceau, "History of the Government Procurement," 89–90; Pomeranz, "Toward a New International Order," 137.

9. Pomeranz, "Toward a New International Order," 137–38.

10. Blank and Marceau, "History of the Government Procurement," 91; Pomeranz, "Toward a New International Order," 139–40.

11. Blank and Marceau, "History of the Government Procurement," 91.

12. The first six rounds of GATT trade negotiations dealt primarily with tariff measures. The Tokyo Round of Multilateral Trade Negotiations (1973-1979) was the first GATT negotiating round to address nontariff barriers.

13. Blank and Marceau, "History of the Government Procurement," 77.

agreement had to be based on conditional most-favored-nation (MFN) treatment. These constraints limited the advantages of the agreement to the countries undertaking its obligations.[14]

3.2 Tokyo Round of Multilateral Trade Negotiations

After the transfer of the procurement negotiations to the Tokyo Round, the GATT members agreed to negotiate government procurement in two stages: they would begin developing the text of an agreement and then move to determine the covered procurement. In developing the text, they sought to eliminate two types of discrimination. The first type was "clearly stated preferences" for domestic goods or suppliers, best exemplified by the Buy American Act and variants maintained by other countries.[15] To address these preferences, they required national treatment to be a fundamental principle of the procurement process.

The second form of discrimination was far harder to eliminate. It arose from the absence of procurement rules and the use of nontransparent practices and procedures allowing an agency to make a purchase by entering a contract with a domestic supplier without the knowledge of other suppliers. To address this type of discrimination, the negotiators devoted "the largest part of the Code" to providing rules and the means for ensuring that those rules would be applied openly and the procurement process would be carried out fairly and equitably.[16] Hence, they designed the code rules to establish transparency and discourage discrimination against foreign suppliers at all stages of the procurement process, including in determining the characteristic of the product

---

14. Pomeranz, "Toward a New International Order," 140–41; Blank and Marceau, "History of the Government Procurement," 92.

15. Pomeranz, "Toward a New International Order," 144.

16. Pomeranz, "Toward a New International Order," 144; Blank and Marceau, "History of the Government Procurement," 96.

to be purchased, tendering procedures, and evaluating contract performance. Those dual procedural and substantive aspects of the non-discrimination principle became permanent elements of procurement agreements.

In market access negotiations to determine the procurement covered under the agreement, the US wanted the agreement to apply to "all entities under the direct and substantial control of the government, and to provide a balance of concessions in terms of quantity (total value) and quality (types of products covered)."[17] To that end, it offered to bring the entire federal establishment under the new disciplines. However, other countries "were not prepared to subject the entire universe of such entities to the Agreement." The US accepted limiting the application of the procurement code only to the entities listed by each country, and as a result, it reduced its coverage to a list of federal agencies.[18]

In the negotiations, the US was particularly interested in gaining access for its suppliers to the procurement of its trading partners in the heavy electrical, telecommunications, and transportation sectors, which were subject to a "high degree of government incursion."[19] In contrast, most US entities in those sectors were private. Thus, their purchasing was essentially open to all suppliers and was governed by commercial considerations. The European Union (EU) refused to include these sectors in the agreement since they were excluded from the EU Directive governing the procurement of its member states. Until its members agreed to open their markets to one another, it was difficult for the EU to commit to cover these markets in an agreement with non-EU

---

17. US Congress, Senate, Committee on Finance, *Trade Agreements Act of 1979*, 96th Cong., 1st Sess., 1979, S. Rep. 96-249, 129.

18. Pomeranz, "Toward a New International Order," 152.

19. US Congress, *Trade Agreements Act of 1979*, 96th Cong., 1st Sess., 1979, S. Rep. 96-249, 128–31, 140–47.

parties.[20] When the EU and other trading partners did not offer entities in those sectors, the US redressed the imbalance in commitments by withdrawing its offer to cover entities that purchased comparable products, namely, the Departments of Energy and Transportation, the Department of Interior's Bureau of Reclamation, the Army Corps of Engineers, the Tennessee Valley Authority, and two sections of the General Services Administration (the National Tool Center and the Federal Supply Regional Office 9).[21]

Eventually, the negotiating parties reached a plurilateral agreement–the GATT Code. They limited its coverage to goods procured by central government entities listed in the Code Annex.[22] They further required that this procurement be subject to a common threshold, a monetary value at and above which procurement was covered. The US Senate reported that the GATT Code opened some $33 billion annually to international competition, based on the value of the offers of the principal participants: US ($12.5 billion), EU ($10.5 billion), Japan ($6.9 billion), and Canada ($1.25 billion). It concluded that the US and its major trading partners were "starting from a base of roughly comparable coverage" with several notable exceptions.[23] The Code represented "a first small attempt to bring a considerable part of international trade, hitherto left out of the scope of multilateral trade rules, under GATT rules," albeit on a plurilateral basis.[24]

---

20. US Congress, *Trade Agreements Act*, 142; Herbert C. Shelley, "The Trade Agreements Act of 1979 and Trade Reorganization," The World Trade Institute at the World Trade Center (Mar 26–28, 1980), 8; Blank and Marceau, "History of the Government Procurement," 105.

21. Pomeranz, "Toward a New International Order," 152; Shelley, "The Trade Agreements Act," 8.

22. See Chapter 9 for a discussion of the negotiations of a bilateral agreement between the US and Japan to address US dissatisfaction with Japan's coverage of its domestic telecommunications carrier under the GATT Code.

23. US Congress, *Trade Agreements Act*, 147.

24. Blank and Marceau, "History of the Government Procurement," 102.

3.3 Entry into Force

The GATT Code was signed in April 1979 and entered into force on January 1, 1981, as a plurilateral agreement with obligations and benefits that only applied to the 20 GATT contracting parties that signed it. They were Austria, Canada, the EU and its nine members,[25] Finland, Hong Kong,[26] Japan, Norway, Singapore, Sweden, Switzerland, and the US.[27] Israel was added as a party in 1983; Greece, Portugal, and Spain were brought under the Code when they acceded to the EU. Several countries, including India, Jamaica, South Korea, and Nigeria, participated in the Code negotiations but did not sign it. The GATT Code remained in effect for 15 years.[28]

4. 1988 REVISION OF THE GATT CODE TEXT

In November 1983, less than three years after implementing the GATT Code, its parties commenced negotiations to broaden and improve the agreement, according to the Code's built-in negotiating mandate. They initially focused on improving the text. They viewed such improvements as equally important, if not more so, as broadening the Code's scope and coverage.[29]

The parties completed the first phase of the GATT Code renegotiations in November 1986 and signed a Protocol of Amendments

---

25. The EU members were Belgium, Denmark, France, the Federal Republic of Germany, Ireland, Italy, Luxembourg, the Netherlands, and the UK.

26. The UK signed the GATT Code on behalf of Hong Kong. In 1986, Hong Kong became a GATT contracting party and began participating in the Code in its own right. Blank and Marceau, "History of the Government Procurement," 102.

27. USTR, "Determination Regarding Application of Agreement on Government Procurement and Waiver of Discriminatory Purchasing Requirements," *Federal Register* 46 (January 6, 1981): 1657.

28. Blank and Marceau, "History of the Government Procurement," 102.

29. Blank and Marceau, "History of the Government Procurement," 102.

in February 1987, which became effective a year later.[30] The amendments included:

- lowering the threshold for the coverage of procurement[31]
- broadening the concept of procurement to include leases
- prohibiting discrimination against locally established suppliers based on the degree of foreign affiliation or ownership
- increasing the minimum tendering period from 30 to 40 days
- awarding contracts based on criteria and essential requirements
- tightening offset provisions[32] and
- requiring publication of post-award notices within 60 days of a contract award.[33]

5. NEGOTIATIONS OF THE GPA 1994

Following the adoption of the 1988 Code amendments, its signatories embarked on negotiations to extend market access commitments beyond the Code's limited coverage of goods purchased by central government entities. They concurred that a new agreement should apply to all types of contracts, including service and construction contracts. It should also extend to two other categories of entities, namely, subcentral (regional and local) government

---

30. Pre-WTO Legal Texts, Tokyo Round Codes, accessed May 16, 2022, https://www.wto.org/english/docs_e/legal_e/prewto_legal_e.htm.

31. A threshold is a monetary value below which procurement is not covered under a procurement agreement.

32. The 1988 amended GATT Code provided entities "should normally refrain from awarding contracts on the condition that the supplier provide offset procurement opportunities." It further directed that in the limited number of cases where such requisites are part of a contract, the concerned parties "shall limit the offset to a reasonable proportion within the contract value and shall not favour suppliers from one Party over suppliers from any other Party." GATT Code, art. V:15(h).

33. Blank and Marceau, "History of the Government Procurement," 106–107.

entities and other entities. 'Other entities' were described as entities "whose procurement policies are substantially controlled by, dependent on, or influenced by central, regional or local government." Lacking a consensus on which 'other entities' should be covered, the negotiators compromised on All Other Entities which Procure in Accordance with the Provisions of this Agreement and let each signatory determine the entities to list, subject to acceptance by its negotiating partners.[34]

While the negotiations derived their authority from the GATT Code, they were conducted in parallel with the Uruguay Round of multilateral trade negotiations, launched in 1986. Nonetheless, "the main players in both sets of negotiations considered them intrinsically linked."[35] The US Trade Representative (USTR), Carla Hills, referred to government procurement as one of the most important aspects of market access in the Uruguay Round.[36]

5.1 Text Negotiations

The negotiations improved and expanded the overall Code text, more than doubling its length from nine to 23 articles. Three improvements were particularly of note. The addition of a bid challenge system was one of the most crucial developments.[37] This addition required the parties to "provide non-discriminatory,

---

34. Blank and Marceau, "History of the Government Procurement," 110–11, 113; De Graaf and King, "Towards a More Global Government," 441.

35. Blank and Marceau, "History of the Government Procurement," 115.

36. Blank and Marceau, "History of the Government Procurement," 114–15.

37. Ping Wang, "Coverage of the WTO's Agreement on Government Procurement: Challenges of Integrating China and Other Countries with a Large State Sector into the Global Trading System," *Journal of International Economic Law* 10, no. 4 (2007): 887–920; Stephen Woolcock and Jean Heilman Grier, "Public Procurement in the Transatlantic Trade and Investment Partnership Negotiations," in *Rule-Makers or Rule-Takers? Exploring the Transatlantic Trade and Investment Partnership*, eds. Daniel S. Hamilton and Jacques Pelkmans (London: Rowman & Littlefield, 2015), 238.

timely, transparent and effective procedures enabling suppliers to challenge alleged breaches of the Agreement." Such challenges had to be heard by a court or an impartial and independent review body.[38]

A second critical improvement was the prohibition of using offsets in procurement covered by the GPA (with exceptions for developing countries). It forbade entities from imposing, seeking, or considering offsets "in the qualification and selection of suppliers, products or services, or in the evaluation of tenders and award of contracts."[39] The third major improvement subjected all disputes that arose under the GPA to binding resolution under the WTO's dispute settlement mechanism, the Understanding on Rules and Procedures Governing the Settlement of Disputes.[40]

Beyond these three improvements, the agreement incorporated other revisions, such as a specific method of calculating the procurement value to determine whether the GPA covers it. It also included a provision stipulating technical specifications should be based on performance (rather than design) requirements and international standards (rather than national standards) and a section expanding information made available to prospective bidders.[41]

5.2 Market Access Negotiations

The US entered the market access negotiations with the perception that the GATT Code had failed to open foreign government procurement markets and the US "had drawn the short straw" in the

---

38. GPA 1994, accessed May 20, 2022, https://www.wto.org/english/docs_e/legal_e/gpr-94_e.pdf, art. XX.

39. GPA 1994, art. XVI:1. It described offsets as "measures used to encourage local development or improve the balance-of-payments accounts by means of domestic content, licensing of technology, investment requirements, counter-trade or similar requirements." GPA 1994, note 7.

40. GPA 1994, art. XXII.

41. De Graaf and King, "Towards a More Global Government," 437–40.

balance of Code benefits.[42] As a consequence, the US believed it "should get its fair share" under a new agreement.[43] Those concerns led Congress to enact Title VII of the Omnibus Trade and Competitiveness Act of 1988.[44] The law provided the president with leverage to persuade foreign governments to open their procurement markets by limiting their access to US government procurement if they refused to do so. Furthermore, Title VII required the president to report annually to Congress on barriers in foreign procurement markets until 1996. The report would identify countries that discriminated in their government procurement practices against US products or services or were not in compliance with the GATT Code (or its successor).[45] The president delegated this authority to the USTR.[46]

In the market access negotiations, the US and the EU, the two largest parties in the Code, came into sharp conflict. As its main objective in the negotiations, the US resumed its 1970s pursuit of access to EU telecommunications and electric utilities procurement. The US negotiators focused on the EU's adoption of a Utilities Directive in September 1990. The Directive brought utilities in the water, energy, transport, and telecommunications sectors into the EU's procurement regime. It subjected this procurement to rules that, among other things, eliminated the use of sole sourcing to

---

42. De Graaf and King, "Towards a More Global Government," 441.

43. De Graaf and King, "Towards a More Global Government," 441.

44. *Omnibus Trade and Competitiveness Act of 1988*, Public Law 100-418, *U.S. Statutes at Large* 102 (1988): 1107; codified in scattered sections of *U.S. Code* 19 (1988).

45. *Omnibus Trade and Competitiveness Act of 1988*, § 7002; US Congress, House of Representatives, Committee on Government Operations, *Foreign Government Procurement and the Unfair Treatment of US Companies*, 96th Cong., 1992, H. Rep. 102-1066, 2.

46. "Executive Order 12661 of December 27, 1988, Implementing the Omnibus Trade and Competitiveness Act of 1988 and Related International Trade Matters," accessed June 30, 2022, https://www.archives.gov/federal-register/codification/executive-order/12661.html.

procure from national suppliers.[47] With the adoption of the Directive, the EU had the authority to offer coverage of the utilities in those sectors in the negotiations.[48]

While the US generally applauded the Directive's adoption, it criticized one provision, Article 29, ultimately exercising its Title VII authority against that provision. Article 29 authorized EU utilities to discriminate against non-EU bids in two ways. First, it required utilities to apply a mandatory 3% price preference to EU products over foreign products when procuring equipment. Second, it allowed utilities to reject any bid with more than 50% foreign content (by value). The EU could waive these provisions if it negotiated a market access agreement that provided comparable access for its suppliers to the same utility sectors of its trading partners. Both the US and the EU aimed to achieve such an agreement, as the EU sought similar access to US utilities.

The EU also wanted unfettered access to US state and major city procurement and the removal of 'Buy American' restrictions[49] attached to federal funding provided to state and local entities.[50] It pressed the US to obligate the states to abide by the GATT Code obligations. It contended that 70% of government purchases in the US were at the state and local levels. It also argued that discrimination in state procurement practices effectively excluded EU firms from $200 billion in procurement awards each year.[51] The US

---

47. EU, Directive on the Procurement Procedures of Entities Operating in the Water, Energy, Transport, and Telecommunications sectors–EEC 90/531. Council Directive 90/531, *Official Journal of the European Union* (L 297). 1990.

48. USTR, *Fact Sheet, Title VII Early Review*, February 21, 1992, 4.

49. The restrictions are conditions attached by the US Congress to federal funds (grants or loans). They require the recipients to use American-made goods when undertaking infrastructure projects with the federal funds.

50. De Graaf and King, "Towards a More Global Government," 443.

51. James D. Southwick, "Binding the States: A Survey of State Law Conformance with the Standards of the GATT Procurement Code," *University of Pennsylvania Journal of International Law* 13 (1992): 57–58, 62.

wanted to offer access to state procurement in exchange for an EU commitment to open its national telecommunications and utilities markets to US companies.[52]

After commencing in 1988, the GATT Code negotiations had effectively stalled by early 1992 over the balance of EU and US offers. A bilateral agreement between them was needed to break the deadlock.[53] In a Title VII report to Congress in April of that year, the USTR cited discrimination by Germany, France, and Italy,[54] as well as the procurement provision in the EU's Utilities Directive. The report contended that the EU Directive would compound this problem by codifying informal 'Buy EU' policies. The US delayed imposing Title VII sanctions on the EU until January 1993, when the Utilities Directive would enter into force. The delay was intended to give the two sides time to complete negotiations of a reciprocal agreement on coverage of utilities that would enable the EU to waive Article 29 when it took effect.[55]

The US's threat of sanctions did not deter the EU from implementing the Utilities Directive, including Article 29, on January 1, 1993. Nonetheless, the two sides continued negotiations, reaching a partial agreement, a Memorandum of Understanding, on May 25, 1993. This two-year interim agreement was characterized by the USTR, Mickey Kantor, as essentially a "down payment" by both parties on a future, more ambitious agreement.[56] It provided comprehensive procurement coverage at the US federal and EU central

---

52. Scott Sheffler, "A Balancing Act: State Participation in Free Trade Agreements with 'Sub-central' Procurement Obligations," *Public Contract Law* 44, no. 4 (2015): 724.

53. De Graaf and King, "Towards a More Global Government," 441–43.

54. USTR contended that all three countries discriminated against foreign suppliers in purchasing heavy electrical equipment and that Germany and France were also discriminating in purchases of telecommunications equipment.

55. USTR, *Fact Sheet, Title VII Announcement*, February 1, 1993, 3; USTR, *Fact Sheet, Title VII*, April 26, 1991, 2.

56. De Graaf and King, "Towards a More Global Government," 443.

government levels for goods, services, and construction services. In this agreement, the EU maintained its GATT Code entity coverage, and the US added several entities that it had withdrawn from its initial GATT Code offer, including the Department of Transportation, the Department of Interior's Bureau of Reclamation, and the US Army Corps of Engineers.[57]

In addition, the US and the EU exchanged national treatment commitments regarding the electric utilities sector for two years. The US offered its federal electric utilities, namely, the Tennessee Valley Authority and five power marketing administrations of the Department of Energy[58] and agreed to waive the application of the Buy American Act for their procurement of goods. It also committed to the utilities' use of procurement procedures substantially equivalent to the Federal Acquisition Regulation (FAR).[59] In response, the EU agreed to waive the discriminatory provision in the Utilities Directive for procurement by its electric utilities. However, the two sides did not reach an agreement on coverage of the telecommunications sector, sub-federal procurement, or procurement by nonfederal entities with federal funds.[60]

Following the US-EU breakthrough with their 1993 interim agreement, the GATT Code parties restarted their talks and concluded a new plurilateral agreement on December 13, 1993, in parallel with the conclusion of the Uruguay Round negotiations. The agreement included MFN treatment for central government entities, with "almost no exemptions or differences of treatment."[61]

---

57. De Graaf and King, "Towards a More Global Government," 443–44.

58. They were Bonneville, Western Area, Southeastern, Southwestern, and Alaska.

59. The FAR applies to most federal procurement at the executive level. It does not apply to Congress or the judiciary.

60. De Graaf and King, "Towards a More Global Government," 444.

61. De Graaf and King, "Towards a More Global Government," 446, n. 47. An exception was the US's exclusion of Japan from the procurement of the National Aeronautics and Space Administration because Japan did not offer access to procurement by its space agencies.

However, the parties departed from MFN treatment with their first-time coverage of subcentral entities and other entities. Instead, they agreed to conditional MFN based on strict reciprocity. Rather than require all parties to open their procurement to all other parties, each party could condition its offer on obtaining access to equivalent procurement from another party. Reciprocity "was instrumental" in expanding the Code from a simple agreement covering central government entities to "a much more far-reaching one."[62] Had the signatories not overcome their initial resistance to the application of reciprocity and derogations from MFN, they would have had to scale down their offers to "the lowest common denominator in order to achieve balance."[63] As a consequence, they might not have reached an agreement on the new categories at all.

Notwithstanding the plurilateral agreement, the US and the EU had not reached a final bilateral package. They continued negotiations and concluded that package, initialing it on April 15, 1994, when the new plurilateral procurement agreement was also signed. In this bilateral pact, the US and the EU expanded upon their 1993 agreement by permanently covering the electric utility sector and subcentral government entities. The agreement also reconfirmed US coverage of all executive branch agencies, except the Federal Aviation Administration, and the EU confirmed coverage of the Council of European Union, the European Commission, and all central government authorities of its member states. The EU excluded procurement of air traffic control equipment since the US did not cover the Federal Aviation Administration.[64]

In this agreement, the US offered coverage of the procurement of 37 of its 50 states. The EU offered all subcentral government entities in its member states in response but scaled down its proposal

---

62. De Graaf and King, "Towards a More Global Government," 446.

63. De Graaf and King, "Towards a More Global Government," 446, n. 49.

64. De Graaf and King, "Towards a More Global Government," 449–50.

to only these entities' procurement of goods (not works or services) in order "to match the U.S. offer dollar for dollar."[65] As part of its offer, the US added procurement by the New York Power Authority, the St. Lawrence Seaway, the Port Authority of New York and New Jersey, and the Port of Baltimore to the 'other entities' category. It also agreed to waive the 'Buy American' restrictions on projects financed by the federal Rural Electrification Administration.[66] The US also reduced its threshold for federal government enterprises to $250,000.[67] With US coverage of three port authorities, the EU agreed to waive Article 29 of the Utilities Directive for procurement of US-origin supplies by EU ports. However, it excluded dredging services and procurement-related to shipbuilding since the US kept them out of its commitments.[68] The EU also did not provide the US with access to procurement by airports, despite its inclusion of several major US airports, because the US would not remove 'Buy American' requirements on federal funds for airport improvements.[69]

Part of the agreement reached by the US and the EU was not incorporated into the plurilateral agreement. Instead, several elements were reserved for a separate bilateral agreement, the 1995 US-EU Memorandum of Understanding on Government Procurement. This agreement was signed on May 30, 1995.[70] It provided the EU with access to procurement by several subcentral entities, including cities that the US did not offer to the other parties, on

---

65. De Graaf and King, "Towards a More Global Government," 449–50.

66. It was later renamed the Rural Utilities Service.

67. European Commission, "EU-US negotiations on public procurement," Press Statement, April 21, 1994, 2–3.

68. European Commission, "EU-US negotiations," 2–3.

69. De Graaf and King, "Towards a More Global Government," 449–50.

70. Agreement in the Form of an Exchange of Letters on Government Procurement between the European Community and the United States of America, May 30, 1995, https://ustr.gov/issue-areas/government-procurement/us-european-communities-1995-exchange-letters.

a national treatment basis.[71] The agreement did not include any EU commitments.

The GPA 1994 was estimated to open procurement "worth around US$350 billion annually, approximately a tenfold increase in the value of contracts open to bidding" under the GATT Code.[72]

The US and the EU were still unable to reach an agreement on procurement by telecommunications operators. The US rejected the EU's proposed application of certain transparency and tendering disciplines to privately owned US telecommunications companies. It argued that the purchases by these companies were already open to EU suppliers on a commercial basis. Furthermore, the EU 'balked' at an agreement covering its telecommunications sector because the US refused to lift all 'Buy American' restrictions on federally funded transit, highway, and airport projects.[73] The two parties could not make progress on such funding "because of its political sensitivity" in the US.[74] As a result, the EU continued to apply Article 29 of the Utilities Directive to US bids in the telecommunications, public transport, water, and airport sectors.

In the absence of a telecommunications agreement, the US imposed sanctions under Title VII on EU bidders. It prohibited them from participating in procurement not covered by an agreement (excluding purchases supporting US national security interests). The sanctions were applied simultaneously with the ratification of the 1995 US-EU agreement.[75] The EU responded with

---

71. For details of the agreement, see Chapter 5.

72. De Graaf and King, "Towards a More Global Government," 435–36.

73. USTR Press Release, "United States and European Union Reach Procurement Agreement," April 13, 1994, 1.

74. De Graaf and King, "Towards a More Global Government," 444.

75. "Federal Acquisition Regulation; Implementation of Memorandum of Understanding Between the United States of America and the European Economic Community on Government Procurement and Sanctions Imposed on the European Community," *Federal Register* 58, no. 102 (May 28, 1993): 31140.

countersanctions against US bidders.[76] Both parties maintained their sanctions until 2006.[77]

5.3 Conclusion of Negotiations

The procurement negotiations concluded with the signing of the GPA at a Ministerial Conference in Marrakesh, Morocco, on April 15, 1994.[78] This conference marked the end of the Uruguay Round negotiations and the signing of the Marrakesh Agreement Establishing the World Trade Organization (WTO Agreement) and its ancillary agreements. The GPA signatories regarded the outcome of their negotiations as an important part of the overall package signed in Marrakesh, even though the GPA was not included in the WTO's single undertaking.[79] Its commitments only applied among a comparatively small number of WTO members.[80] The GPA 1994 entered into force on January 1, 1996, for Canada, the EU and its 15 member

---

76. De Graaf and King, "Towards a More Global Government," 444.

77. USTR, "Termination of Sanctions Imposed on Certain Member States of the European Communities Pursuant to Title VII of the Omnibus Trade and Competitiveness Act of 1988," *Federal Register* 71, no. 39 (February 28, 2006): 10093, https://www.govinfo.gov/content/pkg/FR-2006-02-28/pdf/E6-2810.pdf; EU, Council Regulation (EC) No 352/2006 of February 27, 2006, repealing Regulation (EEC) No 1461/93 concerning access to public contracts for tenderers from the United States of America, L 59/7. Council Regulation (EC) No 352/2006 of February 27, 2006, repealing Regulation (EEC) No 1461/93 concerning access to public contracts for tenderers from the United States of America, L 59/7.

78. GPA 1994.

79. A single undertaking is a fundamental principle of WTO negotiations. It means that "[v]irtually every item of the negotiation is part of a whole and indivisible package and cannot be agreed separately." WTO, *How the negotiations are organized*, accessed June 30, 2022, https://www.wto.org/english/tratop_e/dda_e/work_organi_e.htm.

80. WTO, *Guide to the Uruguay Round Agreements*, Kluwer Law International, 247 (1999).

states,[81] Israel, Japan, Norway, Switzerland, and the US, and on January 1, 1997, for South Korea, which had not been a party to the GATT Code. Two Code parties–Hong Kong[82] and Singapore–did not sign the GPA 1994. They subsequently joined that agreement through accession.

The GPA 1994 remained a plurilateral agreement like the GATT Code. It is one of four plurilateral agreements that are part of the agreement that established the WTO "for those Members that have accepted them" and is binding on them.[83] These plurilateral agreements are listed in Annex 4 of the WTO Agreement.[84] This agreement commits the multilateral organization to provide the GPA (and the other plurilateral agreements) with the framework for their "implementation, administration and operation."[85]

5.4 US-Japan Negotiations

When the parties concluded negotiations of the GPA 1994, the US and Japan had not reached an agreement on bilateral coverage of subcentral government entities and government-related entities. The major outstanding issue was Japan's insistence on applying a threshold for construction services for those entities, which was three times higher than that of the US and other signatories. The two countries finalized their coverage negotiations

---

81. The EU's 15 member states were Austria, Belgium, Denmark, Finland, France, Germany, Greece, Ireland, Italy, Luxemburg, the Netherlands, Portugal, Spain, Sweden, and the UK.

82. On July 1, 1997, the British colony of Hong Kong was transferred to China and is now known as Hong Kong, China.

83. WTO Agreement, 1994, art. II:3.

84. The plurilateral agreements (other than the GPA) concerned specific trade sectors, with memberships comprised essentially of countries with a particular interest in those sectors. Of the three, only the Agreement on Trade in Civil Aircraft continues to operate. The International Dairy Agreement and the International Bovine Meat Agreement were terminated in 1997.

85. WTO Agreement, art. III:1.

and implemented their bilateral agreement on February 25, 1996. Japan maintained its higher threshold, and the US withheld access to the procurement of its entities responsible for the generation or distribution of electricity from Japan.[86]

6. NEGOTIATIONS OF THE GPA 2012

Within two years of implementing the GPA 1994, the parties embarked on a new round of negotiations under a built-in mandate. The mandate called for improving the agreement, extending its coverage based on mutual reciprocity, and eliminating the remaining discriminatory measures.[87] For several years, they focused on simplifying and improving the text. In July 2004, the WTO Committee on Government Procurement (Committee) adopted modalities for the coverage negotiations that recognized they would be largely pursued bilaterally. However, some elements were to be handled by the whole Committee, such as whether there should be further harmonization of thresholds or uniformity of entity coverage.[88] The modalities called for the parties first to exchange requests for improvements in the coverage of the other parties and then market access offers. The market access negotiations duly began with the exchange of requests at the end of 2004, followed by initial offers in late 2005 and early 2006.[89] Subsequently, the parties exchanged revised offers before submitting final offers.

---

86. Jean Heilman Grier, "Japan's Implementation of the WTO Agreement on Government Procurement," *University of Pennsylvania Journal of International Law* 17 (1996): 625.

87. GPA 1994, art. XXIV:7(b).

88. WTO, Committee on Government Procurement, "Modalities for the Negotiations on Extension of Coverage and Elimination of Discriminatory Measures and Practices," WTO Doc. GPA/79, July 19, 2004.

89. USTR, Trade Policy Staff Committee, "Public Comments for Market Access Negotiations Under the WTO Agreement on Government Procurement," *Federal Register* 69, no. 194 (October 7, 2004): 60219, https://www.govinfo.gov/content/pkg/FR-2004-10-07/pdf/04-22574.pdf.

In the negotiations, the US did not have the same strong interest in expanding market access as it had had in the GPA 1994 negotiations. Preparing for the coverage negotiations, the US sought public comments on the improvements needed in the existing coverage of the GPA parties.[90] It found that the US industry was generally satisfied with its access. The US's principal market access aims were expanding the coverage of information technology and eliminating the offsets maintained by Israel.

In contrast to its modest interest in the market access negotiations, the US played a leading role in revising the GPA text. US regarded it as an important opportunity to streamline the agreement and make it more easily understood by current and potential GPA parties and their suppliers. The US interest in the text negotiations could also be attributed to its simultaneous negotiations of the free trade agreements (FTAs) with procurement chapters, which enabled it to incorporate advancements in the GPA text into the FTAs.

6.1 Text Negotiations

In December 2006, the GPA parties reached a provisional agreement[91] on "the first major revision of the text of the GPA since its adoption in 1979."[92] They agreed to a complete overhaul of the GPA 1994 text. That included reorganizing provisions to reflect the order of the procurement process, clarifying obligations, removing ambiguities and redundancies, and defining key terms. The

---

90. USTR, "Public Comments."

91. WTO, "Provisional agreement on text of government procurement," December 8, 2006, https://www.wto.org/english/news_e/news06_e/gproc_8dec06_e.htm; WTO, Committee on Government Procurement, "Revision of the Agreement on Government Procurement as at 8 December 2006," GPA/W/297, December 11, 2006.

92. USTR, *Trade Facts, Provisional Agreement on Text of Revised Government Procurement Agreement*, December 2006, https://ustr.gov/archive/assets/Document_Library/Fact_Sheets/2006/asset_upload_file200_10225.pdf.

revision also incorporated up-to-date procurement practices, such as electronic procurement. It also added an arbitration process for resolving disputes over modifications to coverage and expanded transitional measures available for developing countries. The modifications, however, did not affect the GPA's fundamental principles of non-discrimination, transparency, and procedural fairness or the parties' rights and obligations.[93]

The parties' agreement on the text was provisional because it was subject to a mutually satisfactory outcome of the coverage negotiations and a final legal check.[94] Work on the legal check of the revised text was completed in 2007.[95] Even though the text was provisional, the parties agreed that it would be used as the basis for accession negotiations. The US noted the revised text would be particularly useful for China in preparing its initial GPA offer, which it had committed in a US-China forum to table by the end of 2007.[96]

The GPA parties also applied the provisional text in bilateral agreements. For example, in a 2010 bilateral procurement agreement, the US and Canada agreed that Canada's provinces would apply that text when they opened their government procurement to the US. Similarly, the EU and South Korea agreed to apply the provisional text when they implemented their FTA in 2011.

---

93. For discussion of the revised text, see Chapter 3 and Sue Arrowsmith and Robert D. Anderson, eds., *The WTO Regime on Government Procurement: Challenge and Reform* (Cambridge: Cambridge University Press, 2011).

94. The legal assessment was limited to "rectifications of a purely formal character that do not affect the substance or meaning of the text." WTO, *Report (2006) of the WTO Committee on Government Procurement to the General Council*, GPA/89 December 11, 2006, paras. 20 and 21.

95. "Revised Text of the Agreement on Government Procurement (Articles I–XXI) as of 13 November 2007," WTO Document negs 268, November 19, 2007.

96. USTR, *Trade Facts*.

6.2 Market Access Negotiations

After the GPA parties reached an agreement on the revision of the text, they aimed to conclude their market access negotiations by the spring of 2007. They ultimately missed that goal and spent another five years at the negotiating table attempting to resolve significantly different market access ambitions. The EU aimed for a substantial expansion of coverage, while the other parties were prepared to accept a more modest outcome. For example, the EU was disappointed that the offers of the other parties, in particular the US, did not match its own offer. It "made clear its dissatisfaction with the level of ambition reflected in other major Parties' offers" as it pushed for a significant expansion of their coverage and a rolling back of their exclusions and derogations.[97] Unless the parties improved their offers, the EU reportedly threatened to reduce its existing GPA commitments.[98]

In its initial offer, the US proposed the addition of the Social Security Administration, the Rural Utilities Service's financing of telecommunications projects,[99] and coverage of build-operate-transfer (BOT) contracts, a form of public-private partnerships (PPPs). It also offered to expand its coverage of telecommunications services from enhanced (value-added) services to all federal telecommunications services except for wire-based voice telecommunications services connecting to the public switched network. The US attached a condition to its telecommunications services offer that allowed its government agencies to exclude a supplier with more than 25% foreign government ownership from a procurement.

---

97. "EU Warns It Could Pull Back GPA Commitments Over SME Treatment," *Inside U.S. Trade*, March 2, 2007, https://insidetrade.com/inside-us-trade/eu-warns-it-could-pull-back-gpa-commitments-over-sme-treatment.

98. "EU Warns."

99. This was an addition to the Rural Utilities Service's existing commitment to not impose any domestic purchasing requirement as a condition of its financing of power generation projects.

In subsequent offers, the US added 11 more federal entities.[100] It also elaborated on the entities of seven states covered under the GPA by providing a list of their executive branch agencies.[101] It listed the entities for purposes of clarity and transparency, but it did not expand the states' coverage.

In a February 2010 revised offer, the US offered to all parties a concession that it had given to Canada as a result of their 2010 bilateral agreement and incorporated into its GPA schedule.[102] Under the offer, the US would have provided access to infrastructure projects undertaken by nonfederal entities under seven federal financing programs for a limited period (until September 30, 2010). For those projects, the US would not impose a domestic purchasing requirement on the iron, steel, or manufactured goods of the parties. Ultimately, the funding for the federal programs ended before the parties completed the market access negotiations. The US did not negotiate similar commitments with any other party.

The US withdrew its telecommunications offer when other parties were unwilling to reciprocate by providing expanded access to their telecommunications services. The EU accorded little value to the US telecommunications offer because the possible exclusion of telecommunications companies with 25% or more foreign government ownership would have eliminated most of its suppliers. Instead, the EU and several other parties extended their partial

---

100. The 11 federal agencies were the Advisory Council on Historic Preservation, Court Services and Offender Supervision Agency for the District of Colombia, Federal Energy Regulatory Commission, Federal Labor Relations Authority, Millennium Challenge Corporation, National Assessment Governing Board, National Endowment for the Arts, National Endowment for the Humanities, US Access Board, US Marine Mammal Commission, and the Transportation Security Administration (except for textiles and apparel products).

101. The seven states were Arizona, California, Kansas, Oklahoma, Tennessee, Utah, and Washington.

102. WTO, Committee on Government Procurement, "Modifications to Appendix I of the United States, Notification from the United States under Article XXIV:6(a) of the GPA," GPA/MOD/USA/7, February 18, 2010.

coverage of telecommunication services to full coverage but excluded the US from that broadened coverage.

Only a few parties were prepared to cover PPPs under the GPA. South Korea covered BOT contracts, and Japan covered its private finance initiative. The EU and several other parties offered work concessions on a national treatment basis. When most parties were not prepared to extend construction services coverage to PPPs, the US withdrew its offer to cover BOT contracts.

As the negotiations moved into their fifth year, the GPA parties felt pressure to conclude them before the WTO's Ministerial Conference in 2011 to demonstrate that the WTO could negotiate new agreements, even if they were plurilateral agreements. The GPA parties reached a political agreement on the revision only "hours before the official opening of the 8th Ministerial Conference" on December 15, 2011.[103] Although they did not add any new procurement categories, all parties expanded their coverage. For example, the EU offered comprehensive coverage of the central government entities of its member states, which included both existing entities and any established in the future. Of particular importance to the US, Israel agreed to reduce–and eventually phase out–its use of offsets.[104] The WTO Secretariat estimated that the negotiations expanded covered procurement by approximately $80 billion to $100 billion annually, bringing the total procurement covered by the GPA to an estimated $1.7 trillion.[105]

6.3 Conclusion, Ratification, and Implementation

In the negotiations, the parties disagreed on the final form of the agreement, whether it should be given legal effect as a new WTO

---

103. WTO, "Historic deal reached on government procurement," December 15, 2011, https://www.wto.org/english/news_e/news11_e/gpro_15dec11_e.htm.

104. For a more extensive discussion of the improvements in market access, see Chapter 4.

105. WTO, *What is the GPA?*, accessed May 16, 2022, https://www.wto.org/english/tratop_e/gproc_e/gp_gpa_e.htm.

agreement or as an amendment of the GPA 1994.[106] The EU and other parties preferred that it be treated as a new agreement and based their argument on the substantial revision of the text. The US argued that it should be implemented as an amendment because the text revision had not altered the parties' basic rights and obligations. Furthermore, the US would have found it easier to gain approval of a revision. For a new agreement, the US would likely have had to seek new authorizations from the 37 states covered under the GPA and face the risk that some states might refuse to participate. A new agreement might have also required the US to obtain congressional approval. Either would have likely delayed US ratification.

Beyond the US concerns, there was a potential issue that could have involved all WTO members. If the GPA parties treated the outcome of their negotiations as a new agreement, they might have had to add it to Annex 4 of the WTO Agreement. Such an addition would have required approval of all members of the organization.[107] Ultimately, the GPA parties reached a consensus to implement the GPA 2012 as an amendment of the GPA 1994.

The GPA revision was one of the few WTO achievements recognized at the WTO's 8th Ministerial Conference. The USTR hailed the revision as a demonstration of the WTO's ability "to reach agreements that strengthen and clarify international rules and expand the international trading system."[108] On March 30, 2012, the parties adopted the outcome of the negotiations in a Protocol

---

106. WTO, 2007 Report of the Committee on Government Procurement, GPA/92, December 13, 2006, para. 21.

107. WTO Agreement, art. X:9 provides: "The Ministerial Conference, upon the request of the Members parties to a trade agreement, may decide exclusively by consensus to add that agreement to Annex 4."

108. USTR, "United States Welcomes Opportunities for U.S. Suppliers Under Newly Revised WTO Government Procurement Agreement," December 15, 2011, https://ustr.gov/about-us/policy-offices/press-office/press-releases/2011/december/united-states-welcomes-opportunities-us-suppliers.

Amending the Agreement on Government Procurement, which incorporated the revised text and improvements in parties' market access schedules.[109] Two years later when the GPA 2012 entered into force, WTO Director-General Roberto Azevêdo pointed to it as further evidence that the WTO was "back in business."[110]

The GPA 2012 took effect on April 6, 2014, following ratification by the required two-thirds of its 15 parties: Canada; the EU; Hong Kong, China; Iceland; Israel; Liechtenstein; Norway; Singapore; Chinese Taipei (Taiwan); and the US. Later in 2014, Japan and Aruba ratified it, followed by Armenia in 2015 and South Korea in 2016. Five years later, Switzerland became the last party to ratify the amended agreement.[111] With Switzerland's implementation of the amended agreement, the GPA 2012 replaced the GPA 1994, and the coexistence of the two agreements ended on January 1, 2021.[112]

---

109. WTO, Committee on Government Procurement, "Adoption of the Results of the Negotiations under Article XXIV:7 of the Agreement on Government Procurement, Following Their Verification and Review, as Required by the Ministerial Decision of 15 December 2011 (GPA/112), Paragraph 5; Action Taken by the Parties to the WTO Agreement on Government Procurement at a Formal Meeting of the Committee, at the Level of Geneva Heads of Delegations, on 30 March 2012," GPA/113, April 2, 2012.

110. WTO, "2014 News Items, Government Procurement," April 2014.

111. WTO, "UK and Switzerland confirm participation in revised government procurement pact," December 2, 2020, https://www.wto.org/english/news_e/news20_e/gpro_02dec20_e.htm. Switzerland had delayed its ratification to complete internal legislative procedures to harmonize Swiss procurement legislation at the federal and cantonal levels. WTO, *Report (2020) of the Committee on Government Procurement*, GPA/AR/3, n. 12, December 3, 2020.

112. WTO, Report (2021) of the Committee on Government Procurement, GPA/AR/4, para. 2.1, November 12, 2021.

7. GOVERNMENT PROCUREMENT IN OTHER WTO FORUMS

While the GPA has advanced over four decades, government procurement disciplines in the international arena seem destined to remain a plurilateral endeavor. Efforts to develop multilateral obligations for government procurement have not succeeded. The failures were the initiatives to negotiate multilateral disciplines for the procurement of services and a multilateral agreement on transparency in procurement. The challenges of these two initiatives underscored the difficulties of developing multilateral obligations for procurement across the WTO.

7.1 GATS Mandate for Procurement Negotiations

The WTO's 1995 General Agreement on Trade in Services (GATS) exempted government procurement from its main market access provisions. As a result, when a WTO member opened a particular service sector to participation by suppliers of other WTO members under the GATS, it had no obligation to allow access to its government procurement of that service.[113] Nevertheless, the GATS contains language indicating its framers intended to extend the agreement to the procurement of services.

The GATS established a mandate for multilateral negotiations on the procurement of services.[114] It directed negotiations to commence within two years after it had come into effect. The WTO Council on Trade in Services, which oversees the GATS, established a Working Party on GATS Rules in 1995 to undertake several tasks, including the procurement mandate.[115] The Working Party

---

113. The exception was a GPA party that covered that service in its GPA commitments.

114. GATS, art. XIII:2.

115. It also conducted work on emergency safeguard measures and subsidies of services.

has made little progress on the mandate since the WTO members have disagreed on its scope. Some members held the view that negotiations could involve market access and non-discrimination commitments as well as transparency and other procedural issues. Other members disputed that interpretation and contended that the GATS mandate excludes negotiations on MFN treatment, national treatment, and market access.[116] As of late 2022, the Working Party had not met since 2016.

7.2 WTO Transparency in Government Procurement

In 1996, the WTO's 1st Ministerial Conference established a multilateral Working Group on Transparency in Government Procurement to conduct a study on transparency in government procurement practices and develop elements that could be included in an agreement. The Working Group examined 12 issues relating to a potential agreement on procurement transparency. These issues covered the following four broad subject areas:

(i) the definition of government procurement, the scope, and coverage of a potential agreement

(ii) the substantive elements of an agreement, including access to general and specific procurement-related information and procedural matters

(iii) compliance mechanisms and

(iv) issues relating to developing countries, including the role of special and differential treatment as well as technical assistance and capacity.[117]

---

116. WTO, *Government Procurement and the GATS*, accessed May 16, 2022, https://www.wto.org/english/tratop_e/gproc_e/gpserv_e.htm.

117. WTO, *Government Procurement and Doha Development Agenda*, accessed May 16, 2022, https://www.wto.org/english/tratop_e/gproc_e/gp_dda_e.htm.

Five years later, in 2001, at the WTO's 4th Ministerial Conference in Doha, Qatar, the WTO ministers launched a new round of multilateral trade negotiations, commonly called the Doha Round. They agreed that these negotiations would ultimately include multilateral negotiations on transparency in procurement. They also agreed that the modalities for those negotiations would be set at the 5th Ministerial Conference. Once they had established the modalities, the members would commence negotiations of a procurement transparency agreement. The ministers noted that negotiations would be limited to transparency aspects and would not restrict the ability of countries to provide domestic preferences.[118]

In undertaking its work program, the Working Group drew broad participation from the WTO membership, including many members that were not parties to the GPA. The US, the EU, Canada, and other GPA members were particularly involved in presenting proposals based on their GPA experience.[119]

Despite progress in the Working Group, the WTO members did not agree to launch negotiations on a procurement transparency agreement when the 5th Ministerial Conference convened in Cancún, Mexico. On August 1, 2004, the WTO General Council decided that "no work towards negotiations on [transparency in government procurement] will take place within the WTO during the Doha Round."[120] Although the Working Group has not been abolished, its work has been suspended since 2004.[121]

---

118. WTO, *Report (2003) of the Working Group on Transparency in Government Procurement to the General Council*, WT/WGTGP/7, July 15, 2003; Doha Ministerial Declaration, WTO Doc. WT/MIN(01)/DEC/1, para. 26.

119. Other active participants were Australia; Brazil; Chile; China; Chinese Taipei; Colombia; Cuba; Dominican Republic; Egypt; Hong Kong, China; Hungary; India; Japan; South Korea; Malaysia; Morocco; Pakistan; Peru; Philippines; Poland; Nigeria; Sri Lanka; Switzerland; Thailand; and Venezuela. WTO, *Report (2003) of the Working Group*, para. 6.

120. WTO, *Government Procurement and Doha Development Agenda*.

121. WTO, *Government Procurement and Doha Development Agenda*.

CHAPTER 2

GPA MEMBERSHIP

1. INTRODUCTION

The GPA is open to accession by any WTO member prepared to meet its terms and conditions. A member is expected to provide access to procurement that is comparable to the coverage of the parties and ensure that its procurement system is compatible with the GPA to gain approval of its accession. To make it easier for developing counties, especially least developed countries (LDCs), to join, the GPA offers special measures to facilitate their compliance with the agreement.

When the GPA entered into force in 1996, it had 23 members. In the following 25 years, it added 25 more, almost doubling its membership to 48. These 25 new members came from three sources. The enlargement of the European Union (EU) brought in 13 members. Accessions by former GATT contracting parties contributed another seven. Finally, five countries joined the GPA to fulfill commitments made during their WTO accessions. Even with these additions, the GPA roster still constituted less than a third of the multilateral organization's 164 members in 2022.

2. PARTIES AND OBSERVERS

GPA Parties: The 1979 GATT Code, the first plurilateral procurement agreement, had 24 parties. In 1996, when it was replaced by the GPA 1994, all 24 parties (except Hong Kong and Singapore) became parties to the agreement. Hong Kong and Singapore did not sign the GPA. In contrast, South Korea, which was not a GATT Code party, signed the GPA 1994, deferring its implementation for one year–until January 1, 1997. From 1996 through 2021, Singapore, Hong Kong, and 23 other WTO members joined the GPA.

In late 2022, the GPA had 21 parties comprising 48 WTO members. The EU and its 27 member states constitute one GPA party, even though the member states are individual WTO members. The GPA parties are:

> Armenia; Australia; Canada; the EU and its 27 member states (Austria, Belgium, Bulgaria, Croatia, Cyprus, Czech Republic, Denmark, Estonia, Finland, France, Germany, Greece, Hungary, Ireland, Italy, Latvia, Lithuania, Luxembourg, Malta, the Netherlands, Poland, Portugal, Romania, Slovakia, Slovenia, Spain, and Sweden); Hong Kong, China; Iceland; Israel; Japan; South Korea; Liechtenstein; Moldova; Montenegro; the Netherlands with respect to Aruba (Aruba); New Zealand; Norway; Singapore; Switzerland; Chinese Taipei (Taiwan); Ukraine; the United Kingdom (UK); and the US.

See Appendix 1 for a list of parties to the GATT Code and the GPA.

Observers: By submitting a request, any WTO member may become an observer to the WTO Committee on Government Procurement (Committee).[1] Observers may participate in Committee

---

1. GPA, https://www.wto.org/english/tratop_e/gproc_e/gp_gpa_e.htm, art. XXII:4.

discussions and obtain access to working documents. A WTO member does not incur any obligations as an observer. To attract more WTO members, the GPA 2012 did not incorporate the conditions for observers in the GPA 1994.[2]

In late 2022, 36 WTO members were observers to the Committee. They are listed below (with the year they became observers in parentheses):

> Afghanistan (2017), Albania (2001), Argentina (1997), Bahrain (2008), Belarus (2018), Brazil (2017), Cameroon (2001), Chile (1997), China (2002), Colombia (1996), Costa Rica (2015), Côte D'Ivoire (2020), Dominican Republic (2022), Ecuador (2019), Georgia (1999), India (2010), Indonesia (2012), Jordan (2000), Kazakhstan (2016), Kyrgyzstan (1999), Malaysia (2012), Mongolia (1999), North Macedonia (2013), Oman (2001), Pakistan (2015), Panama (1997), Paraguay (2019), Philippines (2019), Russia (2013), Saudi Arabia (2007), Seychelles (2015), Sri Lanka (2003), Tajikistan (2014), Thailand (2015), Turkey (1996), and Vietnam (2012).[3]

3. SPECIAL MEASURES FOR DEVELOPING COUNTRIES

Beginning with the GATT Code, the parties have made special and differential treatment available to developing countries[4] to encourage their accession. In both accession negotiations and GPA

---

2. The GPA 1994 required observers to comply with requirements relating to technical specifications, publication of notices, and the stability of their procurement regulations. GPA 1994, art. XVII:2.

3. GPA, *Parties, observers and accessions*, accessed May 20, 2022, https://www.wto.org/english/tratop_e/gproc_e/memobs_e.htm.

4. The WTO does not define developing countries. Any WTO member can self-designate as a developing country. WTO, *Who are the developing countries in the WTO?*, accessed May 22, 2022, https://www.wto.org/english/tratop_e/devel_e/d1who_e.htm.

implementation, the parties are directed to "give special consideration to the development, financial and trade needs and circumstances of developing countries." Upon request, the parties must accord special and differential treatment to LDCs.[5] They may also provide such treatment to any other developing country "where and to the extent [it] meets its development needs." This treatment is intended to allow developing countries more time to implement specific GPA obligations fully. Furthermore, it allows special measures to protect the sensitive elements of their business community while they adjust to competition from the GPA parties.[6]

In the GPA 2012, the parties expanded the special measures available to developing countries to make the agreement more attractive to such countries. First, they added measures that a developing country may apply for a specified period with the agreement of the parties. These measures include:

(i)   price preferences that are transparent and clearly described in the procurement notice

(ii) offsets, provided that such requirements are clearly stated in the procurement notice

(iii) the phased-in addition of specific entities or sectors and

(iv) temporary higher thresholds.[7]

In the second set of measures, parties may allow a developing country to delay the application of any specific GPA obligation other than the most-favored-nation obligation. The length of a delay in implementation can be five years after an LDC implements the GPA and up to three years for any other developing country. The

---

5. The United Nations established criteria for the designation of LDCs. United Nations, *Least Developed Countries*, accessed May 21, 2022, https://www.un.org/development/desa/dpad/least-developed-country-category.html.

6. GPA, art. V:1.

7. GPA, art. V:3.

transitional periods may be extended with the approval of the parties.[8]

Although the GPA allows an acceding member to delay the application of specific obligations, the new party may not delay its entire implementation of the agreement after its accession. In the accessions that the Committee approved since the GPA 2012 implementation, it has required the acceding country to provide access to the procurement covered under the GPA to all parties when its accession becomes effective. This Committee position precludes any delay by an acceding member in implementing its GPA obligations (except transitional measures) and allows the parties to participate in its procurement from the date of its accession. The Committee articulated this position for the first time in 2014 in Montenegro's accession.[9]

The GPA also requires each party to provide a developing country joining the agreement with the party's most favorable coverage. However, a party and the developing country may negotiate any terms necessary to maintain a balance of market access opportunities under the agreement.[10]

Since the GPA's implementation in 1996, the parties have approved transitional measures for only four developing countries: Hong Kong, Israel, Chinese Taipei, and Moldova. In 1996, the Committee permitted Hong Kong to delay its application of the bid challenge procedures for one year after it implemented the GPA.[11]

---

8. GPA, art. V:4.

9. WTO, Committee on Government Procurement, "Accession of Montenegro to the Agreement on Government Procurement, Decision of the Committee of 29 October 2014," GPA/124, November 3, 2014. The decision provides in paragraph 4: "[f]rom the date of entry into force of the [GPA] for it, Montenegro shall provide access to the procurement that it covers under Appendix I as set out in Attachment A to this decision to all Parties to the [GPA]."

10. GPA, art. XXII:2.

11. WTO, Committee on Government Procurement, "Accession of Hong Kong Decision," GPA/9, December 9, 1996, para. 3.

When Chinese Taipei became a GPA party more than a decade later (2009), the Committee approved its application of maximum offsets of 50% of the procurement of certain railway-related goods for 10 years, dating from its 2002 WTO accession.[12]

Israel has applied transitional measures for the longest period of any party. When it joined the GATT Code in 1983, it was permitted to maintain offsets. Under the GPA 1994, it was allowed to continue using offsets, subject to the requirement that it gradually reduced the offset level from 35% to 20% of the value of a contract. Israel met the condition on January 1, 2009. In the GPA 2012 negotiations, Israel agreed to phase out its offset regime for covered procurement. As a first step beginning in 2020, Israel committed to limit the entities that apply offsets to those listed in its Offset Note in GPA Appendix I.[13] It also agreed to limit those entities' use of offsets to procurement above 3 million SDRs and 20% of the value of the contract until 2023, when it promised to decrease the level to 18%. Israel committed to further reducing the entities that could apply offsets from 2025 and eliminating offsets entirely for procurement covered by the GPA in 2030.

Since expanding transitional measures for developing countries in the GPA 2012, the Committee has made sparse use of such measures. It has only authorized Moldova's application of higher thresholds for two years after its 2016 accession.[14] Three developing countries–Armenia, Montenegro, and Ukraine–joined the GPA 2012 without any transitional measures.

---

12. WTO, Committee on Government Procurement, "Accession of the Separate Customs Territory of Taiwan, Penghu, Kinmen and Matsu, Decision of the Committee of 9 December 2008," GPA/96, December 9, 2008.

13. GPA, Appendix 1, Israel, Annex 8.

14. WTO, Committee on Government Procurement, "Accession of the Republic of Moldova, Decision of the Committee of 16 September 2015," GPA/131, September 21, 2015.

4. FRAMEWORK FOR ACCESSIONS

All WTO members are eligible to accede to the GPA. A WTO member initiates its accession by submitting an accession application. The accession process has two primary aspects. The first centers on the candidate's negotiations with the parties on the procurement that it will cover under the agreement (market access commitments). The second is the parties' assessment of whether the procurement regime of the accession candidate is consistent with the GPA requirements.[15]

At the same time the WTO member submits its accession application, it is expected to respond to a Checklist of Issues for Provision of Information Relating to Accession to the GPA (Checklist of Issues)[16] and submit an initial market access offer. These documents provide the basis for negotiating accession to the GPA.

The Checklist of Issues seeks a description of the accession candidate's government procurement regime to facilitate the market access negotiations and the assessment of its compliance with the GPA. It asks the candidate to provide information on the following topics:

- its legal framework
- procuring entities
- provisions for non-discrimination (such as requirements to apply preferences for domestic goods, services, or suppliers and use of offsets)[17]

---

15. GPA, Parties.

16. WTO, *Checklist of Issues for Provision of Information Relating to Accession to the Revised Agreement on Government Procurement*, GPA/132, October 14, 2015, https://www.wto.org/english/docs_e/legal_e/rev-gpr-94_01_e.pdf.

17. An offset is "any condition or undertaking that encourages local development or improves a Party's balance-of-payments accounts, such as the use of domestic content, the licensing of technology, investment, counter-trade and similar action or requirement." GPA, art. I(l).

- measures for avoiding conflicts of interest and preventing corrupt practices
- procurement procedures
- domestic review procedures.

The Checklist of Issues also asks the candidate to identify any legal or administrative action needed to align its procurement regime with the requirements and ensure its full implementation of the agreement.

In its initial offer, an accession candidate specifies the procurement it proposes to open to the GPA parties. Its offer is expected to cover four areas of coverage: procuring entities (central, subcentral, and other entities); goods and services, including construction services; thresholds; and any exceptions to its proposed coverage. The offer should be organized in accordance with the annexes to Appendix I of the GPA, which set out the parties' market access commitments.[18]

After submitting its initial offer, the accession candidate engages in bilateral market access negotiations with the existing parties. The parties may request improvements in its offer, such as lowering thresholds, adding entities, expanding coverage of services, including construction services, and removing exclusions or restrictions. The candidate is expected to submit a revised offer based on such requests. This process may continue through multiple rounds of negotiations until the candidate reaches an accord with the parties on the scope of procurement it will open under the GPA.

In the bilateral negotiations, any GPA party or the accession candidate may negotiate reciprocity clauses that allow them to withhold access to certain procurement when the other does not provide comparable coverage. For example, when Montenegro joined the GPA, it withheld elements of its coverage from several

---

18. GPA, art. II:4.

parties, including the US.[19] Similarly, the EU did not provide access to certain procurement to Australia[20] and New Zealand[21] when they acceded to the GPA. In addition, developing countries may request the application of transitional measures, as described above.

The final step in the accession process is the parties' verification that the accession candidate's procurement regime complies with the agreement. If the candidate's procurement system does not conform to the GPA's principles and obligations, the parties will request changes to bring it into compliance and require the candidate to enact the necessary revisions before they approve its accession. Once both the market access negotiations and verification of compliance with the GPA are completed, the Committee adopts a decision inviting the member to accede to the GPA on the agreed terms. An accession becomes effective 30 days after the member deposits its instrument of accession with the WTO Director-General.[22]

5. SOURCES OF MEMBERSHIP

5.1 EU Enlargement

Over half of the growth in GPA membership between 1996 and 2021 was the consequence of the EU's addition of 13 countries to its Union. When the EU added new member states, it incorporated them into its GPA commitments on the same terms and

19. WTO, Committee on Government Procurement, "Accession of Montenegro to the Agreement on Government Procurement, Decision of the Committee of 29 October 2014," GPA/124, November 3, 2014.

20. WTO, Committee on Government Procurement, "Accession of Australia to the Agreement on Government Procurement, Decision of the Committee of 17 October 2018," GPA/CD/1, October 23, 2018.

21. WTO, Committee on Government Procurement, "Accession of New Zealand to the Agreement on Government Procurement, Decision of the Committee of 29 October 2014," GPA/125, November 3, 2014.

22. GPA, art. V:1.

conditions as existing member states. It accomplished this action through the GPA's modification process.[23] Unlike countries that joined the GPA on their own authority, the new EU members did not negotiate their market access offers directly with the GPA parties. With each expansion, the EU proposed modifications of its annexes to Appendix I to add the new member states, along with a list of their central government entities and indicative lists of the subcentral entities and utilities that they would cover. Any party could object to the EU's proposed modification under the modification procedures.

Since the establishment of the GPA, the EU added member states on three occasions. First, on May 1, 2004, it incorporated 10 new member states: Cyprus, Czech Republic, Estonia, Hungary, Latvia, Lithuania, Malta, Poland, Slovakia, and Slovenia. The GPA was applied to them on that same date, based on the Committee's approval of the EU's addition of them to its annexes.[24] Subsequently, Estonia, Latvia, Lithuania, and Slovenia, which had previously applied to join the GPA, withdrew their applications.[25]

The second expansion of the EU took place two years later with the addition of Bulgaria and Romania. On December 8, 2006, the Committee approved their inclusion in the EU's GPA annexes, effective January 1, 2007 (the date they became EU member states).[26] Lastly, in 2013, EU enlargement added Croatia as a member state.

---

23. The modification process is described in Chapter 4.

24. WTO, Committee on Government Procurement, "Decision Pursuant to Article XXIV:6(a) of the Agreement on Government Procurement, "Decision of 23 April 2004," GPA/78, May 4, 2004; WTO, Committee on Government Procurement, "Proposed Modifications to Appendices I, II and IV of the European Communities," GPA/MOD/EEC/1, March 26, 2004.

25. WTO, Committee on Government Procurement, *Report (July 2003 – November 2004) of the Committee on Government Procurement*, GPA/82, para.12, November 26, 2004.

26. WTO, Committee on Government Procurement, "Decision Pursuant to Article XXIV:6(a) of the Agreement on Government Procurement, Decision of 8 December 2006," GPA/90, December 11, 2006.

The Committee approved the proposed addition of Croatia to the EU annexes in a June 27, 2013 decision.[27]

5.2 Accessions by Former GATT Contracting Parties

Former GATT contracting parties that transitioned to the WTO when it replaced the GATT were the second source of GPA membership expansion. Seven of them acceded to the GPA, accounting for less than a third of GPA growth during the 25-year period. Two of them, Hong Kong[28] and Singapore,[29] were parties to the GATT Code but did not sign the GPA, as noted above. Therefore, when in 1997, each decided to join the GPA, they had to join through accession. The other former GATT contracting parties that acceded to the GPA were Aruba in 1996,[30] Liechtenstein in 1997,[31] Iceland in 2001,[32] New Zealand in 2015,[33] and Australia in 2019.[34]

---

27. WTO, Committee on Government Procurement, "Decision Pursuant to Article XXIV:6(a) of the Agreement on Government Procurement, Decision of 27 June 2013," GPA/118, June 27, 2013.

28. WTO, "Accession of Hong Kong."

29. WTO, Committee on Government Procurement, "Accession of Singapore Decision," GPA/6, October 9, 1996.

30. The Caribbean Island of Aruba is part of the Kingdom of the Netherlands. It obtained internal autonomy as a country within the Kingdom on January 1, 1986. WTO, "Application for Accession to the Agreement on Government Procurement, The Kingdom of the Netherlands with Respect to Aruba," GPA/IC/W/14, February 8, 1995; WTO, "Accession of Aruba Decision," GPA/2, March 5, 1996.

31. WTO, Committee on Government Procurement, "Accession of Liechtenstein Decision," GPA/3, March 6, 1996.

32. WTO, Committee on Government Procurement, "Accession of Iceland," GPA/43, October 9, 2000.

33. WTO, Committee on Government Procurement, "Accession of New Zealand to the Agreement on Government Procurement, Decision of the Committee of 29 October 2014," GPA/125, November 3, 2014.

34. WTO, Committee on Government Procurement, "Accession of Australia to the Agreement on Government Procurement, Decision of the Committee of 17 October 2018," GPA/CD/1, October 23, 2018.

The UK's accession to the GPA on January 1, 2021, represented a special case as it only reflected a change in its status under the GPA. The country was covered under the GATT Code and the GPA as an EU member state until its exit from the EU (so-called 'Brexit') when it became an individual GPA party. Hence, even though it acceded to the GPA, it is not counted in the 25-member expansion because it has always been included on the GPA roster.

The process that brought the UK into the GPA as an individual party began nine months after the June 2016 national referendum in which the UK voted to leave the EU. On March 29, 2017, the UK initiated the formal withdrawal process with a notification to the EU. Subsequently, the UK and the EU began negotiations on the terms of their disengagement and future relationship.[35] The UK's preparations for Brexit included applying for GPA membership "in its own right" in June 2018 and submitting an initial market access offer and responses to the Checklist of Issues. The Committee approved the terms of its accession in February 2019, noting that the GPA would cover it as an EU member state until its withdrawal from the EU or the expiration of any transition period.[36] On January 31, 2020, the UK formally left the EU and entered a one-year transition period during which it retained EU benefits and obligations, including GPA membership.[37]

On December 2, 2020, the UK submitted its instrument of accession to the WTO Secretary-General and was added to the GPA

35. For a more detailed discussion of the UK's accession to the GPA, see Robert D. Anderson, "The UK's New Role in the WTO Agreement on Government Procurement: Understanding the Story and Seizing the Opportunity," *Public Procurement Law Review* 30, no. 3 (2021): 159–70.

36. WTO, "UK set to become a party to the Government Procurement Agreement in its own right," February 27, 2019, https://www.wto.org/english/news_e/news19_e/gpro_27feb19_e.htm; WTO, Committee on Government Procurement, Decision, "Accession of the United Kingdom to the Agreement on Government Procurement in its Own Right," GPA/CD/2, February 28, 2019.

37. WTO, "The United Kingdom's Withdrawal from the European Union, Communication from the United Kingdom," WT/GC/206, February 1, 2020.

roll as an independent party on January 1, 2021.[38] When it became a party, the UK replicated the procurement that it covered under the GPA as an EU member, including the reciprocity restrictions.[39] It subsequently updated its GPA annexes, and the Committee approved them on May 31, 2021.[40]

5.3 Accessions to Fulfill WTO Commitments

Commitments by new WTO members to join the GPA after they become members of the multilateral organization constituted the third source of GPA expansion. From the WTO's establishment in 1995 through 2021, two-thirds (24) of the countries or economies that have acceded to it pledged to seek GPA membership as part of their terms of accession. Such commitments were reflected in the members' WTO accession protocols. Nine have fulfilled their promises and became GPA parties, five through accession: Armenia (2011), Chinese Taipei (2009),[41] Moldova (2016), Montenegro (2015), and Ukraine (2016). The other four entered the GPA by way of EU enlargement (Croatia, Estonia, Latvia, and Lithuania).

---

38. WTO, "UK and Switzerland confirm participation in revised government procurement pact," December 2, 2020, https://www.wto.org/english/news_e/news20_e/gpro_02dec20_e.htm.

39. The EU added a footnote to its annexes to Appendix 1, stating: "[a]ll the references to the contracting authorities and contracting entities of the United Kingdom currently contained in the European Union's Appendix I are obsolete."

40. WTO, "Certification of Modifications to Appendix I," WT/Let/1552, May 31, 2021.

41. Completion of Chinese Taipei's accession was delayed for several years due to issues concerning the nomenclature of its listed entities. *WTO, 2008 Report of the Committee on Government Procurement*, GPA/95, para. 16, December 9, 2008.

CHAPTER 3

GPA PRINCIPLES, PROCEDURES, AND INFORMATION

1. INTRODUCTION

The GPA is composed of two parts: the text and the parties' market access schedules.[1] The GPA text builds upon the cornerstone of non-discrimination and establishes fundamental principles and procedures that apply to the conduct of procurement covered by the agreement. The agreement does not impose a single procurement system on its parties. It recognizes that procedural obligations must be sufficiently flexible to accommodate the specific circumstances of each party. To that end, it sets out basic requirements or minimum standards designed to accommodate a variety of procurement systems and simultaneously ensure that procuring entities conduct covered procurement in a non-discriminatory, fair, and transparent manner.

---

1. GPA, https://www.wto.org/english/tratop_e/gproc_e/gp_gpa_e.htm. The market access schedules are detailed in Chapter 4.

In addition to establishing minimum standards for the conduct of procurement, the GPA also provides enforcement measures to ensure that parties adhere to their obligations under the agreement. Furthermore, it imposes a variety of reporting requirements on parties to guarantee the transparency and predictability of their procurement regimes.

2. FUNDAMENTAL PRINCIPLES

Non-discrimination: The cornerstone of the GPA is a non-discrimination obligation with two prongs. The first prong prohibits discrimination in favor of domestic goods, services, and suppliers. This national treatment obligation prohibits parties from applying 'buy local' requirements and preferences for domestic goods, services, or suppliers in GPA-covered procurement. It requires each party and its procuring entities[2] to treat the goods and services and the suppliers of any other party that are offering the goods or services of any party in a manner equivalent to their treatment of domestic sources.

The second prong, most-favored-nation treatment, is the general principle that all parties must be treated equally under the agreement. The GPA prohibits discrimination among other parties' goods, services, and suppliers. It requires that a party and its procuring entities must not treat one GPA party more favorably than another party.

The GPA also prohibits discrimination against locally established suppliers. The parties must not treat one locally established supplier less favorably than another supplier based on the degree of its foreign affiliation or ownership. Such suppliers also may not be discriminated against when they offer the goods or services of another party. It should be noted that the GPA's non-discrimination provisions do not apply to a supplier offering the goods or services of a non-GPA party.[3]

---

2. A procuring entity is an entity covered under a party's Annex 1, 2, or 3 to Appendix I of the GPA. GPA, art. I(o).

3. GPA, art. IV:1 and 2.

Prohibition of Offsets: The GPA also prohibits a party and its procuring entities from seeking, taking account of, imposing, or enforcing any offset.[4] The only exception is for a developing country that negotiates the use of an offset as a transitional measure when joining the GPA.[5]

Conflict of Interest: The GPA 2012 incorporated a conflict-of-interest obligation for the first time in any WTO agreement.[6] It requires procuring entities to avoid conflicts of interest and prevent corrupt practices in conducting covered procurement.[7] The GPA emphasizes the importance of avoiding such practices under applicable international instruments, such as the United Nations Convention Against Corruption.[8]

Rules of Origin: The GPA directs the parties not to apply rules of origin to covered procurement that is different from those applied in the normal course of trade.[9]

3. SECURITY AND GENERAL EXCEPTIONS

The GPA recognizes the need for certain exceptions to its application. First, the agreement provides an exception for a party's actions necessary to protect its essential security interests. It provides a second exception for measures necessary to protect public morals, order, or safety; human, animal or plant life or health; or

---

4. GPA, art. IV:6. An offset is "any condition or undertaking that encourages local development or improves a Party's balance-of-payments accounts," such as requirements to use domestic content, license technology, undertake investment, or engage in countertrade. GPA, art. I(l).

5. GPA, art. V:3.

6. Anderson, "The UK's New Role," 164.

7. GPA, art. IV:4(b) and (c).

8. GPA, preamble.

9. GPA, art. IV:5.

intellectual property. This exception also applies to measures relating to goods or services produced by persons with disabilities,
philanthropic institutions, or prison labor. Measures covered by
this second exception must not be applied in a manner that would
constitute a means of arbitrary or unjustifiable discrimination between parties (where the same conditions prevail) or a disguised
restriction on international trade.[10]

4. PROCUREMENT METHODS

The GPA provides for three types of procurement methods–open,
selective, and limited–but does not prescribe the use of a specific
method.[11] Nonetheless, it effectively sets open tendering as the primary or default method by placing conditions on the use of both
selective and limited tendering.

Open Tendering: Under the GPA, open tendering provides for the
broadest participation by allowing all interested suppliers that meet
the conditions for participation, described in the next section, to
submit a tender.[12]

Selective Tendering: The GPA permits the use of selective tendering to limit participation in a procurement to suppliers that
a procuring entity has determined are qualified, provided certain
requirements are fulfilled.[13] The requirements include inviting
suppliers to submit a request to participate in the procurement
in the notice of intended procurement. In addition, all qualified
suppliers must be invited to submit a tender unless the notice
indicates only a limited number of qualified suppliers will be

---

10. GPA, art. III.

11. GPA, art. 4:4(a).

12. GPA, art. I(m).

13. GPA, art. I(q).

permitted to submit tenders and sets out the criteria for selecting those suppliers.[14]

Limited Tendering: The GPA allows the use of limited tendering in which a procuring entity selects a specific supplier(s) without complying with most of the agreement's transparency and procedural requirements.[15] However, the GPA circumscribes its use. The circumstances in which it is permitted include when no tenders were submitted, no tenders met the essential requirements of the procurement, no suppliers requested participation in the procurement or satisfied the conditions for participation, or only a particular supplier could supply the goods or services, and there was no reasonable alternative. Other permitted situations are for additional deliveries by the original supplier, purchases on a commodity market, procurement of a prototype or a first good or service, or in cases of extreme urgency arising from unforeseeable events.[16]

When a procuring entity uses limited tendering, the GPA requires it to publish a notice of the contract award that includes a description of the circumstances justifying its use.[17] It must also prepare a report on each contract awarded under limited tendering and include the justification for its use and the value and kind of goods or services procured.[18]

5. TRANSPARENCY AND PROCEDURAL REQUIREMENTS

The GPA sets out basic obligations or minimum standards that apply throughout the procurement process.

---

14. GPA, art. IX:4–6.

15. GPA, art. I(h).

16. GPA, art. XIII:1.

17. GPA, art. XVI:2(f).

18. GPA, art. XIII:2.

Publication of Notices: The GPA requires procuring entities to publish a notice of intended procurement for each covered procurement (except where limited tendering is used).[19] The notice must include the information needed by a supplier to determine whether to pursue participation in the procurement. This information includes a description of the procurement, where the supplier may obtain tender documentation, the time limits for delivering the goods or services, the deadline for submitting tenders, and the conditions that a supplier must fulfill to participate in the procurement. The GPA 2012 added the requirement that such notices for central government entities must be accessible by electronic means, free of charge, and through a single point of access[20] to enable suppliers to access notices of intended procurement more efficiently.

The GPA provides for the publication of two notices to facilitate participation by suppliers. It requires the publication of a summary notice in one of the WTO languages (English, French, and Spanish) to enable suppliers to obtain essential information on an intended procurement so they may decide whether to pursue participation.[21] In addition, the agreement encourages procuring entities to publish notices of planned procurement as early as possible in each fiscal year to assist suppliers in preparing to pursue participation in their procurement.[22]

Conditions for Participation of Suppliers: The GPA recognizes that procuring entities must be able to determine whether a supplier would be able to carry out a procurement if awarded a contract. At

---

19. GPA, art. VII:1–2.

20. GPA, art. VII:1(a).

21. GPA, art. VII:3. The summary notice must include the subject matter of the procurement, the date for the submission of tenders, and where to obtain documents relating to the procurement.

22. A notice of planned procurement sets out a procuring entity's future procurement plans. It should include the subject matter of the procurement and the planned date of publication of the notice of intended procurement. GPA, art. VII:4.

the same time, to ensure fair treatment of suppliers, it requires entities to limit conditions to those "essential to ensure that a supplier has the legal and financial capacities and the commercial and technical abilities" to undertake the procurement. Entities must specify these conditions in advance. In addition, to avoid favoritism of local suppliers, the GPA prohibits procuring entities from requiring a supplier to have been previously awarded a contract by a particular party. It also directs entities to evaluate the abilities of a supplier based on its business activities both inside and outside its party's territory. However, they may require a supplier to have relevant prior experience when essential to meet the procurement requirements.[23]

The GPA 2012 expanded the grounds for excluding suppliers from participating in procurement. It permits a procuring entity to exclude a supplier for various reasons, such as bankruptcy, false declarations, significant or persistent deficiencies in performances under prior contracts, criminal convictions, professional misconduct that adversely reflects on its commercial integrity, and failure to pay taxes, provided the entity has supporting evidence.[24]

Registration System: The GPA permits a party to maintain a supplier registration system that requires suppliers to register and provide certain information. However, such systems must not be used to create unnecessary obstacles to participation in its procurement.[25]

Multiuse List: The GPA 2012 replaced the supplier lists used in its predecessor with a multiuse list. This is a list of suppliers that a procuring entity has determined to satisfy the conditions for participation in the list and intends to use more than once.[26] The GPA prescribes requirements for the use of such lists. For example,

---

23. GPA, art. VIII:1–3.
24. GPA, art. VIII:4.
25. GPA, art. IX:1–3.
26. GPA, art. I(j).

procuring entities must invite suppliers annually to apply for inclusion on the list and include all qualified suppliers.[27]

Information on Decisions: The GPA requires procuring entities to inform suppliers promptly of the acceptance or rejection of their requests for participation in a procurement or applications for inclusion on a multiuse list. It also directs entities to provide a written explanation of their decision (when requested by a supplier).[28]

Technical Specifications: The GPA prescribes rules intended to prevent procuring entities from tailoring procurement requirements to the capabilities of certain suppliers. For example, it prohibits procuring entities from seeking or accepting advice in preparing technical specifications that would preclude competition.[29] It also prohibits entities from requiring a particular trademark or trade name, patent, copyright, design, type, origin, producer, or supplier "unless there is no other sufficiently precise or intelligible way of describing the procurement requirements." In such cases, the agreement requires the entity to include words such as "or equivalent" in the tender documentation.[30]

The agreement also directs entities to set technical specifications, where appropriate, in terms of performance or functional requirements rather than design or descriptive characteristics. It further directs these entities to base such specifications on international rather than national standards.[31]

Environmental Considerations: The GPA 2012 clarified that technical specifications promoting the protection of the environment, or the conservation of natural resources might be used.[32] It also

27. GPA, art. IX:7–11.

28. GPA, art. IX:14-15.

29. GPA, art. X:4–5.

30. GPA, art. X:1.

31. GPA, art. X:2–3.

32. GPA, art. X:6.

added a provision that allowed entities to include environmental characteristics in evaluation criteria.[33]

Tender Documentation: The GPA requires procuring entities to provide suppliers with tender documentation containing all the necessary information for preparing and submitting responsive tenders to ensure a level playing field for all suppliers. This includes a complete description of the goods or services to be purchased, the conditions for participation, and all evaluation criteria. The agreement also requires an entity to make tender documentation available (on request) to any interested supplier and with sufficient time for tender preparation. In addition, entities must not provide information to a particular supplier that would give it an advantage over other suppliers.[34]

Modifications: The GPA allows entities to modify their procurement requirements or evaluation criteria before awarding a contract in that procurement. However, they must not use the modifications to advantage certain suppliers over others. Where a procuring entity modifies the procurement criteria or requirements or amends or reissues a notice or tender documentation, the GPA directs it to provide that information to all known participating suppliers. In cases where the entity does not know all the potential suppliers, it must disseminate information about the changes in the same manner as it published the original information.[35]

Time Periods for Tendering: The GPA requires a procuring entity to provide sufficient time for suppliers to prepare and submit requests for participation in procurement and responsive tenders. In setting time periods, entities may consider their own reasonable needs and the nature and complexity of the procurement.[36] The

---

33. GPA, art. X:9.

34. GPA, art. X:7–10.

35. GPA, art. X:11.

36. GPA, art. XI:1.

GPA prescribes a minimum 40-day period for tendering. This is the period between the publication of the notice of intended procurement (in open tendering) or notification that suppliers will be invited to submit a tender (in selective tendering) and the deadline for the submission of tenders. That period may be reduced to a minimum of 10 days where there is a state of urgency or a notice of planned procurement has been published within 12 months.[37] The tendering period may also be reduced when electronic procurement is used, as described below.

Procurement of Commercial Goods and Services: The GPA 2012 recognized the need for more expeditious procurement of commercial goods and services to reflect modern procurement practices.[38] Accordingly, it permits entities when purchasing such 'off-the-shelf' goods and services to reduce the tendering period to a minimum of 13 days, provided they publish both the notice of intended procurement and the tender documentation electronically.[39]

Negotiations: The GPA allows entities to use negotiations in conducting procurement in two circumstances. First, they can engage in procurement negotiations when they have indicated in a notice of intended procurement their intention to do so. In the second, they can employ negotiation when, based on their evaluation, "no tender is obviously the most advantageous." Entities may eliminate suppliers from negotiations only in accordance with published evaluation criteria. In addition, upon the conclusion of negotiations, the entities must provide the remaining participating suppliers with a common deadline for submitting new or revised tenders.[40]

---

37. GPA, art. XI:3.

38. These are "goods or services of a type generally sold or offered for sale in the commercial marketplace to, and customarily purchased by, non-governmental buyers for non-governmental purposes." GPA, art. I(a).

39. GPA, art. XI:7.

40. GPA, art. XII.

Treatment of Tenders: The GPA directs procuring entities to receive, open, and treat all tenders under procedures that guarantee the fairness and impartiality of the procurement process and the confidentiality of tenders.[41]

Awarding of Contracts: The GPA includes requirements to ensure that procuring entities do not award a contract to a supplier based only on unsubstantiated assertions of its ability to meet procurement requirements. The agreement stipulates entities consider only tenders meeting the essential requirements of the procurement from suppliers satisfying the conditions for participation when tenders are opened. The agreement further requires entities to have determined that the supplier can fulfill the contract. They must also establish that, based solely on the evaluation criteria, the supplier has submitted the most advantageous tender or the lowest price, where the price is the sole criterion. Entities may also scrutinize an abnormally low bid and verify that the supplier satisfies the conditions for participation and is capable of fulfilling the terms of the contract. The GPA prohibits procuring entities from circumventing procurement requirements by using options, canceling a procurement, or modifying an awarded contract.[42]

Contract Award Information: The GPA emphasizes the importance of the transparency of contract awards by requiring procuring entities to publish a notice of each award covered by the agreement within 72 days of its award.[43] The notice must include the name of the successful supplier, the value of the successful tender (or the highest and lowest offers considered), and the procurement method used. Entities must also inform participating suppliers of contract awards and explain to unsuccessful suppliers (on request) why their tenders were not selected.[44]

---

41. GPA, art. XV:1.
42. GPA, art. XV:4–7.
43. GPA, art. XVI:2.
44. GPA, art. XV1:1.

Maintenance of Documentation, Reports, and Electronic Traceability: The GPA stipulates that each procuring entities must, for at least three years after they award a contract, maintain documentation and reports on covered procurement and data that ensures the traceability of the conduct of procurement undertaken by electronic means.[45]

Nondisclosure of Information: The GPA prohibits a party from providing information to a particular supplier that might prejudice fair competition between suppliers. It also provides that a party is not required to disclose confidential information that would impede law enforcement, prejudice fair competition between suppliers, prejudice legitimate commercial interests, or otherwise be contrary to the public interest.[46]

6. ELECTRONIC PROCUREMENT

In the GPA 2012, the parties recognized the importance of using and encouraging the use of digital technology.[47] They added several requirements to ensure proper and consistent application of such technology. The GPA requires procuring entities to use information technology (IT) systems and software that are generally available and interoperable with other generally available IT systems and software to enable broad participation. It further directs that when entities conduct procurement electronically, they must maintain mechanisms that ensure the integrity of participation and tender requests submitted electronically.[48]

The GPA encourages electronic procurement by permitting procuring entities to shorten the tendering period when they use

---

45. GPA, art. XVI:3.

46. GPA, art. XVII:2.

47. GPA, preamble and art. II:1.

48. GPA, art. IV:3.

electronic means. It allows entities to reduce the 40-day tendering period by five days for each of the following uses of digital technology in a procurement: (i) publication of the notice of intended procurement; (ii) publication of all tender documentation; and (iii) receipt of tenders.[49] If entities use all three, they can reduce the tendering period to 25 days.[50]

Under certain conditions, the GPA permits entities to conduct procurement using electronic auctions.[51] In conducting such auctions, the entities must provide each participant (before the auction commences) with the automatic evaluation method for the auction. They must also provide participants with the results of any initial evaluation of a tender's elements when the contract is awarded based on the most advantageous tender.[52]

7. SPECIAL PROVISIONS FOR ANNEX 2 AND ANNEX 3 ENTITIES

When the coverage of the GPA 1994 was extended beyond central government entities, the parties adopted certain rules to provide the newly covered entities with more flexibility in conducting procurement than was accorded to central government entities. These rules apply to subcentral government entities covered under Annex 2 of the GPA's Appendix I and utilities and other entities "of more industrial or quasi-commercial character" covered under Annex 3 of the Appendix.[53]

---

49. GPA, art. XI:5.

50. GPA, art. XI:5.

51. GPA, art. I(f).

52. GPA, art. XIV.

53. Gerard De Graaf and Matthew King, "Towards a More Global Government Procurement Market: The Expansion of the GATT Government Procurement Agreement in the Context of the Uruguay Round," *International Lawyer* 29, no. 2 (1995): 437.

Instead of publishing a notice of intended procurement, the GPA gives Annex 2 and 3 entities two options. First, they may publish a notice of planned procurement that provides essential information on the procurement and invites interested suppliers to express their interest in the procurement.[54] Under the second option, these entities can publish a notice inviting suppliers to apply for inclusion on a multiuse list, provided the entities fulfill certain requirements.[55]

The GPA 2012 prescribed different electronic publication requirements for Annex 1 entities and Annex 2 and 3 entities. While it requires Annex 1 entities to make notices of intended procurement accessible by electronic means, it only encourages Annex 2 and 3 entities to do so. If they publish their notices electronically, the notices must be accessible through links in a free gateway electronic site.[56]

The GPA also applies special rules to the use of multiuse lists by Annex 2 and 3 entities. In contrast to the standard requirements, these entities do not need to allow suppliers to apply at any time for inclusion on a multiuse list or include all qualified suppliers on the list. Instead, they can reject a supplier's application if the entity has not had sufficient time to determine the supplier's eligibility for inclusion on the list.[57] In addition when these entities use selective tendering, they may fix the tendering period by mutual agreement with the qualified suppliers and, in the absence of agreement, set the tendering period to a minimum of 10 days.[58]

---

54. GPA, art. VII:5.

55. GPA, art. IX:12.

56. GPA, art. VII:1.

57. GPA, art. IX:13.

58. GPA, art. XI:8.

8. ENFORCEMENT PROVISIONS

The GPA provides two enforcement mechanisms to ensure that the parties properly implement the agreement and conduct procurement according to its principles and procedures. One is a government-to-government dispute settlement mechanism that operates at the international level. The other is a domestic review mechanism at the national level.

8.1 Dispute Settlement

When issues arise relating to the GPA's operation, its parties are encouraged to engage in consultations. If they are unable to resolve their dispute through consultations, a party can initiate a formal dispute settlement case. In such a case, the parties may resort to the WTO's dispute settlement mechanism, the Understanding on Rules and Procedures Governing the Settlement of Disputes (DSU). They are allowed to use this mechanism even though the GPA is not a multilateral WTO agreement.[59]

The GPA specifies the types of government procurement disputes that may be taken to the DSU. They include disputes arising from the failure of a party to carry out its obligations under the agreement or its application of a measure to the detriment of another party.[60]

The DSU applies to consultations and dispute settlement proceedings in procurement disputes, except those concerning retaliation. Any GPA party that utilizes the DSU process cannot cross-retaliate. This means that if a party is authorized to retaliate in a dispute settlement case involving the GPA, it must limit its suspension of concessions or other obligations to those under the GPA. It cannot suspend tariffs or other concessions under any other WTO agreement.[61]

---

59. GPA, art. XX.

60. GPA, art. XX:2.

61. GPA, art. XX:3. Similarly, any dispute arising under any other WTO agreement cannot result in the suspension of concessions or obligations under the GPA.

Parties have made very limited use of dispute settlement provisions under plurilateral procurement agreements. They have brought only three disputes under the GPA and four under the GATT Code on Government Procurement.[62] This limited use may be, as least partially, explained by an unusual feature of the GPA that allows suppliers to directly challenge the conduct of a specific procurement under domestic review procedures. This obviates the need for the supplier's government to consider using the DSU when a supplier alleges that another party's procuring entity has failed to comply with the agreement in a specific procurement.

8.2 Domestic Review

The GPA (unlike most WTO agreements) gives private parties the right to challenge the conduct of procurement covered by the agreement and enforce GPA rules.[63] Any supplier with an interest in a specific covered procurement can bring a challenge. They can challenge either a breach of the agreement directly or a procuring entity's failure to comply with its party's measures that implement it. The GPA 2012 added the second condition to accommodate the legal structures of parties, such as the US, whose domestic law does not allow a supplier to directly challenge a breach of the GPA.[64]

The GPA requires parties to allow suppliers to submit a challenge at least 10 days from when its basis became known or reasonably should have become known to the supplier. It directs the parties to designate at least one impartial administrative or judicial

---

62. For a list of the disputes and links to each dispute, see WTO, *Dispute Settlement*, accessed May 18, 2022, https://www.wto.org/english/tratop_e/gproc_e/disput_e.htm.

63. Sue Arrowsmith, "The Character and Role of National Challenge Procedures under the Government Procurement Agreement," *Public Procurement Law Review* 11, no. 4 (2002): 237.

64. GPA, art. XVIII:1. This distinction had been overlooked when the domestic review provision was added to the GPA 1994.

authority independent of its procuring entities to hear these challenges. When a review body (other than a court) is designated, it must apply court-like procedures, or its decision must be subject to judicial review. The parties must also provide "rapid interim measures" such as suspension of the procurement process to preserve the supplier's opportunity to participate in the procurement.[65]

9. WTO COMMITTEE ON GOVERNMENT PROCUREMENT

The WTO Committee on Government Procurement (Committee) is comprised of a representative of each GPA party.[66] It oversees and administers the implementation of the GPA and provides a forum for the parties to consult on any matters relating to its operation. The Committee reports annually to the WTO General Council on its activities and developments pertaining to the agreement. It is supported by the WTO Secretariat.

10. PROCUREMENT INFORMATION

Information on Procurement Systems: The GPA directs each party to publish information on its procurement system. This information includes laws, regulations, judicial decisions, administrative rulings of general application, standard contract clauses, and procurement procedures.[67] The parties must also list the electronic or paper media in which they publish this information in Appendix II to the GPA.[68]

---

65. GPA, art. XVIII:3–7.

66. GPA, art. XXI:1–3. WTO members and intergovernmental organizations with observer status under the GPA may also participate in the Committee. GPA, art. XXI:4.

67. GPA, art. VI. The reporting obligation extends to any modifications of that information.

68. GPA, art. VI:2(a).

The GPA also requires each party to inform the Committee of any changes to its laws and regulations relevant to the GPA and their administration.[69] When a party's current laws and regulations are available electronically, it may fulfill this reporting obligation with annual notification of any changes that may affect its GPA obligations. However, if the change is substantive, the party must immediately notify the Committee.[70]

Provision of Information to Parties: The GPA directs the parties to provide, on the request of any other party, information necessary to determine whether a procurement was conducted fairly, impartially, and in accordance with the GPA.[71]

Media for Publication of Notices: The GPA requires each party to list in Appendix III to the GPA the electronic or paper media in which it publishes its procurement notices. These include intended procurement notices, summary notices, notices of planned procurement, and notices relating to multiuse lists. The parties must also list in the GPA's Appendix IV the website address(es) where they publish the notices of their contract awards.[72]

---

69. GPA, art. XXII:5; GPA, *Notifications, National Implementing Legislation*, accessed May 18, 2022, https://www.wto.org/english/tratop_e/gproc_e/notnat_e.htm#natLeg.

70. This change was added to the GPA 2012. The GPA Committee's Decision containing the outcome of the renegotiations of the GPA 1994 (GPA/113) specifies that: "[w]here a Party maintains officially designated electronic media that provide links to its current laws and regulations relevant to this Agreement and its laws and regulations are available in one of the WTO official languages, and such media are listed in Appendix II, the Party may fulfil the requirement in Article XXII:5 by notifying the Committee annually, at the end of the year, of any changes unless such changes are substantive, that is, they may affect the Party's obligations under the Agreement; and in such cases, a notification shall be made immediately." GPA, *Notifications, National Implementing Legislation*.

71. GPA, art. XVII:1.

72. GPA, art. VI:2(b) and 2(c)(ii).

Thresholds in National Currencies: The GPA stipulates that each party calculates and converts the value of the coverage thresholds listed in its annexes into its own national currency. It must notify the Committee of the results every two years.[73]

Procurement Statistics: The GPA directs parties to report annually to the Committee on the value of their covered procurement. For the procurement covered for their central government entities under Annex 1, they must report the total number and value of contracts awarded (both in total and by entities).[74] They may provide less detailed statistics (even estimates) for procurement covered under Annex 2 and Annex 3.[75] Since the 2012 revision, the parties are no longer obligated to report the amount of procurement they purchase from one another.[76]

The GPA 2012 also simplified the parties' statistics reporting. When a party publishes its statistics on an official website, it only needs to notify the Committee of the website and explain of how to access the statistics found on it.[77] Parties must list the website

---

73. WTO, Committee on Government Procurement, "Decisions on Procedural Matters Under the Agreement on Government Procurement (1994), GPA/1" (March 5, 1996). For the current thresholds, see GPA, *e-GPA portal*, Thresholds, accessed May 18, 2022, https://e-gpa.wto.org/en/ThresholdNotification/FrontPage.

74. GPA parties must also report on their central government entities' use of limited tendering. GPA, art. XVI:4(a).

75. For procurement covered under Annex 2 and Annex 3, the parties need only report the number and total value of contracts awarded under each Annex (without any breakdown by the entity). When it is not feasible for a party to provide the data, it may provide estimates with an explanation of its methodology for developing the estimates. GPA, art. XVI:4(b) and (c).

76. In the negotiations of the GPA 2012, the parties removed the requirement in GPA 1994, art. XIX:5, that parties submit statistics on the country of origin of products and services purchased by its entities "[t]o the extent that such information is available" because few (if any) parties were providing that information.

77. GPA, art. XVI:4–5; GPA, *Notifications, Parties notifications on procurement statistics*, accessed May 18, 2022, https://www.wto.org/english/tratop_e/gproc_e/notnat_e.htm#notifs.

address(es) where they publish procurement statistics in the GPA's Appendix IV.[78]

WTO e-GPA Portal: The WTO's Integrated Government Procurement Market Access Information Resource (e-GPA portal), available at https://e-gpa.wto.org, provides a single point of access to considerable information relating to the GPA. It contains the following four types of information in all WTO languages:

(i)   the market access commitments of each party based on their Appendix I annexes

(ii) a chart with the thresholds applied by the parties and links to the thresholds in national currencies

(iii) the publication media that parties use to provide information on their procurement systems, notices (including contract awards), statistics, and

(iv) the means for searching the coverage commitments of one or more parties.

The portal also provides information on the parties' modifications of their annexes.[79]

---

78. GPA, art. VI:2(c).

79. Much of the information on modifications is unavailable to the public while modifications are pending.

CHAPTER 4

GPA MARKET ACCESS COMMITMENTS

1. INTRODUCTION

The fundamental aim of the GPA is to open government procurement among its parties.[1] The GPA does not require parties to open all their procurement. Rather, it establishes a framework for each party to specify the procurement that it offers to its counterparts and promises to conduct in accordance with the agreement's principles and procedures.[2] While the principles and procedures apply equally to all parties, the market access commitments are diverse and do not apply uniformly.

The GPA does not require all parties to offer identical market access commitments. It allows each party to offer or withhold procurement based on its economic, social, or political interests and constraints and negotiations with the other parties. If the GPA's market access commitments were limited to the procurement that

---

1. GPA, https://www.wto.org/english/tratop_e/gproc_e/gp_gpa_e.htm.
2. A discussion of the principles and procedures is found in Chapter 3.

all parties could agree to open, it would cover only a small amount of their government procurement.

Not only does the GPA allow parties to diverge in the procurement that they cover, but it also does not require them to provide the same access to all parties. The GPA's market access commitments are based on mutual reciprocity. This enables the parties to grant equivalent rights and benefits to each other and restrict access to elements of their procurement if they are not given equivalent concessions by another party. Allowing parties to derogate from the most-favored-nation (MFN) principle provides for broader coverage than would be possible if the parties had to provide the same access to all parties.

As a result of negotiations between parties, the GPA's market access commitments operate as an accumulation of bilateral agreements. Observing how those bilateral commitments are incorporated into the GPA's framework is central to understanding the GPA. It illustrates how the structure of the market access commitments allows the parties to expand the procurement covered under the GPA to the greatest extent possible and tailor their commitments to reflect their interests and priorities.

2. GENERAL COVERAGE PROVISIONS

2.1 Covered Procurement

In the GPA 2012, the parties added a definition of "covered procurement" that incorporated the factors determining whether procurement is subject to the GPA. It is a procurement for governmental purposes:

(i)   of goods, services, or any combination of goods and services covered in each party's annexes (and that is "not procured with a view to commercial sale or resale")

(ii)   by any contractual means, including purchase, lease, and rental or hire purchase, with or without an option to buy

(iii) for which the value equals or exceeds the relevant threshold specified in the party's annexes

(iv) by a procuring entity (an entity covered under a party's annexes) and

(v) that is not otherwise excluded from coverage.[3]

2.2 Excluded Activities

GPA 2012 also specifies certain activities that generally are not subject to its disciplines. They include the acquisition or rental of land; public employment contracts; noncontractual agreements or assistance such as grants, loans, and fiscal incentives; and the acquisition of fiscal agency or depository services, management services for regulated financial institutions, and services related to the sale of public debt, including government bonds.[4]

2.3 Valuation

The GPA sets out valuation rules for estimating the value of procurement to ascertain whether it is covered under the agreement. Under these rules, procuring entities must include the estimated maximum total value of the procurement over its entire duration and consider all forms of remuneration, such as fees, commissions, interest, and options. A procuring entity may not divide a purchase into separate procurements or use a valuation method to exclude the procurement from the application of the GPA.[5]

---

3. GPA, art. II:2.
4. GPA, art. II:3.
5. GPA, art. II:6–8.

3. RECIPROCITY AND CONDITIONAL MFN

The 1979 GATT Code provided essentially uniform coverage. Its signatories applied the same threshold to the procurement of goods by the central government entities listed in an annex. All GATT Code signatories (except Singapore)[6] accorded comparable access to the other signatories, in accordance with the MFN principle.

Subsequently, in the negotiations that replaced the GATT Code with the GPA 1994, the parties significantly expanded the scope of the procurement covered under the Code. They extended their commitments to include subcentral government entities and other entities such as utilities and government enterprises. In addition, they agreed to cover their procurement of services, including construction services. However, with this expansion, not all parties were able or willing to cover all their entities in the new categories or all their services. The negotiators of the GPA 1994 could have insisted on maintaining uniform coverage, but that would have reduced the expanded coverage to the lowest level that all parties could meet. The result would have been a much smaller agreement with a more limited impact. Instead, they committed to a broad level of coverage based upon conditional MFN. They allowed parties to derogate from the MFN obligation by applying reciprocity conditions that withheld access to specific procurement from counterparts that did not offer equivalent concessions.

Each party effectively negotiated with other interested parties to reach a mutually satisfactory agreement on reciprocity-based

---

6. Singapore conditioned its coverage "on the right of the Singapore Government to grant tenderers from the ASEAN countries a two and a half per cent or US$40,000 preferential margin in accordance with the provisions of the Agreement on ASEAN Preferential Trading Arrangements." GATT Code, Annexes, Lists of Entities Covered by the Agreement, Singapore, Note. For a discussion of the basis for this condition and its removal, see Jędrzej Górski, "CPTPP and Government Procurement," *Transnational Dispute Management* 5 (2019), text surrounding notes 131–45, accessed May 17, 2022, https://www.transnational-dispute-management.com/article.asp?key=2675.

coverage. This resulted in "an accumulation of preferential bilateral agreements" between the parties.[7] Subsequently, the parties added reciprocity clauses in both the negotiations of GPA 2012 and in accessions of WTO members.[8] Incorporating these bilateral agreements into the GPA has resulted in conditional MFN treatment expressed in a complex array of coverage commitments.

The derogations from MFN "are sometimes accompanied with declarations that they will be withdrawn only when the respective signatory has accepted that the other parties have given comparable access to its suppliers."[9] In other cases, parties withhold procurement from specific parties without explanation. The reciprocity conditions are found in all elements of coverage.

The GPA parties located in Europe, led by the European Union (EU), maintained a greater share of derogations. Some GPA parties, in particular the EU, strictly applied reciprocity in undertaking procurement commitments. Other parties, including the US, were less exacting in their reciprocity application. They pursued an overall balance of procurement commitments or access to certain procurement rather than precisely matching coverage. The US sought "appropriate reciprocal competitive procurement opportunities," as required by the Trade Agreements Act of 1979.[10] In applying that directive, the US generally considered whether its trading partners used the same thresholds, covered similar types of

---

7. Arie Reich, "The New GATT Agreement on Government Procurement: The Pitfalls of Plurilateralism and Strict Reciprocity," *Journal of World Trade* 31, no. 2 (1997): 125–51.

8. See, for example, WTO, "Australia accepted as new party to government procurement pact," October 17, 2018, https://www.wto.org/english/news_e/news18_e/gpro_17oct18_e.htm.

9. Kamala Dawar, "The Government Procurement Agreement, the Most-Favored Nation Principle, and Regional Trade Agreements," in *The Internationalization of Government Procurement Regulation*, eds. Aris Georgopoulos, Bernard Hoekman, and Petros C. Mavroidis (Oxford: Oxford University Press, 2017), 111.

10. *Trade Agreements Act of 1979*, Public Law 96-39, *U.S. Statutes at Large* 93 (1979): 144; codified as amended at *U.S. Code* 19, §§ 2501–581.

entities, opened comparable services, and minimized exclusions.[11] Nine parties imposed no reciprocity conditions.[12]

4. MARKET ACCESS COMMITMENTS

The market access commitments are described in each party's annexes in Appendix I of the GPA, based on five fundamental elements of coverage. First, they identify three types of procuring entities whose procurement is subject to GPA rules: central government entities (Annex 1), subcentral government entities (Annex 2), and other entities (Annex 3). Second, the commitments specify thresholds, which are monetary values at and above which procurement is covered. Thresholds may vary by entity type, so they are set out in each of the entity annexes. Third, as a general principle, the parties cover all goods procured by their entities, except those listed as excluded in Annex 4 or other annexes. Fourth, these commitments specify the services (Annex 5) and construction services (Annex 6) that they cover under the GPA, using either a positive list (only listed services are covered) or a negative list (all services are covered except those listed). Finally, they specify exceptions to their coverage commitments, such as small business exceptions, in Annex 7 or other annexes.

4.1 Central Government Entities

Beginning with the GATT Code, parties have specified their central government entity coverage by listing all or most of their ministries and agencies, as well as a wide variety of other central government

---

11. Jean Heilman Grier, "Trade Agreements Open Foreign Procurement Markets," *Thomson Reuters Briefing Papers* 17–10, October 2017, 10.

12. The nine parties were Armenia; Australia; Hong Kong, China; Israel; South Korea; the Netherlands with respect to Aruba; New Zealand; Singapore; and Ukraine.

entities such as judicial authorities and legislative bodies in Annex 1. All parties (except Israel) listed their defense ministries.

The uniformity of central government coverage changed slightly in the GPA 2012 when several parties offered comprehensive coverage of their central government entities. Instead of listing these entities, the EU, Iceland, Norway, and Switzerland covered all their Annex 1 entities with a 'catch-all' clause intended to include existing entities, as well as any entities to be established in the future. They provided indicative lists[13] of their covered entities. The EU applied this approach to the central government entities of its member states. When the United Kingdom (UK) acceded to the GPA in 2021 following its exit from the EU, it also applied this approach, the same as it had when it was an EU member state.

Of the parties that offered comprehensive coverage of their central government entities, only the EU and the UK did not provide that coverage to all other parties. The EU accorded full rights to its comprehensive coverage to only six parties.[14] For the other GPA parties, the EU granted access in three tiers (apparently reflecting its assessment of the scope of their partners' coverage). Its top tier provided Israel, Montenegro, Moldova, and Ukraine with access to all its listed entities but not entities established in the future. The EU gave its second tier of coverage–all listed entities (except for nearly 200 entities marked by an asterisk)–to 10 parties, including the US.[15] Finally, in a third tier, the EU accorded Japan, Chinese Taipei (Taiwan), and the US access to entities marked by a double asterisk. The UK restricted its comprehensive coverage to

---

13. With an 'indicative list,' a party lists entities of the type it covers, but it may make changes to the list without resorting to the GPA's modification process since it has not provided a definitive list.

14. The six parties were Iceland, Liechtenstein, Aruba, Norway, Switzerland, and the UK.

15. The 10 parties were Armenia; Australia; Canada; Hong Kong, China; Japan; South Korea; New Zealand; Singapore; Chinese Taipei; and the US.

five parties[16] but opened all its listed entities to the other parties. Ukraine covered central government entities in six categories and provided an indicative list of 109 entities.[17]

The US was the only party to apply a reciprocity provision to a single central government entity. It withheld procurement by the National Aeronautics and Space Administration from Japan because that country did not cover its space agency.

4.2 Subcentral Government Entities

When the parties decided to bring subcentral entities under international procurement obligations for the first time in the negotiations of the GPA 1994, they could not agree on a uniform level of coverage. This was the result of differences among the parties concerning the types and structures of their subcentral entities and the ability of their central governments to prescribe the conduct of the procurement of these entities. Some parties, such as the US, only covered their first tier of subcentral entities (states) and only when they had authorized such coverage. Other parties, including the EU, listed all subcentral entities subject to its procurement directives. Due to the lack of uniform coverage, several parties applied derogations to their coverage.

The GPA 1994 parties (except Canada), which had subcentral government entities, covered at least some of their entities under the agreement.[18] Canada refused to open the procurement of any subcentral entities because the US would not provide Canadian

---

16. They were the EU, Iceland, Liechtenstein, Norway, Aruba, and Switzerland.

17. Ukraine covered (i) administrative bodies of its parliament, president, and cabinet of ministers; (ii) ministries and other central government bodies in its executive branch; (iii) Constitutional Court, Supreme Court, and higher specialized courts; (iv) institutions and organizations; (v) academies of sciences; and (vi) subordinate entities financed by state budgets.

18. Hong Kong, China; Aruba; and Singapore have no subcentral entities.

businesses with access to its small business set-asides and other procurement that it excluded from the agreement.[19] This gap in coverage remained until Canada offered coverage of its provinces and territories to the US in a 2010 bilateral agreement and then offered it to all the parties in the GPA 2012 negotiations.[20]

To specify their subcentral coverage, parties either listed their covered entities or based their coverage on classifications of entities. The US and eight other parties[21] listed the entities they cover (see Table 4.1).

TABLE 4.1. Subcentral Coverage Based on Listed Entities

GPA Party	Subcentral Coverage
Armenia	Forty-seven local authorities (municipalities), as defined by its Law on Administrative-Territorial Division, No. N-062-I of 7 November 1995
Australia	Eight states and territories with lists of procuring entities for each state and territory
Canada	All 13 provinces and territories with lists of covered entities for some and categories of covered entities for others
Israel	Three municipalities (Jerusalem, Tel-Aviv, and Haifa) and the Local Government Economic Services Ltd.
Japan	Forty-seven prefectures and 19 designated cities covered by its Local Autonomy Law

---

19. Dawar, "The Government Procurement Agreement," 117.

20. For a discussion of the 2010 bilateral agreement, see Chapter 5.

21. The eight other parties were Armenia, Australia, Canada, Israel, South Korea, Japan, New Zealand, and Chinese Taipei.

GPA Party	Subcentral Coverage
South Korea[22]	Group A: 16 entities (Seoul Metropolitan Government, six metropolitan cities, and nine provinces); and Group B: local governments in three cities (Seoul, Busan, and Incheon)
New Zealand	Eleven health boards and seven city and regional councils
Chinese Taipei	Taiwan Provincial Government and city governments for Taipei and Kaohsiung
US	Thirty-seven states with entities covered varying by state

The EU, together with eight other parties, covered their subcentral entities within specified classifications (see Table 4.2).[23] They illustrated that coverage with indicative lists of entities.

TABLE 4.2. Subcentral Coverage Based on Categories of Entities

GPA Party	Categories of Covered Entities
EU	(i) All regional or local contracting authorities; and (ii) all contracting authorities that are bodies governed by public law, as defined by the EU public procurement directive, with indicative lists of entities
Iceland	(i) All contracting authorities of the regional or local public authorities, including municipalities; and (ii) all other entities whose procurement policies are substantially controlled by, dependent on, or influenced by central, regional, or local government and that are engaged in noncommercial or nonindustrial activities

---

22. The GPA formally refers to the Republic of Korea, which is otherwise known as South Korea.

23. They were Iceland, Liechtenstein, Moldova, Montenegro, Norway, Switzerland, Ukraine, and the UK.

GPA Party	Categories of Covered Entities
Liechtenstein	(i) Public authorities at the local level; and (ii) all bodies governed by public law
Moldova	(i) Local authorities defined by the Law on Local Public Administration (Municipalities of Chisinău and Balti) and 32 district authorities (*consilii*); and (ii) public authorities of the Autonomous Territorial Unit of Gagauzia as per the Law on the Special Status of Gagauzia (Gagauz-Yeri) No 344-XIII, dated 23 December 1994
Montenegro	(i) All regional or local contracting authorities; and (ii) all contracting authorities that are bodies governed by public law with an indicative list of 17 authorities
Norway	(i) All subcentral government entities operating at regional (counties) or local (municipalities) level; (ii) all bodies governed by public law; and (iii) all associations formed by one or several of the entities in the first two categories. An indicative list includes 12 bodies plus two categories (state banks and publicly owned and operated museums)
Switzerland	Any centralized or decentralized authority or administrative unit at: (i) the cantonal level under cantonal law; and (ii) the district and communal level (lists 23 cantons)
Ukraine	(i) Bodies of the executive branch (local state administrations and provincial branches); (ii) provincial and local public authorities; (iii) bodies that ensure the functioning of the Autonomous Republic of Crimea; and (iv) other entities financed by state or local budgets, with an indicative list of 52 entities
UK	(i) All regional or local contracting authorities; and (ii) all contracting authorities that are bodies governed by public law

Lacking uniform subcentral coverage, the parties took a wide range of derogations from MFN and attached reciprocity conditions to their subcentral coverage. These included withholding

access to the procurement of all or part of their subcentral entities or the right to use domestic review procedures. For example,
when Canada added its provinces to the GPA 2012, it withheld
that coverage from Iceland and Liechtenstein. Those two countries
responded by withholding their Annex 2 coverage from Canada
until it provided satisfactory access.

In a similar manner, the EU, Iceland, Liechtenstein, Montenegro, Norway, and the UK denied the US the right to participate
in the procurement of services by their Annex 2 entities until it
provided satisfactory reciprocal access. The EU also withheld certain subcentral entity coverage from Australia, Canada, and New
Zealand under the same condition.[24] Other parties did not allow
access to some aspects of their subcentral procurement to specific
parties.[25] Switzerland excluded all parties (except Armenia, the EU,
and the members of the European Free Trade Association)[26] from

---

24. The EU withheld subcentral coverage based on a classification system
referred to as the "NUTS classification" (nomenclature of territorial units
for statistics), which "is a hierarchical system for dividing up the economic
territory of the EU." Eurostat, accessed May 17, 2022, https://ec.europa.eu/
eurostat/web/nuts/background. It withheld the following subcentral procurement from: (i) Australia: EU "procurement by regional and local contracting authorities" (contracting authorities of administrative units listed under
NUTS classification 2 and 3 and smaller administrative units, as referred to
in Regulation 1059/2003 (as amended)); (ii) Canada: procurement by EU
cities-regions listed under NUTS 1 and NUTS 2, local procuring entities,
and bodies governed by public law covered under the EU's Annex 2; and
(iii) from New Zealand: EU procurement by local contracting authorities of
administrative units listed under NUTS 3 and smaller administrative units
and contracting authorities of administrative units listed under NUTS 1 and
2 (unless their procurement is covered under the EU's Annex 3). GPA, Appendix I, EU, Annex 2, n. 1.

25. Montenegro withheld from Canada procurement by its cities-regions with
a population between 800,000 and 7 million, local procuring entities, and bodies governed by public law. Norway limits the access of Australia and Canada
to subcentral government entities operating at the regional level (counties).

26. The European Free Trade Association members are Iceland, Liechtenstein, Norway, and Switzerland, accessed May 17, 2022, https://www.efta.
int/about-efta.

procurement of authorities or administrative units at the district and communal levels. Liechtenstein also denied Australia access to procurement by local public authorities. Finally, the UK withheld access to elements of its subcentral coverage from Canada and New Zealand until the parties were satisfied that they provided reciprocal access.[27]

The EU, Iceland, Liechtenstein, Montenegro, Norway, and the UK applied the second type of reciprocity condition to both Japan and Korea.[28] These parties denied the targeted countries access to their domestic review procedures that enable suppliers to contest the award of contracts by bodies governed by public law until they complete coverage of subcentral entities.

4.3 Other Entities

When the GPA 1994 was extended to the third category of entities, referred to as "other entities," the negotiators allowed each party to determine which entities to include based on negotiations with its counterparts. As a result, the parties covered a broad and diverse range of entities, including utilities, government enterprises, state-owned enterprises, government authorities, banks, and hospitals.[29]

Like their approach to subcentral coverage, the parties defined their Annex 3 coverage by either listing specific entities or covering

---

27. The UK denied Canada access to procurement by cities-regions listed under Territorial Units 1 and 2 and local procuring entities and bodies governed by public law. It also did not accord New Zealand access to two categories of subcentral procurement: (i) local contracting authorities (contracting authorities of administrative units listed under Territorial Unit 3 and smaller administrative units) and (ii) contracting authorities of administrative units listed under Territorial Units 1 and 2, unless their procurement is covered under the UK Annex 3.

28. Norway limited the reciprocal condition to Japan, and Liechtenstein extended its restriction to Israel.

29. Jean Heilman Grier, "What Are the Prospects for Concluding Work on China's GPA Accession in 2015?," *Public Procurement Law Review* 24, no. 6 (2015): 230–31, Table 4.

all entities that fell within certain classifications and providing indicative lists. Only Aruba did not cover any entities under Annex 3 after withdrawing its listed entities in the GPA 2012 because they had been privatized.

The US and nine other parties specified their Annex 3 coverage by listing entities,[30] which ranged from five for Hong Kong, China to 165 for Japan. The parties diverged in whether to list certain "identical government entities" such as their Central Bank in Annex 1 or Annex 3.[31] Japan included several entities in Annex 3 (for example, the Atomic Energy Agency, Environmental Restoration and Conservation Agency, Housing Financial Agency, and International Cooperation Agency), which appear comparable to entities that the US listed in Annex 1 (Nuclear Regulatory Commission, Environmental Procurement Agency, and US Agency for International Development).

The EU and eight other parties[32] based their Annex 3 coverage on entities within certain classifications and undertaking activities in specified sectors (see Table 4.3). The sectors included drinking water, electricity, airports, ports, urban transport, rail services, and postal services. Ukraine also covered entities engaged in a variety of sectors.[33] These parties provided indicative lists of their entities.

---

30. They were Australia; Canada; Hong Kong, China; Israel; Japan; South Korea; New Zealand; Singapore; and Chinese Taipei.

31. Ping Wang, "Coverage of the WTO's Agreement on Government Procurement: Challenges of Integrating China and Other Countries with a Large State Sector into the Global Trading System," *Journal of International Economic Law* 10, no. 4 (2007): 11.

32. The other parties were Iceland, Liechtenstein, Moldova, Montenegro, Norway, Switzerland, Ukraine, and the UK.

33. Ukraine covered entities in the following sectors: gas, heat, sewage, air navigation services, geological exploration, telecommunications, and crude oil.

TABLE 4.3. Utility Sectors Covered

GPA Party	Drinking Water	Electricity	Airports	Ports	Urban Transport	Railways	Postal Services
EU	X	X	X	X	X	X	
Iceland	X	X	X	X	X	X	X
Liechtenstein	X	X	X	X	X		X
Moldova	X	X	X	X	X	X	
Montenegro	X	X	X	X	X	X	
Norway	X	X	X	X	X		
Switzerland	X	X	X	X	X		X
Ukraine	X	X	X	X	X	X	X
UK	X	X	X	X	X	X	X

Moldova included 21 additional legal entities governed by public law with no industrial or commercial character and covered by its Law on Government Procurement. Armenia incorporated three categories of entities governed by public law[34] and published the list of entities.[35]

In the absence of uniform coverage of other entities in Annex 3, the GPA parties imposed numerous reciprocity conditions on other parties that did not offer equivalent or comparable concessions. Those that based their coverage on entities within certain utility sectors imposed more reciprocity conditions than the parties that listed specific entities.

The US excluded Canada from its Annex 3 coverage because it did not open the procurement of its provincial hydro utilities. It also denied Japan access to procurement of US entities in the electric sector and the waiver of the domestic purchasing restriction on financing power generation projects by the Rural Utilities Services because Japan maintained a higher construction threshold for its Annex 2 and 3 entities. In addition, Canada did not extend its Annex 3 coverage to the EU, Iceland, and Liechtenstein. South Korea refused Norway and Switzerland access to procurement by the Korea Railroad Corporation and the Korea Rail Network Authority until they provided comparable access for South Korean undertakings.

Parties opening the procurement of particular utility sectors incorporated a complex array of derogations or reciprocity conditions that restricted the participation of specific parties in various sectors (see Table 4.4).

---

34. The state or community nonprofit organizations, commercial organizations with more than 50% government or community shareholding, and public services (including utilities) whose procurement is covered by its Law on Procurement were three categories of entities included by Armenia.

35. Armenia published the list of entities in its official electronic bulletin for procurement, accessed May 17, 2022, https://gnumner.am/en.

TABLE 4.4. Reciprocity-based Exclusions of Utility Sectors

GPA Party Imposing Conditions	Parties Excluded from Specific Utility Sectors					
	Drinking Water	Electricity	Airport Facilities	Maritime or Inland Ports	Urban Transport	Railways
EU	Australia; Canada; New Zealand; US	Australia; Canada; Japan; South Korea (certain goods)	Australia; Canada; South Korea; New Zealand; US	Australia; Canada; New Zealand; US (dredging services or related to shipbuilding)	Australia; Canada; Israel (bus services); Japan; New Zealand; US	Armenia; Australia; Canada; Japan; Hong Kong, China; South Korea (high-speed railways); Singapore; Chinese Taipei; US
Iceland	Australia; Canada; US	Australia; Canada; Japan; South Korea; Israel (certain goods)	Australia; Canada; South Korea; US	Australia; Canada; US (dredging services or related to shipbuilding)	Australia; Canada; Israel (bus services); Japan (urban railway); US	Armenia; Canada; Japan; Hong Kong, China; South Korea (high-speed railways): Singapore; Chinese Taipei; US
Liechtenstein	Australia; Canada; US	Australia; Canada; Japan			Australia; Canada; Japan; US; Israel; South Korea (bus services)	

Parties Excluded from Specific Utility Sectors

GPA Party Imposing Conditions	Drinking Water	Electricity	Airport Facilities	Maritime or Inland Ports	Urban Transport	Railways
Moldova					Israel	Israel
Montenegro	Canada; US	Canada; Japan; Korea; Israel (certain goods)	Canada; South Korea; US	Canada; US (dredging services or related to shipbuilding)	Canada; Israel (bus services); Japan (urban railways); US	Armenia; Canada; Japan; Hong Kong, China; South Korea (high-speed railways); Singapore; Chinese Taipei; US
Norway	Australia; Canada; US	Australia	Australia; Canada; South Korea; US	Australia; Canada	Australia; Canada; Japan (urban railway); Israel (bus service); US	
Switzerland	Australia; Canada; Singapore; US	Australia; Canada; Japan; Singapore	Australia; Canada; South Korea; US	Australia; Canada	Australia; Canada; Israel; Japan; US	
UK	Australia; Canada; New Zealand; US	Australia; Canada; Japan; South Korea (certain goods)	Australia; Canada; South Korea; New Zealand; US	Australia; Canada; New Zealand; US (dredging services or related to shipbuilding)	Australia; Canada; Israel (bus services); Japan; New Zealand; US	Armenia; Australia; Canada; Japan; Hong Kong, China; South Korea (high-speed railways); Singapore; Chinese Taipei; US

In addition to the Table 4.4 derogations, the EU, Montenegro, and the UK excluded Japan from eight categories of goods and services procured by entities operating in the urban transport sector under Annex 3 until Japan fully opened its procurement of urban transport.[36]

4.4 Thresholds

Under the GATT Code, all parties applied a single uniform threshold of 150,000 special drawing rights (SDRs)[37] to the purchase of goods by their central government entities. They reduced the threshold to 130,000 SDRs when they amended the Code in 1988. When the agreement was replaced by the GPA 1994, the parties diverged in their application of thresholds.[38]

In the GPA 1994, most parties applied a 130,000 SDRs threshold to the purchase of both goods and services by their central government entities and a construction services threshold of 5 million SDRs (except Japan's 450,000 SDRs threshold for architectural, engineering, and other technical services[39]). In the GPA 2012, Aruba and Japan reduced their thresholds.[40]

---

36. See, for example, GPA, Appendix I, EU, Annex 3, n. 8.

37. An SDR is an international reserve asset created by the International Monetary Fund. The value of the SDR is based on a basket of five currencies: the US dollar, the euro, the Chinese renminbi, the Japanese yen, and the British pound sterling. International Monetary Fund, *Fact Sheet: Special Drawing Rights*, accessed May 17, 2022, https://www.imf.org/en/About/Factsheets/Sheets/2016/08/01/14/51/Special-Drawing-Right-SDR.

38. GPA, Integrated Government Procurement Market Access Information (e-GPA) Portal, Thresholds, accessed May 17, 2022, https://e-gpa.wto.org/en/ThresholdNotification/FrontPage.

39. Japan applied this exception to the procurement of its Annex 1 and Annex 3 entities.

40. Aruba and Japan reduced their central government thresholds to 100,000 SDRs for the procurement of goods and services and for construction services—4 million SDRs and 4.5 million SDRs, respectively. In addition, in 2020, Israel reduced its 8.5 million SDRs threshold to 5 million SDRs under its commitment in the GPA 2012.

Parties generally divided into two groups on the thresholds their subcentral government entities applied when buying goods and services. The largest group, led by the EU, used a 200,000 SDRs threshold and the other group (the US, Australia, and Canada) applied a threshold of 355,000 SDRs. The exceptions were Israel's 250,000 SDRs threshold and Japan's threshold of 1.5 million SDRs for architectural, engineering, and other technical services.

With four exceptions, parties applied a 400,000 SDRs threshold for goods and services purchased by their Annex 3 entities. The exceptions were the US's $250,000 threshold for federal government enterprises, Canada's and Israel's 355,000 SDRs threshold, and Japan's 130,000 SDRs threshold. For construction services procured by Annex 2 and Annex 3 entities, all parties used a 5 million SDRs threshold (except Japan and Korea maintained a 15 million SDRs threshold).

In response to the higher thresholds, parties derogated from MFN by imposing two types of reciprocity conditions. They either matched the higher threshold or limited access to their domestic review procedures. In the first category of conditions, Chinese Taipei and the US applied reciprocity provisions in response to higher thresholds. Chinese Taipei limited the access of the higher-threshold parties (except Israel and the US) to its procurement at the same threshold in the same procurement category. The US did not permit South Korea to participate in the procurement of construction services by its Annex 2 and Annex 3 entities below 15 million SDRs.[41]

In addition, the EU, Iceland, Montenegro, and Norway withheld rights to participate in their subcentral entities' procurement of goods and services below 355,000 SDRs from Canada and Australia, while the UK applied this restriction only to Canada. The EU also excluded Australia from procurement between 200,000

41. That contrasts with the US's withholding of access to its federal electric utilities from Japan in response to its higher threshold.

SDRs and 400,000 SDRs by EU bodies governed by public law under Annex 2.

In the second category of derogations, the EU, Iceland, Liechtenstein, Montenegro, Switzerland, and the UK denied suppliers of Japan and Korea access to their domestic review procedures to contest the award of contracts for procurement with a value that is less than the two parties' higher threshold.[42] Japan countered with a reciprocal clause that denied access to its domestic review procedures to service providers from parties that refused Japan such access in the same category of entities. In practice, this condition meant that a supplier from the parties subject to the derogation could participate in covered procurement. However, it could not challenge the conduct of the procurement under the party's domestic review procedures.

4.5 Goods

Following the practice established in the GATT Code, the GPA parties opened the procurement of all goods purchased by their covered entities (except for defense goods and goods explicitly excluded). They generally limited coverage of their defense and security ministries to the goods that each party listed in Annex 1 or Annex 4.

In response to exclusions of specific products, several parties imposed reciprocity-based restrictions. Canada's exclusion of goods in Federal Supply Classification 58[43] drew reciprocal exclusions by Iceland, Liechtenstein, and Norway for procurement of the same category. When Australia acceded to the GPA, it excluded the procurement of motor vehicles for five of its eight states and territories.

---

42. Liechtenstein, Moldova, and Switzerland also applied this condition to Israel, while Norway limited it to Japan.

43. Federal Supply Classification 58 comprises communication, detection, and coherent radiation equipment.

In response, the EU withheld access to several categories of motor vehicles and motor vehicle components procured by its Annex 2 entities from Australia. The US exclusion of the Federal Aviation Administration from its coverage led to the application of reciprocity conditions for the procurement of air traffic control equipment by the EU and several other parties.[44]

Canada and the US excluded from their commitments any good or service of a contract (Canada) or a procurement (US) not covered by the GPA. In response, the EU, Iceland, Montenegro, and the UK matched the exclusion with a reciprocity provision that applied to both the US and Canada.

4.6 Services

When the parties extended their commitments to the procurement of services in the GPA 1994, they did not follow a uniform approach in specifying their coverage as they had with goods. Instead, they used two different methods to define their service commitments. The first one was a negative list, in which they covered all services except those listed. The second approach was a positive list, in which the party listed the services that it opened under the GPA. While the US was the only party initially to use a negative list, it was joined by Australia, New Zealand, and Ukraine when they acceded to the GPA. Table 4.5 records the services they excluded. By contrast, all the other parties based their services coverage on a positive list, in which they opened only the services that each listed in Annex 5.

The use of a negative list is dynamic as it captures new services that are created. With the use of a positive list, new services are covered only when the parties undertake market access negotiations.

---

44. The EU, Iceland, Montenegro, Norway, Switzerland, and the UK applied the restriction to the procurement of all covered entities, while Liechtenstein limited it to Annex 1 and 3 entities.

TABLE 4.5. Services Excluded from Coverage

GPA Party	Services Excluded
Australia	(i) plasma fractionation services; (ii) government advertising services; (iii) health and welfare services; and (iv) research and development (R&D) services
New Zealand	(i) R&D services; (ii) public health; (iii) education; (iv) and welfare services
Ukraine	(i) services of international mediation courts and international commercial arbitrages provided for resolution of disputes involving a procuring entity; (ii) services of financial institutions, including international institutions, related to the raising of credit resources and funds by a procuring entity; and (iii) financial and related services procured or provided by its national bank
US	(i) transportation services, including launching services; (ii) services associated with the management and operation of government facilities or privately owned facilities used for governmental purposes, including federally funded R&D centers; (iii) public utility services (except enhanced or value-added telecommunications services); and (iv) R&D services

In addition to diverging on their approaches to specifying their service coverage, the parties have not uniformly liberalized their services procurement.[45] Because each GPA party has opened different services, two-thirds (13) of them offered access to their services market only on a reciprocal basis.[46] Those parties opened the procurement of a specific service to another party only if that other party opened the same service. As a result, "parties do not

---

45. Robert D. Anderson et al., "The Relationship between Services Trade and Government Procurement Commitments: Insights from Relevant WTO Agreements and Recent RTAs," *WTO Working Paper* ERSD-2014-21, November 18, 2014, 36–37, https://www.wto.org/english/res_e/reser_e/ersd201421_e.htm.

46. The 13 parties were Australia, Canada, the EU, Iceland, South Korea, Liechtenstein, Moldova, Montenegro, Norway, Switzerland, Chinese Taipei, the UK, and the US.

have access to certain services because they have not themselves liberalized the same services sector."[47]

4.7 Construction Services and PPPs

When Liechtenstein expanded its coverage to include all construction services in the GPA 2012, the agreement reached full coverage of construction services (except dredging for Canada and the US and several entity exclusions). Despite the full coverage, nine GPA parties maintained reciprocity conditions relating to construction services.[48] Such restrictions could be applied in the future if a new GPA party did not offer full coverage of construction services.

The GPA 2012 initiated coverage of public-private partnerships (PPPs) by three parties: the EU, Japan, and South Korea. They were followed by Montenegro and the UK when they acceded to the agreement. Korea opened build-operate-transfer contracts. Japan covered procurement in construction projects subject to its Act on Promotion of Private Finance Initiative.[49] The EU, Montenegro, and the UK opened works concessions contracts awarded by their Annex 1 and 2 entities under a national treatment regime. However, they restricted access to these contracts, opening them only to each other and six other GPA parties.[50] In addition, they limited Korea's access to their work concessions valued at and above 15 million SDRs.

---

47. Anderson et al., "The Relationship between Services Trade," 36–37.

48. The nine parties were Canada, the EU, Iceland, Liechtenstein, Montenegro, Norway, Switzerland, Chinese Taipei, and the UK.

49. This is a form of PPP that uses private finance, management abilities, and technical capabilities in the construction, maintenance, and management of public facilities.

50. The six parties were Iceland, South Korea, Liechtenstein, Norway, Aruba, and Switzerland.

4.8 Small Business Preferences

Several parties imposed reciprocity conditions on Australia, Japan, South Korea, and the US because they maintained preferences for their small businesses. The preferences excluded from their commitments varied slightly:

- Australia: any form of preference that benefited its small and medium enterprises (SMEs)
- Korea: any set-asides for SMEs
- Japan: contracts awarded to cooperatives or associations comprised of small businesses
- US: any set-aside on behalf of its small- or minority-owned businesses.

In response to these domestic preferences, the EU, Iceland, Liechtenstein, Montenegro, Norway, Switzerland, and the UK denied access to their domestic review procedures to SMEs of the four parties. They aim to maintain these restrictions until those parties "no longer operate discriminatory measures in favour of certain domestic small and minority businesses."[51]

---

51. See, for example, GPA, Appendix I, EU, Annex 1, n. 2. Canada also maintained an exclusion for set-asides for its small and minority-owned businesses: "[t]his Agreement does not apply to set asides for small and minority owned businesses." GPA, Appendix I, Canada, Annex 7, n. 2. As of June 2022, it had not established a program for small business set-asides. However, in March 2022, Canada commenced a consultations process to solicit views from Canadian stakeholders on, among others, the possible creation of a federal set-aside program for Canadian small businesses. Government of Canada, "Consultations on reciprocal procurement policies in Canada," March 2022, https://www.international.gc.ca/trade-commerce/consultations/RP-AR/index.aspx?lang=eng.

5. MODIFICATIONS OF COVERAGE

5.1 Modification Process

The GPA permits parties to modify their coverage provided they follow a prescribed process.[52] To initiate the GPA's modification process, a party must notify other parties of its proposed modification and provide the required information.[53] Any party whose rights may be affected by a proposed modification is allowed 45 days from the notice to object (increased from 30 days under the GPA 1994). It must set out the reasons for its objection.[54]

Under the GPA 1994, when parties were unable to resolve objections over proposed modifications through consultations, their only recourse was to take the dispute to the WTO's dispute settlement mechanism. However, no party had ever used the mechanism to resolve any dispute over a proposed modification. Instead, these disputes languished unresolved for years, particularly modifications proposed by Japan.

Japan was blocked for more than two decades in its efforts to remove several entities from its coverage commitments. In 2001, it proposed the withdrawal of three railway companies[55] from its Annex 3 coverage, contending the Japanese government no longer had control or influence over them.[56] Both the EU and the US objected to the proposed withdrawals, disputing Japan's argument.

---

52. GPA, art. XIX.

53. When a party proposes to withdraw an entity because government control or influence over the entity's covered procurement has been effectively eliminated, it must provide evidence of such elimination. For other proposed modifications, the party must indicate the likely consequences of the change on the mutually agreed coverage under the GPA, art. XIX:1.

54. GPA, art. XIX:2.

55. They were East Japan Railway Company, Central Japan Railway Company, and West Japan Railway Company.

56. WTO, Committee on Government Procurement, GPA/W/144, 145 and 146, August 29, 2001.

In 2006, the US withdrew its objection based on assurances by the Japanese government that its control over the three companies had ended.[57] When the EU maintained its objection, Japan added a note in its Annex 3 in the GPA 2012 that its coverage of the three companies would end when the EU withdrew its objection.[58] In 2022, Japan was still covering those railway companies, as the EU had not withdrawn its objection.

In a second case, Japan proposed in 2003 to withdraw the National Aerospace Laboratory of Japan from its listed entities on the basis that it had been abolished and a newly established entity, the Japan Aerospace Exploration Agency, would carry out its predecessor's activities.[59] However, Japan did not add the new agency to its covered entities. The EU and the US objected to the proposed modification.[60] Their objections remained unresolved when the GPA 2012 was negotiated. That led Japan to add a note in its Annex 3 like its railway companies' note.[61] This dispute also remained unresolved in 2022.

The US faced a similar objection when it attempted to remove the Uranium Enrichment Corporation from its coverage on the

---

57. WTO, Committee on Government Procurement, GPA/MOD/JPN/25, November 30, 2006.

58. Japan's note stated the East Japan Railway Company, Central Japan Railway Company, and West Japan Railway Company "shall be deemed to be included in Group A with respect to Goods and Services of this Annex until such time as the European Union withdraws its objection against the delisting of these companies." GPA, Appendix I, Japan, Annex 3, n. 5.

59. WTO, Committee on Government Procurement, GPA/W/275, September 23, 2003.

60. WTO, Committee on Government Procurement, GPA/W/279 and GPA/W/280, October 2003.

61. Japan's note provided that the "National Aerospace Laboratory of Japan shall be deemed to be included in Group B with respect to Goods and Services of this Annex until such time as the European Union and the United States withdraw their objections against the delisting of this abolished entity." GPA, Appendix I, Japan, Annex 3, n. 6.

grounds that the company had been privatized and sold to investors. That dispute was resolved only when the US withdrew the corporation from its list of covered entities in the GPA 2012 negotiations.[62]

5.2 Arbitration

The GPA 2012 established an arbitration process to prevent prolonged disputes over proposed modifications.[63] It directed the WTO Committee on Government Procurement (Committee) to adopt procedures governing the arbitration process.[64] Until the Committee implemented arbitration procedures, the parties could unilaterally ignore objections. During that interim period, a party could propose a modification to its coverage and implement that modification over the objections of other parties, provided it met certain requirements.[65]

The Committee adopted the arbitration procedures in 2016.[66] With their adoption, any party to a dispute over a proposed modification of coverage may invoke the arbitration process to resolve the dispute. Any objecting party must invoke the arbitration procedures within 120 days of the notice of the modification proposal. If no party initiates arbitration, the modification becomes effective 130 days after the notification, and no party can withdraw coverage from the modifying party.

---

62. See the discussion in Chapter 6.

63. GPA, art. XIX:7.

64. GPA, art. XIX:8(a).

65. The modifying party was required to notify all other parties of the proposed modification and wait until 150 days had passed before implementing it. In that case, any objecting party could withdraw substantially equivalent coverage from the modifying party to compensate for the loss of access to the withdrawn procurement. GPA, Art. XIX:5(c) and 6.

66. WTO, Committee on Government Procurement, "Decision on Arbitration Procedures Pursuant to Article XIX:8 of the Revised GPA, Decision of the Committee of 22 June 2016," GPA/139, June 23, 2016.

When arbitration is invoked, any party with a substantial interest in the proposed modification may participate as a third party. Any objecting party must participate in the arbitration if it intends to seek compensation for the reduction in coverage or withdraw substantially equivalent coverage from the modifying party. The modifying party cannot implement the proposed modification until the arbitration is completed. The arbitration rules allow the participants to submit written and oral arguments. They also stipulate that meetings of the arbitrators (except their deliberations) must be open to the public to ensure transparency unless a participant requests their closure to protect confidential information.[67]

Typically, the parties to the arbitration select three arbitrators, and if they cannot agree on a selection, the WTO Director-General selects the arbitrators for them.[68] Depending on the type of the proposed modification, the arbitrators must determine whether:

(i) government control or influence over the covered procurement of the entity proposed to be withdrawn has been effectively eliminated; or

(ii) the proposed modification maintains a balance of rights and obligations and a comparable level of mutually agreed coverage provided in the GPA and, where appropriate, the level of compensatory adjustment."[69]

The arbitrators' determination binds the parties to the arbitration. If the party proposing the modification does not comply with a negative decision and implements its proposed modification, it must

---

67. The arbitration procedures include a proposed timeline for the conduct of an arbitration, which generally should be completed within three to four months. WTO, "Decision on Arbitration Procedures," Annex.

68. The arbitrators must meet the same requirements–and follow the same rules of conduct–as panelists in WTO dispute settlement cases. The arbitrators may consult experts in making their determination. WTO, "Decision on Arbitration Procedures," para. 3.

69. WTO, "Decision on Arbitration Procedures," para. 10.

compensate the objecting party or parties, or they may withdraw substantially equivalent coverage from it. The parties may ask the arbitrators to determine the appropriate level of compensation.

To date, the GPA parties have invoked the arbitration procedures in only one dispute. They acted in response to a US-proposed modification in November 2020 to remove more than 300 medicines and medical devices from its GPA commitments.[70] In March 2021, Australia, Canada, the EU, Israel, Japan, South Korea, Switzerland, and the UK invoked the arbitration process to challenge the proposed modification. Before the arbitration could proceed, the Biden administration withdrew the proposed modification in April 2021.[71]

To further facilitate the modification process, the GPA 2012 directed the Committee to adopt two sets of criteria. The first set is "indicative criteria" that provide a means to demonstrate the effective elimination of government control or influence over an entity's covered procurement.[72] The second set determines the level of compensation to be offered by a party that modifies its coverage and the level of substantially equivalent coverage to be withdrawn by a party that objects to a modification.[73] As of late 2022, the Committee had yet to adopt either set of criteria. It indicated in its 2021 annual report that it would do so when appropriate.[74]

---

70. WTO, Committee on Government Procurement, "Proposed Modifications to Appendix I of the United States under the Revised Agreement on Government Procurement," GPA/MOD/USA/18, November 27, 2020.

71. See the discussion in Chapter 8.

72. GPA, art. XIX:8(b).

73. GPA, art. XIX:8(c). In developing these criteria, the parties might, for example, specify that government ownership below a certain percentage indicates no government control or influence.

74. WTO, *Report (2021) of the Committee on Government Procurement*, GPA/AR/4, paras. 2.16 and 2.17, November 12, 2021.

PART TWO

US PROCUREMENT: BALANCING LIBERALIZATION AND PROTECTIONISM

INTRODUCTION

After implementing its first international procurement agreement in 1981, the US pursued a strategy that balanced market liberalization and domestic protection for nearly 30 years. It expanded access to foreign procurement markets for US suppliers through revisions of the plurilateral procurement agreements and negotiations of a series of FTAs. Simultaneously, it had to comply with a myriad of laws mandating domestic preferences in direct procurement by federal agencies and state and local government projects that received federal funds. It was able to find the middle ground between liberalization and protectionism because Congress gave the president the authority to waive the application of several 'Buy American' requirements, provided the US was accorded reciprocal access to foreign procurement markets.

During this period, the US utilized its negotiating authority to gain reciprocal access to government procurement markets with more than 60 countries. The US reached the pinnacle of its push for liberalization in 2012 when it implemented the last FTAs with new trading partners. Since then, the US has followed a more protectionist approach and has not implemented any FTAs with new trading partners.

In addition to the GPA and FTAs, the US augmented its procurement commitments through other kinds of agreements. In one bilateral agreement, the US gave the European Union access to subcentral procurement that was not available to other trading partners. In another agreement, the US and Canada exchanged access to the procurement of their respective states and provinces. In addition, the US Department of Defense has negotiated reciprocal defense procurement agreements with nearly 30 countries.

After President Trump entered the White House in 2017, US efforts to liberalize foreign procurement markets halted. His procurement policies centered on an 'America First' platform supported by a bevy of 'Buy American' orders to maximize the procurement of US goods at the expense of foreign goods. While his administration voiced interest in the liberalization of foreign procurement markets, its rhetoric was not matched with action. It only negotiated one FTA, one that was a renegotiation of an earlier agreement. Of greatest consequence, Trump withdrew the US from the Trans-Pacific Partnership, the most important regional agreement of this era.

The US also negotiated an unusual series of procurement agreements with Japan in the 1980s and 1990s. These agreements were intended to address concerns in Congress and industry that Japan was unfairly limiting access to its procurement markets. Unlike FTAs in which the parties exchanged reciprocal access, the agreements with Japan provided one-sided liberalization. Only Japan committed to opening its procurement and removing barriers to US participation in its government procurement. The US undertook no procurement commitments under those agreements.

CHAPTER 5

LIBERALIZATION OF PROCUREMENT THROUGH US BILATERAL AGREEMENTS

1. INTRODUCTION

After implementing its first international procurement agreement, the 1979 GATT Code, the US embarked on negotiations of procurement chapters in FTAs.[1] Beginning in the mid-1980s, it included government procurement provisions in every FTA it negotiated. The development of these FTAs overlapped with the negotiations of plurilateral procurement agreements, first the revision of the GATT Code and then the establishment of the GPA. As a result, these FTAs built on the plurilateral agreements. The initial FTAs followed the GATT Code and provided a modest expansion

---

1. Office of the US Trade Representative (USTR), Free Trade Agreements, accessed April 28, 2022, https://ustr.gov/trade-agreements/free-trade-agreements. Direct links to the government procurement chapters in the FTAs may be found in USTR, Government Procurement, FTAs with Government Procurement Obligations, accessed April 28, 2022, https://ustr.gov/issue-areas/government-procurement/ftas-government-procurement-obligations.

of government procurement. The last of these early agreements, the 1994 North American Free Trade Agreement (NAFTA), had a full-fledged procurement chapter that anticipated procurement provisions in the GPA. Subsequent FTA government procurement chapters closely followed GPA provisions.

The US pursued a relatively uniform approach in the procurement negotiations of these FTAs, essentially applying a 'one-size-fits-all' model to their procurement chapters. These agreements had nearly identical procedural requirements and most opened comparable procurement. While the FTAs covered basically the same federal procurement, they varied in their coverage of state governments. Like the plurilateral agreements, the FTA procurement chapters were based on the concept of reciprocity. The US applied the concept broadly to open comparable procurement among the parties. It did not measure reciprocity based on the dollar value of the procurement markets of its FTA partners.

Through the FTAs, the US exchanged procurement commitments with 19 countries.[2] As only five FTA partners were also GPA parties,[3] the FTAs expanded market access opportunities for US suppliers in other procurement markets based on GPA disciplines.[4] The US liberalization of procurement markets came to an end in 2012 with the implementation of FTAs that had been negotiated during President George W. Bush's administration. Since then, the

---

2. The FTA parties were Australia, Bahrain, Canada, Chile, Colombia, Costa Rica, Dominican Republic, El Salvador, Guatemala, Honduras, Israel, South Korea, Mexico, Morocco, Nicaragua, Oman, Panama, Peru, and Singapore. An FTA with Jordan had only a single procurement provision.

3. The GPA parties were Australia, Canada, Israel, South Korea, and Singapore. Australia did not join the GPA for nearly 15 years after it implemented an FTA with the US. Furthermore, Canada is no longer subject to an FTA, as it opted out of the procurement obligations in the agreement that replaced NAFTA.

4. US International Trade Commission (USITC), *Economic Impact of Trade Agreements Implemented under Trade Authorities Procedures*, 2021 Report, June 2021, 61. For a summary of the commitments contained in the agreements, see USITC, *Economic Impact*, appendix E, table E.4.

US has not implemented an FTA with any new country. It only re-negotiated one of its first FTAs.

The US also negotiated two unique bilateral agreements in which it undertook government procurement commitments outside of plurilateral agreements or FTAs. The first was with the European Union (EU) and the second was with Canada.

In addition, the US Department of Defense (DoD) negotiated reciprocal defense procurement agreements with 27 countries, which opened defense procurement excluded from the GPA and FTAs. Although these agreements are not trade agreements, they further demonstrate the role of reciprocity as the foundation of the American approach to procurement in international agreements.

2. US FTAS IMPLEMENTED BETWEEN 1985 AND 1994

2.1 US-Israel FTA

The first US FTA, the US-Israel FTA, implemented in 1985, represented a modest beginning for FTA procurement commitments between GATT Code parties.[5] It devoted a mere seven paragraphs to procurement. Under the agreement, the US and Israel expanded on the procurement of goods that they covered under the GATT Code in three ways. First, they applied a lower threshold ($50,000) than the Code threshold of 150,000 SDRs.[6] Furthermore, each party promised to waive 'buy national' restrictions for procurement at or above those values. Second, Israel provided US suppliers with access to the purchases of its Ministry of Defense. This was an important addition because Israel did not

---

5. The US-Israel FTA, April 22, 1985, 24 I.L.M. 653, art. 15, accessed April 28, 2022, https://ustr.gov/trade-agreements/free-trade-agreements/israel-fta/final-text.

6. The GATT Code threshold was reduced to 130,000 SDRs in 1988.

cover this ministry under the Code and does not cover it under the GPA.[7] Third, Israel committed to relaxing the offset requirements on purchases by its government agencies (except the defense ministry).[8] Finally, the FTA applied the Code procedures to its covered procurement. It was the only FTA that did not add procedural obligations.

2.2 US-Canada FTA

The second FTA, the US-Canada FTA, was also between GATT Code parties. When it was implemented in 1989, it established the standard of incorporating a separate government procurement chapter in US FTAs.[9] The parties applied the bilateral agreement to the same federal procurement of goods that they covered under the GATT Code. However, they broadened their commitments by using a lower threshold ($25,000) than the Code threshold.

In the FTA, the US and Canada also reaffirmed their rights and obligations under the GATT Code and expanded on procedural obligations by adding new disciplines. One new discipline required the parties to specify, in advance, the criteria used to qualify potential suppliers and the criteria applied to evaluate bids and award contracts. It further stipulated that these criteria be free of any domestic preferences.

Of particular significance, the Canada FTA was the first FTA to introduce bid challenge procedures that enabled companies to

---

7. The US-Israel FTA provided that the Israeli defense ministry was "subject to exceptions comparable in character and extent" to those of the US Department of Defense in the GATT Code. US-Israel FTA, art. 15.

8. The US-Israel FTA deferred implementation of its procurement provisions for most agencies for one year after it entered into force and for defense agencies until Israel completed the list of defense exceptions comparable to those of the US.

9. US-Canada FTA, December 22, 23, 1987 and January 2, 1988, 27 I.L.M. 281 (1988). The government procurement provisions were in FTA Chapter 13 and Annexes 1304.3 and 1305.3.

seek review of contract award decisions.[10] It directed the parties to establish and maintain bid challenge procedures.[11] It required a reviewing authority with no substantial interest in the outcome of the procurement to receive and decide challenges by suppliers regarding the conduct of procurement covered by the FTA. With the implementation of NAFTA[12] in January 1994, this FTA was suspended; its suspension continued when the US-Mexico-Canada Agreement (USMCA) replaced NAFTA in 2020.[13]

2.3 NAFTA

NAFTA "initiated a new generation of US trade agreements in the Western Hemisphere and other parts of the world."[14] As the most comprehensive FTA negotiated at the time, its groundbreaking rules influenced subsequent agreements negotiated by the US and other countries.[15] Entering into force on January 1, 1994, NAFTA governed trade among the US, Canada, and Mexico for 25 years until it was replaced by the USMCA.

NAFTA's government procurement chapter could not directly incorporate the GATT Code because Mexico was not a Code

---

10. Stephen Woolcock, "Public Procurement in EU FTAs," in *Law and Practice in the Common Commercial Policy*, eds. Michael Hahn and Guillaume Van der Loo (Leiden: Brill Nijhoff, 2020), 238.

11. The US has maintained a bid protest system since the 1920s. Daniel I. Gordon, "In the Beginning: The Earliest Bid Protests Filed with the US General Accounting Office," *Public Procurement Law Review* 13, no. 5 (2004): 147–64.

12. NAFTA, December 8, 1993, http://www.sice.oas.org/trade/nafta/naftatce. asp. The government procurement provisions were in NAFTA's Chapter 10 and Annexes 1001.1a-1 through 1010.1.

13. *US-Mexico-Canada Agreement Implementation Act*, Public Law 116–113, § 601 (2020).

14. US Library of Congress, Congressional Research Service, *International Trade and Finance: Overview and Issues for the 116th Congress*, by Andres B. Schwarzenberg et al., R45474 (2020), 26, http://sgp.fas.org/crs/row/R45474.pdf.

15. Congressional Research Service, *International Trade and Finance*, 26.

signatory. Instead, it became the first US FTA with a procurement chapter comprised of detailed principles and procedures that followed the basic structure of the Code, establishing a precedent for subsequent FTAs. In addition to national treatment and non-discrimination obligations, the agreement prohibited the use of offsets in the qualification and selection of suppliers, goods, or services, the evaluation of bids, and the award of contracts. It prescribed disciplines for each stage of the procurement process to ensure that procurement covered by NAFTA was conducted in a fair, transparent, and non-discriminatory manner. It also built on the Canada FTA's bid challenge provisions by, for example, requiring a minimum 10-day period for suppliers to submit a bid challenge to a procurement.

The NAFTA negotiations overlapped those of the GPA 1994, although NAFTA's implementation preceded that of the plurilateral agreement by two years. Thus, NAFTA became the first US agreement to cover the procurement of services, construction services, and government enterprises. However, unlike the GPA, NAFTA never covered subcentral entities, despite including commitments to seek such coverage.[16]

NAFTA covered federal government entities and government enterprises. Each party listed federal government entities: Canada (78 federal entities), Mexico (23 ministries with numerous subordinate entities), and the US (52 federal departments and agencies). Regarding government enterprises, Canada listed 10 enterprises, such as the Canada Post Corporation and Via Canada Rail Inc., and Mexico covered nearly 50 enterprises, including its oil companies.

The US included several federal entities in NAFTA that it did not cover under the GATT Code but subsequently added in the GPA 1994. These entities were the Departments of Energy and

---

16. NAFTA called for negotiations to further liberalize government procurement markets to begin before the end of 1998 and for the parties "to endeavor to consult with their state and provincial governments with a view to obtaining commitments, on a voluntary and reciprocal basis" to cover procurement under the agreement. NAFTA, art. 1024(3). The negotiations were never undertaken.

Transportation, the Department of Interior's Bureau of Reclamation, and the federal electric utilities, namely, the Tennessee Valley Authority and four power administrations. Applying the reciprocity principle, the US withheld access to procurement by the Bureau of Reclamation and the federal electric utilities from Canada until that country opened the procurement of its provincial hydro utilities. The US also covered the Rural Utilities Service's financing of electric generation and telecommunications projects for the first time, with a commitment to not apply that agency's 'buy national' requirement to products from Canada and Mexico.

The agreement set a threshold of $50,000 for goods and services purchased by federal government entities, except the US and Canada carried over the $25,000 threshold from their bilateral FTA for goods procurement. The $50,000 threshold was adjusted every two years for inflation and was incorporated in subsequent FTAs at the adjusted level.

As the first US FTA to cover the procurement of services, NAFTA established a precedent for the manner of specifying services covered under US agreements. Following the approach used for the coverage of goods, NAFTA required the parties to open the procurement of all services and construction services except those that each party expressly excluded in a 'negative list.'[17] Subsequently, the US followed this approach in all FTAs and the GPA. Canada excluded a number of services. NAFTA permitted Mexico to initially open the procurement of only services listed and convert its service commitments to a negative list by July 1, 1995. However, it was not until 2004 that Mexico reached an agreement with the US and Canada on its permanent list of excluded services. That list became effective in June 2005.[18]

---

17. When a party used a 'negative list,' it covered the procurement of all services except those that it listed. This contrasted with a 'positive list,' which a party used to list only the services it covered.

18. USTR, *2005 National Trade Estimate Report on Foreign Trade Barriers*, 418, March 30, 2005; *Diario Oficial de la Federacion* [Official Gazette of the Federation of Mexico], 95, June 1, 2005.

NAFTA also allowed Mexico to apply several special measures, specifically set-asides, local content requirements, and the exclusion of certain drugs. First, it permitted Mexico to set aside the following from the agreement's obligations:

(i) $1 billion of procurement annually for the first nine years of the agreement (through 2002) and $1.2 billion each year starting from 2003, and

(ii) beginning in 2003, $300 million annually for two government enterprises, *Petróleos Mexicanos* and *Comisión Federal de Electricidad*.

Second, NAFTA allowed a Mexican procuring entity to impose local content requirements up to 40% in labor-intensive turnkey or major integrated projects or 25% in capital-intensive turnkey or major integrated projects. The third special measure permitted several agencies to exclude the procurement of drugs not patented in Mexico or whose Mexican patents had expired from NAFTA requirements for eight years after the agreement was implemented.[19]

3. US-JORDAN FTA

The US-Jordan FTA, which entered into force in December 2001, stands alone as the only US FTA without substantive procurement obligations.[20] It only committed the parties to enter negotiations regarding Jordan's accession to the GPA. Jordan applied for GPA membership in 2000 but had not completed its accession as of late 2022.[21]

---

19. This special measure applied to the Ministry of Health, the Mexican Social Security Institute, the Institute for Social Security and Services for Government Employees, and the Ministry of National Defense.

20. US-Jordan FTA, 2001, art. 9, accessed April 28, 2022, https://ustr.gov/trade-agreements/free-trade-agreements/jordan-fta/final-text.

21. For a discussion of Jordan's negotiations to join the GPA, see Chapter 14.

4. US FTAS IMPLEMENTED BETWEEN 2004 AND 2012

Beginning in 2004, the US entered a series of 11 FTAs with procurement chapters built on NAFTA and incorporated improvements added to the GPA 2012. The new provisions included electronic procurement requirements and opportunities for procuring entities to reduce the tendering period when they purchased commercial goods and services or published notices and tender documentation electronically.

This second set of FTAs incorporated the same fundamental principles as the GPA and most of its procedural obligations. Although these agreements are not identical, the US Government Accountability Office found they "generally have similarities in text, and commitments, potentially because parties negotiated multiple agreements concurrently."[22] It identified nine elements that were common to the agreements: provisions that relate to transparency, non-discrimination, defining scope and coverage, exceptions, procurement procedures, criteria for procurement decisions, supplier challenges, ethical standards, and further improvements.[23] The US International Trade Commission (USITC) also compared procurement provisions in the FTAs.[24]

The FTAs reflected the parties' interests and domestic priorities, as well as the characteristics of their procurement systems. They also included provisions not found in the GPA, such as the integrity of government procurement provisions. These integrity provisions required each party to adopt legislation or other measures to prevent corruption by making both the giving and receiving of a

---

22. US Government Accountability Office (GAO), *Government Procurement Agreements Contain Similar Provisions, but Market Access Commitments Vary*, September 2016. It included a timeline of the negotiations of the GPA and selected FTAs. *Government Procurement Agreements*, 2.

23. GAO, *Government Procurement Agreements*, 8.

24. USITC, *Economic Impact*, table E-4, 312.

bribe a criminal offense. In addition, these FTAs covered a form of public-private partnerships, namely, build-operate-transfer (BOT) and public works concession contracts, as a type of contract for construction services.[25]

In the negotiations of the FTAs, the US allowed its partners to choose NAFTA thresholds, GPA thresholds, or a mixture of the two. For example, they could select the GPA threshold for goods and services and the NAFTA threshold for construction services. But all parties to the FTA were required to apply the chosen thresholds. When a NAFTA threshold was used in an FTA, the FTA would incorporate the value of the latest biannual adjustment of the threshold.[26]

Table 5.1 provides a comparison of several elements of the FTAs: their dates of signing and entry into force (and the president then in office), the thresholds that they applied to federal or central government procurement, and whether the FTA covered subcentral entities and other entities.[27] It shows they are similar but not identical.

---

25. BOT contracts are "any contractual arrangement, the primary purpose of which is to provide for the construction or rehabilitation of physical infrastructure, plant, buildings, facilities, or other government-owned works and under which, as consideration for a supplier's execution of a contractual arrangement, the entity grants to the supplier, for a specified period of time, temporary ownership or a right to control and operate, and demand payment for the use of, such works for the duration of the contract." See, for example, US-Chile FTA, June 6, 2003, accessed April 28, 2022, https://ustr.gov/trade-agreements/free-trade-agreements/chile-fta/final-text, art. 9.20.

26. The biannual adjustment of thresholds is discussed in Chapter 6.

27. For a comparison of the FTA provisions, see GAO, *Government Procurement Agreements*.

TABLE 5.1. US FTA Comparisons

FTA	Year Signed (President in Office)	Year of Entry into Force (President in Office)	Thresholds for Federal or Central Government Entities — Goods and Services	Thresholds for Federal or Central Government Entities — Construction Services	Coverage of Subcentral Entities	Coverage of Other Entities
Australia FTA	2004 (GW Bush)	2005 (GW Bush)	NAFTA threshold	GPA threshold	Yes	Yes
Canada FTA	1988 (Reagan)	1989 (Reagan)	$25,000	n/a	No	No
Bahrain FTA	2004 (GW Bush)	2006 (GW Bush)	GPA threshold	NAFTA threshold	No	Yes
Chile FTA	2003 (GW Bush)	2004 (GW Bush)	NAFTA threshold	GPA threshold	Yes	Yes
Colombia TPA	2006 (GW Bush)	2012 (Obama)	NAFTA threshold	GPA threshold	Yes	Yes
CAFTA-DR FTA	2004 (GW Bush)	2006-2009 (GW Bush)	NAFTA threshold	GPA threshold	Yes	Yes
Israel FTA	1985 (Reagan)	1985 (Reagan)	$50,000 (goods only)	n/a	No	No
South Korea FTA	2007 (GW Bush)	2012 (Obama)	$100,000	GPA threshold	No	No
Jordan FTA	2000 (Clinton)	2001 (GW Bush)	n/a	n/a	No	No

FTA	Year Signed (President in Office)	Year of Entry into Force (President in Office)	Thresholds for Federal or Central Government Entities		Coverage of Subcentral Entities	Coverage of Other Entities
			Goods and Services	Construction Services		
NAFTA	1992 (HW Bush)	1994 (Clinton)	$50,000 (except $25,000 for goods for US and Canada)	$6.5 million	Yes	Yes
Morocco FTA	2004 (GW Bush)	2006 (GW Bush)	GPA threshold	GPA threshold	Yes	Yes
Oman FTA	2006 (GW Bush)	2009 (GW Bush)	GPA threshold	NAFTA threshold	No	Yes
Panama TPA	2007 (GW Bush)	2012 (Obama)	GPA threshold	GPA threshold	Yes	Yes
Peru TPA	2006 (GW Bush)	2009 (Obama)	GPA threshold	GPA threshold	Yes	Yes
Singapore FTA	2003 (GW Bush)	2004 (GW Bush)	NAFTA threshold	GPA threshold	Yes	Yes
USMCA	2018 (Trump)	2020 (Trump)	NAFTA threshold	NAFTA threshold	No	Yes

The following sections highlight elements of each FTA entered between 2004 and 2012 in the order in which they were implemented. Chapter 6 details the procurement that the US covered in these FTAs; hence, the discussion below addresses US commitments only where they diverge from standard US FTA coverage.

4.1 US-Chile FTA

The US began negotiations of its first post-NAFTA FTAs, those with Chile and Singapore, in December 2000. Both FTAs were implemented in January 2004.[28] The US-Chile FTA was the first US FTA with a South American country. It was also the only US FTA with a non-GPA partner to mirror the coverage of the GPA 1994 in all three categories of entities (federal, subcentral, and other entities).[29] For its central government coverage, Chile listed 19 ministries and its presidency, as well as 13 regional governments and 183 *municipalidades*. In addition, Chile covered 10 ports and airports owned by the state and all services (except financial and related services). The Chile FTA provided a 30-day tendering period, in contrast to the standard 40 days found in the GPA and most FTAs.

4.2 US-Singapore FTA

Since the US and Singapore are parties to the GPA, the government procurement chapter of the US-Singapore FTA incorporated most of the GPA provisions.[30] It also included the parties' GPA market

---

28. US-Chile FTA. The government procurement provisions are in the FTA's Chapter 9 and Annex 9.1.

29. The US covered the same federal entities in FTAs with Chile, Australia, Colombia, Panama, and Peru.

30. US-Singapore FTA, May 6, 2003, accessed April 28, 2022, https://ustr.gov/sites/default/files/uploads/agreements/fta/singapore/asset_upload_file708_4036.pdf. The government procurement provisions are in the FTA's Chapter 13 and Annexes 13A and 13B.

access commitments (except Singapore's coverage of services). In the GPA, Singapore listed the services that it covered in a positive list. In contrast, the Singapore FTA based its service coverage on a negative list and excluded 11 categories of services such as security services, certain financial services, and radio and television services. The FTA incorporated a provision tailored to government enterprises in which Singapore had effective influence. In procurement by such enterprises, it prohibited Singapore from exercising "any control or influence, including through any shares that it owns or controls or its personnel selections to corporate boards or positions."[31]

The Singapore FTA was the first US FTA to cover the government procurement of digital products "that are transmitted electronically and are created, produced, contracted for, commissioned, or first made available on commercial terms in the territory of the other Party."[32] It defined digital products as "computer programs, text, video, images, sound recordings and other products that are digitally encoded, regardless of whether they are fixed on a carrier medium or transmitted electronically."[33] The US incorporated similar provisions in subsequent FTAs.

In the FTA, Singapore and the US confirmed "their desire and determination to apply the [Asia-Pacific Economic Cooperation's (APEC)] Non-Binding Principles on Government Procurement, as appropriate, to all their government procurement that is outside

---

31. US-Singapore FTA, art. 13.2.4. The FTA provided that "effective influence exists where the government and its government enterprises, alone or in combination: (a) own more than 50 percent of the voting rights of an entity; or (b) have the ability to exercise substantial influence over the composition of the board of directors or any other managing body of an entity, to determine the outcome of decisions on the strategic, financial, or operating policies or plans of an entity, or otherwise to exercise substantial influence over the management or operation of an entity." US-Singapore FTA, art. 12.8.5.

32. US-Singapore FTA, art. 13.2(6)(a).

33. US-Singapore FTA, art. 14.4.

the scope of the GPA and this Chapter."[34] Even though it was non-binding, the provision indicated interest by the parties in the conduct of procurement not subject to trade agreements.

4.3 US-Australia FTA

On January 1, 2005, nearly 15 years before Australia became a GPA party, it joined the US in implementing the US-Australia FTA (AUSFTA).[35] The FTA facilitated the country's eventual GPA accession by requiring it to make substantial changes in its procurement system. Those changes would have been necessary for Australia to comply with the GPA.

When Australia entered FTA negotiations with the US, it sought to preserve its informal and flexible procurement system, which emphasized the importance of streamlining procurement practices and maintaining flexibility in the procurement process "to keep pace with a rapidly changing world."[36] However, because Australia's system did not comply with the standard provisions in US FTAs, the US insisted that Australia revise its procurement system.

The Australian government was reluctant to convert its principles-based procurement system to one based on specific rules. It was concerned that a rules-based system would unnecessarily constrain its procurement practices. The country eventually agreed to reform its system in part due to complaints from its own business community. Australian businesses argued that they

---

34. US-Singapore FTA, art. 13.1(4).

35. AUSFTA, May 18, 2004, accessed April 28, 2022, https://ustr.gov/trade-agreements/free-trade-agreements/australian-fta/final-text. The government procurement provisions are in the FTA's' Chapter 15 and Annex 15-A.

36. Australian Department of Finance and Administration, "2002 Commonwealth Procurement Guidelines and Best Practice Guidance," February 12, 2002. Jean Heilman Grier, "The Role of International Trade Agreements in the Converging of Procurement Systems" (Conference materials, The Government Contracts Year in Review Conference, Washington, DC, February 17, 2009).

were being shut out of the US federal procurement market by the procurement ban mandated by the US Trade Agreements Act of 1979, while American firms were free to participate in Australia's procurement market.[37]

The two countries eventually reached an agreement on a government procurement chapter modeled on the GPA, albeit with provisions tailored to the Australian procurement system. For example, the FTA set a 30-day tendering period in place of the standard 40-day period and allowed the reduction of the tendering period by an additional five days when the procurement notice and tender documentation were published electronically. It also included extensive provisions on selective tendering intended to both accommodate and restrict Australia's particular use of this tendering method.

US FTAs and the GPA typically include rules for selective tendering that require all suppliers to be allowed to request participation in procurement conducted under that tendering method. In addition, procuring entities must invite all suppliers that meet the qualification requirements to submit a tender. When an entity intends to limit the number of suppliers invited to submit tenders, it must provide notice of its intention. In contrast to these standard provisions and to accommodate Australia's practice, the AUSFTA permitted a procuring entity to restrict its invitation to tender to suppliers that had been granted a license or complied with specific legal requirements unrelated to the procurement.

The AUSFTA procurement chapter covered 77 Australian central government entities, all its states and territories, and 32 other entities. Under the agreement, the US listed 31 states, including one (Georgia) that it did not cover under the GPA or any other FTA.

---

37. The Trade Agreements Act of 1979 generally prohibits federal agencies from purchasing goods and services from countries that are not parties to a trade agreement with the US. *Trade Agreements Act of 1979*, Public Law 96-39, U.S. *Statutes at Large* 93 (1979): 144.

In addition, Australia excluded the procurement of two categories of services: plasma fractionation services and government advertising services.

To bring its procurement system into accord with the AUSFTA, the Australian government issued new Commonwealth Procurement Guidelines that took effect on the same day as the bilateral agreement. These guidelines noted that the revision "represents a change in the Government's policy with regard to procurement, including prescriptions for procurement processes which have not existed in the past" and would "allow agencies to act in a manner consistent with [its] international agreements."[38]

The AUSFTA listed the goods and services that Australia excluded for its Department of Defence and Defence Materiel Organisation, as well as the goods that the US excluded for the DoD (as it did in all FTAs). It was the only FTA to note that certain defense procurement excluded under the FTA was covered by a separate reciprocal defense procurement agreement. In the FTA, the parties reaffirmed their commitments in that defense agreement.[39]

4.4 US-Morocco FTA

The US has negotiated only one FTA with an African country, the US-Morocco FTA, which was implemented on January 1, 2006.[40] It covered 30 Moroccan central government entities, 77 prefectures and provinces, and 137 other entities. It excluded three categories of

---

38. Australian Department of Finance and Administration, "Commonwealth Procurement Guidelines, Financial Management Guidance No. 1," January 2005.

39. The Memorandum of Agreement Between the Government of Australia and the Government of the United States Concerning Reciprocal Defense Procurement, April 19, 1995. For a discussion of reciprocal defense procurement agreements, see Section 6 of this Chapter.

40. US-Morocco FTA, June 15, 2004, accessed April 28, 2022, https://ustr. gov/trade-agreements/free-trade-agreements/morocco-fta/final-text. The government procurement provisions are in the FTA's Chapter 9 and Annex 9-A-1 through Annex 9-G.

services: quality control and inspection services, geological services, and certain utilities management services. It also did not cover certain construction services such as dredging and construction of official and national landmark buildings. Under a transitional measure, Morocco was permitted to delay the implementation of a provision of the FTA relating to the domestic review of supplier challenges.[41]

A side letter between the parties clarified the provision in the government procurement chapter that the FTA applied to an entity procuring by any contractual means. It included Morocco's

> "public concessions of services, under which a procuring entity awards a contract for the provision of a specified public service and, as consideration for a supplier's execution of a contractual arrangement, grants to the supplier, for a specified period, the right to demand payment for the services provided by the supplier under the contract."[42]

4.5 CAFTA-DR

In 2004, the US negotiated a regional FTA with the Dominican Republic and five Central American countries (Costa Rica, El Salvador, Guatemala, Honduras, and Nicaragua). The Dominican Republic-Central America-US FTA (CAFTA-DR) could be implemented only when the US and at least one other signatory had completed their domestic approval process.[43] After the US approved CAFTA-DR in 2005, it executed it with the other parties on a

41. Morocco was given a year to provide for the suspension of a contract award and the performance of a contract pending the resolution of a supplier's challenge of a procurement.

42. US-Morocco FTA, Side Letter on Government Procurement and Services. June 15, 2004.

43. CAFTA-DR, August 5, 2004, accessed April 28, 2022, https://ustr.gov/trade-agreements/free-trade-agreements/cafta-dr-dominican-republic-central-america-fta/final-text. The government procurement provisions are in the FTA's Chapter 9 and Annex 9.1.2 (b)(i).

'rolling basis' after each party had concluded its domestic approval process. CAFTA-DR became operative in 2006 for El Salvador, Guatemala, Honduras, and Nicaragua; 2007 for the Dominican Republic; and 2009 for Costa Rica.

CAFTA-DR specified procurement coverage obligations in three annexes. The primary annex defined the coverage between the US and each of the Central American parties as well as the Dominican Republic.[44] The following discussion considers only the coverage obligations in that annex.

Under CAFTA-DR, the US covered 79 federal entities, and the other parties covered between 11 and 35 central government entities. Regarding subcentral governments, the Central American parties incorporated numerous *municipalidades*, and the Dominican Republic covered regional governments. They also included a variety of other entities. All the parties (except El Salvador) excluded various services, predominantly public services. Following the example of the US, several parties did not cover the management of government-owned facilities (Costa Rica, the Dominican Republic, and Nicaragua) or transport services (the Dominican Republic and Honduras). Costa Rica also excluded gambling and betting services. The parties covered all construction services (except dredging, matching the US exclusion). The Dominican Republic withheld the procurement of construction services from suppliers of Puerto Rico until Puerto Rico provided reciprocal access to its construction services.

The regional FTA permitted each Central American party and the Dominican Republic to apply higher transitional thresholds for three years following its implementation of the agreement. It also allowed the Dominican Republic to maintain certain offsets in construction services, provided it applied them in a transparent

---

44. CAFTA-DR, Annex 9.1.2(b)(i) was the primary annex. The second annex (Annex 9.1.2(b)(ii)) set out the obligations applied among the five Central American countries based on their own community obligations. The third annex (Annex 9.1.2(b)(iii)) specified the market access obligations that applied between the Central American countries and the Dominican Republic.

and non-discriminatory manner. The Dominican Republic could require a foreign supplier participating in the procurement of construction services covered by the agreement to be associated with an enterprise established under its domestic laws and capitalized with Dominican or mixed Dominican and foreign capital. In addition, the agreement permitted the Dominican Republic to limit the foreign supplier's share in the enterprise to 50% under certain conditions and require 50% of the management of procurement covered by the FTA to be comprised of Dominican nationals.[45]

Both Costa Rica and the Dominican Republic excluded government procurement programs on behalf of their small, medium, and micro enterprises. The Dominican Republic's exclusion extended to any form of preference. Nicaragua maintained a price preference of 10% for such enterprises for five years after implementing the agreement. It also agreed to consult with the US on any extension of the price preference or other proposed measures for the benefit of these entities.

4.6 US-Bahrain FTA

The US sought agreements with three members of the Gulf Cooperation Council (GCC), a regional intergovernmental political and economic union consisting of all Arab states of the Persian Gulf, to expand its FTAs in the Middle East beyond Israel. The US successfully negotiated FTAs with two GCC members (Bahrain and Oman) but with more limited market access commitments than other FTAs. However, it was unable to conclude negotiations of an FTA with a third GCC member, the United Arab Emirates.

The US-Bahrain FTA entered into force on January 11, 2006, with Bahrain covering 28 ministries and other central-level

---

45. These percentages were to be reduced over 15 years. Before the end of that period, the Dominican Republic and the US were to consult on the future Dominican Republic's application of offsets. If they were unable to reach an agreement, the US could reduce the country's access to US procurement.

government entities and 17 other entities, including the Bahrain Petroleum Company.[46] The US limited its coverage to 52 federal entities and several federal government enterprises; the agreement did not include subcentral coverage. Bahrain excluded services generally corresponding to those that the US excluded, as well as arbitration, conciliation, and certain financial intermediation services. The FTA authorized Bahrain to apply higher transitional thresholds for two years after its implementation.

4.7 US-Oman FTA

On January 1, 2009, three years after the US implemented its FTA with Bahrain, the US-Oman FTA became effective.[47] It is the only US FTA that does not cover the US DoD due to Oman's refusal to cover its defense agency. Under the FTA, Oman covered 33 central-level government entities, including its refinery, oil companies, and five other entities, such as its gas company.[48] The US covered only 50 federal agencies–the lowest number in any FTA. The agreement did not include any subcentral government entities. Regarding services, Oman excluded seven categories, including utilities, transportation services, and certain financial intermediation services. It also reserved the right to maintain its existing preference program to promote

---

46. US-Bahrain FTA, September 14, 2004, accessed April 28, 2022, https://ustr.gov/trade-agreements/free-trade-agreements/bahrain-fta/final-text. The government procurement provisions are in the FTA's Chapter 9 and Annex 9.

47. US-Oman FTA, January 19, 2006, accessed April 28, 2022, https://ustr.gov/trade-agreements/free-trade-agreements/oman-fta/final-text. The government procurement provisions are in the FTA's Chapter 9 and Annex 9.

48. The agreement included a side letter between the parties on state-owned enterprises. It stated: "[w]ith respect to procurement, the Sultanate of Oman Government does not exercise any undue control or influence in procurement conducted by Omantel, Petroleum Development Oman, and Oman Liquefied Natural Gas. The Sultanate of Oman shall ensure that all procurement by these entities is conducted in a transparent and commercial manner." US-Oman FTA, Side Letter on State-owned Enterprises, January 19, 2006.

the development of its SMEs. The FTA permitted Oman to apply a higher transitional threshold for goods and services for two years.[49]

4.8 US-Peru TPA

In November 2003, the administration of President George W. Bush notified Congress of its intent to negotiate an FTA with four Andean countries: Colombia, Peru, Ecuador, and Bolivia.[50] In May 2004, the US launched negotiations with all of them (except Bolivia). Bolivia became an observer to the negotiations.[51] After multiple rounds of talks, the trading partners were unable to conclude a regional agreement. The US continued bilateral negotiations with each of the three countries, reaching separate arrangements with Colombia and Peru. It failed to reach an agreement with Ecuador.

The US and Peru concluded negotiations of a bilateral agreement, the US-Peru Trade Promotion Agreement (Peru TPA), in December 2005 and signed it in April 2006. Before they implemented the TPA, the two countries agreed to a Protocol of Amendment in May 2007.[52] The Protocol was needed to implement a Bipartisan Agreement on Trade Policy that the Bush administration and congressional Democrats reached on May 10, 2007 (known as the May

---

49. The agreement included a second side letter on impartial review. It recognized that Oman's Administrative Judicature Court satisfied the FTA's requirement of an impartial authority for the domestic review of supplier challenges. US-Oman FTA, Side Letter on Impartial Authority, January 19, 2006.

50. USTR, "USTR Notifies Congress of Intent to Initiate Free Trade Talks with Andean Countries," November 18, 2003, https://ustr.gov/archive/Document_Library/Press_Releases/2003/November/USTR_Notifies_Congress_of_Intent_to_Initiate_Free_Trade_Talks_with_Andean_Countries.html.

51. USTR, "Peru and Ecuador to Join with Colombia in May 18-19 Launch of FTA Negotiations with the US," May 3, 2004.

52. US Congress, House of Representatives, Committee on Ways and Means, *United States-Peru Trade Promotion Agreement Implementation Act* (*US-Peru TPA Implementation Act*), 110th Cong. 1st sess., 2007, H. Rept. 110-421, https://www.congress.gov/congressional-report/110th-congress/house-report/421.

10th Agreement).[53] The May 10th Agreement resolved Congress's concerns with the original TPA and enabled it to approve the bilateral agreement. It called for the inclusion in the text of core labor and environmental standards of pending and future trade agreements. The Peru TPA was the first to incorporate such provisions when it entered into force on February 1, 2009.[54]

The May 10th Agreement required a modification of the Peru TPA's government procurement chapter "to allow conditioning of contracts on adherence to basic and minimum labor standards."[55] This provision clarified the role of TPA parties in enforcing labor laws in government procurement. It allowed the parties to require suppliers to comply with core labor laws in the country where goods were produced or services were performed.[56] The provision was not intended to allow TPA governments to impose protectionist requirements, such as forcing contractors that manufacture their products abroad to comply with labor rules in the importing country. Subsequently, Colombia, South Korea, and Panama agreements added the same provision. The labor provision was similar to a clarification in the GPA and FTAs that government agencies may provide for the promotion of environmental protection in their procurement requirements.[57]

---

53. USTR, "Statement from Ambassador Susan C. Schwab on US trade agenda," May 10, 2007, https://ustr.gov/about-us/policy-offices/press-office/press-releases/archives/2007/may/statement-ambassador-susan-c-schwab-us-trade-; USTR, *Trade Facts*, May 2007, https://ustr.gov/sites/default/files/uploads/factsheets/2007/asset_upload_file127_11319.pdf.

54. US-Peru TPA, April 12, 2006, accessed April 28, 2022, https://ustr.gov/trade-agreements/free-trade-agreements/peru-tpa/final-text. The government procurement provisions are in the FTA's Chapter 9 and Annex 9.1.

55. US Congress, *US-Peru TPA Implementation Act*.

56. The labor laws may range from fundamental principles and rights at work to acceptable labor conditions, such as occupational safety and health requirements.

57. GPA, art. X:6 ("For greater certainty, a Party, including its procuring entities, may, in accordance with this Article, prepare, adopt or apply technical specifications to promote the conservation of natural resources or protect the environment").

Under the Peru TPA's government procurement chapter, Peru covered 61 central government entities, 25 regional governments, and 23 other entities. The agreement also introduced a unique reciprocity provision relating to subcentral procurement that was intended to overcome the reluctance of states to authorize coverage of their procurement in trade agreements. Under this policy, Peru's regional governments could deny access to their procurement to suppliers from US states that did not cover their own procurement under the TPA. Similarly, US states participating in the procurement chapter could decline access to suppliers from any Peruvian subcentral entity that did not provide reciprocal access to its procurement. Only eight states and Puerto Rico agreed to bring their procurement under the TPA. Two more states subsequently authorized coverage of their procurement under the agreement.

Peru covered all construction services and all but five categories of services. It excluded accounting and auditing, architectural, engineering, design services (during construction and installation phases), and arbitration and conciliation services. It also excluded procurement programs on behalf of small and micro-sized companies.

4.9 US-Korea FTA

The US-Korea FTA (KORUS FTA) between the US and South Korea stood out in the second set of FTAs because its coverage was limited to federal and central government procurement. It was one of three FTAs signed by President George W. Bush and implemented under President Obama.[58] It was also one of the few FTAs that the US had negotiated with a GPA party. The KORUS FTA was signed on June 30, 2007, and entered into force five years later, on March 15, 2012.[59]

---

58. The other FTAs were the US-Peru TPA and the US-Panama TPA.

59. KORUS FTA, June 30, 2007, accessed April 28, 2022, https://ustr.gov/trade-agreements/free-trade-agreements/korus-fta/final-text. The government procurement provisions are in the FTA's Chapter 17 and Annex 17-A.

The KORUS FTA's procurement commitments only applied to 51 South Korean central government entities and 79 US federal entities. Its exclusion of subcentral and other entities was the consequence of the US's refusal to pursue coverage of any states under the FTA. South Korea already had the right to participate in the procurement of the 37 states that the US listed under the GPA. The US had concluded that it was unlikely to be able to obtain authorizations from the non-GPA-covered states to cover their procurement under the FTA. South Korea responded to the US position by refusing to cover any other entities in the FTA. Only the Israel and Canada FTAs, restricted to central government procurement of goods, were narrower in scope.

The South Korean agreement introduced a new threshold of $100,000 (or ₩100 million) for the procurement of goods and services. The parties agreed to this threshold because when they negotiated the FTA, all federal procurement up to $100,000 was set aside for US small businesses, and South Korea would not have been able to participate in such procurement.[60] Hence, the threshold was set at that level.

In contrast to other FTAs in which all parties based their service commitments on a negative list of excluded services, the KORUS FTA incorporated both parties' GPA coverage of services. Under the GPA, South Korea covered only listed services, while the US opened the procurement of all services except those it listed. As in other FTAs, the US exchanged access to BOT contracts and public works concession contracts. South Korea excluded set-asides for its small- and medium-sized businesses.

The KORUS FTA incorporated provisions from the GPA 1994, as well as those included in the GPA 2012, which was being negotiated at the same time as the FTA. It further included the labor text that was based on the May 10th Agreement with Congress.

---

60. The small business set-aside threshold was later increased to $250,000, as described in Chapter 7.

The FTA also referred to the parties' cooperation on procurement matters in APEC, similar to the Singapore FTA provision.

4.10 US-Colombia TPA

The US-Colombia TPA resembled other contemporary FTAs. It differed only in its special provisions for certain government enterprises. The parties signed the agreement on February 27, 2006 and implemented it more than six years later–on May 15, 2012.[61]

Under the TPA, Colombia listed 28 central government entities, including all three branches of government as well as four entities labeled "control agencies."[62] At the subcentral level, it covered 32 entities, whereas the US included eight states and Puerto Rico under the reciprocity policy discussed above. The agreement also permitted Colombia to apply a higher transitional threshold for construction services for three years after its implementation.

Colombia covered 22 other government entities, including *Empresa Colombiana de Petróleos, S.A.* (ECOPETROL), a government enterprise subject to special provisions. ECOPETROL was permitted to apply either the procurement procedures in the agreement or equivalent measures. It could also limit its tendering period to 10 business days rather than the FTA's 40-day tendering period. In addition, it excluded several services from its commitments, such as financial auditing, investment banking, insurance, and pension services. Finally, ECOPETROL could convert to a new category of an entity called Special Covered Entities, provided it met the requisite conditions.

---

61. US-Colombia TPA, November 22, 2006, accessed April 28, 2022, https://ustr.gov/trade-agreements/free-trade-agreements/colombia-tpa/final-text. The government procurement provisions are found in the FTA's Chapter 9 and Annex 9.1.

62. The control agencies were the *Contraloría General de la República, Auditoría General de la República, Procuraduría General de la Nación*, and *Defensoría del Pueblo*.

Special Covered Entities was a category created for Colombia. They were Colombian government entities that were not subject to Colombia's procurement law. Instead, they conducted their procurement under private law. The Colombia TPA listed three Special Covered Entities: *Interconexion Electrica S.A., ISAGEN,* and *Colombia Telecomunicaciones.* The TPA required them to conduct their procurement transparently, following commercial considerations, and without any control or influence by the Colombian government. It also limited them to a national treatment obligation in conducting their procurement. This meant they could not discriminate against US goods or services in favor of Colombian goods and services. None of the agreement's procedural obligations applied to them.

Colombia excluded six categories of services, including utilities, engineering, and architectural services. It also exempted set-asides of procurement below $125,000 on behalf of small, medium, and micro enterprises. The set-asides comprised any form of preference, such as the exclusive right to provide goods or services, as well as measures to facilitate the transfer of technology and subcontracting.

4.11 US-Panama TPA

For the US, the most important procurement opened under the US-Panama TPA was access for US suppliers to Panama Canal procurement.[63] The US had a unique history with the Panama Canal. Until December 1999, the US controlled the Canal and listed its operator, the Panama Canal Commission, as a federal entity covered under the GATT Code and the GPA 1994. It removed that entity from US coverage under the plurilateral agreement after the Government of the Republic of Panama assumed authority and

---

63. US-Panama TPA, June 28, 2007, accessed April 28, 2022, https://ustr.gov/trade-agreements/free-trade-agreements/panama-tpa/final-text. The government procurement provisions are in the FTA's Chapter 9 and Annex 9.1.

responsibility for the operation of the Panama Canal in December 1999, based on the 1977 Panama Canal Treaty.

The Panama TPA covered the procurement of the Panama Canal Authority, which replaced the Panama Canal Commission as the operator of the Panama Canal. When the parties signed the TPA in June 2007, Panama was embarking on a major expansion of the Panama Canal. The US anticipated that the TPA would provide opportunities for participation by US firms in the Canal's expansion. But a delay in Congress's approval of the agreement—and hence its implementation—significantly curtailed the ability of US firms to participate in the expansion. This delay lasted for more than five years, until October 31, 2012, when the TPA took effect.

The Panama Canal Authority was subject to special provisions to facilitate its coverage under the TPA and its expansion of the Panama Canal. First, it was permitted to apply a threshold for construction services of $12 million for 12 years after the agreement entered into force (until 2024) and $10.3 million thereafter. These thresholds were much higher than the $7.4 million threshold applied by other government enterprises under the TPA. Second, the Panama Canal Authority could reserve 10% of its procurement to expand the Canal for Panamanian nationals or suppliers owned and controlled by Panamanian nationals, subject to certain conditions. That set-aside was applicable during the first 12 years of the agreement, which coincided with the estimated duration of the Canal's expansion.

The third set of special measures applied to the Panama Canal Authority's procurement procedures. Specifically, it was excused from the minimum 40-day period for tendering and permitted to reduce its tendering period to five business days from when it published a procurement notice online. It was also exempted from two provisions relating to domestic review of supplier complaints. It could reduce the time for a supplier to submit a challenge to procurement to five business days (rather than the 10-day period required for other challenges). In addition, the TPA did not require the Authority to suspend a contract award or performance of a contract during the review of a supplier challenge. Finally, the Canal's procurement could not be challenged under the TPA's dispute settlement provisions relating to nullification or impairment.

In addition to the Panama Canal Authority, Panama listed 13 ministries, its legislative assembly, Comptroller General, and judicial authority at the central government level, as well as 12 provinces and 30 other government entities. Panama excluded several categories of services that generally reflected those excluded by the US.

Moreover, the FTA excluded Panamanian procurement measures designed to promote small, medium, and micro enterprises, which were businesses with 100 or fewer employees and total annual sales not exceeding $2.5 million. For the first five years of the FTA, Panama was permitted to apply a price preference of up to 10% for such enterprises, provided the preference was transparent. In addition, Panama was given two years to comply with the 40-day tendering period; during that time, it had to allow suppliers at least 30 days to submit tenders.

5. BILATERAL PROCUREMENT AGREEMENTS

5.1 1995 US-EU Agreement on Government Procurement

The US and the EU signed a bilateral procurement agreement, the US-European Communities Memorandum of Understanding on Government Procurement, on May 30, 1995.[64] The bilateral

---

64. Agreement in the Form of an Exchange of Letters on Government Procurement between the European Community and the United States of America, May 30, 1995, https://ustr.gov/issue-areas/government-procurement/us-european-communities-1995-exchange-letters. The US and the EU initialed the bilateral agreement on April 15, 1994, the same day they joined in signing the GPA 1994.

agreement resulted from negotiations between the US and the EU on the expansion of coverage under the GPA 1994. The two parties incorporated most of the results of their negotiations into the GPA but reserved certain US subcentral commitments for the EU in the 1995 bilateral agreement. The US agreed to provide the EU with access to procurement not covered under the GPA or any FTA. This coverage included access to procurement of three states,[65] the Massachusetts Port Authority, and seven cities.[66] Unlike other agreements, it did not include entity lists, thresholds, exclusions, or any requirements relating to the conduct of the procurement. It also did not contain any EU commitments.[67]

Though relatively unknown, this bilateral agreement remains important as a US procurement agreement. Its continuing significance was recognized in implementing the American Recovery and Reinvestment Act of 2009 (Recovery Act). That law excluded procurement covered by an international agreement from its domestic purchasing requirement. The bilateral agreement was listed as one of the international agreements covered by the legislation's exclusion.[68]

---

65. The three states were Illinois, North Dakota, and West Virginia.

66. The cities were Boston, Chicago, Dallas, Detroit, Indianapolis, Nashville, and San Antonio.

67. For a description of the procurement covered by the agreement, see Chapter 6.

68. The US-EU agreement was listed as one of the "international agreements that obligate recipients that are covered under an international agreement to treat the goods and services of a Party the same as domestic goods and services." Office of Management and Budget, "Requirements for Implementing Sections 1512, 1605, and 1606 of the American Recovery and Reinvestment Act of 2009 for Financial Assistance Awards," *Federal Register* 75, no. 57 (March 25, 2010): 14323–14330, https://www.govinfo.gov/content/pkg/FR-2010-03-25/pdf/2010-6548.pdf; 2 *Code of Federal Regulations* 2, Part 176, accessed April 28, 2022, https://www.ecfr.gov/cgi-bin/text-idx?node=pt2.1.176&rgn=div5.

5.2 2010 US-Canada Agreement on Government Procurement

Canada's 2009 request for a US waiver of a new 'Buy American' requirement provided an unexpected opportunity for the US to realize a long-held aim of obtaining access to Canada's provincial procurement. Canada made the waiver request for its goods and suppliers to gain access to procurement in a broad array of state and local infrastructure projects funded by the Recovery Act.[69] This law required the use of American-made iron, steel, and manufactured goods in projects that it funded unless the project was covered by an international agreement (or another exception applied). It applied to infrastructure projects undertaken by states and other nonfederal entities. Hence, Canada did not qualify for the exclusion because it had no right to participate in US subcentral procurement under any agreement.

The US and Canada had not exchanged commitments relating to subcentral coverage under NAFTA[70] or the GPA. The US withheld its GPA coverage of states from Canada because Canada was unwilling to open the procurement of its provinces. Canada had refused to cover its provinces under the GPA because the US would not "exempt Canadian businesses from [its] small business set-asides" and other excluded procurement.[71] As a consequence, Canadian suppliers had to comply with the domestic content requirement to participate in Recovery Act projects.

---

69. *American Recovery and Reinvestment Act of 2009*, Public Law 111-15, *U.S. Statutes at Large* 123 (2009): 115. It was enacted at the beginning of President Obama's first term.

70. NAFTA did not cover any subcentral procurement.

71. Kamala Dawar, "The Government Procurement Agreement, the Most-Favored Nation Principle, and Regional Trade Agreements," in *The Internationalization of Government Procurement Regulation*, eds. Aris Georgopoulos, Bernard Hoekman and Petros C. Mavroidis (Oxford: Oxford University Press, 2017), 117.

Canada's request for a waiver of the domestic content requirement led to intensive negotiations between the two neighbors, albeit with different aims. The US insisted that Canada open the procurement of its provinces in exchange for relief from the 'Buy American' requirement. Canada, however, only proposed an exchange of temporary access to construction projects that would enable it to participate in Recovery Act projects without meeting the 'Buy American' restriction. After six months of negotiations, the countries reached an agreement that effectively met both aims. In the US-Canada Agreement on Government Procurement, signed on February 12, 2010, and implemented four days later, they exchanged permanent and reciprocal commitments concerning provincial, territorial, and state procurement under the GPA and temporary enhanced coverage of construction projects.[72]

Most important to the US, for the first time, Canada committed to open the procurement of its provinces and territories (except Nunavut) to the US. Canada also agreed to incorporate that coverage into the GPA. The US provided Canada with access to the procurement of the states covered under the GPA by removing the reciprocity restriction that had excluded Canada from state coverage. Rather than obligate Canadian entities to comply with the GPA 1994 text, the bilateral agreement required them to conduct procurement in accordance with the revised GPA text, which had been approved on an interim basis in 2007. Furthermore, the agreement recognized that the provincial entities would have to comply with the GPA on an expedited basis. As a result, the US agreed not to seek dispute settlement proceedings against Canada for any failure of its entities to comply with specified GPA provisions for one year after implementing the bilateral agreement.

---

72. US-Canada Agreement on Government Procurement, February 10, 2010, https://ustr.gov/issue-areas/government-procurement/us-canada-agreement-government-procurement.

In the second part of the bilateral agreement, the two parties committed to exchange temporary enhanced coverage of certain construction projects through September 30, 2011, the deadline for obligating funds for projects under the Recovery Act. Paramount for Canada, the US pledged not to impose the Act's 'Buy American' restriction on Canadian iron, steel, and manufactured goods in procurement above a threshold of 5 million SDRs in seven programs funded by the legislation.[73] The US also agreed to incorporate that commitment in its GPA coverage, where it could have been enforced through the plurilateral agreement's dispute settlement provisions. Subsequently, the US added this commitment and a list of the Recovery Act programs to its coverage in the GPA 1994.[74]

For its part, Canada offered temporary access for US iron, steel, and manufactured goods to certain provincial and municipal construction projects. Canada only agreed to apply core principles, namely, national treatment and transparency obligations, as well as domestic review procedures for these projects. Canada specified the scope of coverage of each province and territory, either stating that all its Crown Corporations and municipalities were covered or listing those that were covered (or excluded). It did not incorporate this temporary access into the GPA.

The US-Canada Agreement was unusual in requiring the parties to modify their GPA commitments. It also benefited the other

---

73. The US programs were: (i) US Department of Agriculture (USDA), Rural Utilities Service, *Water and Waste Disposal Programs*; (ii) USDA, Rural Housing Service, *Community Facilities Program*; (iii) Department of Energy (DoE), Office of Energy Efficiency and Renewable Energy, *Energy Efficiency and Conservation Block Grants*; (iv) DoE, Office of Energy Efficiency and Renewable Energy, *State Energy Program*; (v) Department of Housing and Urban Development (HUD), Office of Community Planning and Development, *Community Development Block Grants Recovery*; (vi) HUD, Office of Public and Indian Housing, *Public Housing Capital Fund*; and (vii) Environmental Protection Agency, *Clean Water and Drinking Water State Revolving Funds*.

74. The list was not incorporated into the GPA 2012 because the commitment applied only through September 2011.

GPA parties as it obligated Canada to offer the same subcentral coverage to them in the negotiations of the GPA 2012. The bilateral agreement demonstrated the "effective negotiating muscle of GPA parties outside of the venue of the WTO,"[75] as well as the role of reciprocity conditions in opening procurement markets.

6. RECIPROCAL DEFENSE PROCUREMENT AGREEMENTS

The DoD has entered reciprocal defense procurement agreements in the form of memoranda of understanding with its counterparts in several countries. These agreements are not trade agreements but include similar provisions. A country signing a reciprocal defense procurement agreement with the US became a qualifying country under the Defense Federal Acquisition Regulation Supplement,[76] and its products were afforded the same treatment as domestic products in DoD procurement.[77] In these agreements, the US and a qualifying country exchanged commitments to remove barriers to purchases of supplies manufactured in or services provided by the other country. Such agreements generally applied to all DoD procurement, including military items, unless the procurement was excluded for national security purposes.

DoD exempted products covered by a defense agreement from the application of the Buy American Act of 1933 and its Balance of Payments Program based on a determination that it would be in-consistent with the public interest to apply them to products from

---

75. Dawar, "The Government Procurement Agreement," 116.

76. Defense Federal Acquisition Regulation Supplement (DFARS) 225.872-1 and -3.

77. Christopher R. Yukins and Allen Green, "International Trade Agreements and US Procurement Law," in *The Contractor's Guide to International Procurement*, eds. Erin Loraine Felix and Marques Peterson (Chicago: American Bar Association, 2018), 173.

its agreement partners.[78] Similarly, the qualifying country was obligated to exempt US products from any 'buy local' laws or policies applicable to procurement by that country's defense entities. All the qualifying countries[79] (except Egypt and Turkey) are parties to the GPA or a US FTA.

Reciprocal defense procurement agreements included elements similar to provisions in trade agreements. For example, in addition to the national treatment obligation, the defense agreements required defense procurement to be conducted following certain requirements found in trade agreements. The procedures in these defense agreements included the publication of notices of proposed purchases, the content and availability of solicitations for proposed purchases, the notification of unsuccessful offerors, the provision of feedback, upon request, to unsuccessful offerors concerning the reasons they were prohibited from participating in procurement or were not awarded a contract, and the provision for the hearing and review of complaints arising in connection with any phase of the procurement process.[80]

---

78. DFARS 225.872-1(a).

79. The qualifying countries were Australia, Austria, Belgium, Canada, Czech Republic, Denmark, Egypt, Estonia, Finland, France, Germany, Greece, Israel, Italy, Japan, Latvia, Luxembourg, Netherlands, Norway, Poland, Portugal, Slovenia, Spain, Sweden, Switzerland, Turkey, and the United Kingdom of Great Britain and Northern Ireland. DFARS 225.003(10).

80. DoD, "Defense Acquisition Regulation System, Negotiation of a Reciprocal Defense Procurement Memorandum of Understanding With the Ministry of Defense of Japan," *Federal Register* 80, no. 251 (December 31, 2015): 81812, https://www.govinfo.gov/content/pkg/FR-2015-12-31/pdf/2015-32945.pdf.

CHAPTER 6

US PROCUREMENT COVERED UNDER TRADE AGREEMENTS

1. INTRODUCTION

While the US has made commitments in numerous international agreements to open its government procurement to foreign suppliers, it has been remarkably uniform in the procurement covered under these agreements. This uniformity is founded on plurilateral agreements, first the 1979 GATT Code and then the GPA. The US has rarely offered procurement under an FTA that it has not already covered (or was preparing to cover) under a plurilateral agreement.

The US relies on five basic elements to specify the procurement that it covers under the GPA and FTAs. It begins with the lists of the government agencies or enterprises whose procurement is subject to the agreement. These entities are listed in three categories: central government, subcentral government, and other entities, reflecting GPA categories. Another element is thresholds, the monetary value below which procurement is not covered.

Next, the US lists the goods that it excludes from its obligations. Similarly, the US lists the services and construction services that it does not open under the agreement. Finally, it sets out agreement-wide exclusions.

An examination of the procurement that the US covers under international agreements illustrates the breadth and depth of its commitments. It also reveals the limits on its coverage arising from domestic purchasing restrictions. In its efforts to expand procurement, the US has faced substantial challenges in including the purchases made by subcentral entities, principally state governments. Unlike many other trading partners, the US does not require its subcentral entities to cover their procurement under these agreements; rather, it seeks their authorization to participate in agreements.

The US coverage under agreements is not static. It has modified its coverage from time to time, adding and removing entities following modification provisions in the GPA and FTAs. In most cases, the US changed its list of entities in response to laws that created, abolished, or merged entities or transferred functions between entities.

Together, the US procurement commitments and the changes to these commitments illustrate how the US negotiates procurement agreements and maintains uniformity across agreements.

2. FEDERAL GOVERNMENT ENTITIES

In negotiations of the plurilateral procurement agreements, the US started with a core group of federal agencies and subsequently expanded its covered agencies. It began with an initial list of 53 federal entities under the GATT Code in 1981 and then expanded that list to approximately 75 federal entities under the GPA 1994. In the negotiations of the GPA 2012, the US added 12 more federal agencies, including the Social Security Administration and the

Transportation Security Administration.[1] In 2022, the US listed 85 entities under the GPA.[2]

For its coverage under FTAs, the US has–in most cases–incorporated the federal agencies covered under the plurilateral agreement in effect when it negotiated the FTA. The US included the entities listed in the GATT Code in its FTAs with Canada and Israel and the North American Free Trade Agreement (NAFTA). In the US-Chile FTA and subsequently negotiated FTAs, the US generally incorporated the entities listed in the GPA 1994, though with several exceptions. For example, the FTAs with Bahrain and Oman covered around 50 entities, which remain significantly less than the nearly 80 entities listed in most FTAs. In another exception, the US-Oman FTA did not include the Department of Defense (DoD) because Oman did not cover its defense entity. Finally, in the US-Mexico-Canada Agreement (USMCA), the only FTA that the US implemented after expanding its coverage in the GPA 2012, the US did not include the entities added in that agreement. Instead, it replicated its NAFTA coverage of 52 entities.

The US covered all the goods purchased by the federal agencies listed under the GPA and FTAs (except for DoD and exclusions for several civilian agencies). For the procurement excluded for civilian entities under the GPA and FTAs, see Table 6.1.

---

1. The other 10 federal agencies were the Advisory Council on Historic Preservation, Court Services and Offender Supervision Agency for the District of Colombia, Federal Energy Regulatory Commission, Federal Labor Relations Authority, Millennium Challenge Corporation, National Assessment Governing Board, National Endowment for the Arts, National Endowment for the Humanities, US Access Board, and US Marine Mammal Commission.

2. For a list of the covered entities, see GPA, Appendix I, US, Annex 1. GPA, accessed May 18, 2022, https://www.wto.org/english/tratop_e/gproc_e/gp_gpa_e.htm. The number of entities covered under the GPA fluctuated from time to time with modifications to US coverage.

TABLE 6.1. Procurement Excluded for US Civilian Entities

US Federal Entity	Procurement Excluded for the Entity
Department of Agriculture	Agricultural goods made in furtherance of agricultural support or human feeding programs
Department of Commerce	Procurement related to the shipbuilding activities of the US National Oceanic and Atmospheric Administration
Department of Energy	Procurement that supports the safeguarding of nuclear materials or technology where the procurement is conducted under the Atomic Energy Act and oil purchases related to the Strategic Petroleum Reserve
Department of Homeland Security	Procurement by the Transportation Security Administration of Federal Supply Code (FSC) 83 (textiles, leather, furs, apparel, shoes, tents, and flags) and FSC 84 (clothing, individual equipment, and insignia)
Department of Transportation	Procurement by the Federal Aviation Administration[3]
General Services Administration	Hand tools (FSC 51), measuring tools (FSC 52), and cutlery and flatware
US Agency for International Development	Procurement for the direct purpose of providing foreign assistance

Source: GPA, Appendix I, US, Annex 1, notes 1 to 8.

---

3. The Federal Aviation Administration was exempt from the Federal Acquisition Regulation (FAR) and major procurement laws such as the Competition in Contracting Act, which mandated that agencies use full and open competitive procedures for procurement. Robert Brodsky, "TSA contracting exemption to end next month," *Government Executive*, May 27, 2008, https://www.govexec.com/oversight/2008/05/tsa-contracting-exemption-to-end-next-month/26957/.

Consistent with the practice of other parties, the US applied special treatment to the coverage of DoD. The US identified its commitments in four lists under the GPA. Two lists specified goods that are excluded from DOD's commitments because they are subject to domestic purchasing requirements[4] (see Table 6.2).

A third DoD list[5] is comprised of goods that are generally not covered due to the application of the agreement's national security exception.[6] Finally, in a fourth list, for purposes of transparency, the US lists goods that are generally covered for this Department, subject to the application of the national security exception.[7]

TABLE 6.2. Procurement Excluded for the US Department of Defense

Federal Supply Code (FSC)[8]	Procurement Excluded for the Department of Defense
FSC 19	Ships, small craft, pontoons, and floating docks (the part of this classification defined as naval vessels or major components of the hull or superstructure thereof)
FSC 20	Ship and Marine Equipment (the part of this classification defined as naval vessels or major components of the hull or superstructure thereof)
FSC 2310	Passenger motor vehicles (only buses)
FSC 51	Hand tools

---

4. GPA, Appendix I, US, Annex 1, n. 4(a) and (b).

5. GPA, Appendix I, US, Annex 1, n. 4(c).

6. GPA, art. III:1.

7. GPA, Appendix I, US, Annex 1, n. 4(d). This list is not included in FTAs.

8. For a complete list of US Federal Supply Classifications, see the Product and Service Code Manual at https://www.acquisition.gov/psc-manual.

Federal Supply Code (FSC)[8]	Procurement Excluded for the Department of Defense
FSC 52	Measuring tools
FSC 83	Textiles, leather, furs, apparel, shoes, tents, and flags (all elements other than pins, needles, sewing kits, flagstaffs, flagpoles, and flagstaff trucks)
FSC 84	Clothing, individual equipment, and insignia (all elements other than subclass 8460–luggage)
FSC 89	Subsistence (all elements other than sub-class 8975–tobacco products)
N/A	Specialty metals and goods containing a specialty metal[9]

Source: GPA, Appendix I, US, Annex 1, n. 4(a).

3. SUBCENTRAL GOVERNMENT ENTITIES

3.1 State Authorizations to Cover Procurement under Agreements

Under the US federal system of government, its 50 states and territories enjoy substantial autonomy. In addition, even though local governments draw their authority from the states, they have independent authority. State and local governments have their own

---

9. A specialty metal refers to: (i) steel for which the maximum alloy content exceeds one or more of the following levels: manganese, 1.65%; silicon, 0.60%; or copper, 0.60%; (ii) steel that contains more than 0.25% of aluminum, chromium, cobalt, columbium, molybdenum, nickel, titanium, tungsten, or vanadium; (iii) a metal alloy consisting of a nickel, iron-nickel, or cobalt-base alloy that contains a total of other alloying metals (except iron) in excess of 10%; (iv) titanium or a titanium alloy; or (v) zirconium or a zirconium-base alloy. GPA, Appendix I, US, Annex 1, n. 4(b).

procurement laws, which are diverse, resulting in little if any harmonization across federal, state and local governments.[10] However, states that receive funds from the federal government must follow certain minimum procedures and apply domestic purchasing requirements imposed as a condition of their use of federal funds.[11]

In the negotiations of the GPA in the early 1990s, the parties agreed to extend the scope to include subcentral entities for the first time. According to one legal analysis, the US, "as a matter of constitutional law," could have bound state procurement in the negotiations of the GPA 1994 without their consent.[12] Yet, it chose not to do so. That legal analysis has suggested that Congress was reluctant "for political reasons [...] to preempt the states in an area so closely connected with state governmental operations as the purchase of supplies and equipment."[13] Instead, the US sought voluntary commitments from states to bind their procurement under the GPA.

The US Trade Representative (USTR) wrote to the governor of each state, seeking their authorization to cover that state's procurement under the GPA.[14] When a state granted such authorization, the US allowed it to determine the entities it would cover and any

---

10. Christopher R. Yukins and Allen Green, "International Trade Agreements and US Procurement Law," in *The Contractor's Guide to International Procurement*, eds. Erin Loraine Felix and Marques Peterson (Chicago: American Bar Association, 2018).

11. Uniform Administrative Requirements, Cost Principles, and Audit Requirements for Federal Awards, Code of Federal Regulations 2, Part 200.

12. James D. Southwick, "Binding the States: A Survey of State Law Conformance with the Standards of the GATT Procurement Code," *University of Pennsylvania Journal of International Law* 13 (1992): 58.

13. Southwick, "Binding the States," 66.

14. For a detailed discussion of the USTR's correspondence with the states relating to their authorizations to cover their procurement under the GPA, see Scott Sheffler, "A Balancing Act: State Participation in Free Trade Agreements with 'Sub-central' Procurement Obligations," *Public Contract Law Journal* 44, no. 4 (2015): 724–27.

goods or services that it would exclude from its commitments. The US listed the 37 states that provided consent in the GPA.[15]

The US followed this approach in all FTAs that included sub-central coverage (except the first two FTAs to cover states).[16] In the Chile and Singapore FTAs, the US carried over the 37 states covered under the GPA without seeking state authorization. Singapore already had access to state procurement as a GPA party, but Chile did not. In all subsequent FTAs, the USTR sought permission from states to cover their procurement under the FTAs. It only listed a state in an agreement with its explicit approval.

Obtaining state approval to cover its procurement under FTAs grew increasingly difficult in the mid-2000s as states raised concerns that such commitments could mean the loss of state sovereignty. For example, several states withdrew their authorizations to cover state procurement under the Dominican Republic-Central American-US FTA (CAFTA-DR) before it was concluded.[17]

In addition, beginning in 2005, several states, including Maryland, Hawaii, Minnesota, and Rhode Island, enacted laws prohibiting their governors from authorizing the US to cover their state procurement under international agreements and required approval by the state legislature for such coverage.[18] Maryland was the first state to take such action. In 2005, its General Assembly enacted legislation, over the governor's veto, that revoked "the governor's authority to commit Maryland to FTA procurement obligations" without the explicit consent of the legislature.[19]

---

15. GPA, Appendix I, US, Annex 2.

16. Sheffler, "A Balancing Act," 728.

17. Southwick, "Binding the States," 58, 66. "New Hampshire Joins Majority of States in Rejecting CAFTA's Restrictions on State Procurement Policy," *Public Citizen*, May 16, 2005, https://www.citizen.org/news/new-hampshire-joins-majority-of-states-in-rejecting-caftas-restrictions-on-state-procurement-policy/.

18. Sheffler, "A Balancing Act," 742–43.

19. Sheffler, "A Balancing Act," 743–44.

When the government of Chile raised concerns with the effect of the Maryland legislation on that state's coverage under its FTA with the US, Maryland's governor pointed out the state's "'procurement policies do not prohibit businesses in Chile or other foreign nations from applying or competing for contracts with the State [and the legislation] does not alter the State's procurement policies'."[20]

A further challenge to the coverage of state procurement under international agreements is the potential withdrawal of a state's procurement commitments. For example, both Montana and New Hampshire have sought to withdraw from such obligations. However, to date, the US has not withdrawn any state from its coverage under the GPA or FTAs, even though it has recognized that such a mechanism exists.[21]

3.2 States and Cities Covered under Agreements

Forty US states have commitments to open some of their procurement to foreign suppliers under one or more international agreements. Out of these 40 states, 37 cover procurement under the GPA and FTAs with Chile and Singapore.[22] Of the 13 states not covered under the GPA or the Chile and Singapore FTAs,[23] one state–Georgia–is covered under an FTA, the US-Australia FTA (AUSFTA). In

---

20. Sheffler, "A Balancing Act," 745–46 (quoting a letter from the Maryland Governor to the US Ambassador to Chile).

21. Sheffler, "A Balancing Act," 741–43.

22. The 37 states were Arizona, Arkansas, California, Colorado, Connecticut, Delaware, Florida, Hawaii, Idaho, Illinois, Iowa, Kansas, Kentucky, Louisiana, Maine, Maryland, Massachusetts, Michigan, Minnesota, Mississippi, Missouri, Montana, Nebraska, New Hampshire, New York, Oklahoma, Oregon, Pennsylvania, Rhode Island, South Dakota, Tennessee, Texas, Utah, Vermont, Washington, Wisconsin, and Wyoming.

23. The 13 states were Alabama, Alaska, Georgia, Indiana, Nevada, New Jersey, New Mexico, North Carolina, North Dakota, Ohio, South Carolina, Virginia, and West Virginia.

addition, Puerto Rico, a US territory, covered its procurement in FTAs with Central and South American countries.

Moreover, three states have commitments under a bilateral agreement with the European Union (EU), the 1995 Memorandum on Government Procurement (EU MOU).[24] Under the EU MOU, North Dakota and West Virginia, which are not covered by the GPA or any FTA, provide EU suppliers with access to their procurement. A third state, Illinois, which covers procurement under the GPA, opened additional procurement under the EU agreement, such as procurement below GPA thresholds. The only procurement responsibility of these states is a national treatment obligation to provide the best out-of-state treatment to EU suppliers. Although they are not required to accept bids from outside their state, when they do, they must allow EU suppliers to participate in the procurement. The EU agreement also committed the US to open procurement of cities for the first time in any agreement. The US covers seven cities based on best out-of-city treatment.[25] That means the cities have only a national treatment obligation to accept bids from EU suppliers when they accept bids from suppliers outside their cities. Finally, the bilateral agreement committed the Massachusetts Port Authority to provide best out-of-state treatment when it considered offers from non-Massachusetts suppliers.

Table 6.3 shows the agreements under which each state has a commitment to open procurement to foreign participation.

---

24. For a discussion of the negotiations of the EU MOU, see Chapter 1.

25. The cities were Boston, Chicago, Dallas, Detroit, Indianapolis, Nashville, and San Antonio.

TABLE 6.3. States that Cover Procurement under International Agreements

States and Territory	WTO GPA	AUSFTA	CAFTA-DR	US–Chile FTA	US–Colombia TPA	US–Morocco FTA	US–Panama TPA	US–Peru TPA	US–Singapore FTA	1995 US–EU MOU
Arizona	x								x	
Arkansas	x	x	x	x	x	x	x	x	x	
California	x	x		x					x	
Colorado	x	x	x	x	x	x	x	x	x	
Connecticut	x	x	x	x		x			x	
Delaware	x	x	x	x		x		x	x	
Florida	x	x	x	x	x	x	x	x	x	
Georgia		x								
Hawaii	x	x	x	x		x			x	
Idaho	x	x	x	x		x			x	
Illinois	x	x		x	x		x	x	x	x
Iowa	x			x					x	
Kansas	x	x		x		x			x	
Kentucky	x	x	x	x		x			x	
Louisiana	x	x	x	x		x			x	
Maine	x	x		x					x	
Maryland	x	x	x	x		x			x	
Massachusetts	x			x					x	
Michigan	x	x		x					x	
Minnesota	x			x					x	

States and Territory	WTO GPA	AUSFTA	CAFTA-DR	US-Chile FTA	US-Colombia TPA	US-Morocco FTA	US-Panama TPA	US-Peru TPA	US-Singapore FTA	1995 US-EU MOU
Mississippi	x	x	x	x	x	x	x	x	x	
Missouri	x			x					x	
Montana	x			x					x	
Nebraska	x	x	x	x		x			x	
New Hampshire	x	x	x	x		x			x	
New York	x	x	x	x	x	x	x	x	x	
North Dakota										x
Oklahoma	x	x		x				x	x	
Oregon	x	x	x	x		x			x	
Pennsylvania	x	x		x					x	
Rhode Island	x	x	x	x		x			x	
South Dakota	x	x	x	x		x			x	
Tennessee	x	x	x	x		x			x	
Texas	x	x	x	x	x	x	x	x	x	
Utah	x	x	x	x	x	x	x	x	x	
Vermont	x	x	x	x		x			x	
Washington	x	x	x	x		x			x	
West Virginia									x	x
Wisconsin	x	x	x	x					x	
Wyoming	x	x	x	x		x			x	
Puerto Rico	x	x	x		x		x	x		

The US does not cover state procurement under its FTAs with Bahrain, Israel, South Korea, Oman, or the USMCA.[26]

US states covered a wide range of entities under the agreements. Some states listed specific agencies, whereas others broadly included 'executive branch agencies' without naming them. In the GPA 2012 negotiations, the US added specific agencies for seven states whose coverage had previously been described as 'executive agencies.'[27] Except for Texas, each state covered the same procurement and maintained the same exclusions in the GPA and FTAs.[28] The US applied the same thresholds and exclusions for states in the GPA and FTAs, thus ensuring that state obligations were uniform across agreements.

3.3 Reciprocity Policy Applied to State Procurement

President George W. Bush's administration undertook a major effort to persuade states to cover their procurement under FTAs. It negotiated a special reciprocity policy in FTAs with Colombia, Panama, and Peru. That policy was designed to incentivize states to authorize coverage of their procurement in those FTAs. Under the reciprocity policy, when a state did not participate in an FTA by covering its procurement, the FTA partner's subcentral entities could deny that state's suppliers the right to participate in their procurement. Only suppliers from states that covered procurement under the FTA were guaranteed non-discriminatory access to the FTA partner's subcentral procurement. The states that agreed to such coverage could similarly restrict access to their procurement to nonparticipating

---

26. Israel and South Korea had rights to participate in state procurement as parties to the GPA.

27. The seven states were Arizona, California, Kansas, Oklahoma, Tennessee, Utah, and Washington.

28. Texas added several exclusions in authorizing coverage of its procurement in FTAs: the procurement of motor vehicles, travel agencies located in Texas, and certain rubberized asphalt paving from its commitments.

subcentral entities of the FTA partners.[29] The reciprocity policy fell far short of its aim. Only eight states and Puerto Rico agreed to open their procurement under those FTAs–the lowest number of states authorizing coverage under any FTAs.[30] Subsequently, no administration attempted to cover state procurement under any FTA.[31]

3.4 State Procurement Restrictions

The US took two types of restrictions or exclusions for procurement covered by states under the GPA and FTAs. One applied to all states, and the other was limited to specific states. Those that applied to all states were:

(i) preferences or restrictions associated with programs promoting the development of distressed areas and businesses owned by minorities, disabled veterans, and women

(ii) procurement by a covered-state entity on behalf of a non-covered entity at a different level of government (such as a city or county), and

(iii) restrictions in procurement that promote general environmental quality, as long as they are not disguised barriers to international trade (for example, preferences for domestic suppliers).

The states were also covered by the general exclusions that applied to all US procurement subjects to agreements.

In addition, the agreements limited foreign participation in certain infrastructure projects that received federal funding. They

---

29. For a more detailed discussion of the reciprocity policy, see Sheffler, "A Balancing Act," 728–29.

30. After the implementation of the US-Peru Trade Promotion Agreement, two more states were added to it.

31. The US did not offer any subcentral coverage in the USMCA or Trans-Pacific Partnership.

excluded 'Buy American' or other domestic purchasing requirements that were attached to federal funds for mass transit and highway projects undertaken by states. While the states could permit foreign suppliers to participate in such projects, they must require the supplier to meet the 'Buy American' requirement imposed by the federal financing.

The second type of state restrictions were exceptions applied by certain states. Two-thirds of the states covered under the GPA and FTAs excluded certain procurement or limited their market-opening commitments. For example, a dozen states did not cover construction-grade steel, motor vehicles, and coal, and six states excluded construction contracts (see Table 6.4). Fourteen states had no exclusions.[32]

TABLE 6.4. State-specific Exclusions of Procurement

State	State-specific Exclusions
Arizona	None
Arkansas	Construction services
California	None
Colorado	None
Connecticut	None
Delaware	Construction-grade steel (including requirements on subcontracts), motor vehicles, and coal
Florida	Construction-grade steel (including requirements on subcontracts), motor vehicles, and coal
Hawaii	Construction services, software developed in the state
Idaho	None

32. The 14 states with no exclusions were Arizona, California, Colorado, Connecticut, Idaho, Louisiana, Massachusetts, Minnesota, Missouri, Nebraska, Oregon, Utah, Vermont, and Wisconsin.

State	State-specific Exclusions
Illinois	Construction-grade steel (including requirements on subcontracts), motor vehicles, and coal
Iowa	Construction-grade steel (including requirements on subcontracts), motor vehicles, and coal
Kansas	Construction services, automobiles, and aircraft
Kentucky	Construction services
Louisiana	None
Maine	Construction-grade steel (including requirements on subcontracts), motor vehicles, and coal
Maryland	Construction-grade steel (including requirements on subcontracts), motor vehicles, and coal
Massachusetts	None
Michigan	Construction-grade steel (including requirements on subcontracts), motor vehicles, and coal
Minnesota	None
Mississippi	Services
Missouri	None
Montana	Goods
Nebraska	None
New Hampshire	Construction-grade steel (including requirements on subcontracts), motor vehicles, and coal
New York	Construction-grade steel (including requirements on subcontracts), motor vehicles, and coal; procurement by public authorities and public benefit corporations with multistate mandates; transit cars, buses, and related equipment
North Dakota	None
Oklahoma	Construction services, construction-grade steel (including requirements on subcontracts), motor vehicles, and coal
Oregon	None
Pennsylvania	Construction-grade steel (including requirements on subcontracts), motor vehicles, and coal

State	State-specific Exclusions
Rhode Island	Boats, automobiles, buses, and related equipment
South Dakota	Beef
Tennessee	Services, including construction services
Texas	Motor vehicles, travel agencies located in Texas, and certain rubberized asphalt paving (not included in the GPA or FTAs with Chile and Singapore)
Utah	None
Vermont	None
Washington	Fuel, paper products, boats, ships, and vessels
West Virginia	None
Wisconsin	None
Wyoming	Construction-grade steel (including requirements on subcontracts), motor vehicles, and coal

4. GOVERNMENT ENTERPRISES AND OTHER ENTITIES

The US offered relatively modest coverage of government enterprises and other entities under its agreements. Beginning with NAFTA and the GPA 1994, the US opened the procurement of five federal entities engaged in the electricity sector: the Tennessee Valley Authority and four power marketing administrations (Bonneville, Southeastern, Southwestern, and Western Area). It also covered the St. Lawrence Seaway Development Corporation. The US included these entities in its commitments in all agreements that covered other entities. It made few changes in its coverage of these entities after it first offered them.[33]

The US broadened its coverage of government enterprises in the GPA and the Chile and Singapore FTAs by covering several

---

33. The US covered the Alaska Power Administration until it removed the entity from its coverage (see section 7).

subcentral authorities. They were the Port Authority of New York and New Jersey, the New York Power Authority, and the Port of Baltimore. For the Port Authority of New York and New Jersey, the US excluded:

- procurement of maintenance, repair, and operating materials and supplies
- procurement under a multi-jurisdictional agreement (contracts initially awarded by other jurisdictions)
- in exceptional cases, where the Authority's board of directors requires the purchase of certain goods produced in the region.

This Authority's operations include several airports, such as the John F. Kennedy International Airport, Newark Liberty International Airport, and LaGuardia Airport. The New York Power Authority applied the same conditions as the state of New York in its procurement coverage (see Table 6.4). Even though it is not located in that state, the Port of Baltimore also applied New York state's conditions. The US also excluded restrictions attached to federal funds for airport projects. That meant it did not waive the 'Buy American' requirements that were conditions attached to federal funding of such projects.

The US also made a national treatment commitment related to the financing of projects by the Rural Utilities Service. As the only applicable provision of the GPA and FTA, the US committed that this agency would not mandate the recipient of its financing to purchase domestic goods for use in the projects it funded. In both the GPA 2012 and the USMCA,[34] the Rural Utilities Service's commitment extended to its financing of both electric generation and telecommunications projects. In the other FTAs, its commitment was limited to the financing of electric generation projects.

---

34. Under USMCA, as under NAFTA, the Rural Utilities Service's financing is listed with US federal government entities and not in the other entities list, as in the GPA and other FTAs.

Under the GPA, it was subject to a $250,000 threshold, but it was generally subject to a higher threshold under FTAs.

5. THRESHOLDS

A key criterion for determining whether a procurement is covered under an agreement is its value. The US was obligated to open a specific procurement to foreign suppliers under an agreement only when the minimum estimated value of the procurement equaled or exceeded a certain monetary value or threshold. Under the GPA, the US generally applied the same thresholds as most other parties, with two notable exceptions.[35] For the goods and services purchased by its subcentral entities, the US maintained a higher threshold of 355,000 SDRs, whereas most parties applied a 200,000 SDRs threshold. For procurement of goods and services by federal government enterprises, the US used a lower threshold of $250,000, in contrast to a 400,000 SDRs threshold ($563,000 in 2022) applied by most parties.[36]

In each US FTA, all the parties applied the same thresholds (except where developing country partners applied higher transitional thresholds). Under most FTAs, the US and its partners drew thresholds from either the GPA or NAFTA. Two exceptions to this practice were FTAs with Israel and South Korea that provided unique thresholds for central government procurement of $50,000 and $100,000, respectively.[37] The US GPA and FTA thresholds are detailed in Table 6.5.

---

35. For the thresholds applied by the parties to the GPA, see WTO, Integrated Government Procurement Market Access Information (e-GPA) Portal, accessed June 29, 2022, https://e-gpa.wto.org/en/ThresholdNotification/FrontPage.

36. For procurement of goods and services by government enterprises at the subcentral level, the US applies a 400,000 SDRs threshold.

37. Under the US-Canada FTA and NAFTA, Canada and the US applied a $25,000 threshold for the procurement of their goods. These agreements are no longer in effect.

TABLE 6.5. US Thresholds under Trade Agreements (2022–2023)

Trade Agreement	Central Government Entities		Subcentral Government Entities		Other Entities	
	Goods and Services	Construction Services	Goods and Services	Construction Services	Goods and Services	Construction Services
AUSFTA	$92,319	$7,032,000	$499,000	$7,032,000	$461,594 or $563,000	$7,032,000
NAFTA*	$83,099; Canada goods $25,000	$10,802,884	N/A	N/A	$415,495	$13,296,478
US-Bahrain FTA	$183,000	$12,001,460	N/A	N/A	$250,000 or $563,000	$14,771,718
US-Chile FTA	$92,319	$7,032,000	$499,000	$7,032,000	$461,594 or $563,000	$7,032,000
US-Colombia TPA	$92,319	$7,032,000	$499,000	$7,032,000	$250,000 or $563,000	$7,032,000
CAFTA-DR	$92,319	$7,032,000	$499,000	$7,032,000	$250,000 or $563,000	$7,032,000
US-Israel FTA	$50,000 (goods only)	N/A	N/A	N/A	N/A	N/A
US-Korea FTA	$100,000	$7,032,000	N/A	N/A	N/A	N/A

Trade Agreement	Central Government Entities		Subcentral Government Entities		Other Entities	
	Goods and Services	Construction Services	Goods and Services	Construction Services	Goods and Services	Construction Services
US-Morocco FTA	$183,000	$7,032,000	$499,000	$7,032,000	$250,000 or $563,000	$7,032,000
US-Oman FTA	$183,000	$12,001,460,	N/A	N/A	$250,000 or $563,000	$14,771,718
US-Panama TPA	$183,000	$7,032,000	$499,000	$7,032,000	$250,000 or $563,000	$7,032,000
US-Peru TPA	$183,000	$7,032,000	$499,000	$7,032,000	$250,000 or $563,000	$7,032,000
US-Singapore FTA	$92,319	$7,032,000	$499,000	$7,032,000	$250,000 or $563,000	$7,032,000
USMCA	$92,319	$12,001,460	N/A	N/A	$461,594	$14,771,718
WTO GPA	130,000 SDRs ($183,000)	5 million SDRs ($7,032,000)	355,000 SDRs ($499,000)	5 million SDRs ($7,032,000)	$250,000 or 400,000 SDRs ($563,000)	5 million SDRs ($7,032,000)

* For NAFTA, the thresholds are those that applied when it was replaced by the USMCA on July 1, 2020.

Source: USTR, Procurement Thresholds for Implementation of the Trade Agreements Act of 1979, *Federal Register* 86, no. 225, (November 26, 2021): 87579, https://www.govinfo.gov/content/pkg/FR-2021-11-26/pdf/2021-25821.pdf.

The GPA and FTAs require biannual adjustments of threshold values. The GPA requires each party to notify the WTO of its national currency equivalent to the thresholds specified in SDRs.[38] FTAs that incorporate GPA thresholds apply the same adjustment methodology, whereas FTAs that apply non-GPA thresholds require the parties to make an inflation adjustment of the thresholds. Unique thresholds are not adjusted. Every two years, the USTR adjusts the US dollar values of the thresholds and publishes those adjustments.[39] Based on these adjustments, the Federal Acquisition Regulatory Council incorporates the adjusted values into the Federal Acquisition Regulation (FAR).[40]

6. GOODS

Consistent with the practice established in the GATT Code and applied in subsequent agreements, the US opened the procurement of all goods by the entities that it covered under the agreements, except for exclusions for specific agencies, noted above.

---

38. WTO, Committee on Government Procurement, "Decisions on Procedural Matters under the Agreement on Government Procurement (1994)," GPA/1, March 5, 1996.

39. In a November 2021 biannual adjustment, the USTR determined the threshold values that applied to procurement under the GPA and FTAs in calendar years 2022 and 2023. USTR, "Procurement Thresholds for Implementation of the Trade Agreements Act of 1979," *Federal Register* 86, no. 225 (November 26, 2021): 87579, https://www.govinfo.gov/content/pkg/FR-2021-11-26/pdf/2021-25821.pdf.

40. "Federal Acquisition Regulation: Trade Agreements Thresholds," *Federal Register* 86, no. 248 (December 30, 2021): 74528, https://www.govinfo.gov/content/pkg/FR-2021-12-30/pdf/2021-28083.pdf. For the current thresholds, see FAR 25.402(b), table 1.

7. SERVICES

In its coverage of services, the US follows the same approach as it does for goods. It uses a 'negative list' that opens the procurement of all services purchased by its listed entities except for those that it explicitly excluded. The US's use of a negative list contrasts with that of most GPA parties that base their coverage on a 'positive list,' by which they only liberalize the sectors that they list.[41]

Under the GPA, the US excluded four categories of services:

(i) all transportation services, including launching services[42]

(ii) research and development (R&D) services

(iii) public utility services, including telecommunications and automated data processing-related telecommunications services (except enhanced or value-added services), and

(iv) services associated with the management and operation of government facilities or privately owned facilities used for governmental purposes, including federally funded R&D centers.

The federal R&D centers undertake, support, or manage basic or applied R&D for the federal government. These centers have more access to government and supplier data, employees, and facilities than is common in contractual relationships. A federal agency sponsors each center under a broad charter. The National Science Foundation maintains a master list of the federal R&D centers.[43] They include the Los Alamos National Laboratory (sponsored by

---

41. The FAR listed the services that the US excluded from its commitments under the GPA and FTAs. FAR subpart 25.401(b).

42. The excluded transportation services were the Provisional Central Product Classification (CPC Prov.) 71, 72, 73, 74, 8859, and 8868. The CPC Prov. is found at http://unstats.un.org/unsd/cr/registry/regcst.asp?Cl=9&Lg=1.

43. National Science Foundation, *Master Government List of Federally Funded R&D Centers*, last updated February 2022, https://www.nsf.gov/statistics/ffrdclist/.

the Department of Energy), the Jet Propulsion Laboratory (administered by the California Institute of Technology and sponsored by the National Aeronautics and Space Administration), and the National Defense Research Institute (administered by the RAND Corporation and sponsored by DoD).[44]

In addition to the excluded categories of services, the US did not cover procurement of any service in support of military forces located overseas. It also excluded printing services purchased by state entities and specific services for several states. Mississippi and Tennessee did not cover any services under the agreements. FTAs excluded the same services as the GPA, with some differences in their description of the services. FTAs also did not apply to the maintenance, repair, modification, rebuilding, and installation of equipment related to ships and non-nuclear ship repair.

8. CONSTRUCTION SERVICES

Under the GPA and FTAs, the US covered the procurement of all construction services (except dredging). Beginning with the FTAs with Chile and Singapore and continuing in subsequent FTAs, the US also offered coverage of build-operate-transfer (BOT) and public works concession contracts, a form of public-private partnership. BOT contracts provide for the construction of infrastructure, facilities, or other government-owned works under a specific arrangement. The arrangement posits that a procuring entity grants to a supplier temporary ownership or a right to control and operate (and demand payment for the use of) those works for the contract duration. At the end of the contract, the private party transfers the facilities to the government. A typical example of such a contract is toll roads, which allow a private company that builds the road to collect tolls from those using it during the duration of the contract.

---

44. For the policy and rules for federally funded R&D centers, see FAR subpart 35.017.

Subsequently, the company transfers the road to the government at the end of the contract.

9. EXCLUSIONS FROM COVERAGE

In addition to the exclusions described above, the US took other exceptions to its commitments under the GPA and FTAs. Its most extensive exclusion was procurement set aside for small- and minority-owned businesses. The US broadly defined a 'set-aside' in its commitments in the GPA to include "any form of preference, such as the exclusive right to provide a good or service, or any price preference."[45] It also clarified that the GPA and FTAs did not apply when the government provided "goods and services to persons or governmental authorities not specifically covered" under the annexes to the agreements.[46]

10. MODIFICATIONS OF COVERAGE

From time to time, the US has modified its coverage under the GPA and FTAs, in accordance with the modification processes provided in the agreements. It has both withdrawn listed entities and added new entities to replace those that have been abolished or taken on functions of covered entities. US modifications under the GPA since 2001 arc outlined in Table 6.6. The Table lists both the entities removed and the entities added, as well as an explanation provided for the modification.[47]

---

45. GPA, Appendix I, US, Annex 7, n. 1.

46. GPA, Appendix I, US, Annex 7, n. 2.

47. When the US proposed modifications to its GPA coverage, it submitted similar proposals under FTAs.

TABLE 6.6. Modifications of US Federal Entity Coverage

Entity Removed	Entity Added	Explanation
2001 Proposed Modifications[48]		
Panama Canal Commission		Under the 1977 Panama Canal Treaty of 7 September 1977, the Government of the Republic of Panama assumed all authority and responsibility for the operation of the Panama Canal, effective December 13, 1999.[49]
US Information Agency (USIA)	Broadcasting Board of Governors	The Foreign Affairs Reform and Restructuring Act of 1998 abolished the USIA and assigned its procurement functions to the Broadcasting Board of Governors and the Department of State.
Board for International Broadcasting		The United States International Broadcasting Act of 1994 eliminated the entity, and the Broadcasting Board of Governors assumed responsibility for its procurement functions.
ACTION	Corporation for National and Community Service (CNCS)	The National and Community Service Trust Act of 1993 created the CNCS and required its merger with ACTION.
Arms Control and Disarmament Agency (ACDA)		The Foreign Affairs Restructuring Act of 1998 eliminated the ACDA, and its functions were assigned to the Department of State.

---

48. WTO, "Proposed Modifications to Appendix I of the United States," GPA/W/153, September 25, 2001.

49. US firms regained access to procurement of the Panama Canal in 2012 when the US implemented the US-Panama Trade Promotion Agreement, which covered the Panama Canal Authority, the operator of the Canal.

Entity Removed	Entity Added	Explanation
Interstate Commerce Commission (ICC)		The Interstate Commerce Commission Termination Act of 1995 dissolved the ICC, and its remaining responsibilities were assigned to the Department of Transportation.
Administrative Conference of the United States		Public Law 104-52 abolished the Administrative Conference, and its procurement functions ceased.
Alaska Power Administration (APA)		The Alaska Power Administration Asset Sale and Termination Act authorized the termination of the APA and the sale of its assets.
Rural Electrification Administration Financing	Rural Utilities Service Financing	Section 232 of Public Law 103354 eliminated the Rural Electrification Administration (REA), and REA's financing functions were assumed by the Rural Utilities Service of the Department of Agriculture.
Uranium Enrichment Corporation (UEC)		Public Law 104-134 required the reorganization of UEC from a government corporation to a private, forprofit corporation and renamed it the US Enrichment Corporation (USEC). The USEC came under private sector control on July 23, 1998, when it issued 100 million public shares on the New York Stock Exchange.
Resolution Trust Corporation (RTC) Oversight Board		The Resolution Trust Corporation Refinancing and Restructuring Act of 1991 required the termination of the Resolution Trust Corporation, and, as a result, the RTC Oversight Board was renamed the Thrift Depositor Protection Oversight Board. That Oversight Board was subsequently dissolved by the Homeowner's Protection Act of 1998, which transferred its remaining functions to the Department of the Treasury.

Entity Removed	Entity Added	Explanation
2004 Proposed Modification[50]		
Federal Emergency Management Agency (FEMA)	Department of Homeland Security (DHS)	The Homeland Security Act of 2002 (Public Law 107-296) established the DHS and incorporated FEMA and various organizational elements and functions transferred from other covered entities, including the US Coast Guard, transferred from the Department of Transportation. The US Secret Service and US Customs Service were transferred from the Department of Treasury.
2006 Proposed Modifications[51]		
Pennsylvania Avenue Development Corporation (PADC)		The PADC was dissolved under Section 3 of Public Law 92578 in 1996. Its procurement functions were transferred to the National Parks Service under the Department of Interior, and the General Services Administration under Section 313 of the Omnibus Appropriations Act of 1996 (Public Law 104-134).

50. WTO, "Proposed Modifications to Appendix I of the United States, Notification from the United States under Article XXIV:6 of the GPA," GPA/MOD/USA/1, January 15, 2004.

51. WTO, "Proposed Modifications to Appendix I of the United States, Notification from the United States under Article XXIV:6(a) of the GPA," GPA/MOD/USA/4, February 14, 2006.

Entity Removed	Entity Added	Explanation
	2013 Proposed Modifications[52]	
Advisory Commission on Intergovernmental Relations (ACIR)		The ACIR was terminated by Public Law 104-52. Following its termination in 1996, Public Law 104-328 called for the ACIR to exist solely to complete any contracts regarding the National Gambling Impact Study Commission, which terminated 60 days after it issued its final report on June 18, 1999.
National Commission on Libraries and Information Science (NCLIS)		The National Commission on Libraries and Information Science Act, which authorized the NCLIS, was repealed by Public Law 111-340 in 2010. NCLIS's functions were transferred to the Institute of Museum and Library Science, which is part of the National Foundation on the Arts and the Humanities, a covered entity.
Office of the Nuclear Waste Negotiator (ONWR)		The Nuclear Waste Policy Amendments Act of 1987 directed that the ONWR "shall cease to exist not later than 30 days after the date seven years after 22 December 1987." ONWR was terminated when Congress did not reauthorize its funding in 1995.
Office of the Thrift Supervision (OTS)		The Dodd-Frank Wall Street Reform and Consumer Protection Act abolished OTS. It transferred its functions to three covered entities: the Office of the Comptroller of the Currency in the Department of the Treasury, the Federal Deposit Insurance Corporation, and the Federal Reserve Board of Governors.

---

52. WTO, "Proposed Modifications to Appendix I of the United States under the Revised Agreement on Government Procurement," GPA/MOD/USA/14, December 9, 2013. These modifications were certified on January 8, 2014.

A closer look at two modifications under the GPA illustrates how US coverage has evolved and how the US has utilized the modification process. In the first case, the US resorted to market access negotiations to resolve a long-standing objection to withdrawing an entity under the modification process. In 2001, the US proposed removing several entities, including the Uranium Enrichment Corporation (UEC), from its list of covered federal entities.[53] Several parties objected to the proposed modifications. Subsequently, the objections were resolved except for those relating to the UEC. The other entities were taken off the list of covered entities on October 1, 2004.[54] At that point, Japan and the EU continued their objections to the removal of the UEC. In 2006, Japan withdrew its objection "based upon explanations and information provided by the Government of the United States."[55] However, the EU maintained its opposition. Finally, in the negotiations of the GPA 2012, the US did not include the UEC in its list of covered federal entities in its final offer, which removed it from coverage when the GPA 2012 entered into force in 2014.

The second case demonstrates how the US used the modification process to expand its coverage by adding a major new agency and avoiding a reduction in US coverage. In 2004, after establishing the Department of Homeland Security (DHS),[56] the US proposed adding that agency to its covered entities under the GPA and FTAs. In the same proposed modification, the US presented other related

---

53. WTO, "Proposed Modifications to Appendix I."

54. WTO, Committee on Government Procurement, Report (July 2003-November 2004) of the Committee on Government Procurement, GPA/82, para. 13(e)(i), November 26, 2004.

55. WTO, "Japan's Withdrawal of Objections to the United States' Proposed Modification to Appendix I of the Agreement on Government Procurement to Withdraw Uranium Enrichment Corporation," GPA/W/153, GPA/MOD/USA/5, November 30, 2006.

56. The DHS was established in 2002. *Homeland Security Act of 2002*, Public Law 107-296, *U.S. Statutes at Large* 116 (2002): 2135.

changes. Those changes included removing the Federal Emergency Management Agency as a separate covered entity because it had been transferred to the new department and hence would be covered under it. In addition, several organizations were transferred from other covered entities to the DHS. They included the US Coast Guard, which was transferred from the Department of Transportation, and the US Secret Service and US Customs Service were transferred from the Department of Treasury. These proposed modifications to US coverage under the GPA became effective on October 1, 2004.[57]

When the US added the DHS to the agreements, it excluded the Transportation Security Administration (TSA) because it was exempt from the FAR. Congress had created this agency in the wake of the September 11 attacks (2001) on the US to strengthen the security of the nation's transportation systems. It was initially established under the Department of Transportation and applied the acquisition management system of the Federal Aviation Administration (FAA) in conducting its procurement, rather than the FAR.[58]

In 2003, the TSA was transferred to DHS, but it continued to apply the FAA's acquisition management system.[59] However, in 2007, Congress removed the TSA's exemption from the FAR,[60] citing "the lack of urgency in its procurement operations and the agency's ongoing problems with contract management."[61] As a

57. WTO, "Certifications to Modifications of Agreement," WT/LET/482rev1, November 23, 2004.

58. DHS, "Revision of Department of Homeland Security Acquisition Regulation; Technical Amendments (HSAR Case 2008–001)", *Federal Register* 73, no. 102 (May 27, 2008): 30317, https://www.govinfo.gov/content/pkg/FR-2008-05-27/pdf/E8-11560.pdf.

59. DHS, "Revision;" Brodsky, "TSA contracting exemption."

60. *Consolidated Appropriations Act*, 2008, Public Law 110-161, Div. E, § 568, *U.S. Statutes at Large* 121 (2007): 1844, 2092.

61. Brodsky, "TSA contracting exemption."

result, this agency was required to follow the FAR.[62] Subsequently, the US added TSA (except its procurement of textiles and apparel) to federal entities covered under the GPA and the USMCA.

---

62. DHS, "Revision."

CHAPTER 7

PROTECTIONISM: US DOMESTIC PREFERENCES

1. INTRODUCTION

In its negotiations to open government procurement, the US has had to address domestic restrictions on purchasing foreign products. Domestic "preferences in procurement are deeply embedded in US politics and law," notes one guide to the US procurement system, "and, once in place, are difficult to erase."[1] An example of such restrictions is the 1933 Buy American Act, which limits the ability of the federal government to purchase foreign goods. Controversial at the time of its passage, it remains in force and is only one of a plethora of US laws aimed at limiting foreign purchases.

During the 1970s, Congress began extending domestic preferences beyond direct federal procurement to infrastructure projects

---

1. Christopher R. Yukins and Allen Green, "International Trade Agreements and US Procurement Law," in *The Contractor's Guide to International Procurement*, eds. Erin Loraine Felix and Marques Peterson (Chicago: American Bar Association, 2018), 148–77.

undertaken by state and local governments with federal funds, especially in the transportation sector.

Such laws that require domestic preferences conflict with US obligations under the GPA and FTAs. The US pursued two strategies to reconcile the conflict between domestic purchasing restrictions and the national treatment obligation at the heart of the GPA and FTAs. It either waived the domestic preference for its trade agreement partners, or it excluded the restricted procurement from US commitments, depending on whether Congress had given it authority to waive the requirement.

2. DOMESTIC PREFERENCES WITH WAIVER AUTHORITY

2.1 Trade Agreements Act of 1979

When the US signed the GATT Code, it needed congressional authority to implement it. Congress provided that authority in the Trade Agreements Act of 1979 (TAA).[2] This law authorizes the president to waive the application of "any law, regulation, procedure, or practice regarding government procurement" that would treat eligible goods and services and suppliers of such goods and services less favorably than those from the US or another foreign country. That authority applied to the GATT Code, its successors, and other agreements that provide "appropriate reciprocal competitive government procurement opportunities" to US goods, services, and suppliers. President Carter delegated the waiver authority to the US Trade Representative (USTR).[3] With that authority, USTR

---

2. *Trade Agreements Act of 1979*, Public Law 96-39, *U.S. Statutes at Large* 93 (1979): 144; *U.S. Code* 19, §§ 2501-2581. The government procurement provisions are in *U.S. Code* 19. §§ 2511-2518.

3. "Executive Order 12260 of December 31, 1980, Agreement on Government Procurement," December 31, 1980, https://www.archives.gov/federal-register/codification/executive-order/12260.html.

issued waivers for parties to the GATT Code (and its successors), the North American Free Trade Agreement (NAFTA) (and its successor), and FTAs.

2.1.1 Scope of Waiver Authority

Although the TAA provides broad authority for the executive branch to waive discriminatory provisions, Congress intended the authority to be applied narrowly. It explicitly prohibited the use of the waiver for any small business or minority preference.[4] Furthermore, it implicitly acknowledged that the waiver authority would have a narrow application. The congressional reports on the legislation listed the laws and procurement that would not be affected by US commitments under the GATT Code (or subsequent agreements) and thus not subject to the waiver (see Table 7.1).

TABLE 7.1. Laws and Procurement Excluded from the GATT Code

Small Business and Minority Business Programs (*U.S. Code* 15, § 637 and implementing laws and regulations, and Public Law 95-507): "Set-asides, that is, purchases reserved for small and minority businesses, are excluded from the agreement's coverage."

"Berry Amendment" Types of Restrictions on the Department of Defense (DoD) (DoD Appropriations Act, Public Law 95-457): "[t]he Defense Department will continue to purchase, solely from US sources, its needs for textiles, clothing, shoes, food, stainless-steel flatware, certain specialty metals, buses (Public Law 90-500, § 404), ships, and components thereof" (Byrnes-Tollefson Amendment to DoD Appropriations Act).

Hand tools (General Services Administration Appropriations Act): "[f]ifty percent differential in favor of domestic suppliers for all procurements of hand tools will not be affected." They were not affected because the entities that purchased them (National Tool Center and Regional 9 Office in San Francisco) were not covered by the agreement.

Prison- and Blind-Made Goods (*U.S. Code* 18, § 4124 and *U.S. Code* 41, § 48) "are an exception to agreement coverage."

---

4. *TAA, U.S. Code* 19, § 2511(f).

Cargo Transportation Preferences (*U.S. Code* 10, § 2631, *U.S. Code* 46, § 1241(b)(1), International Air Transportation Fair Competitive Practices Act of 1974, Public Law 92-623) "are specifically not considered by the United States to be a service 'incidental' to a procurement."

Purchases by State and Local Governments: "are not affected by the agreement, since the agreement applies only to purchases made by specified Federal agencies."

Federal Grant Funds to State and Local Governments: "[p]urchases by State and local governments which are financed with Federal Grant Funds (for example State purchases made with Federal funds under the Surface Transportation Act and the Clean Water Act), are not covered by the agreement."

Source: US Congress, Senate, Committee on Finance, *Trade Agreements Act of 1979*, 96th Cong., 1st sess., Sen. R. 96-249, July 17, 1979, 132.

Congress recognized that the waiver authority would apply only to two domestic purchasing requirements: the Buy American Act of 1933 (BAA) and the special preferences of the Department of Defense (DoD). The US confirmed the narrow application of the waiver authority in its report to the GATT procurement committee on its implementation of the GATT Code.[5] Twenty-five years later, the US Government Accountability Office (GAO) noted that the US had only used the waiver authority for the BAA and the DoD's Balance of Payments program.[6] In 2009, Congress implicitly acknowledged that the TAA's waiver authority did not apply to new domestic purchasing restrictions when it added a provision to a major infrastructure law that had essentially the same effect as the

---

5. The US informed the GATT procurement committee that the president had waived the Buy American Act and the DoD's special preferences for products originating in the GATT Code countries. GATT, Committee on Government Procurement, "Implementation and Administration of the Agreement, Addendum, Legislation of the United States," GPR/3/Add.1, March 11, 1981.

6. GAO, *Federal Procurement: International Agreements Result in Waivers of Some U.S. Domestic Source Restrictions*, GAO-05-188 (Washington, DC, 2005), 2, www.gao.gov/products/GAO-05-188. See also Morton Pomeranz, "Toward a New International Order in Government Procurement," *Public Contract Law Journal* 12, no. 2 (March 1982): 129–61.

waiver under the TAA.[7] Congress included a similar provision in several subsequently enacted laws, including the 2021 Infrastructure Investment and Jobs Act (Infrastructure Act or IIJA).

2.1.2 Designated Countries

USTR waives domestic purchasing restrictions for eligible products and services for two categories of designated countries.[8] The primary type consists of countries that are parties to the GPA or FTAs with the US that provide reciprocal government procurement opportunities to US goods, services, and suppliers. When a country joins the GPA or the US implements an FTA with procurement commitments, USTR issues a waiver (referred to as a "trade agreements waiver"), which applies to the procurement of goods and services from that country.[9] After USTR issues a waiver for a new GPA or FTA party, the Federal Acquisition Regulatory Council (FAR Council)[10] adds it as a designated country in the Federal Acquisition Regulation (FAR), thus codifying access under the GPA and FTAs.[11]

The second type of designated country is developing countries that benefit from US trade preferences. These countries may participate in federal procurement without providing the US with

---

7. The provision excluded the application of the 'Buy American' requirement to goods covered under international agreements.

8. The Federal Acquisition Regulation (FAR) lists designated countries. FAR 25.003.

9. See, for example, the first waiver under the Trade Agreements Act. USTR, "Determination Regarding Application of the Agreement on Government Procurement and Waiver of Discriminatory Purchasing Requirements," *Federal Register* 46 (January 6, 1981): 1657.

10. The FAR Council consists of the Administrator of the Office for Federal Procurement Policy, the Secretary of Defense, the Administrator of General Services, and the Administrator of National Aeronautics and Space. Public Law 111-350, § 3, *U.S. Statutes at Large* 124 (2011): 3691; *U.S. Code* 41, § 1302.

11. Christopher R. Yukins, "The U.S. Federal Procurement System: An Introduction," 2017 *Upphandlingsrättslig Tidskrift* [Procurement Law Journal] 69, GWU Law School, Legal Studies Research Paper No. 2017-75, 78.

reciprocal access to their own procurement. They are the 47 least developed countries (LDCs) designated by USTR[12] and countries under the Caribbean Basin Trade Initiative.[13]

2.1.3 Eligible Products

A trade agreement waiver does not apply to all goods and services from a designated country. It only applies to "eligible products," which include both goods and services.[14] To be eligible for a waiver, goods must be (i) "wholly" grown, produced, or manufactured in the US or a designated country or (ii) "substantially transformed [in the US or a designated country][15] into new and different articles

---

12. They were Afghanistan, Angola, Bangladesh, Benin, Bhutan, Burkina Faso, Burundi, Cambodia, Central African Republic, Chad, Comoros, Democratic Republic of Congo, Djibouti, Equatorial Guinea, Eritrea, Ethiopia, Gambia, Guinea, Guinea-Bissau, Haiti, Kiribati, Laos, Lesotho, Liberia, Madagascar, Malawi, Mali, Mauritania, Mozambique, Nepal, Niger, Rwanda, Samoa, Sao Tome and Principe, Senegal, Sierra Leone, Solomon Islands, Somalia, South Sudan, Tanzania, Timor-Leste, Togo, Tuvalu, Uganda, Vanuatu, Yemen, and Zambia. FAR 25.003 and 25.400(a)(3).

13. The countries covered by the Caribbean Basin Trade Initiative were Antigua and Barbuda, Aruba, Bahamas, Barbados, Belize, Bonaire, British Virgin Islands, Curacao, Dominica, Grenada, Guyana, Haiti, Jamaica, Montserrat, Saba, Saint Kitts and Nevis, Saint Lucia, Saint Vincent and the Grenadines, Sint Eustatius, Sint Maarten, and Trinidad and Tobago. FAR 25.003 and 25.400(a)(4).

14. *TAA, U.S. Code 19*, § 2518.

15. Until 2000, the substantial transformation test was not applied in the US. A substantially transformed product in the US with less than 50% US components "did not meet the domestic end product test and therefore was treated as a 'foreign end product'." That gave products substantially transformed in a designated country an advantage over products comparably manufactured in the US. To remedy this discrepancy, the FAR Council added the term 'U.S.-made end product' to the FAR and applied the same substantial transformation standard to US manufacturers. Eric Cho, "Purchased in the USA: An Examination of Emerging Issues Surrounding Foreign Acquisition," *The National Contract Management Association (NCMA)*, October 2012, 34; "Federal Acquisition Regulation; Foreign Acquisition (Part 25 Rewrite)," *Federal Register 64*, (December 27, 1999): 72416.

of commerce with names, characters, or uses distinct from that of the article or articles from which it was so transformed."[16] This is referred to as the 'substantial transformation' test.[17]

In the analysis of whether a good is an eligible product, the country of origin of the underlying components incorporated into the end product is largely irrelevant. The TAA allows a waiver for products with 100% foreign, non-designated country components, provided that those components are substantially transformed in the US or a designated country.

In contrast to the rules for determining the eligibility of goods, the rules to determine whether services are eligible for a trade agreements waiver "are woefully inadequate."[18] The FAR includes a single provision on the origin of services, added after the procurement of services was first covered in the GPA 1994. That provision directs contracting officers "to determine the origin of services by the country in which the firm providing the services is established."[19] Thus, the trade agreement compliance test for a service is whether the firm providing the service is established in the US or a designated country. However, the FAR does not define 'established.' It could be where the supplier is incorporated or where it has its principal place of business. Moreover, even if a supplier is established in the US or a designated country, it could provide services in a US procurement that were performed in a non-designated country since

---

16. *TAA*, *U.S. Code* 19, § 2518.

17. In evaluating a foreign offer, a contracting officer may rely on the offeror's certification of the origin of the end product. FAR 25.501(b). A recent decision by the US Court of Appeals for the Federal Circuit, Acetris Health, LLC v. United States, 949 F.3d 719 (Fed. Cir. 2020) "confirmed that in resolving issues of foreign or domestic origin in the federal procurement system, the contracting officer has first responsibility." Christopher R. Yukins, "International Procurement Developments in 2021–Part I: Buy American and the Biden Administration," in *2021 Thomson Reuters' Government Contracts Year in Review Conference Briefs*, 77, February 2022.

18. Cho, "Purchased in the USA," 30.

19. FAR 25.402(a)(2).

the federal regulation does not define the place of performance of the service.[20]

The trade agreement waiver applies when three conditions exist:

(i)   the value of the anticipated procurement is at or above the threshold established in the relevant trade agreement

(ii)   the procurement involves goods or services covered in the applicable agreement, and

(iii) none of the other exceptions provided in the agreement apply, such as limited tendering.[21]

In addition to authorizing waivers for trade agreement partners, the TAA restricts purchases from countries that are not parties to such agreements.[22]

2.2 Buy American Act of 1933

2.2.1 Scope and Application

The BAA is the primary domestic preference law that governs the procurement of goods (but not services) by the federal government.[23] It was enacted during the Great Depression to foster American industry by protecting it from foreign competition in federal government procurement of goods and generate and preserve jobs for Americans.[24]

---

20. Cho, "Purchased in the USA," 130.

21. Stuart B. Nibley, Amy Conant Hoang, and Erica L. Bakies, "Real Steps Towards 'Buy American' Compliance–Part III: Understanding and Avoiding Common Areas of Noncompliance that Lead to Enforcement Actions," *The Government Contractor* 60, no.16, *Thomson Reuters* (2018): 8.

22. *TAA, U.S. Code 19*, § 2512.

23. *BAA*, Public Law 72-428, *U.S. Statutes at Large 47* (1933): 1520; 41 *U.S. Code 41*, §§ 8301–8305.

24. For a discussion of the development of the BAA, see Pomeranz, "Toward a New International Order," 129–61.

The Act mandates that federal agencies purchase only (i) "unmanufactured articles, materials, and supplies that have been mined or produced" in the US and (ii) "manufactured articles, materials, and supplies that have been manufactured in the United States substantially all from articles, materials, or supplies mined, produced, or manufactured" in the US.[25] However, this law is not implemented as an outright ban on the purchase of foreign products. Rather, based on presidential executive orders, the FAR implements its requirements as a preference for American products and construction materials.[26]

In implementing the BAA, federal agencies apply a 'two-part test' to determine whether a manufactured product is considered a "domestic end product." Under this test, a manufactured end product qualifies as such a product if (i) it is manufactured in the US and (ii) the cost of its domestic components exceeds 60% of the cost of all its components (referred to as the component or domestic content test[27]). However, for iron or steel products, domestic components must comprise 95% of the cost.[28] That means if more than 40% (or 5% for iron and steel products) of the cost of all components is attributable to foreign content, federal agencies may not purchase the foreign product unless an exception applies.

The domestic content requirement is scheduled to increase to 65% in 2024 and to 75% in 2029. These scheduled increases are subject to two exceptions. First, after consultation with the Office of Management and Budget (OMB), a federal agency's senior

---

25. *BAA, U.S. Code* 41, § 8302.

26. FAR subpart 25.1.

27. This component test was redesignated the 'domestic content test' by the Trump administration. "Federal Acquisition Regulation: Maximizing Use of American-Made Goods, Products, and Materials," *Federal Register* 86, no. 11 (January 19, 2021): 6180, https://www.govinfo.gov/content/pkg/FR-2021-01-19/pdf/2021-00710/pdf.

28. FAR 25.101(a).

procurement executive could allow for the application of "an alternate domestic content test." The second exception, available until January 1, 2030, is a 55% 'fallback' threshold that agencies may apply when they have determined that no products or construction materials meet the higher domestic content threshold or the cost of such products is unreasonable. They may not use the fallback threshold for products or construction materials consisting wholly or predominantly of iron or steel or that are commercially available off-the-shelf (COTS) items.[29]

Federal agencies do not apply the BAA's component test when they purchase COTS items.[30] In 2009, the Administrator of the Office for Federal Procurement Policy, a unit of the OMB, waived the component test for such acquisitions based on its authority to reduce administrative burdens resulting from government-unique requirements. The Administrator concluded that manufacturers make component purchasing decisions based on factors such as cost and quality, and not the country of origin. Thus, it was difficult for them to guarantee the source of a product's components over the term of a contract. Furthermore, the component content requirement could limit the government's ability to purchase products already in the commercial distribution systems.[31]

---

29. "Federal Acquisition Regulation: Amendments to the FAR Buy American Act Requirements," *Federal Register* 87, no. 44 (March 7, 2022): 12780, https://www.govinfo.gov/content/pkg/FR-2022-03-07/pdf/2022-04173.pdf. As the domestic content thresholds increase, contractors must adjust the domestic content of their product throughout the performance of a contract. David Hickey et al., "Buy American Final Rule Ups the Domestic Content Ante," Kelley Drye Client Advisory, March 11, 2022, https://www.kelley-drye.com/News-Events/Publications/Client-Advisories/Buy-American-Final-Rule-Ups-the-Domestic-Content-A.

30. FAR 12.505(a) and 25.101(a)(2)(i). COTS are defined in FAR 2.101.

31. OMB, Memorandum for Heads of Executive Departments and Agencies, "Increasing Opportunities for Domestic Sourcing and Reducing the Need for Waivers from Made in America Laws," M-21-26, June 11, 2021, 14–15, https://www.whitehouse.gov/wp-content/uploads/2021/06/M-21-26.pdf.

A COTS item meets the BAA's definition of "domestic end product" when it is manufactured in the US, regardless of its foreign content.[32]

In determining whether a product is of domestic origin, the place of mining, production, or manufacture is controlling, and the nationality of the manufacturer or producer is not considered. However, if manufacturers or suppliers falsely assert that their products comply with BAA requirements, they can be subject to civil, criminal, and contractual liability, including competitor claims under the Lanham Act and lawsuits under the False Claims Act.[33]

The BAA's 'two-part test' differs from the TAA's 'substantial transformation' test by taking into consideration the origin of the components of goods. By contrast, under the TAA test, a product could be composed of 100% foreign components and still qualify for a trade agreement waiver, provided the product was substantially transformed into a new product.

2.2.2 Exceptions

Federal agencies can purchase foreign products under certain exceptions to the BAA. The Act does not apply when:

- the cost of the domestic product is unreasonable
- domestic products are not available
- the purchase of domestic products would be inconsistent with the public interest
- the purchase is specifically for commissary resale
- the procurement is of information technology that is a commercial item

---

32. Nibley, Hoang, and Bakies, "Real Steps Towards," 8.

33. Hickey et al., "Buy American Final Rule;" see also, Yukins, "The U.S. Federal Procurement System," 73.

- the value of the purchase is below the micro-purchase threshold ($10,000), and

- the items are procured for use outside of the US.[34]

The primary exceptions are examined below.

Unreasonable cost of domestic products: Federal agencies may purchase a foreign product if they determine that it is less costly (and the cost of a domestic product is unreasonable). Using a comparative price evaluation test, civilian agencies add a price evaluation factor or price preference of 20% to the price of the lowest acceptable foreign offer if the lowest domestic offer is from a large business or 30% from a small business.[35] The DoD applies a 50% differential for its procurement. If the domestic price exceeds the foreign price with the differential or price preference, it is determined to be unreasonable. The agency may purchase the foreign product at the offered price–not the increased evaluated price.[36]

Nonavailability exception: Another exception to the 'Buy American' requirement is when domestic products are not produced or manufactured in the US in sufficient and reasonably available commercial quantities of satisfactory quality. The FAR allows procuring agencies to make two types of nonavailability determinations. The first type is a class determination made by the FAR Council that domestic sources can meet only 50% or less of total US government and non-government demand for a specific product.[37] The products subject to class determinations are listed in the FAR.[38] Before

---

34. FAR 25.103.

35. Until January 2021, when the Trump administration increased the price evaluation factors, they were 6% for most procurement and 12% when small businesses participated.

36. FAR 25.105(b).

37. FAR 25.103(b)(2).

38. FAR 25.104.

purchasing an article from the list, the procuring agency must conduct market research appropriate to the circumstances, including seeking domestic sources. The Council reviews the list every five years.[39] The second type of nonavailability determination is an exception made by a federal agency for a specific procurement.[40]

Inconsistent with the public interest: When the head of a federal agency determines that imposing the domestic purchasing preference would not be consistent with the public interest, the agency may purchase foreign products. This exception is used when an agency has an agreement with a foreign government that provides for a blanket exception to the BAA.[41] For example, the DoD has determined that it would be inconsistent with the public interest to apply the BAA's restrictions to the procurement of products from countries that have entered a reciprocal defense procurement agreement with the US.

The 2021 Infrastructure Investment and Jobs Act also made trade agreements and reciprocal defense procurement agreements exceptions to the BAA. Because these agreements are already treated as exceptions to that law through trade agreement waivers, as discussed above, the infrastructure law merely codified the existing legal regime.[42]

Procurement that is not covered by the GPA or FTAs and is subject to the BAA includes:

---

39. In May 2020, the FAR Council initiated a five-year review of the nonavailability list and requested public comments. It requested information to determine whether some articles should be removed from the list because they are now mined, produced, or manufactured in the US in sufficient and reasonably available commercial quantities and of a satisfactory quality. "Federal Acquisition Regulation: List of Domestically Nonavailable Articles," *Federal Register* 85, no. 93 (May 13, 2020): 28596. As of late 2022, the Council had not published a revised nonavailability list.

40. FAR 25.103(b)(2).

41. FAR 25.103(a).

42. *Infrastructure Investment and Jobs Act*, Public Law 117-58 (2021), § 70922(e).

(i)   small business set-asides

(ii)   acquisition of arms, ammunition, war materials, purchases indispensable for national security, or for national defense purposes

(iii)   acquisitions from Federal Prison Industries Inc. or non-profit agencies employing the blind or severely disabled

(iv)   sole-source or limited tendering awards.[43]

Based on the trade agreements waiver, the BAA does not apply to procurement that the US covers under the GPA or FTAs. As a result, a procurement scholar has pointed out that "generally only those smaller procurement that fall below the coverage threshold of the GPA and other trade agreements are affected by the Buy American Act."[44]

Assessment of Exceptions: In 2018, the GAO assessed the extent to which the federal government procured foreign products through exceptions and waivers of the BAA.[45] GAO examined the federal government's expenditure of $508 billion in contract obligations for goods and services for fiscal year (FY) 2017. It found that 40% ($196 billion) of the obligated funds went to the procurement of end products. Most of these were domestic products that could be subject to the BAA. Only approximately $7.8 billion, less than 5% of the total, was used to purchase foreign end products. The foreign products were purchased under four conditions, and three did not involve trade agreements. They were:

---

43. Nibley, Hoang, and Bakies, "Real Steps Towards," 6.

44. Yukins, "The U.S. Federal Procurement System," 77.

45. GAO, *Buy American Act: Actions Needed to Improve Exception and Waiver Reporting and Selected Agency Guidance*, GAO-19-17 (Washington, DC, 2018), accessed May 12, 2022, https://www.gao.gov/products/GAO-19-17. GAO prepared the report in response to a congressional request for a review of federal agency implementation of the BAA.

(i) $3.7 billion for products such as fuel used outside the US and not subject to the BAA (about 47% of the total foreign end products)

(ii) $2.9 billion for products under the DoD's exception for countries under a reciprocal defense procurement agreement

(iii) $700 million for products under a government-wide BAA exception.[46]

Only the fourth case involved purchases under a trade agreement. In this case, GAO found that the government purchased just $550 million of foreign products under a waiver of a trade agreement–less than 1% of the government's spending for FY 2017.[47]

GAO found that its FY 2017 data analysis was consistent with the information agencies reported in the federal procurement data system for the previous four years (FY 2013-2016). According to the agency data, foreign end products accounted for approximately 3% to 8% of goods subject to BAA restrictions during that period. For FY 2017, the foreign end products primarily came from South Korea, the United Kingdom, Afghanistan, Canada, Mexico, and the United Arab Emirates. Those countries together accounted for almost half of the total foreign end products. The DoD was responsible for more than 80% (roughly $6.4 billion) of the total obligations for foreign end products in FY 2017. Its purchases were primarily for products for use outside of the US or, due to its public interest exception, for countries under a reciprocal defense procurement agreement.[48]

Buy American Act Waivers (2016 2021): In October 2021, the Biden administration published information on over 100,000 "historical waivers," which were issued by federal agencies over five

46. GAO, *Buy American Act*, 11–13.
47. GAO, *Buy American Act*, 12.
48. GAO, *Buy American Act*, 12.

fiscal years (October 1, 2016, through September 30, 2021).[49] Of these waivers, 63% were for the nonavailability of domestic products, followed by 24% for the unreasonable cost of domestic products, 10% for commercial information technology, 2.6% for resale, and a mere 0.16% for public interest determinations.

The waiver information included the country benefiting from the waiver. Nearly half of the products subject to waivers were produced in China (47%), followed distantly by Mexico (14%), and even more distantly by Taiwan (4.4%), France (3.4%), Canada (3.2%), and South Korea (1.7%). Most of China's waivers were the result of the nonavailability of US products, while Mexico led in waivers based on the unreasonable cost of domestic products.[50]

Ten federal agencies issued most of the waivers. The General Service Administration's Federal Acquisition Services issued 40% of the waivers, the Defense Logistics Agency–33%, the Coast Guard–4.6%, the State Department–3%, and the Department of the Navy–2.7%. Four other agencies issued slightly more than 1% of the waivers.[51]

2.3 DoD's Balance of Payments Program

The second domestic preference that the US waives under the TAA is the DoD's Balance of Payments Program. This Program originated in the 1950s when the DoD established a policy to correct balance of payments deficits. It was implemented by a defense

---

49. *Historical Waivers*, Made in America, accessed May 11, 2022, https://www.madeinamerica.gov/waivers/. For each waiver, the Made in America website lists the federal agency issuing the waiver, the basis for the waiver (e.g., nonavailability, unreasonable cost, resale, public interest, or commercial information technology), the country of origin of the product or service purchased, a description of the product or service, the name and address of the supplier, the type of contract, and the total contract value.

50. *Historical Waivers*.

51. The four agencies were the Bureau of Printing and Engraving, the Department of the Army, the National Institute of Standards and Technology, and the National Institutes of Health. *Historical Waivers*.

procurement regulation with restrictions similar to BAA restrictions.[52] It requires the DoD to purchase only US-made end products (supplies) for use outside the US and domestic construction materials for construction to be performed outside of the US with certain exceptions.[53] As described in Chapter 1, this Balance of Payments Program played a historical role in creating the GPA. In 1962, Belgium filed a complaint with the Organisation of Economic Cooperation and Development concerning the US increase of the Program's domestic preference from 6% to 50%. That complaint eventually led to the negotiations of the GATT Code.

2.4 Rural Utilities Service's 'Buy American' Requirement

The Rural Utilities Service (formerly the Rural Electrification Administration), a unit of the US Department of Agriculture, provides funding for power generation and telecommunications projects. Congress requires all materials and equipment financed with loans or guarantees from the Rural Utilities Service must meet a 'Buy American' requirement.[54] Congress waived this requirement for Canada and Mexico in legislation that implemented NAFTA.[55]

---

52. Defense Federal Acquisition Regulation Supplement (DFARS) subpart 225.75; Nibley, Hoang, and Bakies, "Real Steps Towards," 3.

53. Exceptions to the DoD's Balance of Payments Program include: acquisitions at or below the simplified acquisition threshold; acquisitions of certain listed items, such as petroleum products, industrial gases, brand drugs specified by the Defense Medical Materiel Board; information technology that is a commercial item; products on the FAR nonavailable articles list; or the contracting officer determines the requirement can best be filled by foreign construction material, and the cost of the domestic construction material would exceed the cost of the foreign construction material by more than 50%. DFARs 225.75.

54. *Rural Electrification Act of 1936*, Public Law 74-605, *U.S. Statutes at Large* 49 (1936): 1363; *U.S. Code 7*, § 903 note.

55. *North American Free Trade Implementation Act*, Public Law 103-182, *U.S. Statutes at Large* 107 (1993): 2057, § 381(d).

Subsequently, as part of the implementation of the GPA 1994, Congress removed this 'Buy American' requirement for countries determined by the USTR to provide "reciprocal access" for US products, services, and suppliers to their power generation and telecommunications markets under an agreement with the US.[56]

3. DOMESTIC PREFERENCES WITH NO WAIVER AUTHORITY

As illustrated in Section 2.1, Congress did not intend for the executive branch to waive numerous specific domestic preferences or restrictions when undertaking procurement commitments in international agreements. For example, for more than 100 years, Congress has required dredging in US waters to be limited to US-registered vessels.[57] To comply with this law, the US excluded dredging from its commitments under the GPA and FTAs. The Congressional Research Service has provided an extensive list of other procurement that the BAA does not cover.[58] The major domestic preference requirements, which the US does not waive under its agreements, warrant examination to provide a more comprehensive understanding of the scope of domestic preferences and their treatment under trade agreements.

---

56. *Uruguay Round Agreements Act*, Public Law 103-465, § 342(g), *U.S. Statutes at Large* 108 (1994): 4809; Jean Heilman Grier, "Trade Agreements Open Foreign Procurement Markets," *Thomson Reuters Briefing Papers*, October 2017.

57. *The Dredging Act*, Ch. 2566, Sec. 1, *U.S. Statutes at Large* 34 (1906): 206 ("A foreign-built dredge shall not, under penalty of forfeiture, engage in dredging in the United States unless documented as a vessel of the United States"). Yukins and Green, "International Trade Agreements," 2, n. 3.

58. US Library of Congress, Congressional Research Service, *The Buy American Act and Other Federal Procurement Domestic Content Restrictions*, by David H. Carpenter and Brandon J. Murrill, R46748 (2021), 18–25, https://crsreports.congress.gov/product/pdf/R/R46748.

3.1 Small Business Set-asides

Congress has enacted various laws, notably the Small Business Act of 1953,[59] that have a goal of ensuring that a fair proportion of federal procurement is awarded to small businesses. The legislation established government-wide and agency-specific goals for awarding a percentage of federal contracts and subcontract dollars to small businesses. They also require or authorize agencies to conduct procurement competitions where only small businesses may participate (i.e., set-asides) or make sole-source awards to small businesses under certain circumstances. The laws also direct the Small Business Administration (SBA) and other federal agencies to help restructure proposed procurement to maximize opportunities for small businesses to participate in federal procurement.[60]

Congress requires federal agencies to award annually at least 23% of all federal procurement contracting dollars to small businesses.[61] In addition to this general target, federal agencies apply subgoals to the following small business categories:

(i) 5% for small businesses owned by socially and economically disadvantaged individuals

(ii) 5% for women-owned small businesses

(iii) 3% for small businesses in Historically Underutilized Business Zones (HUBZones)

(iv) 3% for service-disabled veteran-owned small businesses.

---

59. *Small Business Act of 1953*, Public Law 83-163, Title II, *U.S. Statutes at Large 67* (1953): 232.

60. US Library of Congress, Congressional Research Service, *Legal Authorities Governing Federal Contracting and Subcontracting with Small Businesses*, by Kate M. Manual and Erika K. Lunder, R42391 (2015), 1, https://sgp.fas.org/crs/misc/R42391.pdf.

61. Yukins and Green, "International Trade Agreements," 11.

A contract can count toward fulfilling more than one subgoal. For example, an award to a small, disadvantaged business in a HUB-Zone owned by a service-disabled woman veteran would contribute to satisfying all three subgoals. Table 7.2 describes the eligibility requirements for the subgoals.

TABLE 7.2. Small Business Subgoals

Small Business Category	Goal	Eligibility Requirements
Small businesses owned by socially and economically disadvantaged individuals	5%	An entity that is 51% or more owned, controlled, and operated by a person(s) who is socially and economically disadvantaged. African Americans, Hispanic Americans, Asian Pacific Americans, Subcontinent Asian Americans, and Native Americans are presumed to qualify; other individuals can qualify if they show, by a "preponderance of the evidence," that they are disadvantaged. The SBA certifies eligibility.
Women-owned small businesses	5%	A small business that is 51% or more owned and controlled by one or more women and whose management and daily business operations are controlled by one or more women, who must be US citizens. They may use a third-party certifier to demonstrate eligibility for the program or self-certify.
Small businesses in HUBZones	3%	A business must be certified by the SBA as a small business residing in a HUBZone, be owned, and controlled by 51% or more US citizens, have its principal office in a HUBZone, and have at least 35% of its employees residing in a HUBZone.
Service-disabled veteran-owned small businesses	3%	A small business that is 51% or more owned and controlled by service-disabled veterans, whose management and daily business operations are controlled by one or more service-disabled veterans or, in the case of a service-disabled veteran with permanent and severe disability, by the veteran's spouse or permanent caregiver.

Source: SBA, Contracting Assistance Programs, https://www.sba.gov/federal-contracting/contracting-assistance-programs.

Federal contracting officers must automatically reserve all procurement with an anticipated value between the micro-purchase threshold ($10,000) and the simplified acquisition threshold ($250,000) exclusively for small businesses. The only exception to this requirement is insufficient competition, a condition determined according to the so-called 'rule of two.' This rule requires procurement to be set aside for small businesses unless the contracting officer concludes that the agency is unlikely to receive offers from two or more responsible small business concerns, representing competitive market prices, quality, and delivery. The contracting officer must also set aside procurement above $250,000 for small businesses when there is a 'reasonable expectation' that at least two responsible small businesses will submit offers and the award will be made at fair market prices. Goods purchased under set-asides for small businesses must comply with the BAA.

Foreign firms are not prohibited from participating in procurement set aside for small businesses, provided they meet the eligibility requirements.[62] A small business must be:

> "a business entity organized for profit, with a place of business located in the United States, and which operates primarily within the United States or which makes a significant contribution to the U.S. economy through payment of taxes or use of American products, materials or labor"[63]

to be eligible to participate in a set-aside. These eligibility requirements make it very difficult–if not virtually impossible–for foreign small businesses to participate.

---

62. Yukins, "The U.S. Federal Procurement System," 78.
63. *Code of Federal Regulations* 13, § 121.105(a)(1).

The TAA prohibits a waiver of any preference for small and minority-owned businesses from the GPA and FTAs.[64] To comply with this TAA provision, the US excludes procurement set-aside for such businesses from its commitments under agreements. Its exclusion in the GPA provides:

> "[t]his Agreement does not apply to any set aside on behalf of a small- or minority-owned business. A set-aside may include any form of preference, such as the exclusive right to provide a good or service, or any price preference."[65]

Because of this broad carve-out of set-asides, the US is able to increase their mandatory level without acting inconsistently with its trade obligations.[66]

3.2 Berry Amendment

The Berry Amendment requires the DoD to purchase certain items only if they are "grown, reprocessed, reused, or produced" in the US.[67] It was enacted in 1941 "to ensure that US troops wore uniforms and consumed food products that were wholly produced

---

64. The TAA provides that the authority of the president "to waive any law, regulation, procedure, or practice regarding Government procurement does not authorize the waiver of any small business or minority preference." *U.S. Code* 19, § 2511(f).

65. GPA, Appendix I, US, Annex 7, n. 1.

66. In 2017, Congress established an automatic increase of the threshold for small business set-asides. It amended the Small Business Act to remove its $100,000 threshold for small business set-asides and permanently tied the small business set-aside threshold to the simplified acquisition threshold. It also raised that threshold to $250,000. *National Defense Authorization Act for Fiscal Year 2018*, Public Law 115-91 (2017). Hence, the small business set-aside threshold increases automatically with future increases in the simplified acquisition threshold.

67. *Fifth Supplemental National Defense Appropriations Act*, Public Law 77-29, *U.S. Statutes at Large* 55 (1941): 123. The Berry Amendment became permanent law in 1993. *Department of Defense Appropriations Act*, 1994, Public Law 103-39, § 8005, *U.S. Statutes at Large* 107 (1993): 1488; *U.S. Code* 10 (2001), § 2533a.

in the US."[68] Subsequently, its scope was expanded when other products were added through defense appropriations acts. It now applies to purchases above the simplified acquisition threshold ($250,000) of food, clothing, tents, certain textile fabrics and fibers, hand or measuring tools, flags, and stainless-steel flatware and dinnerware.[69] The Berry Amendment allows various exceptions to the 100% American-made requirement, including the nonavailability of domestic products, procurement of food and tools outside of the US in support of contingency operations, procurement by vessels in foreign waters, and emergency procurement.[70]

Specialty Metals Restriction: Specialty metals, which consist primarily of certain types of steel, including certain metal alloys made of nickel, iron-nickel, cobalt, titanium and titanium alloys, and zirconium and zirconium alloys, are subject to a domestic sourcing restriction. The restriction prohibits the DoD "from purchasing aircraft, missile and space systems, ships, tank and automotive items, weapon systems, ammunition, or any components thereof, if they consist of a specialty metal not melted or produced" in the US. In addition to applying to defense purchases of certain items and components that contain specialty metal, the restriction also covers specialty metal that was not melted or produced in the US. The specialty metals restriction is subject to several exceptions, including those of the Berry Amendment. This restriction was included in the Berry Amendment in 1972[71] and codified in a separate law in 2002.[72]

The US excludes both products covered by the Berry Amendment and specialty metals restriction from its coverage of the DoD in the GPA and FTAs.

---

68. GAO, *Federal Procurement*, 12.

69. GAO, *Federal Procurement*, 12.

70. DFARS § 225.7002.

71. *Department of Defense Appropriations Act*, Public Law 92-570, § 742, *U.S. Statutes at Large* 86 (1972): 1200.

72. *U.S. Code* 10 (2002), § 2533b; DFARS 225.7003.2.

3.3 Kissell Amendment

The Department of Homeland Security (DHS) is subject to a domestic purchasing requirement that is modeled on the Berry Amendment. This requirement originated in the American Recovery and Reinvestment Act of 2009 (Recovery Act) in a provision (Section 604), known as the 'Kissell Amendment' after its author, Representative Larry Kissell of North Carolina.[73] The Homeland Security Acquisition Regulation made it permanent in March 2013.[74]

The Kissell Amendment generally prohibits the DHS from procuring certain textiles and clothing directly related to US national security interests if the item is not grown, reprocessed, reused, or produced in the US. It applies to the purchase of textiles, clothing, and footwear for the Coast Guard and the Transportation Security Administration (TSA).[75] Its coverage includes clothing, tents, tarpaulins, covers, and protective equipment, as well as the fibers used for fabrics such as cotton and other natural and synthetic fabrics.

This legislative measure was intended to apply to the procurement of uniforms and other textile items by all DHS agencies. However, the Recovery Act required its domestic purchasing restriction to be applied consistent with US obligations under international agreements. Most of the DHS's procurement is covered by the GPA and FTAs. The exception is the TSA, whose procurement was excluded from the GPA and all FTAs (except the US-Chile FTA and NAFTA) until the US added it. When it was added to the GPA, its procurement of textiles and apparel was excluded as required by

---

73. *American Recovery and Reinvestment Act of 2009*, Public Law 111-15, § 604, *U.S. Statutes at Large* 123 (2009): 115; *U.S. Code 6*, § 453-b.

74. US Library of Congress, Congressional Research Service, *Buying American: The Berry and Kissell Amendments*, by Michaela D. Platzer, IF10605 (2021), https://crsreports.congress.gov/product/pdf/IF/IF10605.

75. Nibley, Hoang, and Bakies, "Real Steps Towards," 2–3.

the Kissell Amendment.[76] Under the US-Mexico-Canada Agreement (USMCA), the successor to NAFTA, the US also excluded the TSA's procurement of textiles and apparel from that agreement.

In addition to excluding procurement covered by trade agreements, the Kissell Amendment restriction is subject to other exceptions. These exceptions include purchases below the simplified acquisition threshold, the nonavailability of domestic products at a satisfactory quality and in sufficient quantity at the US market prices, procurement by vessels in foreign waters, and emergency procurement.[77]

3.4 Transportation Services

Several laws require the federal government to purchase transportation services from domestic sources. Because domestic sourcing requirements are inconsistent with the US national treatment obligation under agreements that cover the procurement of services, the US excludes the procurement of all transportation services from its commitments.

Cargo Preference Acts of 1904 and 1954: The Cargo Preference Acts require all supplies bought for the DoD, and at least 50% of all equipment, materials, or commodities purchased or financed with federal funds by nondefense entities,[78] to be carried on privately owned, US-flag commercial vessels when transported to and from international destinations.[79] The Cargo Preference Act of 1904

---

76. In a 2017 report to Congress on the Kissell Amendment's effectiveness in restricting DHS's purchase of foreign textile products, GAO concluded only a limited number of procurements were affected due to multiple factors. Furthermore, the restriction had not fully limited DHS's purchase of textiles from foreign sources. GAO, *Effect of Restriction on DHS's Purchasing of Foreign Textiles Is Limited*, GAO-18-116, November 21, 2017, https://www.gao.gov/products/GAO-18-116.

77. OMB, "Increasing Opportunities," 6.

78. 46 *U.S. Code* § 55305(b); includes foreign military sales financed and managed by the DoD.

79. OMB, "Increasing Opportunities," 6–7.

requires the DoD to use only US government-owned ships or US-flag vessels for ocean transportation when shipping supplies bought by the Army, Navy, Air Force, or Marine Corps or for a defense agency (unless such vessels are not available at fair and reasonable rates).[80] The OMB described these restrictions as necessary for

> "the development and maintenance of an American merchant fleet (and mariner base) sufficient to carry our waterborne domestic commerce and a substantial part of our international trade at all times, and to serve as a naval and military auxiliary in time of war or national emergency."[81]

While these laws require the vessels suitable for carrying cargoes to be US-flag, US-crewed, and US-owned, they do not need to be constructed in the US.[82] Certain exceptions apply.[83]

Jones Act: The Jones Act, formally known as the Merchant Marine Act of 1920,[84] generally provides that merchandise may not be transported between two points in the US unless the vessel is US-built, US-owned, and endorsed by the US Coast Guard with a coastwise endorsement document. The Jones Act may be waived in limited circumstances when it is in the interests of national defense.[85]

Fly America Act: This Act[86] "aims to help domestic carriers compete against foreign carriers by requiring that foreign transportation of

---

80. *U.S. Code* 10, § 2631.

81. OMB, "Increasing Opportunities," 7.

82. OMB, "Increasing Opportunities," 7.

83. FAR subpart 47.5 stipulates the policy, procedures, and exceptions for the use of US-flag vessels when transportation of supplies by ocean vessel.

84. *Merchant Marine Act of 1920*, Public Law 66-261, *U.S. Statutes at Large* 41 (1920): 988; *U.S. Code* 46, § 50101.

85. OMB, "Increasing Opportunities," 6.

86. *The International Air Transportation Fair Competitive Practices Act of 1974*, Public Law 93-623, § 5; *U.S. Statutes at Large* 88 (1975): 2102; *U.S. Code* 49, § 40118; see also FAR subpart 47.4.

persons or property funded by the US government be furnished by US air carriers."[87] It requires federal employees, consultants, contractors, and grantees to use US-flag air carriers for US government-financed international air travel and transportation of their personal belongings. It allows the use of a foreign-flag carrier only where no US-flag carrier is available, or the use of a US-flag carrier would involve an excessive time delay. In 1980, Congress amended the Fly America Act to allow the use of foreign carriers for government-financed air transportation as part of a negotiated bilateral agreement.[88] Based on that authority, the US has negotiated Open Skies Agreements with foreign governments that allow travelers to use foreign air carriers from these countries for government-funded international travel.[89] In addition, a codeshare exception applies when a US-flag air carrier has an arrangement to provide foreign air travel, using a foreign carrier's aircraft through a codeshare arrangement. In that case, the airline ticket includes a US-flag carrier's code.[90]

4. FEDERAL FINANCIAL ASSISTANCE

4.1 Treatment in Agreements

Most trade agreements with procurement commitments do not apply to financial assistance, such as grants and loans. For example, the GPA 2012 does not apply to "non-contractual agreements or any form of assistance that a Party provides, including cooperative agreements, grants, loans, equity infusions, guarantees and fiscal

---

87. David Kelly, "The Fly America Act Controversy: An Analysis of GSA Contracts involving Foreign Carriers and Important Considerations," *Public Contract Law Journal* 47, no. 4 (2018): 510.

88. Kelly, "The Fly America Act," 513.

89. GSA, *Fly America Act*, Open Skies Agreements, accessed May 11, 2022, https://www.gsa.gov/policy-regulations/policy/travel-management-policy/fly-america-act.

90. Kelly, "The Fly America Act," 511.

incentives."[91] US FTAs include similar provisions. When an agreement such as the GPA 1994 did not have such a provision, the US excluded financial assistance in its coverage schedules. Although grants or loans are not considered procurement under the GPA or FTAs, they may fund procurement that is covered under trade agreements.

Beginning in the late 1970s, Congress attached 'Buy American' requirements to funding provided to state and other sub-federal entities for infrastructure projects under various laws. These domestic purchasing requirements generally mandated the use of US-produced iron, steel, and manufactured goods in federally funded projects. They did not conflict with trade agreements until the US covered subcentral entities that received federal funds subject to such requirements under the GPA 1994 and FTAs. When states covered by a trade agreement received federal funds for projects subject to a 'Buy American' requirement, they could not comply with both the federal directive to purchase American-made goods for use in the projects and a national treatment obligation under an agreement. To avoid such a situation, the US excluded the domestic purchasing restrictions from US commitments when it added coverage of procurement of states and other sub-federal entities to the GPA and FTAs.[92] These exceptions allow suppliers from US trading partners to participate in the procurement, provided they satisfy the 'Buy American' requirements.

4.2 Domestic Preferences in Federal Financial Awards

In 2020, the OMB incorporated a domestic preference for purchasing American-made goods by nonfederal agencies that receive

---

91. GPA, art. II:3(b).

92. For example, the US exclusion under the GPA provides: "[f]or the state entities included in this Annex, this Agreement does not apply to restrictions attached to federal funds for mass transit and highway projects." GPA, Appendix I, US, Annex 2, note 5.

federal funds. Although the preference did not mandate the purchase of domestic products, it encouraged federal fund recipients to maximize their use of US-produced goods, products, and materials in procurement under federal awards.[93] This preference has been broadly applied by federal entities.[94]

4.3 Transportation Projects

In the Surface Transportation Assistance Act of 1978, Congress extended–for the first time–domestic content requirements beyond direct procurement by federal agencies to highway and transit projects undertaken by nonfederal entities with federal funding.[95] It authorized the Secretary of Transportation to waive the Act's 'Buy American' requirement when its application would be inconsistent with the public interest, in case of the nonavailability of domestic

---

93. OMB, "Guidance for Grants and Agreements," *Federal Register* 85, no. 157 (August 13, 2020): 49506 https://www.govinfo.gov/content/pkg/FR-2020-08-13/pdf/2020-17468.pdf. It incorporated the preference in the Uniform Administrative Requirements, Cost Principles, and Audit Requirements for Federal Awards. The addition provided: "[a]s appropriate and to the extent consistent with law, the non-Federal entity should, to the greatest extent practicable under a Federal award, provide a preference for the purchase, acquisition, or use of goods, products, or materials produced in the United States (including but not limited to iron, aluminum, steel, cement, and other manufactured products). The requirements of this section must be included in all subawards including all contracts and purchase orders for work or products under this award." *Code of Federal Regulations*, title 2 (2020): § 200.322.

94. For example, the National Endowment for the Humanities applied the preference to all its awards. National Endowment for the Humanities, Infrastructure Programs Subject to the *Build America, Buy America Act*, *Federal Register* 87, 13 (January 20, 2022): 3129, https://www.govinfo.gov/content/pkg/FR-2022-01-20/pdf/2022-01077.pdf.

95. *Surface Transportation Assistance Act of 1978*, Public Law 95-599, *U.S. Statutes at Large* 92 (1978): 2689. The 'Buy American' provision in Title VI, Section 401, of that law stipulated that the Secretary of Transportation could not obligate any funds authorized by the Act, with a total cost above $500,000, unless the articles, materials, and suppliers were mined, produced or manufactured in the US "substantially all" from American-made products.

materials, or if the use of domestic materials would increase the cost of the overall project by more than a certain percentage. Congress, subsequently, enacted numerous laws that impose 'Buy American' requirements on infrastructure projects administered by the Department of Transportation (DoT).

The DoT and its agencies administer many federal financial assistance programs for infrastructure with 'Buy American' requirements. The Department provided over $70 billion in grants and loans for the development of transportation infrastructure improvements and purchases of equipment in FY 2020.[96] The domestic preference requirements in DoT's programs vary among the agencies, as described below, but have certain common elements.

Federal Highway Administration (FHWA): The FHWA's 'Buy American' requirement for the federal-aid highway program was first established in 1978 and modified in 1982.[97] It prohibits the use of federal-aid highway funds for projects unless American-produced steel, iron, and manufactured products are used in the projects. The agency may waive the 'Buy American' requirement where its application would be inconsistent with the public interest, the domestic steel and iron products are unavailable, and the inclusion of domestic material would increase the cost of the overall project by more than 25%.[98] In a 1983 rulemaking, the FHWA made a public interest finding that the 'Buy American' requirement did not apply to raw materials. It also waived the requirement for manufactured

---

96. By contrast, the DoT's direct purchases of products covered under the BAA and other laws in FY 2020 totaled only $700 million. DoT, *Identification of Federal Financial Assistance Infrastructure Programs Subject to the Build America, Buy America Provisions of the Infrastructure Investment and Jobs Act*, January 2022, 2-3, https://www.transportation.gov/office-policy/transportation-policy/made-in-america/build-america-buy-america-60-day-report.

97. *Surface Transportation Assistance Act*, Public Law 97-424, § 165 (1983); *U.S. Code* 23, § 313. See also DoT, *Identification*, 9–10.

98. DoT, *Identification*, 10–11.

products. In 1995, the agency issued a nationwide waiver for pig iron and processed, pelletized, and reduced iron ores due to a lack of adequate domestic supply.[99] The FHWA posts all proposed waivers on its website for a 15-day comment period before publishing the final decision in the *Federal Register*.

Two cases illustrate the FHWA's use of waivers to the 'Buy American' requirement. The first involved the New International Trade Crossing over the Detroit River, which linked Detroit, Michigan to Windsor, Ontario. Even though this project was solely funded by Canadian public and private sources and its financial risk was assumed by Canadian entities, the FHWA insisted that the 'Buy American' requirement be applied to the whole project. It based its position on the state of Michigan's intention to use Canada's financial contribution to the international crossing as the state's matching share on other federal-aid highway projects. The FHWA's position would have meant that Canadian iron and steel could not have been used in the project. That result was averted when the FWHA, based on a request from Michigan's governor, issued a public interest waiver of the domestic purchasing requirement, citing the "unique financing structure."[100] As a result, both American and Canadian steel and iron products were eligible for use in the construction of the international crossing.

The FHWA resolved a second dispute with Canada over the application of its 'Buy American' requirement to the repair of a bridge in Morrison, Colorado. The federal agency initially concluded that the town would have to dismantle a bridge repaired using an FHWA grant because it included Canadian steel. However,

---

99. DoT, *Identification*, 26.

100. DoT, Federal Highway Administration, "Buy America Waiver Notification," *Federal Register* 77, no. 239 (December 12, 2012): 74048, https://www.federalregister.gov/documents/2012/12/12/2012-29917/buy-america-waiver-notification.

it reversed its position and decided in 2014 that the foreign steel did not need to be removed, provided no federal grant money was used for the Canadian beams in the bridge.[101]

Federal Transit Administration: The Transit Administration must require the use of US-produced iron, steel, and manufactured goods in projects that it funds. For manufactured goods (other than rolling stock) to be considered produced in the US, all components must be of US origin, and all the product's manufacturing processes must take place in the US. The agency's statutory authority includes a waiver for rolling stock, covering train control, communication, traction power equipment, and rolling stock prototypes. The waiver applies if the cost of US-produced components and subcomponents is more than 70% of the cost of all components and the final assembly of the rolling stock takes place in the US.[102]

The Transit Administration may issue waivers similar to those of the FHWA. However, it is subject to a unique requirement. If the Secretary of Transportation denies an application for a waiver based on the nonavailability of domestic products, the department head must provide the waiver applicant with a certification that the steel, iron, or manufactured goods are produced in the US in a sufficient and reasonably available amount and of satisfactory quality. The Secretary must also provide a list of known manufacturers in the US from which the item can be obtained.[103]

---

101. Barrie McKenna, "Buy America ruling reversed on Colorado bridge made with Ontario steel," *The Globe and Mail*, October 7, 2014, https://www.theglobeandmail.com/report-on-business/international-business/buy-america-ruling-toppled-in-colorado-over-ontario-made-steel/article20971036/.

102. DoT, *Identification*, 13–15. In 2015, Congress increased the domestic content requirements for rolling stock from 60% of the cost of all components in FY 2016-17 to 65% for FY 2018-19 and to 70%, beginning in FY 2020. The 2015 *Fixing America's Surface Transportation Act*, Public Law 114-94, *U.S. Statutes at Large* 129 (2015): 1312.

103. DoT, Identification, 15.

Federal Railroad Administration: When the Federal Railroad Administration provides grants, it must require the use of US-produced steel, iron, and manufactured goods in the project.[104] Except for the Transit Administration's rolling stock waiver provision, the two agencies' general 'Buy American' provisions are very similar. As a result, the Railroad Administration uses applicable Transit Administration rules.[105]

Federal Aviation Administration (FAA): The FAA provides grants for infrastructure projects under the Airport Improvement Program. Its 'Buy American' statute requires 100% of the steel and manufactured goods (but not iron) used in an airport improvement project to be produced in the US.[106] In addition to the other types of DoT waivers, the FAA may waive the 'Buy American' requirement where the cost of US-made components and subcomponents exceeds 60% of the total components cost, and the final assembly of the facility or equipment has occurred in the US.[107]

4.4 American Recovery and Reinvestment Act of 2009

The Recovery Act was an $800 billion stimulus package enacted by Congress at the beginning of President Obama's administration.[108] It included a broad 'Buy American' provision that required the use of US-made iron, steel, and manufactured goods in projects financed with Recovery Act funds.

When the House of Representatives passed the Recovery Act legislation in January 2009, its 'Buy American' provision was

---

104. *U.S. Code* 49, § 22905(a).

105. DoT, *Identification*, 11–12.

106. *U.S. Code* 49, § 50101.

107. DoT, *Identification*, 6–7.

108. *Recovery Act*, § 1605.

silent regarding its application to procurement covered under trade agreements. That omission prompted an outcry from US trading partners, who contended that the provision would be inconsistent with US commitments under international agreements. The Senate added a provision to the House-passed legislation that required the 'Buy American' restriction to be applied consistently with US obligations under international agreements. That provision was included in the final legislation enacted by Congress and signed by President Obama in February 2009. Consequently, when a project covered by an agreement used Recovery Act funds, goods from parties to those agreements did not have to meet the 'Buy American' requirement.

The Recovery Act's domestic purchasing requirement applied to numerous state and sub-federal projects for the first time.[109] The requirement was subject to the exceptions that commonly apply to domestic preferences.[110] Based on a 2010 bilateral procurement agreement between the US and Canada, the US agreed not to apply the domestic purchasing requirement to Canada in several programs funded by the Recovery Act, in exchange for Canada opening the procurement of its provinces to the US.[111] This case

109. These included projects funded through the Department of Agriculture's Community Facilities Program, Department of Energy's Energy Efficiency and Conservation Block Grant and State Energy Program, and Department of Housing and Urban Development's Community Development Block Grants Recovery and Public Housing Capital Fund. FAR subpart 25.6. The White House issued guidance on the implementation of the 'Buy American' requirement. OMB, "Requirements for Implementing Sections 1512, 1605, and 1606 of the American Recovery and Reinvestment act of 2009 for Financial Assistance Awards," *Federal Register* 74, no. 77 (April 23, 2009): 18449, https://www.govinfo.gov/content/pkg/FR-2009-04-23/pdf/E9-9073.pdf.

110. Its exceptions were inconsistency with the public interest, nonavailability of domestic products, and unreasonable cost (domestic products use would increase the overall project cost by more than 25%).

111. See the discussion of the US-Canada Agreement on Government Procurement in Chapter 5.

demonstrated that when the benefits to the US were substantial, a trading partner could be excluded from a specific domestic preference without explicit waiver authority.

4.5 Water-related Infrastructure Projects

Congress also applied 'Buy American' requirements to water infrastructure projects receiving funds from the Environmental Protection Agency. The Water Resources Reform and Development Act of 2014[112] imposed 'Buy American' restrictions on iron and steel used in large water infrastructure projects that received federal funding, as well as on projects funded by the agency's Clean Water and Drinking Water State Revolving Fund programs.[113] The law stipulated that its domestic content requirement must be applied in a manner consistent with US obligations under international agreements.

4.6 Infrastructure Investment and Jobs Act

The IIJA, which became law on November 15, 2021, authorized $1.2 trillion in spending on a broad range of infrastructure projects. It included the Build America, Buy America Act (BABA Act),[114] which requires federal agencies to impose a domestic preference on every infrastructure project that receives federal financial assistance. Under this law, no federal funds can be obligated for an infrastructure project "unless all of the iron, steel, manufactured products, and construction materials used in the project are produced in the

---

112. *Water Resources Reform and Development Act of 2014*, Public Law 113-21.

113. US Library of Congress, Congressional Research Service, *Effects of Buy America on Transportation Infrastructure and U.S. Manufacturing*, by Michaela D. Platzer and William J. Mallett, R44266 (2019), 21, https://sgp.fas.org/crs/misc/R44266.pdf.

114. *IIJA*, §§ 70901–70927.

United States."[115] This requirement constituted a significant expansion of domestic preferences for infrastructure projects.

The mandate applied to programs not subject previously to any such laws, as well as those that had been subject to 'Buy American' laws limited to specific materials or products.[116] Because BABA's domestic preference is not limited to the funds appropriated or authorized in the Infrastructure Act, it "will have enduring, permanent impact" on participation in its funded projects.[117]

The BABA Act broadly defined infrastructure to include roads, highways, and bridges; public transportation; dams, ports, harbors, and other maritime facilities; intercity passenger and freight railroads; freight and intermodal facilities; airports; water systems, including drinking water and wastewater systems; electrical transmission facilities and systems; utilities; broadband infrastructure; and buildings and real property.[118] In addition, the Act broadened the application of the 'Buy American' requirement beyond iron, steel, and certain manufactured goods, which were covered previously. It extended to nonferrous metals, such as copper used in electric wiring; plastic- and polymer-based products; glass, including optical fiber; and other construction materials, such as lumber and drywall.[119]

The Infrastructure Act specifies three 'Buy American' preferences:

---

115. *IIJA*, § 70912(5).

116. Dustin Painter, "U.S. Lawmakers Adopt Historic and Far Reaching Buy America Laws in Bipartisan Infrastructure Agreement," Kelley Drye Client Advisory, November 10, 2021, https://www.kelleydrye.com/News-Events/Publications/Client-Advisories/U-S-Lawmakers-Adopt-Historic-and-Far-Reaching-(1).

117. Painter, "U.S. Lawmakers Adopt."

118. *IIJA*, § 70912(5).

119. US Library of Congress, Congressional Research Service, *Congress Expands Buy America Requirements in the Infrastructure Investment and Jobs Act (P.L. 117-58)*, by Christopher Watson, IF11989 (2021), https://crsreports.congress.gov/product/pdf/IF/IF11989. The IIJA's list of construction materials subject to 'Buy American' requirements did not include cement and aggregates, comprising sand, gravel, and crushed stone.

(i)   all iron and steel used in the project are produced in the US, which means all manufacturing processes, from the initial melting stage through the application of coatings, occurred in the US;

(ii) all manufactured products used in the project are produced in the US, which requires the product to be manufactured in the US and the cost of its US-produced components to be greater than 55% of the total cost of all components (unless another domestic content standard applies);

(iii) all construction materials are manufactured in the US, which requires all manufacturing processes to take place in the US.[120]

Put simply, the BABA Act requires all covered iron and steel products and construction materials to be produced in the US.[121]

The domestic preferences in the BABA Act may be waivered under circumstances that are typically found in other 'Buy American' laws.[122] Before issuing a waiver, an agency must publish the proposed waiver on its own website and an OMB-designated website and provide 15 days for public comments. General applicability waivers must be reviewed every five years to determine whether a waiver should be continued.[123]

---

120. *IIJA*, § 70912(6).

121. Yukins, "International Procurement Developments." The IIJA directed OMB to issue standards that define the relevant manufacturing processes as they relate to construction materials. *IIJA*, § 70915(b)(1).

122. *IIJA*, § 70914(b) (d). They are when: (i) application of the domestic preference would be inconsistent with the public interest; (ii) the iron, steel, manufactured products, and construction material used in the project are not produced in the US in sufficient and reasonably available quantities or of a satisfactory quality; and (iii) inclusion of the domestic products or construction materials would increase the overall project cost by more than 25%.

123. The Biden administration's measures implementing the IIJA are examined in Chapter 12.

In enacting the BABA Act, Congress stipulated–as it did in the 2009 Recovery Act–that the 'Buy American' requirement must be applied in a manner consistent with US obligations under international agreements.[124] That means that the domestic content requirement does not apply to infrastructure projects covered under the GPA, FTAs, or a 1995 bilateral agreement with the European Union.

---

124. *IIJA*, § 70914(e).

CHAPTER 8

PIVOT FROM LIBERALIZATION TO PROTECTIONISM: TRUMP ERA

1. INTRODUCTION

The 2016 election of Trump as the US president marked a pivot in the American approach to international trade. Trump was elected as a Republican candidate, yet he espoused positions on trade that deviated from traditional Republican orthodoxy and were more aligned with views held by Democrats. Historically, Republican presidents have negotiated more FTAs than their Democratic counterparts, included liberalization of government procurement markets in their FTA negotiating objectives, and insisted on robust government procurement chapters. At the same time, they complied with the domestic purchasing requirements in US laws, demonstrating that liberalization and protectionism in the procurement arena could coexist.

Instead of maintaining this balance of his Republican predecessors, President Trump made 'Buy American' directives a centerpiece of his 'America First' policy to protect the domestic procurement market from foreign products. He issued numerous executive orders to federal agencies to maximize the purchase of goods produced in the US in their direct procurement and funding of state and local infrastructure projects to implement his policy.

President Trump expressed scorn for trade agreements on the campaign trail and in the White House. He most vividly displayed it when he pulled the US out of the Trans-Pacific Partnership (TPP), which had been signed by his predecessor, President Obama. TPP was considered the most significant regional trade agreement that the US had ever signed. It was intended to serve as the cornerstone for US policy in the Asia-Pacific region and a counterweight to China. Subsequently, the Trump administration negotiated only one FTA, which was a revision of the North American Free Trade Agreement (NAFTA), an agreement that Trump had threatened to abandon. This agreement failed to liberalize government procurement. Indeed, Canada chose to opt out of its procurement chapter rather than accept the Trump administration's terms.

President Trump further alarmed the business and trade communities and US trading partners when he threatened to withdraw the US from the GPA. His administration also sought to reduce the procurement that the US covered under this agreement and FTAs.

Trump's efforts to promote 'Buy American' policies were only partially successful, yet they suggested that the US might be beginning to adopt a more protectionist approach to government procurement. Just two of his orders that proposed specific action were incorporated into US regulations and two were reversed by his successor. Nonetheless, President Biden did not repudiate his protectionist policies. Instead, he built upon the foundation that Trump had laid.[1]

2. "BUY AMERICAN" ORDERS

2.1 American Iron and Steel in Pipelines

In his initial "Buy American" order, President Trump sought to extend the reach of domestic purchasing requirements beyond federal

---

1. See discussion in Chapter 12.

government procurement and federally funded projects to private sector projects. In his first week in office, he directed the Secretary of Commerce to develop a plan to require pipelines to use American-made materials and equipment to the extent permitted by law.[2] In preparing for the pipeline plan, the Commerce Department asked for public comments on the use of domestic iron and steel in pipelines, including the extent to which pipe manufacturers obtained domestic material, the share of their inventory that was fully produced in the US, and the extent to which domestic content requirements would affect their operations.[3] In responding to this request, industry representatives and US trading partners sharply criticized the president's attempt to bring private projects under 'Buy American' requirements. The European Union (EU), Canada, Mexico, and Australia were among the critics. They contended that it "would be unprecedented" to impose mandates for American-made iron and steel on privately funded, commercial projects and would violate fundamental principles of the WTO and US trade agreements.[4] The

2. US President, "Presidential Memorandum Regarding Construction of American Pipelines," January 24, 2017, https://trumpwhitehouse.archives.gov/presidential-actions/presidential-memorandum-regarding-construction-american-pipelines/.

3. Department of Commerce, "Construction of Pipelines Using Domestic Steel and Iron," Federal Register 82, no. 50 (March 16, 2017): 13973, https://www.govinfo.gov/content/pkg/FR-2017-03-16/pdf/2017-05197.pdf.

4. Jennifer A. Dlouhy, "Trump's America-First Pipeline Plan Upsets Oil Industry," *Industry Week*, July 21, 2017, https://www.industryweek.com/supply-chain/article/22023276/trumps-americafirst-pipeline-plan-upsets-oil-industry. For example, see business and government responses to the Department of Commerce's request for comments. Department of Commerce, "Construction of Pipelines Using Domestic Steel and Iron," Docket Number: 170309252–7252–01, https://www.regulations.gov; US Chamber of Commerce, "Comments to the U.S. Department of Commerce on Construction of Pipelines Using Domestic Steel and Iron," April 6, 2017; and Canadian Embassy, "Comments by the Government of Canada to the International Trade Administration US Department of Commerce," April 7, 2016.

proposed action "never materialized" and the Commerce Department plan was never made public.[5]

2.2 "Buy American and Hire American" Order

Less than three months after his pipeline order, in April 2017, President Trump issued a broad "Buy American and Hire American" order that declared a policy maximizing the use of US-made products and minimizing waivers of 'Buy American' requirements in federal procurement and financial assistance awards.[6] The president set out three key mandates to implement his policy. First, he directed all agencies to assess their compliance with–and waivers of–'Buy American' laws[7] and report their findings to the Secretary of Commerce and the Director of the Office of Management and Budget (OMB). Second, the president required the Commerce Secretary and the US Trade Representative (USTR) to assess the GPA's and US FTAs' impact on the operation of 'Buy American' laws, including the implementation of domestic procurement preferences. Finally, based on these assessments, he instructed the Commerce Secretary to submit a 'Buy American' report with recommendations on strengthening the implementation of 'Buy American' laws, including domestic procurement preference policies and programs. This report was due in November 2017.

In preparing their assessment of the impact of trade agreements on 'Buy American' laws, Commerce and USTR invited

5. Don Lee, "Why Trump's 'Buy American' campaign went nowhere," *Los Angeles Times*, August 31, 2020, https://www.latimes.com/politics/story/2020-08-31/trumps-buy-american-campaign-went-nowhere.

6. "Executive Order 13788 of April 18, 2017, Buy American and Hire American," *Federal Register* 82, no. 76 (April 21, 2017): 18837, https://www.govinfo.gov/content/pkg/FR-2017-04-21/pdf/2017-08311.pdf.

7. The executive order broadly defined 'Buy American' laws as all statutes, regulations, rules, and executive orders requiring or providing a preference for US-produced goods, products, or materials. "Executive Order 13788."

public comments on the costs and benefits to US industry of government procurement obligations under trade agreements, the effect of those agreements on the operation of domestic preference laws, and the domestic firms' participation in the US and foreign procurement markets.[8] Nearly 50 businesses, trade associations, firms, foreign governments, and others submitted comments.[9] Over half of the comments detailed the benefits of the GPA and FTAs, including that their non-discrimination provisions and transparency requirements ensured a level playing field for US firms in foreign procurement markets. They also pointed to the costs of complying with existing 'Buy American' requirements. In addition, the supporters of trade agreements expressed concerns that potential Trump policies might jeopardize US access to foreign procurement markets and lead to possible retaliation by foreign trading partners. The possible abandonment of existing agreements and the expansion of procurement restrictions were of particular concern.

A broad range of business associations identified multiple benefits of US participation in the GPA, NAFTA, and other trade agreements with procurement obligations. These business groups included those with broad membership, such as the US Chamber of Commerce and the National Foreign Trade Council, along with associations representing specific US sectors and companies. Citing US procurement data, they challenged the "misconception that foreign companies are heavy beneficiaries of U.S.

---

8. Department of Commerce and USTR, "Request for Comment on the Costs and Benefits to U.S. Industry of U.S. International Government Procurement Obligations for Report to the President on 'Buy American and Hire America'," *Federal Register* 82, no. 160 (August 21, 2017): 39561, https://www.govinfo.gov/content/pkg/FR-2017-08-21/pdf/2017-17553.pdf.

9. "Comments on Costs and Benefits to US Industry of US International Government Procurement Obligations for Report to the President on Buy American and Hire American," Docket Number ITA-2017-006, 2017, https://www.regulations.gov/docket?D=ITA-2017-0006.

procurement,"[10] illustrating with data from the US government procurement database "that foreign firms secure few U.S. procurements in practice."[11] They also contended that "U.S. businesses are far more successful in securing procurement opportunities in foreign markets than are foreign firms seeking to secure U.S. government procurement."[12]

The Coalition for Government Procurement, a nonprofit association of firms that sell to the federal government, noted the value of procurement opportunities offered by both the US and foreign governments. It opposed additional restrictions on foreign-made products in domestic federal procurement, the expansion of 'Buy American' laws, or the renegotiations of FTAs "that provide government procurement opportunities to US companies internationally."[13]

Associations that represented specific sectors detailed the benefits of trade agreements to their members. They included the Advanced Medical Technology Association, Coalition of Service Industries (CSI),[14] Information Technology Industry Council and IT

10. "Comments on Costs and Benefits, Coalition of Services Industries (CSI) Submission."

11. "Comments on Costs and Benefits, Statement of the U.S. Chamber of Commerce," September 7, 2017. The US Chamber of Commerce pointed out that "across the entire federal government, just 2% of all contracts were secured by foreign-headquartered companies in FY 2016. Of this small portion, about 80% were Department of Defense contracts, nearly all of which went to the U.S. affiliates of British or other European firms."

12. "Comments on Costs and Benefits, Written Submission of the National Foreign Trade Council," September 18, 2017.

13. "Comments on Costs and Benefits, Letter from Roger Waldron, President, The Coalition for Government Procurement, September 18, 2017. It represents a broad scope of industries, including information technology (IT), professional services, medical products and pharmaceuticals, furniture, and office supplies.

14. According to CSI, in 2016, the US "held over 40 percent (or $128.4 billion) of the global IT procurement market, which includes data center systems, devices, IT services, and software, and covers all IT procurements at every government level." "Comments on Costs and Benefits, CSI Submission."

Alliance for Public Sector,[15] the National Association of Manufacturers,[16] Security Industry Association,[17] and the Telecommunications Industry Association.[18]

Individual firms also submitted comments. For example, the General Electric Company emphasized that it "benefits immensely from multilateral and bilateral government procurement agreements in terms of market access." It also noted that its major markets (health care and energy) were often subject to "much higher degrees of government involvement" in other countries than in the US. It further commented that if the US were to go back on its commitments in government procurement agreements with partner

---

15. The two associations pointed out that: "[w]ithout U.S. participation in the WTO GPA or government procurement market access commitments in U.S. free trade agreements (FTAs), U.S.-based companies would have significantly fewer export opportunities for technology products and services to government procurement markets around the world." "Comments on Costs and Benefits, Response of the Information Technology Industry Council and the IT Alliance for Public Sector to the Request for Comments on the Costs and Benefits of U.S. International Government Procurement Obligations and 'Buy American' Policies."

16. "Comments on Costs and Benefits, National Association of Manufacturers (NAM), Comments on Costs and Benefits to U.S. Industry of U.S. International Government Procurement Obligations," September 18, 2017. NAM commented that its "members from manufacturers of water and wastewater and other infrastructure equipment, energy, medical devices, pharmaceuticals and chemicals to information and communications technology and transportation and capital equipment products have been able to use [the GPA, NAFTA, and other trade agreements] to gain access to foreign government procurements."

17. "Comments on Costs and Benefits, Statement of Security Industry Association," September 14, 2017. It pointed out that for the US security manufacturers, Mexico was one of their most significant export markets as they exported roughly $1 billion in safety and security equipment annually. In addition, under NAFTA, US firms were not subject to Mexico's 15% price preference.

18. "Comments on Costs and Benefits, Telecommunications Industry Association (TIA) Comments," September 18, 2017. TIA commented that the GPA and FTAs shielded US firms from "domestic preferences and discriminatory purchasing requirements that foreign governments could otherwise use to unfairly favor their own suppliers."

countries, "foreign public procurement markets may be closed off in retaliation."[19] Another US company that submitted comments was MetLife, Inc., a provider of insurance, annuities, employee benefits, and asset management with operations in 44 countries. It cited Mexico, its third-largest market–after the US and Japan–to illustrate the importance of the government procurement obligations in US FTAs "in terms of our access to and participation in Mexico's government procurement market."[20]

The governments of Australia[21] and Canada (represented by its national government and the Alberta and Ontario provincial governments)[22] and the EU[23] expressed concerns about the further tightening of 'Buy American' rules. They pointed out the importance of trade agreements in providing guaranteed access to foreign

---

19. "Comments on Costs and Benefits, The General Electric Company, Comments," September 18, 2017.

20. MetLife, Inc. credited NAFTA's rules on government procurement with ensuring that it and other firms "can compete for Mexican government contracts on a fair and transparent basis" while not being subject to Mexico's 15% price preferences for Mexican participants in procurement. "Comments on Costs and Benefits, Statement of MetLife, Inc.," September 18, 2017.

21. The Australian government noted that many companies from the US participate in its procurement and singled out several US companies engaged in specific procurement in Australia, such as Bechtel, General Electric, and Jacobs Engineering Group. It also emphasized that US support of the GPA "was critical to Australia's decision to apply to accede to the WTO GPA." "Comments on Costs and Benefits, Australian Embassy Submission to the Department of Commerce and USTR pursuant to Notice 82 FR 39561."

22. "Comments on Costs and Benefits, Embassy of Canada, Comments by the Government of Canada," September 18, 2017. The Canadian government pointed out that in 2015 11% of its federal procurement contracts were awarded to foreign suppliers, and, of the total, close to 90% went to US suppliers, contrasted with only 0.15% of U.S. federal procurement contracts awarded to Canadian suppliers in 2015.

23. The EU cited a 2017 report that "concluded that eliminating existing US domestic content requirements would increase US GDP by $22 billion and create 363,000 new jobs." "Comments on Costs and Benefits, Letter from Damien Levie, Delegation of the European Union to the United States," September 18, 2017.

procurement markets based on the principle of reciprocity. They also highlighted the role of open government procurement regimes in attracting foreign investment by providing the certainty and predictability businesses need to make investment decisions.

Comments were also submitted that supported 'Buy American' requirements. Several trade associations whose members benefit from such requirements stressed the importance of maintaining 'Buy American' exemptions in trade agreements and even expanding them to more state and local infrastructure projects.[24] Those associations included the Alliance for American Manufacturing, the American Footwear & Apparel, the American Iron and Steel Institute, the American Institute of Steel Construction, and the Parachute Industry Association, as well as companies such as Nucor Corporation.

Public Citizen, a nonprofit consumer advocacy organization, submitted the most extensive criticisms of trade agreements, particularly contending that the US provided access to more procurement than its trading partners. It recommended that the US withdraw from or renegotiate trade pacts, including eliminating the national treatment obligation, or limiting trading partners' access to a set amount of US procurement "that reflects the limited opportunities in each prospective trade agreement partners' procurement markets and the history of the amount of contracts actually obtained by US firms."[25] Others, such as the Municipal Castings Association, a coalition of US manufacturers of iron,

---

24. "Comments on Costs and Benefits," Letter from Scott N. Paul, President, Alliance for American Manufacturing, American Footwear & Apparel, September 18, 2017; Letter from Thomas J. Gibson, American Iron and Steel Institute, September 18, 2017; Letter from Charles Carter, President, American Institute of Steel Construction, September 18, 2017; and Letter from Alan H. Price et al. on behalf of Nucor Corporation, September 18, 2017.

25. "Comments on Costs and Benefits, Public Citizen, Comments Concerning the Costs and Benefits to US Industry of US International Government Procurement Obligations," September 18, 2017.

steel, aluminum, and other cast products used in infrastructure projects, also expressed concern that the US opened more procurement than its trading partners.[26]

Following the submission of these extensive comments to the Commerce Department and USTR (and perhaps because of them), the Trump administration never made public any report on the GPA and FTAs nor even acknowledged preparing such a report.

Trump's 2017 order also called for a limited "judicious use" of public interest waivers of 'Buy American' laws to maximize the use of American goods, products, and materials. Furthermore, it required agencies before issuing a waiver to consider "whether a significant portion of the cost advantage of a foreign-sourced product" was the result of the use of dumped (sold below cost) or injuriously subsidized steel, iron, or manufactured goods and incorporate the findings into their waiver determinations.[27] President Biden revoked this order in January 2021.[28]

2.3 "Buy American" Order to Strengthen Preferences in Infrastructure Projects

The first Trump "Buy American" order reflected in federal regulations applied to infrastructure projects. That order, "Strengthening Buy-American Preferences for Infrastructure Projects," was directed at federal agencies that provide financial assistance to state and local governments for infrastructure projects. It required these agencies to "encourage" the sub-federal recipients of federal funds to use US-produced iron, steel, aluminum, cement, and

---

26. "Comments on Costs and Benefits, Comments of the Municipal Casting Associations," September 18, 2017.

27. "Executive Order 13788."

28. "Executive Order 14005 of January 25, 2021, Ensuring the Future Is Made in All of America by All of America's Workers," *Federal Register* 86, no. 17 (January 28, 2021): 7475, https://www.govinfo.gov/content/pkg/FR-2021-01-28/pdf/2021-02038.pdf.

other manufactured products in their projects.[29] The requirement applied to a broad range of infrastructure projects, including roads, bridges, railroads, transit, airports, and ports, as well as water and sewer, electric, oil, gas and propane, pipelines, broadband internet, and cybersecurity.

In August 2020, the OMB cited both the 2019 infrastructure order and the 2017 "Buy American and Hire American" order when it imposed a 'soft' preference on federal awards to nonfederal entities.[30] Although the agency did not mandate the purchase of domestic products, it strongly encouraged nonfederal recipients of federal funds to provide a 'Buy American' preference "to the greatest extent practicable" for American-made goods, products, or materials.[31] This guidance became effective in November 2020.

2.4 "Buy American" Order to Increase Domestic Content

The Federal Acquisition Regulatory Council (FAR Council) implemented a second Trump 'Buy American' directive as one of the final acts of his administration. The genesis of the FAR Council's action was a 2019 presidential order to tighten the application of the Buy American Act of 1933 and restrict the ability of federal agencies to purchase foreign products.[32] The FAR Council

---

29. "Executive Order 13858 of January 31, 2019, Strengthening Buy-American Preferences for Infrastructure Projects," *Federal Register* 84, no. 24 (February 5, 2019): 2039, https://www.govinfo.gov/content/pkg/FR-2019-02-05/pdf/2019-01426.pdf.

30. OMB, "Guidance for Grants and Agreements," *Federal Register* 85, no. 157 (August 13, 2020): 49506. https://www.govinfo.gov/content/pkg/FR-2020-08-13/pdf/2020-17468.pdf.

31. *Code of Federal Regulations*, title 2, sec. 200.322(a) (2020).

32. "Executive Order 13881 of July 15, 2019, Maximizing Use of American-Made Goods, Products, and Materials," *Federal Register* 84, no. 138 (July 18, 2019): 34257, https://www.govinfo.gov/content/pkg/FR-2019-07-18/pdf/2019-15449.pdf.

implemented those presidential instructions when it issued a final rule that revised the Federal Acquisition Regulation (FAR) on January 19, 2021, the last full day of President Trump's term.[33] One revision increased the domestic content required for a product to be treated as American-made under the Buy American Act from 50% to 95% for iron and steel products and 55% for all other products.[34] As a consequence, iron and steel end products are considered of foreign origin when the cost of foreign iron and steel used in such products constitutes 5% or more of the cost of all components.

The final rule also modified the FAR provision that allows federal agencies to purchase a foreign product if they determine that the cost of a domestic product is unreasonable. It increased the price preferences applied to the price of the foreign product from 12% to 30% when the lowest domestic offer is from a small business and from 6% to 20% when the offer of other businesses is the lowest domestic offer. Thus, the Trump administration's revisions allowed a domestic product offered by a small business to be 30% more expensive than a foreign product and 20% more expensive when offered by other businesses. Only then would the price of a domestic product be deemed unreasonable, and the purchase of a foreign product would be allowed. In defending this revision against claims that it would result in higher prices for the federal government, the FAR Council contended that new competition would assist in holding down prices. It argued that "robust competition among vendors offering domestic products will decrease the extent to which the Government could pay an additional 20 to 30% for domestic products above and beyond the cost of

33. "Federal Acquisition Regulation: Maximizing Use of American-made Goods, Products, and Materials," *Federal Register* 86, no. 11 (January 19, 2021): 6180, https://www.govinfo.gov/content/pkg/FR-2021-01-19/pdf/2021-00710.pdf.

34. At the direction of President Biden, the FAR Council increased the domestic content, as described in Chapter 12.

otherwise equivalent foreign products."[35] These FAR changes constituted the last 'Buy American' action implemented by the Trump administration.[36]

2.5 "Buy American" Order for Essential Medicines

In August 2020, President Trump issued a long-promised "Buy American" order for essential medicines, a category that included key medicines, medical countermeasures, and critical inputs.[37] The administration argued that the order was needed to reduce US dependence on foreign manufacturers for these products and ensure long-term domestic production and resilient supply chains. The order was issued despite reservations expressed by industry, members of Congress, and scholars, who pointed out the insufficiency of US capacity to meet immediate public health care needs. For example, the manufacturing of 72% of pharmaceutical ingredients for US markets occurred outside the US. They also argued that closing off the federal government's access to foreign suppliers could raise supply chain vulnerabilities in the event of disruptions within the US.[38]

A central element of the order was aimed at reducing US obligations under international agreements. The president wanted essential medicines removed from US commitments under the GPA

---

35. "FAR: Maximizing Use."

36. The FAR Council did not act on the president's request to review the feasibility and desirability of reducing to 25% the foreign content threshold for products (other than iron or steel) to be considered domestic.

37. "Executive Order 13944 of August 6, 2020, Combating Public Health Emergencies and Strengthening National Security by Ensuring Essential Medicines, Medical Countermeasures, and Critical Inputs Are Made in the United States," *Federal Register* 85, no. 158 (August 14, 2020): 49929, https://www.govinfo.gov/content/pkg/FR-2020-08-14/pdf/2020-18012.pdf.

38. US Library of Congress, Congressional Research Service, *COVID-19: International Trade and Access to Pharmaceutical Products*, by Nina M. Hart, LSB10436 (2020): 3, https://crsreports.congress.gov/product/pdf/LSB/LSB10436.

and FTAs. As a first step, under the president's directive, the Food and Drug Administration (FDA) published two sets of crucial medicines "that are medically necessary to have available at all times" on October 30, 2020. One listed 223 essential medicines most needed for patients in US acute care medical facilities and urgent medical conditions. Another was a list of 96 medical devices.[39] The FDA invited public comments on the lists, including whether items should be added to or removed from the lists and the frequency and process for updating them.

The FDA's publication of the lists triggered another element of the president's order. It required USTR to take all appropriate action within 30 days of the FDA's publication to remove the items from its lists of US obligations under the GPA and FTAs. Accordingly, on November 27, 2020, USTR submitted a proposed modification to the WTO Committee on Government Procurement (Committee) to withdraw the FDA-listed essential medicines from US commitments for federal government entities covered under the GPA.[40] It contended that the removal of these goods was "necessary for responding to threats arising from chemical, biological, radiological, and nuclear (CBRN) threats and public health emergencies, including emerging infectious diseases such as COVID-19."[41] Rather than include a list of the products to be removed, USTR provided a link to the FDA website for a complete list of the goods to be removed.[42]

---

39. Stephen M. Hahn, "FDA Publishes List of Essential Medicines, Medical Countermeasures, Critical Inputs Required by Executive Order," US Food and Drug Administration, October 30, 2020, https://www.fda.gov/news-events/press-announcements/fda-publishes-list-essential-medicines-medical-countermeasures-critical-inputs-required-executive.

40. WTO, "Proposed Modifications to Appendix I of the United States under the Revised Agreement on Government Procurement, Communication from the United States," GPA.MOD/USA and GPA/MOD/USA/18, November 27, 2020.

41. WTO, "Proposed Modifications to Appendix I."

42. USTR proposed similar modifications of US commitments in FTAs.

Fifteen GPA parties, including Australia, Canada, the EU, Japan, South Korea, and Switzerland, objected to the US's proposed reduction in coverage.[43] They pointed to deficiencies in the US proposal, especially the US's failure to provide the information required by the GPA as to the likely consequences of the proposed modification on the mutually agreed coverage.[44] The Trump administration ended before these objections were addressed.

When the Biden administration inherited the dispute, it initially appeared to support the proposed modifications. It responded to the objections by providing data on the value of the US procurement to be removed. Relying on the fiscal year 2014 procurement statistics (the latest year for which the US then had complete statistics), it pointed out that the products on the FDA list comprised $393 million of the $8.7 billion worth of medical products that the US covered for federal entities under the GPA. Moreover, the products on the FDA list represented only 4.5% of federal medical procurement covered under the GPA. More broadly, the proposed removal would affect only 0.3% of the approximately $129 billion of the total value of federal procurement that the US covered under the GPA.[45]

The US data submission did not satisfy the objecting parties or address all their objections. For example, Canada and

---

43. WTO, *Report (2021) of the Committee on Government Procurement*, GPA/AR/4, paras. 2.12 and 5.7, n. 63, November 12, 2021; Hannah Monicken, "U.S.: Proposed GPA-exempted medicines total $393 million in procurement," *Inside U.S. Trade*, February 11, 2021, https://insidetrade.com/daily-news/us-proposed-gpa-exempted-medicines-total-393-million-procurement.

44. The GPA requires a party proposing a modification of its coverage (other than the withdrawal of an entity) to provide "information as to the likely consequences of the change for the mutually agreed coverage provided for in this Agreement." GPA, art. 19:1(b).

45. WTO, Committee on Government Procurement, "Proposed modifications and rectifications to coverage under the Agreement on Government Procurement 2012," GPA/MOD/USA/37, February 8, 2021; Monicken, "U.S.: Proposed GPA-exempted."

the EU objected to the open-ended scope of the goods to be re-moved. They argued that the US did not provide "a definitive list of goods" but rather relied on a nonpermanent link to the FDA website, where the goods listed could be revised without notice.[46] The EU further contended that making the proposed removal per-manent rather than for a limited period was "disproportionate to the stated objective of responding to specific threats and public health emergencies." On March 26, 2021, eight GPA parties–the EU, Canada, Japan, Australia, Korea, Switzerland, the United Kingdom (UK), and Israel–requested arbitration to resolve their objections.[47]

On April 16, 2021, the Biden administration reversed course and notified the Committee that it was withdrawing the proposed modification "effective immediately."[48] The withdrawal avoid-ed what would have been the first use of the GPA's arbitration procedures and a precedent-setting resort to the GPA's modi-fication process to withdraw goods (rather than entities) from coverage.[49]

2.6 "Buy American" Order for the US Postal Service

In the last week of his term, President Trump sought to extend 'Buy American' policies to the US Postal Service, which is an independent

---

46. The parties also complained that the affected products were not identified by an internationally recognized uniform classification system, such as the Federal Supply Codes.

47. WTO, *Report (2021) of the Committee*, para. 5.7, n. 64; Hannah Mon-icken, "WTO members refer objections to U.S. GPA modification to arbitra-tion," *Inside U.S. Trade*, April. 2, 2021, https://insidetrade.com/daily-news/wto-members-refer-objections-us-gpa-modification-arbitration.

48. WTO, *Report (2021) of the Committee*, para. 2.12; Hannah Monick-en, "U.S. withdraws push to exempt essential medicines from GPA cover-age," *Inside U.S. Trade*, April 20, 2021, https://insidetrade.com/daily-news/us-withdraws-push-exempt-essential-medicines-gpa-coverage.

49. See Chapter 3 for a discussion of the arbitration process.

federal agency not required to apply the FAR. However, it applies its own domestic procurement preferences.[50] In an executive order, Trump strongly encouraged the Postal Service to apply the same increases in price preferences and domestic content that his administration had added to the FAR "[t]o ensure consistency across the Federal Government" and further promote his 'Buy American' policy goals.[51] Before the agency could act on the order, President Biden revoked it.[52]

3. TREATMENT OF GOVERNMENT PROCUREMENT IN TRADE AGREEMENTS

The Trump administration strove to protect domestic procurement even when it pursued new trade agreements. It set broad objectives for increasing opportunities for US firms to sell US goods and services in foreign markets. At the same time, it aimed to maintain domestic preferences and exclude coverage of subcentral entities. It requested an extension of negotiating authority to facilitate its negotiations of trade agreements.

3.1 Renewal of Trade Promotion Authority

When President Trump withdrew the US from the TPP at the beginning of his presidency, he expressed the intention of negotiating bilateral agreements. For such negotiations, he asked Congress in March 2018 for a three-year extension of the Trade Promotion

---

50. US Postal Service, Supply Principles and Practices, 2-36, February 2010, https://about.usps.com/manuals/spp22010/html/welcome.htm.

51. "Executive Order 13975 of January 14, 2021, Encouraging Buy American Policies for the United States Postal Service," *Federal Register* 86, no. 12 (January 21, 2021): 6547, https://www.govinfo.gov/content/pkg/FR-2021-01-21/pdf/2021-01469.pdf.

52. "Executive Order 14005."

Authority (TPA)[53] under the Bipartisan Congressional Trade Priorities and Accountability Act of 2015.[54] The president justified his request by pointing to the administration's negotiations to revise the NAFTA, its aim of negotiating an FTA with the UK, and interest in pursuing trade agreements with countries in the Asia-Pacific region (notably Japan), Africa, and Southeast Asia. On July 1, 2018, the TPA was renewed automatically for three years (until July 1, 2021) based on the fulfillment of the prerequisites for renewal, namely the president's request and the absence of any congressional resolution of disapproval. The Trump administration relied on the renewed negotiating authority only in its renegotiation of NAFTA.[55]

3.2 US-Mexico-Canada Agreement

3.2.1 Preparations for Negotiations to Revise NAFTA

Based on his extensive criticism of NAFTA during the 2016 presidential campaign, upon taking office, President Trump was expected to take immediate steps to renegotiate that agreement or even carry out his threats to withdraw from it. However, Congress's insistence that the administration had to comply with TPA

---

53. White House, *Report to the Congress on the Extension of Trade Promotion Authority, Consistent with Section 103(c)(2) of the Bipartisan Congressional Trade Priorities and Accountability Act of 2015*, March 20, 2018.

54. *Bipartisan Congressional Trade Priorities and Accountability Act of 2015*, Public Law 114-26, *U.S. Statutes at Large* 129 (2015): 320, § 102. This law defined the US negotiating objectives and priorities for trade agreements and established notification and consultation requirements that the president must follow throughout the negotiation process. At the end of the process, Congress committed to an up or down vote on the agreement without amendment, provided the president fulfilled the statutory obligations. For a discussion of the TPA, see Appendix 2.

55. The Trump administration did not invoke TPA in its other negotiations, which produced limited agreements with China, Japan, South Korea, and the EU.

in renegotiating NAFTA, as well as a prolonged congressional confirmation process for the USTR, forced a delay in negotiations. The additional time enabled a broad array of interested parties from Congress, industry, agriculture, the business community, and labor and environmental groups to promote their priorities and views of what should–and what should not–be changed in the agreement. A prevailing view was that the renegotiation should 'do no harm' but instead should modernize the 1994 agreement and not take away what was working.

TPA required the president to specify negotiating objectives at least 30 days before commencing negotiations. On March 29, 2017, the administration submitted to Congress a draft notice of the president's intention to initiate NAFTA negotiations. The draft laid out objectives for negotiations in 19 areas, generally following those in TPA but also including new issues, such as "to level the playing field on tax treatment." Its objectives for government procurement aimed to "establish rules that require government procurement to be conducted in a manner that is consistent with US law and the Administration's policy on domestic procurement preferences" and expand market access opportunities for the US in the procurement markets of the NAFTA countries.[56]

In May 2017, USTR formally notified Congress of the president's intention to renegotiate NAFTA under TPA,[57] triggering a 90-day congressional consultation period after which the administration could begin negotiations. The notice set out the administration's objectives for the negotiations in broad terms, emphasizing the need to modernize NAFTA and improve its implementation and the enforcement of its commitments. Subsequently, USTR issued

---

56. "Draft NAFTA notice shows administration's intent to address core complaints, including Chapter 19," *Inside U.S. Trade*, March 29, 2017, https://insidetrade.com/daily-news/draft-nafta-notice-shows-administrations-intent-address-core-complaints-including-chapter.

57. USTR, "Notification of Intent to Renegotiate NAFTA," May 18, 2017, https://ustr.gov/sites/default/files/files/Press/Releases/NAFTA%20Notification.pdf.

detailed objectives for the negotiations, including five for government procurement.[58]

The first two procurement objectives reflected statements in the draft notice to increase opportunities for US firms to sell US products and services to the NAFTA countries and establish fair, transparent, predictable, and non-discriminatory rules for government procurement, including rules mirroring existing US government procurement practices. The third objective set defensive parameters for the negotiations, specifying that state and local procurement would be excluded, and that the US would maintain exceptions, such as those for small business preferences, domestic preferential purchasing programs, and key defense procurement.[59] A final objective sought to maintain the ability to include labor and environmental criteria in contracting requirements. In a November 2017 update of the objectives, USTR amplified its procurement aims to ensure reciprocity in market access opportunities for US goods, services, and suppliers in Canada and Mexico and combat corruption.[60]

3.2.2 Negotiations and Conclusion of a New Agreement

The US, Canada, and Mexico commenced negotiations in August 2017 without a prior consensus on the form of the agreement to be negotiated. Canada and Mexico wanted a single agreement, while the Trump administration had not indicated whether it would seek

58. USTR, "Summary of Objectives for the NAFTA Renegotiation," July 17, 2017, https://ustr.gov/sites/default/files/files/Press/Releases/NAFTAObjectives.pdf.

59. These objectives were also included in the US's negotiating objectives for the Trans-Pacific Partnership. USTR, "The Trans-Pacific Partnership, Detailed Summary of U.S. Objectives," September 2015, 37-38.

60. USTR, "USTR Releases Updated NAFTA Negotiating Objectives," November 17, 2017, https://ustr.gov/about-us/policy-offices/press-office/press-releases/2017/november/ustr-releases-updated-nafta.

separate bilateral agreements with Canada and Mexico or maintain NAFTA's trilateral structure. After four negotiating rounds, in October 2017, the NAFTA parties reported progress while acknowledging new proposals had "created challenges" and the existence of a "significant conceptual gap among the Parties."[61] USTR emphasized two overarching objectives: to update NAFTA and reduce the US's $500 billion deficit in trade with its NAFTA partners.[62]

Canada and Mexico, along with the US business community, opposed several of the US's new proposals–labeled by the US Chamber of Commerce as "poison pills."[63] The proposals contributed to a growing fear that President Trump would fulfill his threats to withdraw the US from NAFTA without a replacement agreement. One of the controversial US proposals would have capped Canadian and Mexican access to US government procurement at the monetary level of the combined procurement they opened to the US. This strategy was recommended by Public Citizen in 2017, as is discussed in Section 2.3. In response to the proposal, the Canadian Foreign Minister, Chrystia Freeland, was reportedly "incredulous at the stinginess of America's offer on government procurement," pointing out that it meant that businesses from small, distant countries such as Bahrain would have more access than Mexican and

---

61. USTR, "Trilateral Statement on the Conclusion of the Fourth Round of NAFTA Negotiations," October 17, 2017, https://ustr.gov/about us/policy-offices/press-office/press-relcases/2017/october/trilateral-statement-conclusion.

62. USTR, "Closing Statement of USTR Robert Lighthizer at the Fourth Round of NAFTA Renegotiations," October 17, 2017, https://ustr.gov/about-us/policy-offices/press-office/press-releases/2017/october/closing-statement ustr-robert.

63. Brett Fortnam, "Business groups form coalition to urge protection of NAFTA, oppose some U.S. proposals," *Inside U.S. Trade*, October 19, 2017, https://insidetrade.com/daily-news/business-groups-form-coalition-urge-protection-nafta-oppose-some-us-proposals; "Chamber: White House factoring in election implications of NAFTA withdrawal," *Inside U.S. Trade*, January 10, 2018, https://insidetrade.com/daily-news/chamber-white-house-factoring-election-implications-nafta-withdrawal.

Canadian businesses.[64] Moreover, applying strict reciprocity based on a 'dollar-for-dollar' match under this capping proposal would have substantially altered the US's reciprocity approach used successfully to open procurement markets in more than 60 countries.[65]

In a September 2018 letter to USTR, three leading US business groups–the US Chamber of Commerce, Business Roundtable, and National Association of Manufacturers–outlined their priorities for the NAFTA negotiations. They put an agreement that included both Canada and Mexico at the top of their list. They also called for expansion of access for US firms to the Canadian and Mexican procurement markets, rather than limiting it with the US 'dollar-for-dollar' proposal. They further pointed out that "American businesses secure billions of dollars in business opportunities" in the two countries.[66]

In late 2018, the Trump administration concluded the negotiations in two stages, first reaching a bilateral agreement with Mexico and then finalizing a three-party agreement that included Canada. The US and Mexico wanted the outgoing Mexican president, Enrique Peña Nieto, to sign the agreement before the end of his term on November 30, 2018. They had to conclude their negotiations by August 31, 2018, to meet this deadline and comply with the TPA requirement that the president must provide Congress with

---

64. "On NAFTA, America, Canada and Mexico are miles apart," *The Economist*, October 21, 2017, https://www.economist.com/news/finance-and-economics/21730420-a...can-demands-are-so-extreme-some-suspect-it-not-wanting-deal-all.

65. Under its typical approach to reciprocity, the US sought equivalent coverage through the parties' application of the same thresholds, coverage of comparable entities, limits on the exclusion of services, and other exceptions. If the trading partner did not offer comparable coverage, the US would withhold access to corresponding US procurement. Jean Heilman Grier, "Trade Agreements Open Foreign Procurement Markets," *Thomson Reuters Briefing Papers*, October 2017.

66. US Chamber of Commerce, Business Roundtable, and National Association of Manufacturers, Letter to USTR, September 2018.

a 90-day notice of his intent to sign the agreement. The two parties completed the negotiations on a NAFTA replacement by that deadline. President Trump notified Congress of his intention to sign an agreement with Mexico "and with Canada if it is willing, in a timely manner, to meet the high standards for free, fair, and reciprocal trade contained therein."[67] To comply with a second TPA obligation that required the administration to submit the agreement text to Congress 60 days before it signed the pact, the US had to complete negotiations with Canada by September 30, 2018. The three NAFTA parties concluded the US-Mexico-Canada Agreement (USMCA) on September 30 and signed it on November 30, 2018.[68]

3.2.3 Procurement Chapter

USMCA modernized NAFTA's government procurement chapter but also represented a major backward step by omitting Canada from the procurement obligations. The USMCA procurement text was based on the GPA and the FTAs that had been negotiated after NAFTA. It also followed closely the government procurement chapter in the TPP, consistent with a side letter negotiated on the margins of that agreement.[69] The US did not incorporate the expanded procurement that it included in the TPP, other FTAs, and

---

67. White House, "Text of a Letter from the President to the Speaker of the House of Representatives and the President of the Senate," August 31, 2018, https://trumpwhitehouse.archives.gov/briefings-statements/text-letter-president-speaker-house-representatives-president-senate-33/.

68. USMCA, 2020, accessed May 13, 2022, https://ustr.gov/trade-agreements/free-trade-agreements/united-states-mexico-canada-agreement. On November 30, 2018, the "Protocol Replacing the North American Free Trade Agreement with the Agreement Between the United States of America, the United Mexican States, and Canada" was signed to replace NAFTA. *United States-Mexico-Canada Agreement Implementation Act (USMCA Implementation Act)*, Public Law 116-13, *U.S. Statutes at Large* 134 (2020) 11, § 601.

69. The NAFTA parties had agreed to replace NAFTA's procurement procedures with those in the TPP.

the GPA 2012 in the USMCA. Instead, both the US and Mexico rolled over their coverage from NAFTA, with one exception. In that exception, the US withdrew Mexico's access to purchases of textiles and apparel by the Transportation Security Administration following the so-called Kissell Amendment in the American Recovery and Reinvestment Act of 2009. This exclusion aligned USMCA with the entity's exclusion in other FTAs.

Under USMCA, the US replicated its NAFTA coverage of 52 federal entities and six government enterprises, and Mexico covered the same 23 federal entities and 36 government enterprises as in NAFTA. USMCA allowed Mexico to continue to apply the set-asides permitted by NAFTA for Mexican suppliers (with the amounts adjusted for inflation). Mexico's federal entities could set aside procurement up to $2.328 billion annually, within which the total value of contracts set aside by *Petróleos Mexicanos* and *Comisión Federal de Electricidad* could not exceed $466 million each year.

USMCA, like NAFTA, is the only FTA that waives the 'buy national' requirements imposed as conditions of funding by the Rural Utilities Service for both power generation and telecommunications projects. As in other FTAs, USMCA provided coverage of build-operate-transfer contracts. However, as a practical matter, it did not result in any new opportunities for suppliers because Mexico excluded such contracts from its commitments, and the US withheld them from Mexico until it provided reciprocal access.

In a significant departure from other FTAs, USMCA became the first FTA in which a party did not undertake any procurement commitments. Apparently, Canada opted out of the USMCA's government procurement chapter rather than accept restrictions on its access to US procurement. In addition, the US refused to modify its domestic purchasing requirements, which the Canadian business community had made a priority for the negotiations. Canadian business had sought "to roll-back 'Buy America' provisions on government procurement that have disadvantaged both Canada and Mexico."[70]

With the omission of Canada from the USMCA's procurement provisions, US firms only have access to Canadian government procurement under the GPA. Although Canada's GPA thresholds are higher than the NAFTA thresholds, the US and Canada had agreed in a side letter to the TPP negotiations to raise their NAFTA thresholds to the level of GPA thresholds.[71] US access to Canadian procurement may be affected by the loss of NAFTA's coverage of services based on a negative list, which covered all services purchased by its covered entities, except those listed. In contrast, under the GPA, Canada covered only the services that it listed. Canada and Mexico continued to enjoy the same access to one another's markets as parties to the Comprehensive and Progressive Trans-Pacific Partnership (CPTPP), the successor to the TPP.

The USMCA article on "Ensuring Integrity in Procurement Practices" provided more specific obligations than those found in other US FTAs. It sets out potential penalties such as the debarment of suppliers that engage in corruption or fraud relating to government procurement and requires measures to address potential conflicts of interest in procurement. The USMCA procurement chapter allowed for the promotion of compliance with laws relating to labor rights in the territory in which the goods are produced or the services are performed.[72]

---

70. Meredith Lilly, Hugo Perezcano Díaz, and Christine McDaniel, "The Future of North America's Economic Relationship: From NAFTA to the New Canada-United States-Mexico Agreement and Beyond," Centre for International Governance Innovation, February 11, 2019, https://www.cigionline. org/publications/future-north-americas-economic-relationship-nafta-new-canada-united-states-mexico.

71. The side letter was not implemented after the US pulled out of the TPP.

72. This provision resembles requirements in the May 10th Agreement between President George W. Bush's administration and Congress in 2007 that applied to several FTAs, as described in Chapter 5.

3.2.4 Domestic Measures Required for US Approval

After signing USMCA, the US undertook the approval procedures required by TPA. The US's completion of negotiations with Mexico and Canada a month apart hampered the review of the agreement by the US trade advisory committees,[73] which TPA required.

Following the president's notification of Congress of his plans to sign an agreement with Mexico, the advisory committees had to prepare their reports within 30 days (by September 30, 2018). Their review was limited to the agreement between the US and Mexico because negotiations with Canada had not been completed. When Canada joined the agreement a month later, only about half of the committees updated their reports to provide their assessment of the full agreement. These committees were also impeded in preparing their initial reports on government procurement because they were only given the text of the procurement chapter and not its market access annexes.[74]

The upgraded USMCA procurement text received positive comments from the committees, including the top US advisory committee, the Advisory Committee for Trade Policy Negotiations, various industry trade advisory committees (ITACs), and other committees.[75] Several committees also cited specific provisions with approval. For example, the Intergovernmental Policy Advisory Committee (IGPAC) supported the provision that explicitly allowed procuring entities to promote compliance with labor laws,[76] and the Small and Minority Business Committee

---

73. For a discussion of the US trade advisory committee system, see Appendix 3.

74. USTR, USMCA, *Advisory Committee Reports*, accessed May 13, 2022, https://ustr.gov/trade-agreements/free-trade-agreements/united-states-mexico-canada-agreement/advisory-committee.

75. USTR, USMCA, *Advisory Committee Reports*.

76. USTR, USMCA, *Advisory Committee Reports*, Intergovernmental Policy Advisory Committee.

applauded provisions to facilitate small business participation in government procurement.[77]

The advisory committees criticized the exclusion of Canada from the government procurement chapter, as well as the exclusion of the procurement of financial services from the financial services chapter.[78] The ITAC on Automotive Equipment and Capital Goods called the exclusion of Canada from the USMCA's procurement commitments "a bad precedent" for future FTAs. It further worried that US firms would have less access to Canadian government tenders than suppliers from the 11 members of the CPTPP and EU member states under a 2017 EU-Canada FTA. This ITAC was also wary of relying on US and Canadian commitments under the GPA because of the "not inconceivable" possibility that the US could withdraw from that agreement, as President Trump had threatened. In such a case, US suppliers would lose access to the Canadian procurement market.[79]

The IGPAC and the ITAC on the Digital Economy opposed the US 'dollar-for-dollar' market access proposal. The IGPAC characterized it as "disproportionate given the relative size of the economies of the three countries." Several committees had hoped for coverage of subcentral entities, but others, particularly the IGPAC, opposed such coverage. The IGPAC reiterated "its longstanding position that any subcentral procurement commitments must be voluntary positive list commitments to be determined by each state or local government." The ITAC on Steel sought the protection of 'Buy American' preferences,[80] while the Labor Advisory Committee criticized the USMCA's retention of the NAFTA obligation to

---

77. USTR, USMCA, *Advisory Committee Reports*, ITAC 9–Small and Minority Business.

78. USMCA, art. 17.2(4).

79. USTR, USMCA, *Advisory Committee Reports*, ITAC 2–Automotive Equipment and Capital Goods.

80. USTR, USMCA, *Advisory Committee Reports*, ITAC 7–Steel.

provide Mexican bidders with the same 'Buy American' preferences as US bidders.[81]

The ITAC on Services focused on access to Mexico's procurement market, pointing out that NAFTA had led to important access that enabled the Mexican subsidiaries of US insurers to provide insurance "to two-thirds of all Mexican government employees, as well as supplying auto insurance to the Mexican government." This ITAC argued that USMCA's exclusion of government procurement from its financial services chapter, in contrast to its inclusion under NAFTA, created uncertainty relating to continued access to government procurement for financial services. The committee contended that because of this USMCA carve-out, important rules requiring non-discriminatory treatment of financial services did not apply to government procurement.[82]

In accordance with TPA requirements, the US International Trade Commission reviewed the USMCA. Its April 2019 report concluded that USMCA would likely have only a "moderate" impact on the US economy.[83] It estimated that it would raise US's real GDP by $68.2 billion (0.35%) and US employment by 176,000 jobs (0.12%).[84] Since NAFTA had eliminated duties on most goods and significantly reduced nontariff barriers among the three countries, the Commission considered the USMCA's most significant elements to be its digital trade provisions and rules of origin applied to the automotive sector. It pointed out that since USMCA's procurement chapter largely extended provisions in NAFTA without additional commitments, it would

---

81. USTR, USMCA, *Advisory Committee Reports*, Labor Advisory Committee for Trade Negotiations and Trade Policy.

82. USTR, USMCA, Advisory Committee Reports, ITAC 10–Services.

83. US International Trade Commission (USITC), *U.S.-Mexico-Canada Trade Agreement: Likely Impact on the U.S. Economy and on Specific Industry Sectors*, April 2019, https://www.usitc.gov/publications/332/pub4889.pdf, April 2019, 15.

84. USITC, *USMCA: Likely Impact*, 14.

have little impact on US firms. However, it noted that the loss of the lower thresholds that Canada applied under NAFTA could negatively affect some US firms.[85]

3.2.5 Approval and Implementation

Before USMCA could be implemented, the US had to remove tariffs on steel and aluminum imports from Canada and Mexico and renegotiate certain elements of the agreement to address congressional concerns.

Controversy over US tariffs on steel and aluminum products threatened approval of the agreement. In March 2018, President Trump imposed a 10% tariff on aluminum imports and a 25% tariff on steel imports from all countries (except Canada and Mexico) under section 232 of the Trade Expansion Act of 1962.[86] He based this action on a Department of Commerce determination that imports of the two products were a threat to US national security. The administration "implicitly and explicitly linked a successful outcome of the [NAFTA] renegotiation to maintaining the exemptions."[87] On June 1, 2018, the president imposed the tariffs on Canada and Mexico because they had not negotiated "a satisfactory alternative means to remove the threatened impairment to

---

85. USITC, *USMCA: Likely Impact*, 245.

86. US President, Proclamation 9704 of March 8, 2018, "Adjusting Imports of Aluminum into the United States," March 15, 2018, *Federal Register* 83, no. 51 (March 15, 2018): 11619, https://www.govinfo.gov/content/pkg/FR-2018-03-15/pdf/2018-05477.pdf; Proclamation 9705 of March 8, 2018), "Adjusting Imports of Steel into the United States," *Federal Register* 83, no. 51 (March 8, 2018): 11625, https://www.govinfo.gov/content/pkg/FR-2018-03-15/pdf/2018-05478.pdf. For more information, see US Library of Congress, Congressional Research Service, *Section 232 Investigations: Overview and Issues for Congress*, by Rachel F. Fefer et al., R45249 (2020), https://www.everycrsreport.com/files/20200331_R45249_54cce0909ceb0bd653331394abe-172b92a6a3a57.pdf.

87. Congressional Research Service, *Section 232 Investigations*, 8.

the national security by imports."[88] Both countries retaliated against the US and imposed their own tariffs on US goods.[89] Canada and Mexico, along with members of Congress, conditioned their approval of USMCA on the removal of the tariffs.

In May 2019, the Trump administration reached an agreement with its USMCA partners on measures to prevent the importation of aluminum or steel that was unfairly subsidized or sold at dumped prices and the transshipment of aluminum and steel articles.[90] As a result, the president lifted tariffs on steel and aluminum imports from Canada and Mexico, concluding that their imports would no longer threaten to impair national security.[91] The US removed these tariffs "in part to secure congressional support for the [USMCA]."[92] Canada and Mexico, in turn, removed their retaliatory tariffs on US imports.[93]

After resolving the tariff issue, the Trump administration had to address congressional concerns with elements of the USMCA. USTR engaged in extensive negotiations with Democrats in the House of Representatives on revisions to the USMCA to address

---

88. Congressional Research Service, *Section 232 Investigations*, 8.

89. Congressional Research Service, *Section 232 Investigations*, 34–35.

90. USTR, "Joint Statement by the United States and Mexico on Section 232 Duties on Steel and Aluminum," May 17, 2019, https://ustr.gov/sites/default/files/Joint_Statement_by_the_United_States_and_Mexico.pdf; Department of Commerce, "Modification of Regulations Regarding the Steel Import Monitoring and Analysis System," *Federal Register* 85, no. 61 (March 30, 2020): 17515.

91. US President, Proclamation 9893 of May 19, 2019, "Adjusting Imports of Aluminum into the United States," *Federal Register* 84, no. 100 (May 23, 2019): 23983, https://www.govinfo.gov/content/pkg/FR-2019-05-23/pdf/2019-10999.pdf; Proclamation 9894 of May 19, 2019, "Adjusting Imports of Steel into the United States," *Federal Register* 84, no. 100 (May 23, 2019): 23987, https://www.govinfo.gov/content/pkg/FR-2019-05-23/pdf/2019-11002.pdf.

92. Congressional Research Service, *Section 232 Investigations*, 2.

93. Congressional Research Service, *Section 232 Investigations*, 2.

their issues with the agreement.[94] The resolution of the congressional concerns led to a Protocol of Amendment to the USMCA signed by the three countries on December 10, 2019. The Protocol amended several provisions, including those relating to state-to-state dispute settlement, labor, environment, intellectual property rights, and rules of origin.[95] The Protocol also strengthened the enforcement provisions by establishing a new and enhanced labor-specific enforcement mechanism and removing the ability of a party to block the formation of a dispute settlement panel. It did not include any procurement provisions.

With strong bipartisan support, Congress approved USMCA's implementing legislation[96] by a 385 to 41 vote in the House of Representatives on December 19, 2019, and an 89 to 10 vote in the Senate on January 16, 2020. President Trump signed it on January 29, 2020.[97] Mexico had already ratified USMCA. It approved the original agreement in June 2019 and the Protocol of Amendment in December 2019. Canada completed its ratification on March 13, 2020.[98] USMCA entered into force on July 1, 2020.[99]

---

94. US Congress, House of Representatives, Committee on Ways and Means, "Improvements to the USMCA," accessed May 13, 2022, https://waysandmeans.house.gov/sites/democrats.waysandmeans.house.gov/files/documents/USMCA%20win%20factsheet%20.pdf.

95. USMCA, Protocol of Amendment, December 10, 2019, https://ustr.gov/trade-agreements/free-trade-agreements/united-states-mexico-canada-agreement/protocol-amendments.

96. *USMCA Implementation Act.*

97. Jeff Stein, "Trump signs USMCA, revamping North American trade rules," *The Washington Post,* January 29, 2020, https://www.washingtonpost.com/business/2020/01/29/trump-usmca/.

98. USTR, "Ambassador Lighthizer Statement on Canada's Approval of the USMCA," March 13, 2020, https://ustr.gov/about-us/policy-offices/press-office/press-releases/2020/march/ambassador-lighthizer-statement-canadas-approval-usmca.

99. USMCA, July 1, 2020, https://ustr.gov/trade-agreements/free-trade-agreements/united-states-mexico-canada-agreement/agreement-between.

USMCA's implementing legislation repealed the NAFTA implementation act but only suspended the 1988 US-Canada FTA. Therefore, if USMCA were to terminate 16 years after it took effect, as it provides, "unless each Party confirms it wishes to continue this Agreement for a new 16-year term," the bilateral agreement with Canada could be resurrected. In the Statement of Administrative Action, the Trump administration characterized USMCA as "a comprehensive overhaul of the NAFTA" while recognizing that its replication of many NAFTA provisions meant that US obligations remained essentially the same.[100] Furthermore, the USMCA left US procurement obligations with respect to Mexico largely unchanged. As a result, only technical amendments in US law and administrative actions were needed to implement the USMCA's procurement chapter.[101]

3.3 FTA Negotiations

After the conclusion of USMCA negotiations, in October 2018, USTR notified Congress of the administration's intent to negotiate trade agreements with three trading partners.[102] It subsequently published negotiating objectives for each: the EU,[103] Japan,[104] and

100. *USMCA Implementation Act*, The Statement of Administrative Action, accessed May 13, 2022, https://www.finance.senate.gov/imo/media/doc/FINAL%20SAA%20USMCA.pdf.

101. USTR, "Determination Regarding Waiver of Discriminatory Purchasing Requirements With Respects to Goods and Services Covered by Chapter Thirteen of the USMCA," *Federal Register* 85 (June 29, 2020): 39037.

102. USTR, "Trump administration Announces Intent to Negotiate Trade Agreements with Japan, the European Union and the United Kingdom," October 16, 2018, https://ustr.gov/about-us/policy-offices/press-office/press-releases/2018/october/trump-administration-announces.

103. USTR, "United States-European Union Negotiations, Summary of Specific Negotiating Objectives," January 2019, https://ustr.gov/sites/default/files/01.11.2019_Summary_of_U.S.-EU_Negotiating_Objectives.pdf.

104. USTR, "United States-Japan Trade Agreement (USJTA) Negotiations, Summary of Specific Negotiating Objectives," December 2018, https://ustr.gov/sites/default/files/2018.12.21_Summary_of_U.S.-Japan_Negotiating_Objectives.pdf.

the UK.[105] In March 2020, it followed with a notification to Congress that it also planned to negotiate an agreement with Kenya.[106] The US's government procurement objectives for all four negotiations mirrored its NAFTA renegotiation goals. Subsequently, it negotiated only limited agreements with the EU[107] and Japan,[108] and neither included any procurement commitments. The US commenced–but did not conclude–negotiations with the UK and Kenya before the end of the Trump administration.

---

105. USTR, "United States-United Kingdom Negotiations, Summary of Specific Negotiating Objectives," February 2019, https://ustr.gov/sites/default/files/Summary_of_U.S.-UK_Negotiating_Objectives.pdf.

106. USTR, "Trump Administration Notifies Congress of Intent to Negotiate Trade Agreement with Kenya," March 17, 2020, https://ustr.gov/about-us/policy-offices/press-office/press-releases/2020/march/trump-administration-notifies-congress-intent-negotiate-trade-agreement-kenya.

107. USTR, "Joint Statement of the United States and the European Union on a Tariff Agreement," August 21, 2020, https://ustr.gov/about-us/policy-offices/press-office/press-releases/2020/august/joint-statement-united-states-and-european-union-tariff-agreement. Under the agreement, the EU eliminated tariffs on imports of US lobster for five years, and the US committed to reducing by 50% its tariff rates on certain EU products of comparable economic value, including prepared meals, certain crystal glassware, surface preparations, and propellant powders.

108. The US and Japan signed two agreements. The first one, the US-Japan Trade Agreement, provided for eliminating or reducing tariffs on certain agricultural and industrial products. USTR, "U.S.-Japan Trade Agreement Text," October 7, 2019, https://ustr.gov/countries-regions/japan-korea-apec/japan/us-japan-trade-agreement-negotiations/us-japan-trade-agreement-text. The second agreement, the US-Japan Digital Trade Agreement, prohibited duties on digital products distributed electronically and data localization requirements that restrict where data can be stored and processed. USTR, "U.S.-Japan Digital Trade Agreement," October 7, 2019, https://ustr.gov/countries-regions/japan-korea-apec/japan/us-japan-trade-agreement-negotiations/us-japan-digital-trade-agreement-text.

3.3.1 US–UK FTA Negotiations

The Trump administration displayed a strong interest in negotiating an FTA with the UK early in the president's term. In July 2017, the two countries established a Trade and Investment Working Group to lay the groundwork for a potential FTA once the UK had officially exited the EU and gained the authority to enter trade agreements on its own.[109] The two countries formally launched trade negotiations three years later in March 2020.[110]

The UK's negotiating objectives for government procurement clashed with those of the US in two key areas. First, it sought "new and more secure access to the US procurement market [. . .] at all levels of Government."[111] In contrast, the US intended to exclude subcentral coverage from any agreement. In a second area, Britain's aim of addressing 'Buy American' requirements as a procurement barrier conflicted with the US intent to maintain its domestic preferences. The UK also wanted to develop improved rules to support and build on the two countries' GPA commitments.

US business and industry groups supported the inclusion of government procurement in a US-UK agreement. The US Chamber of Commerce and the US-UK Business Council called for a procurement chapter that expanded access beyond the GPA and applied to both countries' national and sub-national levels. Furthermore, they advocated covering the procurement of financial services as it had been omitted from USMCA. They also supported

109. USTR, "U.S.-UK Trade Agreement Negotiations," accessed May 13, 2022, https://ustr.gov/countries-regions/europe-middle-east/europe/united-kingdom/us-uk-trade-agreement-negotiations.

110. USTR, "Statement of USTR Robert Lighthizer on the Launch of U.S.-UK Trade Negotiations," May 5, 2020, https://ustr.gov/about-us/policy-offices/press-office/press-releases/2020/may/statement-ustr-robert-lighthizer-launch-us-uk-trade-negotiations.

111. UK Department for International Trade, "UK-US Free Trade Agreement," March 2, 2020, https://www.gov.uk/government/publications/the-uks-approach-to-trade-negotiations-with-the-us.

a value-based system for government procurement with objective criteria based on best value rather than an exclusive focus on the lowest price.[112]

In a 2019 joint report, the US Chamber of Commerce and the Coalition for Services Industries noted the UK's "relatively liberal government procurement policy" and its political sensitivity to introducing private sector competition in certain public sectors, particularly the health sector. They also urged that state-owned enterprises be subject to the same disciplines as domestic and foreign enterprises, including "parity of treatment" regarding public procurement. The business groups also pointed to the size of the UK's procurement market: it had accounted for around 25% of the EU procurement market (when it was an EU member).[113]

In its negotiations with the UK, the Trump administration reportedly opposed including a government procurement chapter in an agreement, even though it had stated its desire to expand access to British procurement in its negotiating objectives. After several rounds of negotiations, the Trump presidency ended before the two countries could reach such an agreement.

3.3.2 US-Kenya FTA Negotiations

The Trump administration proposed an FTA with Kenya that would serve as a model for other agreements in Africa and lead "to a network of agreements that [would] contribute to Africa's

---

112. US Chamber of Commerce and US-UK Business Council, "U.S.-UK Trade Negotiations: Private Sector Priorities," May 5, 2020, 12, https://www.uscham ber.com/comment/us-united-kingdom trade-negotiations-private-sector-prior-ities. The business group's promotion of best value rather than lowest price echoed similar requests that the US had made of Japan in negotiations for bilateral procurement agreements in the 1980s and early 1990s, as discussed in Chapter 9.

113. US Chamber of Commerce and Coalition of Services Industries, Services Priorities for a Future US-UK Trade Agreement, November 7, 2019, 16, https://www.uschamber.com/report/services-priorities-future-us-uk-trade-agreement.

regional integration objectives."[114] Kenya's proposed negotiating objectives included taking note of its "policy of using Procurement as an instrument to build entrepreneurship in the Kenyan economy," securing access to US government procurement, and applying "the principle of asymmetry geared towards non reciprocity in Government Procurement."[115] The Trump administration commenced negotiations with Kenya but held only two negotiating rounds before its term ended.

As of late 2022, President Biden had not restarted any of the FTA negotiations nor indicated any intention to do so.

4. THREAT OF WITHDRAWAL FROM THE GPA

A February 2020 press report that President Trump was considering the withdrawal of the US from the GPA sent alarm bells ringing in the business and procurement communities.[116] They regarded the report as plausible since he had withdrawn the US from the TPP and threatened to pull it out of NAFTA.

A coalition of 20 business groups rallied to support the GPA with a letter to the USTR, the secretaries of Commerce and Treasury, and the National Economic Council Director urging continued

---

114. USTR, "United States-Kenya Negotiations, Summary of Specific Negotiating Objectives," May 2020, https://ustr.gov/sites/default/files/Summary_of_U.S.-Kenya_Negotiating_Objectives.pdf.

115. Kenya Ministry of Industrialization, "Trade and Enterprise Development, Proposed Kenya - United States of America Free Trade Area Agreement, Negotiation Principles, Objectives, and Scope," June 22, 2020, https://agoa.info/downloads/general/15775.html.

116. Bruce Baschuk, "Trump Considers Withdrawing From WTO's $1.7 Trillion Purchasing Pact," *Bloomberg News*, February 4, 2020, https://www.bloomberg.com/news/articles/2020-02-04/trump-mulls-withdrawal-from-wtos-1-7-trillion-purchasing-pact; see also "Business groups tout WTO procurement pact, warn against withdrawal," *Inside U.S. Trade*, February 19, 2020, https://insidetrade.com/trade/business-groups-tout-wto-procurement-pact-warn-against-withdrawal.

US participation in the GPA and warning of the consequences of a withdrawal.[117] They pointed to a broad range of sectors that had benefited from access to foreign procurement markets under the GPA and would be disadvantaged in competition with foreign companies in GPA markets if the US withdrew.[118] They argued that the GPA and other US trade agreements provided more market access for the US than the US provided in exchange. They noted that "only about three percent of U.S. federal contracts by value have been awarded to foreign industries" over the prior five years. They contended that the low foreign participation reflected the competitiveness of US industry. Furthermore, they pointed out that the significant exceptions to US procurement commitments, including sensitive national security procurement, limited participation by foreign firms.[119]

Without GPA membership, the US would also lose its leverage to negotiate greater market access and better terms with China and other WTO members in their negotiations to accede to the

---

117. The letter was signed by the Advanced Medical Technology Association, Aerospace Industries Association, American Apparel & Footwear Association, American Council of Life Insurers, American Property Casualty Insurance Association, American Wind Energy Association, Association of Equipment Manufacturers, BSA | The Software Alliance, Business Roundtable, Coalition of Services Industries, Computing Technology Industry Association, Information Technology Industry Council, Internet Association, National Association of Manufacturers, National Electrical Manufacturers Association, National Foreign Trade Council, Telecommunications Industry Association, US Chamber of Commerce, United States Council for International Business, and Water and Wastewater Equipment Manufacturers Association. Business Letter, February 14, 2020, https://www.uschamber.com/assets/archived/images/2020-2-14-industry-letter-on-wto-gpa.pdf.

118. The sectors benefiting from the GPA were infrastructure, energy and power, medical devices and equipment, pharmaceutical, chemical, information and communications technology, transportation, and capital equipment. Business Letter.

119. Business Letter. The business groups also noted that "U.S. firms win more than 9% of Canadian federal contracts while Canadian suppliers win just 0.15% of U.S. federal contracts, according to Canadian data."

GPA.[120] As a party to the GPA, the US is "entitled to block the admission of new parties to the GPA (such as China and Russia)" unless it is satisfied with their market access offers and reforms to their national procurement systems.[121] In addition, US withdrawal from the GPA could "require U.S. businesses to restructure their supply chains–including, for example, by changing suppliers or relocating facilities–to comply with domestic sourcing laws."[122] Furthermore, if the US withdrew from the GPA, foreign governments would be free to discriminate against US companies in their government procurement or even ban purchases from US firms.[123]

The more significant ramifications of a US withdrawal from the GPA could center on the coverage of subcentral procurement for at least two reasons. Firstly, the US would lose the rights to participate in the subcentral procurement of the GPA parties (except Australia).[124] Subcentral procurement is typically greater than the level of central government purchases. For instance, more than half of the EU's GPA-covered procurement is undertaken at the subcentral level.[125] Similarly, Canada's provinces and territories

---

120. Business Letter.

121. Robert D. Anderson and Christopher R. Yukins, "Withdrawing the United States from the WTO GPA: Assessing Potential Damage to the U.S. and Its Contracting Community," *The Government Contractor* 62, para. 35, *Thomson Reuters*, February 12, 2019, https://ssrn.com/abstract=3540413.

122. Anderson and Yukins, "Withdrawing the United States," 2.

123. Business Letter.

124. The US has an FTA with Australia that covers the procurement of subcentral entities.

125. In a February 2020 report to the WTO, EU statistics for 2014-2016 showed that the greatest value of EU contracts covered by the GPA in each of the three years was procured by subcentral entities: 54% in 2014, 52% in 2015, and 62.5% in 2016. EU procurement under the GPA totaled €403 billion in 2016, with subcentral procurement accounting for €252 billion, central government entities €83 billion, and utilities €68 billion. (Those figures included the UK's procurement before its exit from the EU.)

purchase more than twice as much as its federal government.[126] In China, local governments comprised 91.9% of China's total procurement in 2019.[127]

Secondly, if the US lost access to the subcentral procurement of its GPA partners, regaining the same level of access, whether it negotiated a return to the GPA or bilateral FTAs with GPA parties, would be difficult. It would be highly unlikely that all the 37 states covered under the GPA would provide new authorizations to bind their procurement under the GPA or a new FTA. After delivering their initial GPA authorizations, many states showed increasing reluctance to authorize coverage under FTAs.[128]

If the US were unable to offer coverage of a critical mass of states, its FTA partner would be unlikely to open all its subcentral procurement to the US.[129] The US faced that situation in the US-Australian FTA negotiations. Australia conditioned the offer of its provinces and territories on the US's offering of at least half of its states. If the US refused to cover any subcentral procurement in a new FTA or re-entry to the GPA, it could expect a repeat of the experience of negotiating the US-Korea FTA. When the US would not pursue state coverage in those negotiations, South Korea refused to cover any government enterprises (or subcentral entities), resulting in an FTA limited to central government procurement.[130]

A GPA withdrawal would mean a loss of access to Canada's procurement market since the US no longer has an FTA with Canada.

---

126. Canadian subcentral procurement totaled Can$8 billion versus Can$3 billion at the federal level in 2016 (the most recent statistics reported to the WTO).

127. WTO, *Trade Policy Review, Report by the Secretariat*, WT/TPR/S/415, para. 3.210, September 15, 2021, https://www.wto.org/english/tratop_e/tpr_e/s415_e.pdf.

128. For a discussion of the challenges of covering state procurement under trade agreements, see Chapter 6.

129. Even with its coverage of 37 states under the GPA, the EU withheld procurement of services by its subcentral entities from the US.

130. The FTAs with Australia and South Korea are discussed in Chapter 5.

The loss of access to the procurement of Canada's provinces and territories would be a particular disappointment because the US had sought that access for 15 years before the two countries exchanged subcentral coverage in a 2010 bilateral agreement.

More broadly, in withdrawing from the GPA, "the U.S. could lose its leadership role (which dates back to World War II) in shaping global standards in public procurement."[131] Trump did not carry out the threat of withdrawal at that time, but fears that he would act on it continued until the end of his term. For example, shortly after the 2020 presidential election, GPA withdrawal seemed once more imminent[132] but again did not materialize. After debating withdrawal from the GPA for more than a year, the Trump administration apparently recognized that the costs would outweigh any perceived benefits.

---

131. Anderson and Yukins, "Withdrawing the United States," 1.

132. Doug Palmer, "Senators urge Trump not to withdraw from Government Procurement Agreement," *Politico*, November 19, 2020, https://www.politico.com/news/2020/11/19/senators-trump-not-withdraw-government-procurement-act-438324.

CHAPTER 9

TARGETED APPROACH: US-JAPAN PROCUREMENT AGREEMENTS

1. INTRODUCTION

During the 1980s, trade relations between the US and Japan were severely strained as a result of record bilateral trade deficits and corresponding concerns that Japan unfairly limited US firms' access to its markets. The heightened trade friction led to "implicit and explicit threats of retaliation by the U.S. government against Japanese exports unless Japan's markets [were] opened further."[1]

Government procurement was a key element of the bilateral trade tensions. Japanese government procurement practices caused protests from American industry in sector after sector. US firms complained of a lack of success in entering Japan's lucrative procurement market despite their international success. The

---

1. US General Accounting Office (GAO), *U.S.-Japan Trade, Evaluation of the Market-Oriented, Sector-Specific Talks*, 13, July 1988, https://www.gao.gov/assets/nsiad-88-205.pdf.

US government responded by pursuing negotiations with Japan to address the perceived barriers. While these negotiations have never quite resulted in fully opening Japan's procurement market, they provide a window into one facet of American trade strategy during that period, a strategy that was shaped by limitations in the international trading system and facilitated by congressional authorizations.

Over 15 years, the US and Japan engaged in nearly continuous negotiations on procurement issues. Their negotiations resulted in more than a dozen procurement agreements aimed at increasing participation by foreign firms in a variety of sectors. Unlike plurilateral agreements and FTAs, these bilateral agreements were not based on reciprocity. They imposed obligations only on Japan. Moreover, their benefits were not limited to the US, as they extended to all of Japan's trading partners on a most-favored-nation (MFN) basis.

The US and Japan engaged in bilateral negotiations even though they were parties to the 1979 GATT Code and its successor, the GPA. The US pursued bilateral remedies for at least four reasons. First, the GATT Code did not cover several areas of concern to US suppliers, namely public works, services, and quasi-governmental entities. Second, when the GATT Code did cover the procurement at issue, its procedures were often inadequate to address the specific obstacles encountered by US industry. Third, when the procurement was covered by the GATT Code and its obligations were possibly breached, its nonbinding dispute settlement procedures would not have provided a viable means of resolving US complaints. Finally, and perhaps most importantly, Congress prodded the administration to take action and provided the president with authority to impose sanctions on Japan if Japan did not make efforts to address US concerns. Moreover, the US could impose unilateral sanctions without contravening its international obligations. While Japan strongly resisted the US tactics, it made some concessions to avoid sanctions and reduce trade tensions.

The US targeted this negotiating strategy only at Japan. It did not employ this strategy after the creation of the WTO and its binding dispute settlement mechanism, which constrained the US's ability to impose sanctions unilaterally. In addition, the GPA 1994 significantly expanded procurement subject to international obligations. This expansion in coverage limited, to an extent, the need for the agreements produced by the US-Japan negotiations. Although those bilateral agreements have a limited current effect, they remain in effect and illustrate an approach the US used to address procurement issues.

2. JAPANESE PROCUREMENT PRACTICES

Prior to implementing the GATT Code, Japan had little experience with open competitive bidding in government procurement, even though its law was premised on the use of open tendering. By one estimate, in the 1970s, it conducted 90% of its central government procurement through private contracts (single tendering) without any public notice of the procurement.[2] Japan's procurement was also subject to the legacy of 'Buy Japan' policies.[3] Even though these policies were rescinded in the early 1970s, they continued to influence Japan's conduct of procurement and created barriers to foreign participation in its public procurement. As a consequence, most of Japan's public sector procurement was conducted with long-term local suppliers. With these restrictive practices, Japan's government procurement was essentially closed to foreign firms.[4]

---

2. Kenneth W. Abbott and Conrad D. Totman, "'Black Ships' and Balance Sheets: The Japanese Market and U.S.- Japan Relations," *Northwestern Journal of International Law and Business* 3 (1981): 124.

3. Jean Heilman Grier, "U.S.-Japan Government Procurement Agreements," *Wisconsin International Law Journal* 14 (1995): 10.

4. Grier, "U.S.-Japan Government Procurement," 11.

Another barrier to foreign participation in Japanese procurement was its heavy reliance on public and quasi-governmental corporations to carry out public policy. These corporations were created by special legislative acts and designated by the Japanese government as public enterprises. Nonetheless, the government denied any control over their procurement policies.[5]

When US firms were unable to penetrate the Japanese government procurement market, they took their complaints to the US government and Congress. As evidence of their own competitiveness, they pointed to their success in other overseas markets and even in Japan's private sector. The US raised these complaints with the Japanese government in various forums, such as the Market-Oriented Sector Selective (MOSS) talks beginning in 1985,[6] and the two countries engaged in extensive discussions on the issues.[7]

3. US LAWS INVOLVED IN NEGOTIATIONS

Congress responded to industry complaints by strengthening the US's negotiating leverage. It enacted legislation that authorized the US to impose sanctions on Japan if it did not open its markets. That authority provided an impetus for negotiations to remove procurement barriers as the US often threatened to impose sanctions, such as closing its procurement market to Japan. Two laws bolstered US negotiations by providing authority for the US to impose sanctions. Both were broad trade laws, but one directly targeted foreign government procurement practices, specifically those of Japan. Despite the authority, the US seldom imposed sanctions.

---

5. Grier, "U.S.-Japan Government Procurement," 12.

6. For a discussion of the MOSS talks, see GAO, *U.S.-Japan Trade.*

7. Grier, "U.S.-Japan Government Procurement," 26.

3.1 Section 301 of the Trade Act of 1974

The first of these two laws was Section 301 of the Trade Act of 1974.[8] It was often "the silent, if unwelcome, presence" at negotiating sessions with Japan, "rarely mentioned, but never forgotten."[9] The US used Section 301 to pressure its trading partners to eliminate trade barriers and open their markets to US exports. It contributed to bringing Japan to the negotiating table to address procurement issues and negotiate resolutions of the issues.

Congress enacted Section 301 to provide the US with "negotiating leverage" to address foreign trade barriers.[10] Section 301 supplied the US Trade Representative (USTR) with authority to impose trade sanctions on foreign countries violating US trade agreements or engaging in acts that were unjustifiable, unreasonable, or discriminatory and burden US commerce. It required USTR to conduct an investigation and request consultations with the targeted trading partner. If the investigation, consultations, and any dispute settlement proceedings did not result in an agreement, USTR determined whether the foreign practice was "unfair" and actionable under Section 301. If so, it then decided on action or retaliation (if any) for the US to take to counterbalance the effect of the unfair practice on US commerce.[11]

The leverage of Section 301 derived from its authorization of sanctions. It authorized USTR to take action to eliminate a foreign

8. *Trade Act of 1974*, Public Law 93-618, § 301, *U.S. Statutes at Large* 88 (1974) 1978; *U.S. Code* 19, § 2411.

9. Jean Heilman Grier, "The Use of Section 301 to Open Japanese Markets to Foreign Firms," *North Carolina Journal of International Law & Commercial Regulation* 17 (1992): 2.

10. US Congress, Senate, Committee on Finance, *Trade Reform Act of 1974*, 93rd Cong., 2d Sess., 1974, S. Rep. 93-1298, 3-4.

11. For a description of the Section 301 process, see US Library of Congress, Congressional Research Service, *Section 301 of the Trade Act of 1974*, by Andres B. Schwarzenberg, IF11346 (2022), https://crsreports.congress.gov/product/pdf/IF/IF11346.

trade practice or compensate the US with satisfactory trade benefits. USTR could impose duties or other import restrictions, withdraw or suspend trade agreement concessions, or enter into a binding agreement with a foreign government. In its negotiations with Japan, the US relied more on the threat of sanctions than their actual imposition.[12]

3.2 1988 Trade Act

The second law was the Omnibus Trade and Competitiveness Act of 1988 (1988 Trade Act).[13] Its provisions included Title VII, directed at foreign procurement barriers, and variations of Section 301.

Title VII: Congress enacted Title VII of the 1988 Trade Act to strengthen the president's ability to negotiate access to foreign government procurement markets.[14] It also authorized the president to close US procurement to countries that refused to open their procurement to the US. The US repeatedly threatened to use this law to impose sanctions on Japan, but it did not do so.[15]

'Super 301:' In the 1988 Trade Act, Congress amended Section 301 to create a so-called 'Super 301'[16] provision based on its concern "that certain foreign countries, most notably Japan, engage in broad and consistent patterns of unfair practices that serve to keep their home markets free of significant competition from US and other foreign firms."[17] It directed USTR to identify priority practices and

---

12. Grier, "The Use of Section 301," 4–10.

13. *Omnibus Trade and Competitiveness Act of 1988 (1988 Trade Act)*, Public Law 100-418, *U.S. Statutes at Large* 102 (1988): 1107; codified in scattered sections of *U.S. Code* 19.

14. See Chapter 1 for a description of Title VII.

15. The US also used Title VII against the European Union in the negotiations of the GPA 1994, as described in Chapter 1.

16. *U.S. Code* 19, § 2420.

17. US Congress, Senate, Committee on Finance, *Omnibus Trade Act of 1987*, 100th Cong., 1st Sess., 1987, S. Rep. 71, 77.

initiate Section 301 investigations. Congress believed that "[m]erely initiating such an investigation can give the President enormous leverage in negotiating an end to a foreign unfair trade practice."[18]

'Construction 301': In another provision of the 1988 Trade Act (Section 1305), Congress targeted Japan's construction practices.[19] Perceiving that US firms had made little progress in entering the Japanese construction market, it created a so-called 'Construction 301' provision. This provision directed USTR to initiate a Section 301 investigation of the acts, policies, and practices of the Japanese government and the entities that it owned, financed, or otherwise controlled that were barriers to the offering or performing US architectural, engineering, construction, and consulting services in Japan.[20]

4. JAPANESE PROCUREMENT AGREEMENTS

4.1 US-Japan NTT Procurement Agreements

The US pursuit of bilateral commitments by Japan began when the US, Japan, and other GATT contracting parties concluded negotiations of the GATT Code. When these negotiations ended, the US and Japan had not reached an agreement on equivalent reciprocal procurement opportunities. The US was dissatisfied with Japan's refusal to cover the procurement of telecommunications equipment by its monopoly domestic telecommunications carrier, Nippon Telegraph and Telecommunications Public Corporation (NTT), under the Code. Japan had limited NTT's commitments to three categories of products[21] and planned new services. The US contended that unless Japan subjected at least NTT's procurement of public

---

18. *Omnibus Trade Act*, 13.

19. *1988 Trade Act*, § 1305.

20. Grier, "The Use of Section 301," 30.

21. General materials, non-telephone type terminals, and machinery, such as computers, were three categories of products covered by NTT.

telecommunications equipment to Code disciplines, it would not open US procurement to Japanese suppliers.[22]

The US sought access to more NTT procurement because the company was the largest purchaser of telecommunications equipment in Japan, and it was essentially closed to foreign firms. As a public corporation under the Ministry of Posts and Telecommunications, NTT served as a prime example of 'Buy Japan' procurement policies. It purchased virtually all its telecommunications equipment from domestic suppliers, and its procurement practices made it very difficult for foreign suppliers to participate in its procurement. Japan resisted US demands to open NTT's procurement of telecommunications equipment, arguing that no GATT Code party had covered entities that purchased such equipment under the Code.[23]

After intense bilateral negotiations in 1979-1980, the two countries concluded the US-Japan NTT Agreement. It entered into force on the same day as the GATT Code, on January 1, 1981, and applied for three years. Under the bilateral arrangement, Japan agreed to open NTT's procurement of telecommunications equipment to foreign bidders on an MFN basis, but it did not bring this equipment under the Code. The Agreement prescribed procedures for NTT's procurement of telecommunications equipment under the following three 'tracks,' with each track applying to a different type of procurement:

- Track I applied to products covered by the Code

- Track II covered telecommunications equipment that already existed in the marketplace or only required modifications to meet NTT requirements

- Track III applied to telecommunications equipment that did not exist in a suitable form in the marketplace and had to be developed especially for–or with–NTT.

---

22. Grier, "U.S.-Japan Government Procurement," 8–9.
23. Grier, "U.S.-Japan Government Procurement," 19.

The procurement procedures applied to participation by all foreign suppliers, except a nonbinding arbitration provision reserved for disputes between the US and Japan.[24]

Subsequently, the US and Japan renewed and revised the NTT Agreement through 1999. In the renewals, the US sought improvements in NTT's procurement procedures to address obstacles US firms encountered when trying to sell to NTT. The difficulties included a lack of access to key procurement information, such as evaluation criteria and procurement plans and practices that favored Japanese suppliers. The revisions required NTT to modify its procurement procedures. For example, the 1984 revised Agreement called for NTT to provide specifications and evaluation criteria to potential suppliers and accord foreign and domestic firms equal access to its research and development (R&D) programs. A decade later, the 1994 NTT Agreement directed NTT to provide more information on its procurement plans, allow earlier participation by foreign firms in its procurement, and include evaluation criteria in its procurement documentation.[25]

After NTT was partially privatized in 1985, three of its new subsidiaries announced they would voluntarily comply with the procedures in the NTT Agreement in response to US pressure.[26]

4.2 Supercomputer Agreements

4.2.1 1987 US-Japan Supercomputer Agreement

Eight years after the US and Japan signed their first bilateral agreement, the US sought to open the Japanese government's procurement of supercomputers to US firms. In the 1970s, the US industry dominated the global supercomputer market. For instance, one US firm had installed more supercomputers than

---

24. Grier, "U.S.-Japan Government Procurement," 20–21

25. Grier, "U.S.-Japan Government Procurement," 21–24.

26. Grier, "U.S.-Japan Government Procurement," 23.

all its competitors combined.[27] As early as 1980, the US industry had sold two supercomputers to the Japanese private sector but none to its government. In 1983, Japan's government made its first supercomputer purchase, a Japanese-made machine that had just entered the market. By 1986, it had purchased 22 supercomputers, and all but one were domestic. Japan effectively excluded US firms from its public sector procurement by not announcing publicly its plans to purchase supercomputers, accepting bids from Japanese firms that were heavily discounted (by as much as 80% off list prices), and using technical specifications that favored Japanese suppliers.[28]

When talks with Japan failed to improve access for US firms, the American government conducted a study of Japan's supercomputer procurement under Section 305 of the Trade and Tariff Act of 1984.[29] The US concluded in that 1987 study that "U.S. firms were being excluded unfairly from Japan's government and public university market [and] that deep Japanese price discounting [. . .] could harm the U.S. industry."[30] Following the report, the US and Japan negotiated the 1987 US-Japan Supercomputer Agreement, which became effective in August 1987. It aimed to improve the transparency of the procurement process for supercomputers and

27. Peter Schuyten, "The Battle in Supercomputers: Control Data's Comeback Bid Against Cray, The Battle in Supercomputers Cray Fills Computer Gap Control Data's Corporate Pride," *New York Times*, July 22, 1980, https://www.nytimes.com/1980/07/22/archives/the-battle-in-supercomputers-control-datas-comeback-bid-against.html.

28. Grier, "U.S.-Japan Government Procurement," 25–26; Grier, "The Use of Section 301," 12; see also GAO, *U.S.-Japan Trade*, 45–46.

29. *Trade and Tariff Act of 1984*, § 305, Public Law 98-573, *U.S. Statutes at Large* 98 (1984): 2948. The law provided the US negotiating objectives for high technology products, including "to obtain commitments that official policy of foreign countries or instrumentalities will not discourage government or private procurement of foreign high technology products and related services."

30. USTR, 1989 National Trade Estimate Report on Foreign Trade Barriers, 103, March 1989.

ensure non-discriminatory treatment of foreign suppliers. It applied to Japanese entities that were covered by the GATT Code.[31]

As a result of the 1987 Agreement, Japan's supercomputer procurement became more transparent. Still, it remained inaccessible to foreign firms, primarily because of discounting, which the agreement had not addressed. After signing the agreement, the Japanese government purchased only two US supercomputers and did so "on a noncompetitive basis under a special 1987 import promotion budget," which were thus not attributable to the 1987 agreement.[32]

4.2.2 1990 US-Japan Supercomputer Agreement

When the 1987 agreement failed to provide US firms with effective access to Japan's supercomputer market, the US ratcheted up the pressure by using the new legislative authority in the 1988 Trade Act. In May 1989, the USTR identified Japan's exclusionary supercomputer procurement practices as a "priority practice" under the 'Super 301' provision in that legislation.[33] It singled out discounting and using technical specifications that favored domestic supercomputers as "especially problematic" when initiating a Section 301 investigation of the practices in June 1989.[34] It also requested consultations with Japan as required by the law.[35]

Although Japan maintained that it would not negotiate under the threat of sanctions, it eventually engaged in what it labeled as "discussions or consultations" with the US.[36] The two sides reached

---

31. Grier, "U.S.-Japan Government Procurement," 26–27.

32. USTR, *1990 National Trade Estimate Report on Foreign Trade Barriers*, 114, March 1990; Grier, "U.S.-Japan Government Procurement," 27–28.

33. USTR, "Notice," *Federal Register* 54 (May 12, 1989): 24438.

34. USTR, "Initiation of Section 302 Investigation and Request for Public Comment; Exclusionary Government Procurement of Supercomputers by the Government of Japan," *Federal Register* 54 (June 21, 1989): 26137.

35. Grier, "U.S.-Japan Government Procurement," 28.

36. Grier, "The Use of Section 301," 11.

a preliminary agreement in March and signed the 1990 US-Japan Supercomputer Agreement on June 15, 1990, the day before USTR could have imposed sanctions under Section 301. On the same day, USTR suspended its Section 301 investigation.[37]

The 1990 Agreement detailed requirements for each stage of the procurement process to ensure supercomputer purchases by Japanese governmental and quasi-governmental entities were competitive, transparent, and non-discriminatory. The accord directed entities to consider only bids of supercomputers built and tested before a bid was submitted (to prevent purchase of nonexistent machines) and evaluate supercomputer systems based on their actual capabilities (and not theoretical peak performance). It also required Japan to evaluate bids based on the 'overall greatest value,' which considered both performance and price. To address the discounting issue, the agreement committed the Japanese government to base its supercomputer budgets on prices in the private sector for supercomputer systems operating in environments similar to those in the government, seek sufficient funds for the procurement of supercomputers, and eliminate bids with deep discounts to address the discounting issue. Finally, Japan agreed to establish its first comprehensive complaint mechanism that enabled suppliers to challenge a supercomputer procurement before an independent Procurement Review Board.[38]

Drawing on its long experience with a bid challenge system, the US had sought Japan's establishment of such a mechanism to enable suppliers to challenge the conduct of procurement and obtain a review of their complaints by an independent review body. Such direct action by a supplier would eliminate the need for the US government to intervene on the supplier's behalf. At the time

---

37. Grier, "The Use of Section 301," 11–12; Grier, "U.S.-Japan Government Procurement," 28.

38. Grier, "The Use of Section 301," 12–14; Grier, "U.S.-Japan Government Procurement," 28–30.

when the 1990 Supercomputer Agreement was implemented, Japan did not have such a mechanism,[39] nor did the GATT Code require it to have one.[40] Later, when Japan was obligated under the GPA 1994 to implement challenge procedures, it created a system that was closely patterned after the supercomputer process.[41]

After Japan established its complaint mechanism, a US supercomputer manufacturer, Cray Research, Inc., brought the first complaint under the new mechanism. It challenged the procurement of a Japanese-made supercomputer by the National Institute of Fusion Sciences. The US firm contended that the procurement unfairly favored the domestic system. In its review, Japan's Supercomputer Review Board did not find any significant issues in the conduct of the challenged procurement. However, it had limited its review to a determination of whether the procurement had been conducted in accord with the procedures in the Supercomputer Agreement. It did not attempt to address the merits of the domestic and foreign supercomputers. Following the review, the US government expressed concerns with the narrow scope of the Board's review.[42]

In its 1995 Title VII report, the US recognized that its access to Japan's supercomputer market had improved considerably over the prior two years while expressing continued concerns with the agreement's implementation.[43]

---

39. Jean Heilman Grier, "Japan's Implementation of the WTO Agreement on Government Procurement," *University of Pennsylvania Journal of International Economic Law* 17 (1996): 643.

40. The GPA required Japan and the other parties to establish domestic challenge procedures. GPA 1994, art. XX.

41. Grier, "Japan's Implementation," 644.

42. Grier, "Japan's Implementation," 653–57.

43. USTR, *Annual Report on Discrimination in Foreign Government Procurement*, 8, April 29, 1995.

4.3 Public Works Agreements

Since the 1980s, the US had pressured Japan to allow US firms to participate in its large public works sector. At that time, Japan had no international obligation to allow foreign firms to participate in its public works.[44] Nonetheless, Japan reluctantly opened portions of its public works under four bilateral public works agreements negotiated with the US over a period of nearly 15 years. In the first three agreements, Japan only allowed foreign firms to participate in select projects under special measures, which were intended to familiarize firms with its public works market. Japan contended that once foreign firms became accustomed to its system, they would be able to compete without the need for such measures. These limited agreements failed to provide effective access for US firms. The final agreement, entered on the eve of the GPA 1994's conclusion, provided for major reform of Japan's public works system, consistent with Japan's commitment to open its public works under the GPA.

The US identified a single practice as the greatest obstacle to foreign firms' entry into Japan's public works, namely the designated bidder system. Under that system, the government first ranked firms according to their ability. The ranking determined the size and type of project on which they were eligible to bid. Then, based on their ranking, government entities selected approximately 10 firms to bid on a particular project. The US considered two elements of this system as particularly problematic. One was the opaque nature of the ranking and designation processes. The second was a 'catch-22' situation that made it virtually impossible for foreign firms to get high rankings. In evaluating bidders and determining their ranking, Japanese entities only considered the bidder's prior work in Japan. Foreign firms were unable to gain such experience

---

44. Procurement of construction works was not covered by an international agreement until it was added to the GPA 1994.

because they did not have a sufficiently high ranking to win their first contract in Japan.[45]

The designated bidder system not only posed a substantial barrier to foreign firms but was also conducive to bid-rigging, a practice the Japanese called *dangō*. For example, firms designated for a project would together decide informally which of them would win a particular contract before submitting bids. The other firms participating in the bid-rigging would submit bids that exceeded the government's ceiling price (which was confidential but was often surreptitiously obtained by these firms) and thus would be rejected. In subsequent procurement, the designated firms repeated that process and selected another firm to 'win' the procurement. Eventually, all the participating firms would obtain a contract. The collusion among bidders was linked to widespread government corruption.[46] The US sought Japan's elimination of the designated bidder system and bid-rigging and adoption of an open bidding system like that of the US.

4.3.1 1987 Kansai International Airport Agreement

The first of the four US-Japan bilateral public works agreements applied to just one project–the Kansai International Airport. From the mid-1980s, the US sought participation in that multibillion-dollar project for foreign firms as a way to open Japan's public works and encourage the adoption of an open bidding system. Japan resisted US efforts and contended that the project's developer, the Kansai International Airport Company (KIAC), was under no obligation to provide an open bidding system because it was a private company. KIAC was established to construct the airport as a third sector project (one financed by private as well as public funds).[47]

---

45. Grier, "U.S.-Japan Government Procurement," 32–33.

46. Grier, "U.S.-Japan Government Procurement," 33–34.

47. Grier, "U.S.-Japan Procurement Agreements," 34–35.

The US disagreed, pointing to the Japanese government's role in the financing, staffing, and control of KIAC and the airport project. After long and intense negotiations, the two countries finalized the Kansai International Airport Agreement (KIA Agreement) in November 1987. Although Japan refused to bring KIAC under the GATT Code, it did agree to apply certain Code provisions, including the publication of invitations to participate in the procurement of KIAC. It also committed KIAC to treat foreign companies in a fair and non-discriminatory manner, in particular treating their overseas experience as equivalent to work in Japan.[48]

4.3.2 1988 Major Projects Arrangements

Following the conclusion of the KIA Agreement, the US and Japan continued negotiations as the US pursued more access to Japan's public works. When Japan refused to apply that agreement to other projects (as it had promised), Congress added a so-called Brooks-Murkowski Amendment to an appropriations bill in December 1987. This legislation shut Japanese firms out of US public works projects for one year.[49] Under this pressure, the two countries concluded negotiations on the second public works agreement–the 1988 Major Projects Arrangements (1988 MPA).[50]

The 1988 MPA specified 14 major projects in which foreign firms were given opportunities to participate. It separated the projects into three categories. In the first group, Japan required two more projects undertaken by private commissioning entities (the Trans-Tokyo Bay Highway and the NTT Headquarters Building) to follow the procedures in the KIA Agreement. In the second category, Japan designated seven major projects in which foreign firms

48. Grier, "U.S.-Japan Government Procurement," 35.

49. Grier, "U.S.-Japan Government Procurement," 36.

50. Grier, "U.S.-Japan Government Procurement," 36.

would be allowed to participate in the Japanese government-commissioned portion of the project. Those projects had to apply special measures similar to those in the KIA Agreement and consider foreign firms as qualified without prior experience in Japan. For the final category, Japan designated portions of five more projects, which were to be undertaken by private or third sector entities. Although the Japanese government contended it had no authority to impose requirements on those projects, it promised to "actively encourage" the third sector entities undertaking them to follow non-discriminatory policies.[51]

4.3.3 1991 Major Projects Arrangements

Despite the two agreements, US firms continued to struggle to gain entry to Japan's public works market. Congress expressed frustration with the lack of progress by targeting a provision of the 1988 Trade Act at Japan's construction practices. Section 1305 of that Act directed USTR to conduct a Section 301 investigation of the barriers to entry of US architectural, engineering, construction, and consulting services firms into Japanese construction projects. After conducting a Section 301 investigation, in November 1989, USTR concluded that Japan's procurement policies in the construction sector limited competition and facilitated collusive bidding practices. It singled out the designated bidder system as restricting competition by limiting the number of firms allowed to bid on a project and basing its designation decisions on vague and subjective criteria. It also cited the lack of open bidding procedures outside of 1988 MPA projects and the exclusion of foreign firms from bidding on projects unless they had prior experience in Japan.[52]

---

51. Grier, "U.S.-Japan Government Procurement," 36–38.

52. Grier, "The Use of Section 301," 30-32; Grier, "U.S.-Japan Government Procurement," 38–39.

When negotiations failed to resolve US concerns, USTR proposed sanctions under Section 301 that would bar Japanese firms from public works projects undertaken by the Departments of Energy, Transportation, the US Army Corps of Engineers, and the Department of Interior's Bureau of Reclamation. These were entities that the US did not cover under the GATT Code, and thus, barring Japan from their procurement would not violate any international obligation. Under this increased pressure, Japan reached a third public works pact with the US–the 1991 Major Projects Arrangements (1991 MPA). With the completion of the agreement, the US stated that it would not impose sanctions.[53]

In the 1991 MPA, Japan agreed to improve the special measures in the 1988 MPA by increasing transparency of the procurement process, considering foreign experience as equivalent to prior work in Japan, and establishing a complaint system. It also committed to opening 23 more projects for participation by US firms. Of these projects, 17 were available immediately and six would be available only if the projects were initiated. Under the three public works agreements, Japan agreed to open at least some portion of 38 projects to American firms.[54]

4.3.4 1994 Public Works Agreement

Disappointed with the results that followed the 1991 MPA, USTR cited Japan in its 1993 Title VII report for discrimination in the procurement of construction, architectural, and engineering services. It particularly noted long-standing anticompetitive practices, extensive use of the designated bidder system, and a nontransparent procurement process that disadvantaged US firms.[55] In

---

53. Grier, "U.S.-Japan Government Procurement," 39; Grier, "The Use of Section 301," 32–33.

54. Grier, "U.S.-Japan Government Procurement," 39–40.

55. USTR, *Title VII Report*, 1–2, April 30, 1993.

1994, Japan finally undertook a major reform of its public works system due to a convergence of factors. The most significant factor was the imminent extension of international disciplines to public works and services under the GPA 1994, as the bilateral negotiations coincided with the GPA negotiations. Without its reforms, Japan would not have been able to meet its new GPA obligation to open construction services, as well as design and consulting services.[56] A second factor was the US threat to impose sanctions against Japan under Title VII.[57] The US again postponed sanctions on Japan after it expressed its intent to reform its public works.[58]

In January 1994, the US and Japan concluded their fourth (and final) public works agreement, the 1994 US-Japan Public Works Agreement (1994 Agreement). Its centerpiece was an Action Plan on Reform of the Bidding and Contracting Procedures for Public Works (adopted by the Japanese Cabinet with extensive US input). Japan's public works reform replaced the designated bidder system with a transparent and competitive system and provided detailed procedures for different types of procurement.[59] Based on the new agreement, USTR concluded that Japan had addressed the US's major concerns and terminated its Title VII determination. Japan applied the Action Plan to the entities listed under the GPA 1994, subject to the same thresholds. It continued to apply the 1991 MPA to procurement not covered by the Action Plan and below the GPA 1994 thresholds.[60]

---

56. Grier, "U.S.-Japan Government Procurement," 41.

57. Japan also faced domestic pressure for reform following a series of scandals involving payoffs of Japanese politicians by construction firms. Grier, "U.S.-Japan Government Procurement," 41.

58. Grier, "U.S.-Japan Government Procurement," 41.

59. They were open and competitive bidding for construction services and a public invitation for design and consulting services.

60. Grier, "U.S.-Japan Government Procurement," 42–45.

In the 2000 Title VII report, the US expressed disappointment with the results of the public works agreements. It emphasized that even though American companies were world-renowned for their expertise and competitiveness in design, consulting, and construction projects, they won only $50 million (0.02%) in contracts in Japan's $250 billion public works market in 1999.[61] At the same time, Japanese firms conducted 12 times as much public construction business in the US as American firms did in Japan. The 2000 USTR report also found that Japan had "engaged in a significant and persistent pattern of practices of discrimination that impedes American companies from participating in Japan's public works sector."[62]

4.4 1990 US-Japan Satellite Procurement Agreement

The US applied the 'Super 301' provision of the 1988 Trade Act for a second time to Japanese procurement practices when it challenged Japan's ban on the procurement of foreign satellites. Even though the US had long been the world leader in satellite production, its firms were locked out of Japan's satellite procurement.[63] Japan's 1983 Long Range Vision on Space Development prohibited

---

61. USTR, *Annual Report on Discrimination in Foreign Government Procurement (2000 Title VII Report)*, 3–4, April 30, 2000.

62. USTR, *2000 Title VII Report*, 3–4. The report noted that US participation was at the same level as in 1998, with only half of the $100 million in Japanese public works contracts awarded to US firms in 1997, and well below US participation in this market in the late 1980s. The practices cited in the report included rampant bid-rigging, unreasonable restrictions on the formation of joint ventures, the use of vague and discriminatory qualifications and evaluation criteria, and structuring procurement to avoid the application of the agreements.

63. USTR, "Suspension of Section 302 Investigation; Ban on Government Procurement of Foreign Satellites by the Government of Japan," *Federal Register* 55, no. 121 (June 22, 1990): 25761.

the procurement of foreign satellites when such purchases would interfere with the development of its indigenous production capability.[64] The policy applied to Japan's entire range of satellites: broadcast, communications, earth resources, and weather, and extended to two major quasi-governmental entities: NTT and the Japan Broadcast Corporation (NHK), Japan's public radio and television network. USTR identified Japan's satellite procurement ban as its second "priority practice" under 'Super 301' and initiated a Section 301 investigation, which proceeded in parallel with its supercomputer investigation.[65]

The two countries reached a preliminary agreement in April 1990 and finalized the US-Japan Satellite Agreement on June 15, 1990. Japan agreed to remove the ban on the procurement of foreign satellites. It pledged to open the procurement of all satellites by the government or any entity under its control to foreign competition, excluding R&D satellites and R&D payloads on non-R&D satellites.[66] In addition to embodying a reversal of the satellite policy, the agreement obligated Japan to adopt procedures to ensure that its satellite procurement was open, transparent, non-discriminatory, and competitive. The procedures were generally comparable

---

64. In an April 27, 1984 announcement, Japan stated that its "government agencies would be enabled to purchase satellites from abroad only if those satellites are 'not necessary for the autonomous development of technology under the space development policy.'" USTR, *1990 National Trade Estimate Report*, 114.

65. USTR, "Initiation of Section 302 Investigation and Request for Public Comment; Ban on Government Procurement of Foreign Satellites by the Government of Japan," *Federal Register* 54 (June 21, 1989): 26136; Grier, "U.S.-Japan Government Procurement," 45–46.

66. R&D satellites were "satellites designed and used entirely, or almost entirely, for the purpose of in-space development and/or validation of technologies new to either country, and/or non-commercial scientific research." R&D satellites do not encompass satellites "designed or used for commercial purposes or for the provision of services on a regular basis." Grier, "U.S.-Japan Government Procurement," 47, n. 380.

to the US procurement system and those in the 1990 Supercomputer Agreement.[67]

The Satellite Agreement applied directly to NTT and other governmental entities. However, its application to NHK was more circumscribed. The Japanese government committed not to influence NHK's procurement of non-R&D satellites. The NHK chairman, in a letter to USTR, stated that as "an independent and autonomous organization," NHK would adopt policies and procedures for satellite procurement equivalent to those in the bilateral agreement.[68]

4.5 1992 US-Japan Computer Procurement Agreement

In 1990, the US pursued a reversal of a 'Buy Japan' legacy in computer procurement. It was concerned that foreign computer manufacturers held less than 1% of Japan's relevant central government market, in contrast to their 41% share of Japan's private sector mainframe computer market. The US criticized Japanese procurement practices that reinforced the incumbency advantage of domestic firms. These practices included relying on its own firms for technical advice on procurement issues and making extensive use of single tendering to purchase from domestic suppliers.[69]

US pressure on Japan to address these issues led to negotiations of the US-Japan Computer Procurement Agreement, signed on January 22, 1992. The agreement applied to the procurement of computer products, including peripherals and packaged software, and services above a threshold of 100,000 SDRs, by entities covered by the GATT Code and quasi-governmental entities not covered by the Code. It became effective on April 1, 1992 for procurement of computer products and a year later for computer services.[70]

---

67. Grier, "U.S.-Japan Government Procurement," 46–48.

68. Grier, "U.S.-Japan Government Procurement," 47.

69. Grier, "U.S.-Japan Government Procurement," 49–50.

70. Grier, "U.S.-Japan Government Procurement," 50.

The overall aim of the Computer Procurement Agreement was to address the lack of market access by foreign firms rather than remedy specific problems as in other agreements. Japan committed to providing foreign and domestic suppliers with "equal access" to pre-solicitation information, disclosing all bid evaluation factors, reducing its use of single tendering, and establishing a bid complaint review mechanism. The agreement included undertakings indirectly related to the conduct of procurement. For example, Japan promised to ensure its entities would give all potential suppliers the same opportunities to participate in technical reference committees, advisory groups, study councils, and other groups that discussed the technology, budget, specifications, functions, or any other aspect of planned procurement of computer products and services.[71]

In its 1994 and 1995 Title VII reports, USTR noted concerns with Japanese computer procurement practices but concluded they did not meet the statutory criteria for action under Title VII. In 1995, US industry data indicated that foreign firms were penetrating Japan's public sector but still lagged behind Japanese firms.[72]

4.6 1994 US-Japan Framework Procurement Agreements

In 1994, the US and Japan completed their portfolio of bilateral procurement agreements with the negotiation of two agreements under the US-Japan Framework for a New Economic Partnership (Framework), which was established to address structural and sectoral trade issues, including government procurement. Under the Framework, the US sought to eliminate the disparity between its firms' strong presence in global markets and limited role in Japan's medical technology and telecommunications sectors. The US pointed to its firms' 52% share of the global medical technology

---

71. Grier, "U.S.-Japan Government Procurement," 50–51.
72. Grier, "U.S.-Japan Government Procurement," 51–52.

market in contrast to only a 21% share of Japan's market. The US attributed the disparity, in part, to inadequate transparency in Japan's procurement process and its reliance on domestic suppliers.[73]

In the telecommunications sector, the US contended that its firms' worldwide competitiveness was not reflected in their position in Japan due to obstacles encountered in its procurement. They included Japanese entities' failure to provide sufficient access to information on upcoming procurement, use of technical specifications that favored domestic suppliers, evaluation of bids that focused on the lowest prices without sufficient consideration of technical merit, and excessive use of single tendering. The US also pointed to the lack of competitive bidding procedures for subcontracts and the lack of an effective bid protest mechanism.[74]

US and Japan began the Framework talks in September 1993. When they did not produce results, USTR identified Japan in its 1994 Title VII report for discriminatory government procurement of telecommunications and medical technology and prepared to impose sanctions on Japan on September 30, 1994. That led to a resumption of negotiations with the two sides concluding the US-Japan Medical Technology Agreement and the US-Japan Telecommunications Agreement on October 1, 1994, averting sanctions. The parties signed these agreements on November 1, 1994.[75]

The two sectoral agreements cover the same central government entities but differ in their coverage of other entities. The Medical Technology Agreement applied to NTT, but the Telecommunications Agreement did not (as it was bound by a separate agreement). Both sectoral agreements included procurement procedures, built on other bilateral agreements, with provisions tailored to their specific sectors. Perhaps the most significant aspect of the agreements

73. Grier, "U.S.-Japan Government Procurement," 52.

74. Grier, "U.S.-Japan Government Procurement," 52–53.

75. Grier, "U.S.-Japan Government Procurement," 53–55. They signed the 1994 NTT Agreement on the same day.

was the requirement that entities evaluate tenders based on the 'overall greatest value' instead of the lowest price in the procurement of products or services above a certain threshold that were modified, specially developed, or off-the-shelf.[76]

The Medical Technology Agreement required all covered entities (and hospitals under their jurisdiction) to apply specified procedures for all procurement of medical technology products and services. A provision particularly important to the US medical technology industry obliged the head of each entity to encourage all procurement officials under its jurisdiction to treat competitive foreign products and services in a fair and non-discriminatory manner. Because most medical technology procurement was below the 100,000 SDRs threshold, special provisions were included to enhance the transparency of such procurement.[77] The Telecommunications Agreement also incorporated provisions related to subcontracts.[78]

The Framework agreements marked the end of the bilateral procurement agreements between the US and Japan. They also coincided with the creation of the WTO, with ramifications for the US negotiating approach, as discussed below.

5. IMPLEMENTATION AND ENFORCEMENT OF AGREEMENTS

Common Elements of the Bilateral Agreements: While each bilateral procurement agreement was tailored to obstacles encountered

---

76. Grier, "U.S.-Japan Government Procurement," 56–59.

77. For example, each hospital was required to publish information annually on the top 10 medical technology products and services that it planned to purchase during that year, regardless of the value of the procurement. Grier, "U.S.-Japan Government Procurement," 56–57, 60.

78. One provision required entities to invite suppliers to express interest in subcontracts in procurement when it published a request for comments for that procurement and its plans for future procurement. Another required entities to make a list of subcontractors available to suppliers. Grier, "U.S.-Japan Government Procurement," 60.

in a particular industry sector, the agreements shared several common characteristics. First, they generally provided more detailed procedures than the GATT Code. Second, they typically applied only to procurement meeting certain thresholds and conducted by specified central government and quasi-governmental entities.[79] Third, they required Japan to accord the benefits of the bilateral agreements to all foreign suppliers on an MFN basis. Fourth, the agreements were not reciprocal as they did not impose any obligations on the US.[80]

Different Views on Results of the Negotiations: The negotiations between the US and Japan were memorialized in exchanges of letters that included applicable measures. They were never entitled 'agreements' at the insistence of the Japanese, who resisted the perception that they had entered agreements with the US under the threat of sanctions.[81] The Japanese generally regarded them as "voluntary measures, the outcome of bilateral negotiations with the United States, to facilitate foreign suppliers' opportunities to access its government procurement markets."[82] Nonetheless, the US considered the results as trade agreements enforceable under Section 301.[83] In its 2021 trade barriers report, for example, USTR

---

79. For a comparison of the sectoral measures in terms of thresholds, entities, and relation to the GPA, see WTO, Trade Policy Review Body, *Trade Policy Review, Report by the Secretariat, Japan*, WT/TPR/S/351, para. 3.165 and Table 3.24, January 18, 2017.

80. Grier, "U.S.-Japan Government Procurement," 62–63.

81. Grier, "The Section 301," 39, n. 238.

82. WTO, *Trade Policy Review, Report by the Secretariat, Japan*, WT/TPR/S/397, January 22, 2020, para. 3.166.

83. For example, USTR determined that the exchange of letters of June 15, 1990, with its attachment, relating to Japanese procurement of supercomputers constituted an agreement under Section 310(c)(1) of the 1974 Trade Act. USTR, "Suspension of Section 302 Investigation; Exclusionary Government Procurement of Supercomputers by the Government of Japan," *Federal Register 55*, no. 121 (June 22, 1990): 25764.

stated that Japan had "made commitments to the United States under bilateral agreements."[84]

In the WTO's trade policy review of Japan in 2020, the Secretariat observed that

> "due to the fact that the 2014 revised GPA has 'caught up' with voluntary measures as compared to the GPA 1994, the benefits that can be drawn from these voluntary measures have become marginal. Details on the remaining value added of these voluntary measures is essentially of a procedural nature."[85]

US Industry Assessment: A US advisory committee offered an assessment of the Japanese agreements in a 2019 report to USTR. The US Industry Trade Advisory Committee on the Digital Economy contended the US-Japan bilateral agreements "were only partially successful" and had become increasingly less relevant over time. It urged the negotiation of new bilateral procurement commitments as part of a comprehensive agreement to enable US firms to compete effectively in Japan's procurement market, which it characterized as "historically-closed."[86]

Restraints on Use of Section 301: While the US and Japan were negotiating the procurement agreements in the early 1990s, they

---

84. USTR, 2021 National Trade Estimate Report on Foreign Trade Barriers, 295, March 31, 2021.

85. WTO, *Trade Policy Review*, para. 3.166. For example, the voluntary measures "encourage the adoption of the overall-greatest-value evaluation method (OGV) where the lowest-price-award method was deemed inadequate." In addition, it was obligatory to apply the OGV in large procurements in products and services in the computer, telecommunication, and medical technology sectors. WTO, *Trade Policy Review*, para. 3.171.

86. USTR, *Report of the Industry Trade Advisory Committee on the Digital Economy, Advisory Committees Reports pursuant to The Bipartisan Congressional Trade Priorities and Accountability Act of 2015 and the Trade Act of 1974, Trade Agreement Between the United States and Japan*, 90, October 2019.

were also actively participating in the Uruguay Round of multilateral trade negotiations to create the WTO and a dispute settlement mechanism. In the negotiations, the use of Section 301 was an issue. For Japan, a primary goal of the Uruguay Round negotiations "was to contain aggressive unilateralism of the United States, embodied in the frequent recourse to unilateral actions under Section 301."[87]

When the Uruguay Round negotiations resulted in the establishment of the WTO with its Understanding on Rules and Procedures Governing the Settlement of Disputes (DSU), the US, in effect, agreed to limit its use of Section 301. It indicated the intention to resort to the DSU to resolve future disputes rather than pursue unilateral action. The administration stated that USTR would use the DSU procedures for Section 301 investigations involving an alleged violation or the impairment of US benefits under WTO agreements. However, it also made clear that neither Section 301 nor the DSU required USTR to use the DSU for matters not covered by WTO agreements.[88]

With the establishment of an enforceable dispute settlement mechanism under the WTO (with strong US support), the US significantly reduced its use of Section 301. It primarily relied on Section 301 to build dispute settlement cases and litigate those cases at the WTO. [89] However, during the Trump administration, the US once again resorted to the use of Section 301 to resolve trade issues unilaterally.[90]

---

87. Ichiro Araki, "Beyond Aggressive Legalism: Japan and the GATT/WTO Dispute," in *WTO and East Asia: New Perspectives*, eds. Mitsuo Matsushita and Dukgeun Ahn, 154 (London: Cameron May, 2004).

88. *Uruguay Round Trade Agreements Act*, Statement of Administrative Action, Understanding on Rules and Procedures Governing the Settlement of Disputes, US Congress, House, H.R. Doc. No. 316, 103d Cong., 2d Sess., Vol. 1, 1027–1029, 1032–1036 (September 27, 1994).

89. Congressional Research Service, *Section 301 of the Trade Act*.

90. Congressional Research Service, *Section 301 of the Trade Act*.

PART THREE

EXPANSION OF INTERNATIONAL PROCUREMENT THROUGH REGIONAL AGREEMENTS

INTRODUCTION

Since the implementation of the GPA 2012, the international procurement system has expanded through regional trade agreements and FTAs. These agreements build on the GPA and incorporate GPA parties and non-GPA countries alike as well as developed and developing countries. The most prominent regional agreement is the 11-member Comprehensive and Progressive Trans-Pacific Partnership (CPTPP), while the most active advocate of FTAs is the European Union (EU), which has been expanding its roster of agreements. These agreements have served as a force of liberalization. They also demonstrate that the leadership of the international procurement system has expanded beyond the US.

Outside of the GPA, the CPTPP is the largest agreement with government procurement provisions that are comparable to the plurilateral agreement. The US played a crucial role in the development of that agreement's predecessor, the Trans-Pacific Partnership (TPP). It led the negotiations of the TPP and signed the final document. However, President Trump withdrew the US from the TPP at the beginning of his presidency. The other signatories then moved forward with the slightly revised CPTPP, which they implemented at the end of 2018.

The EU's FTAs are contributing significantly to the liberalization of procurement markets. In agreements with GPA parties, the EU and its partners have opened procurement not covered under the plurilateral agreement. In negotiating FTAs with developing countries, the EU has made the opening of procurement a key objective.

CHAPTER 10

COMPREHENSIVE AND PROGRESSIVE TRANS-PACIFIC PARTNERSHIP: GOVERNMENT PROCUREMENT

1. INTRODUCTION

Even though the US never implemented the TPP, the predecessor to the CPTPP, it viewed that agreement as the most ambitious FTA that it had negotiated and had high expectations for it. The US intended it to set the standards for 21st-century trade agreements and insisted that it cover more than the usual elements of FTAs. In addition to removing tariff and nontariff barriers, the US also wanted the agreement to promote new technologies and emerging economic sectors and provide new trade rules on such issues as state-owned enterprises and regulatory coherence. It also intended for the agreement to enhance environmental protection, transparency, and workers' rights.[1]

---

1. Office of the US Trade Representative (USTR), *2011 Trade Policy Agenda and 2010 Annual Report*, 146, March 2011.

The US conceived the TPP as both a trade initiative and a way to rebalance its role in the Asia-Pacific region. As a trade initiative, the TPP agreement would bind together a group of countries representing nearly 40% of global GDP and about a third of world trade.[2] Strategically, the TPP would provide an avenue for the US and its partners to play a leading role in reshaping the economic architecture of the Asia-Pacific region.[3] Overall, the US considered the TPP a platform for economic integration across the region and "a means to advance US economic interests with the fastest-growing economies in the world."[4]

In 2017, shortly after the start of his presidency, Donald Trump abruptly pulled the US out of the TPP and ended America's leadership in developing it. Following the US departure, Japan picked up the leadership mantle and, with the other signatories, brought the TPP into force. The final agreement was a slightly slimmed-down version of the original, renamed the CPTPP.

The CPTPP is now the world's most comprehensive FTA and leading Asia-based trade agreement. It brings together a broad range of countries, from highly developed Japan to emerging economies, such as Vietnam. Its importance will grow as it expands its membership and geographical scope. While it is possible the US could return to the agreement, as many advocate, it seemed unlikely in 2022.[5]

---

2. USTR, "Remarks by Ambassador Michael Froman at the Council on Foreign Relations: The Strategic Logic of Trade," June 16, 2014, https://ustr.gov/about-us/policy-offices/press-office/speeches/transcripts/2014/June/Remarks-US-TR-Froman-at-Council-Foreign-Relations-Strategic-Logic-of-Trade.

3. USTR, "Remarks by Ambassador" and US Library of Congress, Congressional Research Service, *The Trans-Pacific Partnership (TPP) Negotiations and Issues for Congress*, by Ian F. Fergusson, Mark A. McMinimy, and Brock R. Williams, R42694 (2015), 1, https://sgp.fas.org/crs/row/R42694.pdf.

4. USTR, *2011 Trade Policy Agenda and 2010 Annual Report*, 146.

5. Wendy Cutler, "America Must Return to the Trans-Pacific Partnership," *Foreign Affairs*, September 10, 2021, https://www.foreignaffairs.com/articles/2021-09-10/america-must-return-trans-pacific-partnership.

The CPTPP's government procurement chapter represents an important addition to the international procurement system. It is the most notable agreement with procurement commitments outside the plurilateral GPA. Including both GPA parties and non-GPA countries, the CPTPP has a more diverse membership than the GPA. It demonstrates how a procurement agreement can integrate developed and developing countries under common GPA-based rules and, at the same time, address the sensitivities of members at different developmental levels. It has facilitated the participation of developing economies, such as Malaysia and Vietnam, by offering extensive and tailored transitional measures.

The CPTPP has been compared to the 2022 Regional Comprehensive Economic Partnership (RCEP), another major Asia-based trade agreement. They share the broad aims of reducing trade barriers and establishing trade rules among their parties. While the RCEP has more members than the CPTPP, it is less comprehensive and includes only a limited government procurement chapter.

Although the US is not a party to the CPTPP, it did play an instrumental role in developing the agreement. As a result, the CPTPP reflects the US approach to government procurement between 2012 and 2020, a period when it completed no other agreement with procurement commitments beyond a revision of the US-Mexico-Canada Agreement (USMCA).[6]

2. DEVELOPMENT OF THE TPP AND CPTPP

2.1 US Negotiations and Signature of the TPP

As an instrument of economic integration and trade liberalization in the Asia-Pacific region, the TPP began modestly as the Trans-Pacific Strategic Economic Partnership Agreement (P-4 Agreement) among Brunei, Chile, New Zealand, and Singapore. The P-4 Agreement

---

6. During that period, the US also attempted–unsuccessfully–to negotiate a major FTA with the European Union.

entered into force in 2006, except for chapters on financial services and investment.[7]

In 2008, the US joined three rounds of negotiations of the P-4 Agreement's financial services and investment chapters. Nearing the end of his term in office, President George W. Bush notified Congress he intended to negotiate a full agreement with the P-4 members plus Australia, Peru, and Vietnam,[8] which later became the TPP. His successor, President Obama, delayed a year before committing the US to re-engage with those countries. In doing so, he set a goal "of shaping a regional agreement that will have broad-based membership and the high standards worthy of a 21st-century trade agreement."[9] Obama formally notified Congress of his intention to enter into negotiations of the TPP in December 2009.[10] The US goal was a regional pact with the scope, coverage, and trade rules that would unify the Asia-Pacific economies that were parties to the agreement.

The TPP negotiations began in March 2010 among the US, Australia, Brunei, Chile, New Zealand, Peru, Singapore, and Vietnam, with Malaysia joining in the fall.[11] The 15th round of negotiations of the TPP in December 2012 brought in Canada and Mexico. The TPP negotiating roster was completed the following year with the addition of Japan.[12]

---

7. Trans-Pacific Strategic Economic Partnership Agreement, 2006, https://investmentpolicy.unctad.org/international-investment-agreements/treaties/treaties-with-investment-provisions/3215/p4-agreement.

8. Congressional Research Service, *The TPP Negotiations*, 1.

9. Remarks of President Obama at Suntory Hall, Tokyo, Japan, November 14, 2009.

10. USTR, *2011 Trade Policy Agenda and 2010 Annual Report*, 146.

11. USTR, *TPP Statements and Actions to Date*, accessed June 7, 2022, https://ustr.gov/about-us/policy-offices/press-office/fact-sheets/2009/december/tpp-statements-and-actions-date.

12. USTR, *2014 Trade Policy Agenda and 2013 Annual Report of the President of the United States on the Trade Agreements Program*, March 2014, 142, https://ustr.gov/about-us/policy-offices/press-office/reports-and-publications/2014-0.

Congress renewed the Trade Promotion Authority (TPA) to provide authority for President Obama to conclude negotiations and sign the TPP.[13] After months of often-acrimonious debate,[14] it enacted the Bipartisan Congressional Trade Priorities and Accountability Act of 2015.[15] With that authority, the US joined the other 11 countries[16] in concluding TPP negotiations in October 2015 and signing the agreement on February 4, 2016.[17]

Implementation of the TPP required ratification by a minimum of signatories, accounting for at least 85% of the combined GDP of all signatories. That would have required ratification by both the US and Japan. Along with New Zealand, Japan ratified the agreement,[18] but the US did not. President Obama never submitted the agreement to Congress for approval because of congressional opposition.[19]

---

13. For a discussion of US trade negotiating authority, see Appendix 2.

14. "The 2015 battle over renewal of Trade Promotion Authority was one of the most divisive in US trade history, with most Democrats opposed to approving the legislation" that President Obama needed to finish negotiations of the TPP. Congress voted for TPA renewal but "[m]ost Democrats in both chambers voted against the TPA bill." Doug Palmer, "Say goodbye to Trade Promotion Authority," *Politico*, June 28, 2021, https://www.politico.com/newsletters/weekly-trade/2021/06/28/say-goodbye-to-trade-promotion-authority-796173.

15. *Bipartisan Congressional Trade Priorities and Accountability Act of 2015*, Public Law 114-26, *U.S. Statutes at Large* 129 (2015): 320.

16. The other TPP signatories were Australia, Brunei, Canada, Chile, Japan, Malaysia, Mexico, New Zealand, Peru, Singapore, and Vietnam.

17. TPP Agreement, accessed June 8, 2022, https://ustr.gov/trade-agreements/free-trade-agreements/trans-pacific-partnership/tpp full-text. The government procurements provisions were in the TPP's Chapter 15 and Annex 15-A.

18. "New Zealand Ratifies TPP despite U.S. Withdrawal," *The Japan Times*, May 11, 2017, http://www.japantimes.co.jp/news/2017/05/11/business/new-zealand-ratifies-tpp-despite-u-s-withdrawal/#.WRUOa1KZO1s.

19. Alan Yuhas, "Congress will abandon Trans-Pacific Partnership deal, White House concedes," *The Guardian*, November 12, 2016, https://www.theguardian.com/business/2016/nov/12/tpp-trade-deal-congress-obama.

2.2 US Withdrawal from the TPP

Throughout the 2016 presidential campaign, Donald Trump expressed strong opposition to the TPP and announced his intention to withdraw from it if elected president.[20] Nonetheless, following his election, TPP supporters harbored the hope that the president would moderate his opposition after he entered the White House and could be persuaded to support the agreement–perhaps after a renegotiation–as with earlier FTAs.[21]

President Trump dashed any hope that he might moderate his opposition to the TPP when, on his first business day in the Oval Office, he ordered the US Trade Representative (USTR) to withdraw the US from the TPP negotiations and remove it from the list of signatories.[22] On January 30, 2017, the USTR duly informed the other TPP parties the US did not intend to become a party to the agreement. Still, it noted that the US remained "committed to taking measures designed to promote more efficient markets and higher levels of economic growth," both domestically and worldwide.[23]

---

20. Megan Cassella, "Trump's first-day agenda: Kill TPP, renegotiate NAFTA," *Politico*, November 9, 2016, https://www.politico.com/tipsheets/morning-trade/2016/11/trumps-first-day-agenda-kill-tpp-renegotiate-nafta-217318.

21. The US had seen other agreements declared dead when a new administration assumed office, only to be resurrected with negotiations of improvements. For example, during the 2008 campaign, presidential candidate Barack Obama opposed the US FTA with South Korea, which President Bush had signed. However, after renegotiation of several elements of the FTA, President Obama signed the legislation implementing it. USTR, *US-Korea Free Trade Agreement, Legal Texts Reflecting December 3, 2009 Agreement*, accessed June 8, 2022, https://ustr.gov/trade-agreements/free-trade-agreements/korus-fta/legal-texts-reflecting-december-3-2010-agreement.

22. US President, Memorandum for the United States Trade Representative, "Withdrawal of the United States from the Trans-Pacific Partnership Negotiations and Agreement," January 23, 2017, *Federal Register* 82, no. 15 (January 25, 2017): 8497, https://www.govinfo.gov/content/pkg/FR-2017-01-25/pdf/2017-01845.pdf.

23. USTR, "The United States Officially Withdraws from the Trans-Pacific Partnership," January 2017, https://ustr.gov/about-us/policy-offices/press-office/press-releases/2017/january/US-Withdraws-From-TPP.

In withdrawing from the TPP, the US lost the opportunity to participate in the government procurement markets in Brunei, Malaysia, and Vietnam, with which it did not have trade agreements.[24] (In 2022, it still did not have agreements with those countries.) The loss of access to Vietnam's government procurement also placed US suppliers at a disadvantage relative to those from the European Union (EU). The EU, in 2020, had implemented a comprehensive FTA with Vietnam with procurement commitments comparable to those of the TPP. In its report on the likely impact of the TPP on the US economy, the US International Trade Commission concluded that these three countries represented the most significant procurement opportunities for the US because it did not have access to their procurement under any other agreement.[25]

With its withdrawal from the TPP, the US was also unable to participate in new procurement opened under the agreement by its GPA and FTAs partners and align other FTAs with the TPP. It could not implement a side agreement with Australia to apply the same thresholds in the TPP, their 2005 FTA, and the GPA for goods and services purchased by their central government entities.[26] The US withdrawal also ended two other side letters relating to the North American Free Trade Agreement (NAFTA).[27]

---

24. This assumes Brunei ratifies the CPTPP.

25. US International Trade Commission, *Trans-Pacific Partnership Agreement: Likely Impact on the U.S. Economy and on Specific Industry Sectors*, 448, May 18, 2016, https://www.usitc.gov/publications/332/pub4607.pdf.

26. The US and Australia agreed to a side letter on the margins of the TPP negotiations that would have applied their TPP (and GPA) threshold to their FTA-covered procurement. TPP Agreement.

27. In one side letter, the three NAFTA partners agreed to update NAFTA's procurement procedures by replacing them with those in the TPP. That aim was accomplished when the US-Mexico-Canada Agreement replaced NAFTA and included government procurement text aligned closely with the TPP and the GPA. In a second letter, Canada and the US agreed to apply their TPP (and GPA) thresholds to procurement covered by NAFTA. TPP Agreement.

2.3 Negotiations, Signature, and Implementation of the CPTPP

When the US exited the TPP, the remaining signatories did not accept its departure as the agreement's death knell. Instead, led by Japan, they moved forward with a renamed agreement to realize the TPP's benefits of opening markets and promoting regional economic integration. They reached a ministerial agreement in November 2017 on the core elements of the renamed CPTPP and concluded negotiations of the agreement in January 2018.[28] Eleven countries signed the CPTPP.[29]

The CPTPP modified the TPP's entry into force provision to require ratification by at least six of its original signatories, accounting for a minimum of 85% of the combined GDP of the original signatories.[30] The agreement took effect on December 30, 2018, after Australia, Canada, Japan, Mexico, New Zealand, and Singapore ratified it. Vietnam's ratification followed in January 2019, Peru's–in September 2021, and Malaysia's a year later, on September 30, 2022. The agreement had yet to be ratified by Brunei and Chile as of late 2022.

The CPTPP incorporated the TPP text, except for some 20 provisions, which had been promoted by the US.[31] The provisions, constituting a small fraction of the text, were suspended. Although these provisions remain part of the CPTPP, Australia has explained

---

28. CPTPP, 2018, accessed June 6, 2022, https://www.mfat.govt.nz/en/trade/free-trade-agreements/free-trade-agreements-in-force/cptpp/comprehensive-and-progressive-agreement-for-trans-pacific-partnership-text-and-resources/. The government provisions are in the CPTPP's Chapter 15 and Annex 15-A.

29. The countries that signed the CPTPP were Australia, Brunei, Canada, Chile, Japan, Malaysia, Mexico, New Zealand, Peru, Singapore, and Vietnam.

30. CPTPP, art. 30.5(2).

31. New Zealand Foreign Affairs and Trade, Annex II, List of Suspended Provisions, accessed June 8, 2022, https://www.mfat.govt.nz/assets/Trade-agreements/CPTPP/ANNEX-II_LIst-of-suspended-Provisions.pdf.

that "they will have no application under international law."[32] The suspended provisions could be reinstated if, for example, the US rejoined the agreement.

2.4 Expansion of CPTPP Membership

With its implementation, the CPTPP opened to accession by any state or separate customs territory subject to the agreement of the parties. In September 2021, the CPTPP Commission reaffirmed it welcomed "economies committed to the Agreement's objectives, able to meet and adhere to its high standards and ambitious market access commitments," and had "demonstrated a pattern of complying with trade commitments."[33] After receiving its first accession application from the United Kingdom (UK) on February 1, 2021,[34] the Commission established an Accession Working Group in June 2021 to conduct accession negotiations.[35]

In September 2021, China formally applied for CPTPP membership, followed by Taiwan (Chinese Taipei) less than a week

---

32. Australian Government, Department of Foreign Affairs and Trade, "CPTPP suspensions explained," https://www.dfat.gov.au/trade/agreements/in-force/cptpp/outcomes-documents/Pages/cptpp-suspensions-explained.

33. Australian Government, Department of Foreign Affairs and Trade, "Comprehensive and Progressive Agreement for Trans-Pacific Partnership (CPTPP). Joint Ministerial Statement on the occasion of the Fifth Commission Meeting," September 1, 2021, https://www.dfat.gov.au/trade/agreements/in-force/cptpp/news/cptpp-joint-ministerial-statement-occasion-fifth-commission-meeting.

34. UK Department for International Trade, "UK applies to join huge Pacific free trade area CPTPP," January 30, 2021, https://www.gov.uk/government/news/uk-applies-to-join-huge-pacific-free-trade-area-cptpp.

35. Government of Canada, "Comprehensive and Progressive Agreement for Trans-Pacific Partnership (CPTPP). Joint Ministerial Statement on the occasion of the Fourth Commission Meeting," June 2, 2021, https://www.international.gc.ca/trade-commerce/trade-agreements-accords-commerciaux/agr-acc/cptpp-ptpgp/2020-08-06-cptpp-statement_declaration-ptpgp.aspx?lang=eng.

later.[36] In December 2021, Ecuador became the fourth applicant for CPTPP membership,[37] and other countries are reportedly considering applying for accession.[38]

2.5 Prospects for the US Return to the CPTPP

Many advocated the US's return to the CPTPP.[39] The calls to rejoin the agreement came from US lawmakers in both political parties, the business community, CPTPP members, and Asian and trade experts. These calls were reinforced by China's application to join the agreement. The US Chamber of Commerce's Chief Executive Officer pointed out that the US answer to China's "rise as a formidable commercial and strategic competitor" had been the TPP. Instead, with its withdrawal, the US is now on the "outside looking in" as China and other countries seek CPTPP membership.[40] Although China's CPTPP application "creates strong geopolitical reasons for US membership," it may not be enough to overcome

36. US Library of Congress, Congressional Research Service, *China and Taiwan Both Seek to Join the CPTPP*, by Brock R. Williams and Michael D. Sutherland, IN11760 (2021), https://crsreports.congress.gov/product/pdf/IN/IN11760.

37. Hidetake Miyamoto, "Ecuador applies for CPTPP membership to diversify trade," *Nikkei Asia*, December 29, 2021, https://asia.nikkei.com/Politics/International-relations/Ecuador-applies-for-CPTPP-membership-to-diversify-trade.

38. See, for example, Yonhap, "S. Korea decides to join CPTPP trade agreement," *The Korea Herald*, April 15, 2022, https://www.koreaherald.com/view.php?ud=20220415000647; Theodore, "Lacalle Pou announces that Uruguay will request adhesion to the CPTPP," *The Postedia*, July 27, 2022, https://thepostedia.com/market/61802.html; and Kosuke Shimizu, "Costa Rica wants to join CPTPP, president says," *Nikkei Asia*, July 30, 2022, https://asia.nikkei.com/Politics/International-relations/Indo-Pacific/Costa-Rica-wants-to-join-CPTPP-president-says.

39. Cutler, "America Must Return."

40. Suzanne P. Clark, "The Competition for the Future," State of American Business 2022 Keynote Address, US Chamber of Commerce, January 11, 2022, https://www.uschamber.com/on-demand/economy/5-takeaways-from-suzanne-clarks-first-state-of-american-business-address?autoplay=1.

congressional resistance.[41] Despite bipartisan calls for the US to re-enter that agreement, even if it means renegotiating parts of the deal, President Biden indicated he had no plans to do so. Even if he were to seek a return to the CPTPP, "such a move would face fierce opposition on Capitol Hill."[42]

3. GOVERNMENT PROCUREMENT CHAPTER

Under the US leadership, the TPP negotiators developed a government procurement chapter. The chapter was based on the 2012 revision of the GPA (GPA 2012) and incorporated provisions from US FTAs and the P-4 Agreement.[43] It fulfilled the US negotiating objective to "establish fair, transparent, predictable, and non-discriminatory rules to govern government procurement in TPP countries."[44] It also generally met the US aim of liberalizing the TPP countries' government procurement markets, "with comparable levels of coverage by all TPP countries, taking into account the particular sensitivities of specific countries."[45]

Even though most of the TPP's procurement provisions followed US FTAs, the market access commitments, especially regarding thresholds and services, lacked the uniformity found in

41. Gary Clyde Hufbauer, "President Biden's elusive trade policy," *East Asia Forum*, October 31, 2021, https://www.eastasiaforum.org/2021/10/31/president-bidens-elusive-trade-policy/?utm_source=newsletter&utm_medium=email&utm_campaign=newsletter2021-10-31?utm_source=newsletter&utm_medium=email&utm_campaign=newsletter2021-10-31.

42. Steven Overly, "Japan's role in selling Biden's Indo-Pacific agenda," *Politico*, January 24, 2022, https://www.politico.com/newsletters/weekly-trade/2022/01/24/japans-role-in-selling-bidens-indo-pacific-agenda-00001050.

43. Jean Heilman Grier, "Government Procurement in the Trans-Pacific Partnership (TPP)," *The Government Contractor, Thomson Reuters* 58, no. 7 (February 17, 2016): 1.

44. USTR, "Trans-Pacific Partnership: Summary of U.S. Objectives," https://ustr.gov/tpp/Summary-of-US-objectives, 2015.

45. USTR, "TPP: Summary of U.S. Objectives."

these agreements. It may be explained by the need to accommodate participants at different levels of development. In response, the TPP created extensive transitional and other special measures for Malaysia and Vietnam. These measures were designed to protect local businesses as their countries opened procurement markets to foreign participation for the first time.

The CPTPP incorporated the TPP's government procurement chapter and its annex with schedules of the market access commitments of each signatory. Only two suspended provisions were excluded. One suspended provision set a deadline of three years after the TPP took effect to commence negotiations on expanding procurement covered by the agreement, including coverage of subcentral entities.[46] The second provision clarified that a procuring entity could promote compliance with labor laws in the territory where goods were produced or services were performed in its conditions for participation in a procurement. This provision was similar to one the US added to four FTAs beginning with the US-Peru Trade Promotion Agreement, resulting from a 2007 agreement between the Bush administration and Congress on labor provisions, referred to as the May 10th Agreement.[47]

3.1 Procurement Rules

The TPP's government procurement chapter specified principles and rules for the conduct of procurement covered under the agreement (covered procurement). It aimed to ensure such procurement was conducted in a fair, non-discriminatory, transparent, and predictable manner. It established national treatment and non-discrimination as fundamental principles. Those principles prohibited parties from favoring domestic goods, services, and suppliers over those of other parties and one party over another in procurement conducted under

---

46. Several TPP signatories, including the US, did not offer any subcentral entities.
47. The May 10th Agreement is discussed in Chapter 5.

the agreement. The TPP also prohibited the use of offsets (except as a transitional measure for developing countries).[48] The TPP's principles reflected the cornerstones of the GPA and the US FTAs.

As in the GPA and US FTAs, the TPP's procurement rules specified baseline requirements for the conduct of covered procurement. They applied to each stage of the procurement process, including the development of technical specifications, conditions for the participation of suppliers, qualification procedures, notices of intended procurement, tender documentation, submission of tenders, evaluation of tenders, selection of the winning tender, providing information to suppliers that were not selected, post-award notices, use of limited tendering, and bid protest mechanisms.[49]

3.2 Market Access Commitments

The US market access commitments in the TPP negotiations are included in this examination as they likely affected the coverage of the other participants. They also contribute to an understanding of the evolution of US procurement commitments in trade agreements.[50]

At the time of the TPP negotiations, the US had exchanged procurement commitments with most of the TPP's participants: six in FTAs (with Australia, Canada, Chile, Mexico, Peru, and Singapore) and four under the GPA (with Canada, Japan, New Zealand, and Singapore).[51] Those participants incorporated most of their GPA or FTA procurement commitments into the TPP. Generally, they made modest additions to their existing coverage, although several offered less procurement than in other agreements.

---

48. Grier, "Government Procurement," 1.

49. Grier, "Government Procurement," 1.

50. Since this discussion includes US commitments, the agreement is referred to as the TPP, with the understanding that for all the participants, except the US, their market access commitments were incorporated into the CPTPP.

51. New Zealand became a GPA party in 2015 before the TPP negotiations concluded; Australia joined the GPA in 2019.

The TPP signatories applied a broad array of thresholds to three categories of entities (central, subcentral, and other entities), in contrast to the uniformity in thresholds found in other US FTAs (see Table 10.1).

TABLE 10.1. TPP Thresholds

TPP Signatory	Central Government Entities		Subcentral Government Entities		Other Entities	
	Goods and Services	Construction Services	Goods and Services	Construction Services	Goods and Services	Construction Services
Australia	130,000 SDRs	5 million SDRs	355,000 SDRs	5 million SDRs	400,000 SDRs	5 million SDRs
Brunei	130,000 SDRs	5 million SDRs	N/A	N/A	130,000 SDRs	5 million SDRs
Canada	130,000 SDRs	5 million SDRs	355,000 SDRs	5 million SDRs	355,000 SDRs	5 million SDRs
Chile	95,000 SDRs	5 million SDRs	200,000 SDRs	5 million SDRs	220,000 SDRs	5 million SDRs
Japan	100,000 SDRs*	4.5 million SDRs	200,000 SDRs*	15 million SDRs	130,000 SDRs	15 million SDRs
Malaysia	130,000 SDRs	14 million SDRs	N/A	N/A	150,000 SDRs	14 million SDRs
Mexico	$79,507	$10.3 million	N/A	N/A	$397,535	$12.7 million
New Zealand	130,000 SDRs	5 million SDRs	N/A	N/A	400,000 SDRs	5 million SDRs
Peru	95,000 SDRs	5 million SDRs	200,000 SDRs	5 million SDRs	160,000 SDRs	5 million SDRs
Singapore	130,000 SDRs	5 million SDRs	N/A	N/A	400,000 SDRs	5 million SDRs
US	130,000 SDRs	5 million SDRs	N/A	N/A	$250,000	5 million SDRs
Vietnam	130,000 SDRs	8.5 million SDRs	N/A	N/A	2 million SDRs	15 million SDRs

* Japan applies higher thresholds for architectural, engineering, and other technical services.

The TPP signatories covered a wide variety of central government ministries and agencies. The US offered 86 federal entities, including the entities it added in the GPA 2012 negotiations and a small federal agency (the Denali Commission), which it had not covered previously. Based on the reciprocity principle, the US limited Vietnam's access to the procurement of the Department of Defense to two units: the Department's Education Activity and the Defense Commissary Agency. That was in response to Vietnam's coverage of only two departments of its defense ministry.

Mexico replicated its government procurement commitments under NAFTA, including its permanent offsets and set-asides. It also included the transitional measures it applied under NAFTA (between 1994 and 2002), the Japan-Mexico Economic Partnership Agreement, and the Additional Protocol to the Pacific Alliance Agreement with Chile and Peru.

New Zealand incorporated its GPA coverage, except for its subcentral entities and about half of its other entities. It withheld its other entities from Mexico. Peru offered only 32 central government entities in the TPP, in contrast to 67 entities in the US-Peru TPA. It also omitted 31 universities listed in the TPA. Chile added three ministries not listed in its US FTA.

Australia, Canada, Chile, Japan, and Peru covered subcentral government entities, closely following their GPA or FTA coverage.[52] They generally did not extend this coverage to the US and other signatories that did not cover their own subcentral entities.[53] Brunei and Singapore have no subcentral entities.

---

52. Several Australian states and territories listed more entities under the TPP than under the GPA. Japan added one designated city.

53. The other signatories that did not cover subcentral entities were Malaysia, Mexico, New Zealand, and Vietnam. The US's exclusion of subcentral coverage under the TPP was consistent with its negotiating objectives. USTR, "TPP: Summary of U.S. Objectives."

Australia listed slightly fewer government enterprises than under its FTA with the US. Japan added 12 other entities to its GPA coverage (but did not include all GPA-listed entities). Singapore added 10 authorities, boards, and councils and the Civil Service College to its GPA entity coverage but excluded two GPA-listed universities.[54] The US denied Malaysia access to the procurement of its electric utilities and the Rural Utilities Service's funding of power generation projects.

In an unusual move, the US overrode a long-standing reciprocity condition when it offered Canada access to the procurement of the federal electric utilities covered under other FTAs and the GPA, namely, the Tennessee Valley Authority and the power administrations. It offered that coverage without receiving access to comparable Canadian procurement. Ever since the US covered government enterprises for the first time under NAFTA and the GPA 1994, it had withheld that coverage from Canada because Canada refused to provide access to the procurement of its provincial hydro utilities. Canada continued to withhold that coverage in the TPP. It did, however, add 12 other entities not covered under the GPA or NAFTA.[55]

As in other US FTAs and the GPA, the TPP covered the procurement of all goods (except defense and specific agency exclusions). Other than Brunei, all TPP signatories defined coverage of their defense agencies by listing the covered procurement. Brunei covered all procurement of its defense ministry. Brunei was also the only country to open the procurement of all services by its covered entities. The other signatories diverged on their coverage of services. In contrast to US FTAs, where all parties (except South

---

54. The universities are Nanyang Technological University and the National University of Singapore.

55. Its added entities included museums, PPP Canada Inc., Canada Development Investment Corporation, Canada Lands Company Limited, and several bridge and pilotage authorities.

Korea) based their services coverage on a negative list (opening all services except those listed), the TPP did not apply a uniform approach.[56]

Peru covered three services in the TPP that it excluded in its US TPA,[57] and Singapore added placement services to the services that it opened under the GPA and its US FTA. The parties provided full coverage of construction services, except those listed as excluded. By contrast, Singapore listed its covered construction services.

The TPP procurement chapter applied to public-private partnerships (PPPs) in two ways. First, following the approach used in US FTAs, the TPP treated build-operate-transfer (BOT) and public works concession contracts as a type of contractual arrangement that applied to all parties (except for those that opted out).[58] Second, Japan included its GPA coverage of its Private Finance Initiative.

More than half the TPP signatories excluded preferences and other measures benefiting SMEs from their commitments.[59] The US excluded procurement set aside for its small and minority-owned businesses and maintained exclusions of procurement subject to domestic preferences as in the GPA and other FTAs. In addition, Chile excluded preferences for micro-, small-, and medium-sized enterprises and procurement of storage and hosting of government data. Canada excluded an entity enigmatically described as "an international crossing between Canada and another country, including

---

56. The US, Australia, Chile, Mexico, New Zealand, and Peru based their coverage on a negative list, while Canada, Japan, Malaysia, Singapore, and Vietnam listed the services they opened. In contrast, Canada had based its services coverage under NAFTA on a negative list.

57. Peru excluded architectural services, engineering and design services, and engineering services during the construction and installation phases.

58. Those excluding such contracts were Malaysia, Mexico, and Vietnam. Even though Mexico excluded BOT contracts, it covered turnkey and major integrated projects as it did in its US FTAs.

59. The others were Australia, Brunei, Canada, Chile, Peru, and Vietnam.

the design, construction, operation or maintenance of the crossing as well as any related infrastructure." This appears to refer to the New International Trade Crossing project between Canada and the state of Michigan, which was undertaken through "Public-Private Agreements with one or more private sector Concessionaires."[60]

Brunei offered broad coverage with minimal exclusions. Its central government coverage included its Prime Minister's Office and 11 ministries but only two other entities.[61] It was the only TPP signatory, as noted above, to cover all goods purchased by its Ministry of Defence and all services. Brunei was authorized to apply two types of transitional measures: higher thresholds[62] and delayed implementation of several obligations.[63]

The TPP also permitted Malaysia, Mexico, and Vietnam to apply transitional measures. Mexico brought into the TPP the same measures it applied under NAFTA, USMCA, and an FTA with the EU. An examination of the commitments of Malaysia and Vietnam and the extensive transitional and special measures they were accorded under the TPP illustrates how an FTA can facilitate the first-time opening of procurement by developing countries. Their

---

60. US Department of Transportation, Federal Highway Administration, "Buy America Waiver Notification," *Federal Register* 77, no. 239 (December 12, 2012): 74048, https://www.govinfo.gov/content/pkg/FR-2012-12-12/pdf/2012-29917.pdf.

61. They were the Authority Monetary Brunei Darussalam and the Employee Provident Fund.

62. For four years after it implemented the TPP, Brunei was permitted to apply higher thresholds for the procurement of goods and services. Those thresholds started at 250,000 SDRs for central government entities and 500,000 SDRs for other entities.

63. For three years after the TPP's implementation, Brunei could omit certain information from its procurement notices, provide information on its contract awards upon request (in place of publishing an award notice), and, in the procurement of certain services, notify suppliers on multiuse lists of procurement opportunities (rather than publish a notice of intended procurement). Finally, for five years after it implemented the TPP, Brunei was not required to establish an impartial domestic review authority to handle supplier complaints.

treatment under the FTA could provide a useful precedent for the inclusion of developing countries in the GPA and other FTAs.[64]

3.3 Malaysia's Procurement Commitments

In the TPP negotiations, the US had been especially interested in opening Malaysia's government procurement as it had been unable to negotiate an FTA with the country. In 2006, the US and Malaysia commenced FTA negotiations, in which gaining access to Malaysia's government procurement market was a particular interest of US firms.[65] However, Malaysia's government procurement policies became "a major sticking point in the negotiations."[66] It refused to engage in negotiations on its government procurement or undertake any procurement commitments. This refusal contributed to ending the FTA negotiations without an agreement.

Highlights of Coverage: Under the TPP, Malaysia made relatively modest government procurement commitments. It opened the procurement of 24 ministries and the Prime Minister's Department.[67] Although its central government coverage was generally comparable to other signatories, its listing of only four other entities fell short of the coverage of such entities by other parties.[68] It specified

---

64. Vietnam applied similar measures in an FTA with the EU, as discussed in Chapter 11.

65. USTR, *2008 Trade Policy Agenda and 2007 Annual Report of the President of the United States on the Trade Agreements Program*, 119, March 2008, https://ustr.gov/archive/assets/Document_Library/Reports_Publications/2008/2008_Trade_Policy_Agenda/asset_upload_file649_14563.pdf.

66. US Library of Congress, Congressional Research Service, *The Proposed U.S.-Malaysia Free Trade Agreement*, by Michael F. Martin, RL33445 (2007), 9, https://crsreports.congress.gov/product/pdf/RL/RL33445/19.

67. Its coverage included government hospitals and clinics under the Ministry of Health.

68. Those entities were the Malaysian Investment Development Authority, Malaysia External Trade Development Corporation, SME Corporation Malaysia, and Malaysia Productivity Corporation.

the services it would open, which included computer and related services. It agreed to open all construction services (except dredging and hillside surfacing) but did not cover any PPPs.

Transitional Measures: The TPP permitted Malaysia to apply several transitional measures when it implemented the agreement. First, it could apply high thresholds during transitional periods ranging from seven to 20 years. It applied the highest and longest threshold to the procurement of construction services.[69] Second, for up to 25 years, Malaysia could exempt "procurement funded by an economic stimulus package in response to a severe nationwide economic crisis" from the TPP requirements. Under a third transitional measure, Malaysia was able to impose offsets on procurement above RM50 million in value for 12 years. Those offsets were restricted to procurement conducted by its Prime Minister's Department or 16 listed ministries. Furthermore, for the first four years, Malaysia could fix the offsets at 60% of the value of the contract, followed by periodic reductions. As a final transitional measure, Malaysia was allowed to delay the implementation of two TPP provisions.[70]

Bumiputera Measures: Traditionally, Malaysia has used government procurement to support national policy objectives such as encouraging greater participation in its economy of Bumiputera, ethnic Malays, who comprised a majority of Malaysia's population. Under the TPP, it was able to protect its Bumiputera by negotiating high thresholds, offsets, permanent set-asides, price preferences, and special measures. It was able to reserve the right to accord Bumiputera status to eligible companies and use set-asides

---

69. Malaysia's construction threshold began at 63 million SDRs, approximately RM315 million, with gradual reductions over 20 years to 14 million SDRs.

70. Malaysia could delay the establishment of an impartial domestic review authority for three years after it entered the TPP. In addition, it was also exempted from dispute settlement provisions relating to government procurement for five years.

and price preferences under its Bumiputera policy.[71] It could set aside annually up to 30% of the total annual value of its covered construction services for Bumiputera. In addition, Malaysia could apply price preferences to Bumiputera suppliers in procurement valued between RM500,000 and RM15 million. The preferences ranged from 3% to 7% for goods and services from a TPP country and between 1.25% and 3.5% for goods and services originating in non-TPP parties. Malaysia reserved the highest price preferences (up to 10%) for Bumiputera goods manufacturers.[72]

According to studies commissioned by its government, Malaysia largely shielded its Bumiputera and SMEs from the impact of the TPP through concessions secured in the negotiations. The concessions applied to government procurement, state-owned enterprises, services, investment, and tariffs.[73] These studies concluded that under the TPP, Malaysia would be able to maintain its practice of using government procurement as a tool for Bumiputera protection and development of SMEs, in particular, in the construction sector, through several measures.

These studies found that Malaysia's ability to apply an initial high threshold for construction services under the TPP excluded all but a small number of construction contracts from coverage. The studies pointed out that in 2014, only 0.7% of government contracts for construction services were above RM300 million. Even when that threshold is reduced to 14 million SDRs after the 20-year transition period, it would likely open very few contracts to the TPP suppliers

---

71. Grier, "Government Procurement," 4.

72. Malaysia also made certain price preferences available to Malaysian suppliers that are not Bumiputera.

73. Institute of Strategic and International Studies (ISIS), *National Interest Analysis of Malaysia's Participation in the Trans-Pacific Partnership*, https://fta.miti. gov.my/miti-fta/resources/ISIS_The_Grand_Finale.pdf, 2015; and PwC, *Study on Potential Economic Impact of TPPA on the Malaysian Economy and Selected Key Economic Sectors*, December 2015, https://fta.miti.gov.my/miti-fta/resources/TPPA_PwC_CBA_-_Final_Report_021215_FINAL_(corrected).pdf.

based on past experience. For example, in 2014, less than 3% of Malaysia's construction service contracts exceeded that level. The reports also pointed out Malaysia's exclusion of PPPs, its economic stimulus packages (for 25 years), and annual set-asides of construction services would allow it to channel procurement to Bumiputera construction companies. Thus, the studies concluded Bumiputera construction firms would be largely unaffected by the TPP.[74]

3.4 Vietnam's Procurement Commitments

During approximately the same period Vietnam engaged in negotiations of the TPP, it was also negotiating an FTA with the EU. It implemented the CPTPP in January 2020 and the EU FTA in July of that year, for the first-time opening its government procurement to foreign suppliers under the two agreements. Vietnam's market access commitments under the agreements illustrated how a developing country could be integrated into major agreements with provisions that facilitate opening its procurement markets.

Covered Entities: Vietnam covered 18 ministries and three other entities at the central government level.[75] It opened only two units of its Ministry of National Defence (Economics and Rescue Departments), limiting the units' obligations to a positive list of goods and services and excluding construction services. It restricted the procurement commitments of its Ministry of Public Security to listed goods, excluding both services and construction services. It also removed construction services from its Ministry of Transport's commitments. In the other entities category, Vietnam listed 38 entities, including the Vietnam News Agency, three national academies, and 34 national hospitals.

---

74. ISIS, *National Interest Analysis*; and PwC, *Study on Potential Economic Impact*.

75. The other central government entities were the Vietnam Social Security, Government Inspectorate, and Committee on Ethnic Minority Affairs.

Goods and Services: Vietnam excluded the procurement of goods such as rice, petroleum oils, books, newspapers, transmission, radar, and other apparatus. Under the TPP, Vietnam opened a relatively minimal list of services. In addition, it applied a condition to its coverage of several services, specifically data network services, electronic message and information services, and computer and related services. For these services, Vietnam required the supplier to be established and operate in Vietnam or be a Vietnamese national. Vietnam also covered most construction services.

Exclusions: Vietnam excluded any form of preference for its SMEs as well as BOT contracts and public works concession contracts from its commitments.

Pharmaceutical Measures: Vietnam applied special measures to its purchase of pharmaceutical products. First, it used different thresholds for its 34 national hospitals to determine whether a pharmaceutical product was covered under the TPP.[76] As a second measure, Vietnam reserved the right to set aside a portion of its annual procurement of pharmaceutical products from its TPP obligations.[77] In a third measure, Vietnam excluded the procurement of distribution services for pharmaceutical products from its commitments. When distribution services are included in

---

76. The thresholds for pharmaceutical products are: (i) for a hospital's consolidated pharmaceutical contract of at least one-year duration or a centralized contract conducted by the Ministry of Health on behalf of hospitals, the threshold starts at 3 million SDRs and is reduced to 2 million SDRs after five years; (ii) for a contract of less than one year, the threshold is 500,000 SDRs; and (iii) for a contract for a single pharmaceutical product, it is 180,000 SDRs.

77. Vietnam could set aside 100% of the value of pharmaceutical contracts during the first three years of the TPP; 65% of the total value in the next seven years; 60% in years 11 to 15; and 50% from the 16th year. Vietnam started with innovative (patented) pharmaceuticals and then moved through five categories of generics (as classified by the Ministry of Health) until it reached the share that was covered for that year to fulfill the share of pharmaceuticals that it committed to open under the TPP each year.

a procurement contract, the supplier, including foreign-invested enterprises, must choose a licensed pharmaceutical distributor in Vietnam to deliver the pharmaceuticals.

Transitional Measures: The TPP permitted Vietnam to apply extensive transitional measures. For the procurement of goods and services, transitional thresholds started at 2 million SDRs for central government entities (to be reduced over 25 years to 130,000 SDRs) and at 3 million SDRs for other entities (to be reduced over five years to 2 million SDRs). For construction services, the transitional threshold for all entities began at 65.2 million SDRs. For central government entities, they would be reduced to 8.5 million SDRs over 15 years. For other entities, they would be reduced to 15 million SDRs over 20 years.

Under the TPP, Vietnam was allowed to impose offsets of any form, including a price preference, for 25 years after it implemented the agreement. It could set an offset level at up to 40% of the annual value of total covered procurement for the first 10 years. But it was required to decrease the offset level to 30% for the next 15 years. Vietnam could request an offset of any amount on a specific contract, provided it did not exceed its annual percentage of total covered procurement subject to offsets.

As another transitional measure, Vietnam could delay the implementation of several TPP obligations. First, it was exempt from certain requirements until its e-procurement system was operational. In the interim, Vietnam could charge a fee for access to its procurement notices when it made them available electronically. It could also omit conditions for participation and limitations on the number of qualified suppliers invited to tender from its notices (provided it included the information in tender documentation). For seven years, it was permitted to limit the period for the submission of tenders to 25 rather than 40 days. Finally, Vietnam was not obligated to include a justification for using limited tendering in post-award notices on the condition it provided such information to any party on request.

The TPP gave Vietnam three years from its implementation of the TPP to establish an impartial domestic review authority.[78] It was also exempted from the agreement's dispute settlement process with respect to government procurement for five years.

4. REGIONAL COMPREHENSIVE ECONOMIC PARTNERSHIP

4.1 Overview

The RCEP was signed in November 2020 by the 10 members of the Association of Southeast Asian Nations (ASEAN)[79] and five countries with which ASEAN had FTAs.[80] The additional five countries, referred to as the 'plus five,' were Australia, China, Japan, South Korea, and New Zealand. The Partnership entered into force on January 1, 2022,[81] following ratification by six ASEAN members (Brunei, Cambodia, Laos, Singapore, Thailand, and Vietnam) and four non-ASEAN countries (Australia, China, Japan, and New Zealand).[82] In 2022, Indonesia, South Korea, and Malaysia

---

78. During that period, suppliers may take their procurement complaints to the procuring entity, as provided in Vietnam's Public Procurement Law.

79. The ASEAN members were Brunei, Cambodia, Indonesia, Laos, Malaysia, Myanmar, Philippines, Singapore, Thailand, and Vietnam.

80. ASEAN, "ASEAN hits historic milestone with signing of RCEP," November 15, 2020, https://asean.org/asean-hits-historic-milestone-with-signing-of-rcep/#:~:-text=JAKARTA%2C%2015%20NOVEMBER%202020%E2%80%93%20It,Economic%20Partnership%20(RCEP)%20Agreement.

81. RCEP, 2022, https://rcepsec.org/legal-text/. The government procurement provisions are in RCEP's Chapter 16 and Annex 16A.

82. ASEAN, "Regional Comprehensive Economic Partnership (RCEP) to enter into force on 1 January 2022," November 3, 2021, https://asean.org/regional-comprehensive-economic-partnership-rcep-to-enter-into-force-on-1-january-2022/.

implemented the agreement, leaving two countries yet to ratify it: Myanmar and the Philippines. RCEP is the world's largest FTA in terms of membership and the first FTA between China, Japan, and South Korea.

India participated in the RCEP negotiations but dropped out at the conclusion of the agreement in 2019. In opting out, India was concerned that the agreement would lead to an influx of goods from China and New Zealand. Such imports could have had a negative impact on India's small businesses as well as its agricultural and dairy sectors. India's issues with RCEP included its major trade deficits with all the RCEP countries and a lack of assurance that it would lead to access to their markets.[83]

The RCEP was intended as an integration instrument. ASEAN countries had negotiated a free trade area among themselves as well as several external FTAs (collectively known as the ASEAN+1 FTAs). The RCEP was designed to integrate the disparate trade agreements between ASEAN nations and their key trading partners into a unified agreement.[84] Since ASEAN+1 FTAs already covered more than 80% of trade liberalized by RCEP, RCEP's economic

83. Suhasini Haider and T.C.A. Sharad Raghavan, "India storms out of RCEP, says trade deal hurts Indian farmers," *The Hindu*, November 4, 2019, https://www.thehindu.com/news/national/india-decides-against-joining-rcep-trade-deal/article29880220.ece?homepage=true; Julien Chaisse, "The Case for Hong Kong Joining RCEP," *East West Forum*, September 2, 2021, https://www.eastasiaforum.org/2021/09/02/the-case-for-hong-kong-joining-rcep/?utm_source=subscribe2&utm_medium=email&utm_campaign=postnotify&utm_id=379496&utm_title=The%20case%20for%20Hong%20Kong%20joining%20RCEP; see also, Asha Sundaram, "India's RCEP exit and its regional future," *East Asia Forum*, April 13, 2022, https://www.eastasiaforum.org/2022/04/13/indias-rcep-exit-and-its-regional-future/?utm_source=subscribe2&utm_medium=email&utm_campaign=postnotify&utm_id=805493&utm_title=India%26rsquo%3Bs%20RCEP%20exit%20and%20its%20regional%20future.

84. Niels Graham, "The RCEP ratification and its implications," *Atlantic Council*, December 3, 2021, https://www.atlanticcouncil.org/blogs/econographics/the-rcep-ratification-and-its-implications/.

impact on ASEAN and its five partners would "not be ground-breaking."[85] Nonetheless, it was "a significant achievement for free trade in Asia through its advancements in rules of origin, intellectual property protection, and tariff reduction."[86]

Common rules of origin governing the amount of a product produced within the region to qualify for tariff benefits was one of the RCEP's most significant elements. According to the US Congressional Research Service, "[t]his simplified regime could facilitate the deepening of regional supply chains by reducing tariffs on semi-finished goods and inputs across RCEP members."[87]

The RCEP and CPTPP share certain similarities. Both are major regional agreements based in Asia. In addition, they have overlapping members: nearly half of RCEP's members and more than 60% of CPTPP's members are parties to both agreements. The countries that are parties to both are Australia, Brunei, Japan, Malaysia, New Zealand, Singapore, and Vietnam. That number will expand if China and other RCEP parties join the CPTPP.

The two regional agreements also shared similarities in their texts. A comparative study found that 30% of RCEP's text duplicated CPTPP's provisions.[88] However, the RCEP's commitments were generally less extensive than those in the CPTPP. For example, the CPTPP's regulatory requirements were far more ambitious in scope and depth than those of the RCEP. It also included chapters on state-owned enterprise reform, the environment, and labor protections, which were not found in the RCEP.[89] Government procurement was another area in which the CPTPP exceeded the RCEP.

85. Graham, "The RCEP ratification."

86. Graham, "The RCEP ratification."

87. US Library of Congress, Congressional Research Service, *Regional Comprehensive and Economic Partnership (RCEP)*, by Cathleen D. Cimino-Isaacs et al., IF11891 (2021), 2, https://crsreports.congress.gov/product/pdf/IF/IF11891.

88. Congressional Research Service, *RCEP*, 2.

89. Graham, "The RCEP ratification."

4.2 Government Procurement Chapter

When the RCEP negotiations were launched in 2013, they did not include government procurement. The RCEP negotiators added procurement in 2017, albeit with narrower aims than the CPTPP. They focused on promoting transparency and developing cooperation across the participating nations,[90] concluding negotiations of the procurement chapter in 2018.[91] The RCEP procurement chapter was modest but represented a small step forward since earlier ASEAN FTAs with the 'plus five' countries did not include any procurement commitments.

The RCEP procurement chapter recognized "the role of government procurement in furthering the economic integration of the region"[92] and limited its commitments to transparency and cooperation. Its transparency obligation required the RCEP parties to make their laws and regulations on procurement by central government entities publicly available and try to make their procurement procedures public. In a nod to international procurement practices, the RCEP required its parties to endeavor to make procurement information available by electronic means and in English.[93]

The RCEP's procurement cooperation provision aimed to develop an understanding of each party's procurement system. It called for an exchange of information that could include procurement measures, electronic procurement systems, technical assistance, and best practices, including those relating to SMEs.[94] The agreement had a single market access provision applying to the procurement

---

90. ASEAN, "Joint leaders' statement on the negotiations of the Regional Comprehensive Economic Partnership (RCEP)," November 14, 2017.

91. ASEAN, "Joint leaders' statement on the Regional Comprehensive Economic Partnership (RCEP) negotiations," November 2018.

92. RCEP, art. 16.3.

93. RCEP, art. 16.4.

94. RCEP, art. 16.5.

opened to international competition. It called on the parties to conduct this procurement in accordance with generally accepted government procurement principles as applied by that party.[95] Its procurement chapter did not impose any obligations on the participating least developed countries: Cambodia, Laos, and Myanmar. In addition, the RCEP's dispute settlement mechanisms did not apply to the procurement chapter.

Finally, the procurement chapter called for a review of the procurement provisions every five years to improve their facilitation of government procurement. Such a review could provide an opportunity to add more extensive procurement rules and market access commitments.[96] If the RCEP parties undertake more substantial procurement commitments, the CPTPP could provide a relevant model, given the overlapping membership in the two agreements.

---

95. RCEP, art. 16.3.

96. "RCEP is designed in the 'ASEAN Way' meaning members must make it a living and evolving agreement." One way that is accomplished is through five-year reviews. Fukunari Kimura, "A framework for ongoing commitments to RCEP success," *East Asia Forum*, April 5, 2022, https://www.eastasiaforum.org/2022/04/05/a-framework-for-ongoing-commitments-to-rcep-success/.

CHAPTER 11

EU AGREEMENTS AND NEGOTIATIONS: PROCUREMENT

1. INTRODUCTION

The European Union (EU) has overtaken the US in negotiating FTAs[1] and now has more FTAs than any other country. It has 50 FTAs in force or provisionally applied,[2] while the US has implemented just 16 FTAs with 20 countries.[3] Furthermore, the EU's FTA negotiations have been particularly active in the decade since the US implemented its last FTAs with new trading partners in 2012.

The EU has been markedly effective in liberalizing procurement markets through negotiations of FTAs with parties to the GPA.

---

1. US Library of Congress, Congressional Research Service, *Bilateral and Regional Trade Agreements: Issues for Congress*, by Brock R. Williams, R45198 (2018), 48, https://fas.org/sgp/crs/row/R45198.pdf.

2. Cecilia Malmström, "The EU should use its trade power strategically," The Peterson Institute for International Economics, January 4, 2022, https://www.piie.com/blogs/realtime-economic-issues-watch/eu-should-use-its-trade-power-strategically.

3. The US FTA with Jordan has only a single provision.

In those FTAs, the EU has offered access to procurement that it withheld in the GPA under its application of strict reciprocity. In return, the other GPA parties have opened procurement they did not cover under the GPA.

The EU has also actively pursued FTAs with developing countries. Its FTA with Vietnam is its most ambitious agreement with such a country. It has completed negotiations of several FTAs with Latin American countries that have not yet been implemented. In 2022, it embarked on negotiations of an FTA with India, with opening procurement as one of the EU's objectives.

Despite its success in negotiating FTAs with other GPA parties, the EU has not been able to negotiate an FTA with the US. Its attempt to negotiate one during President Obama's administration failed, in part as the result of mismatched government procurement goals between the two parties.

While the EU's FTAs are based on the text of the GPA, they often include additional provisions tailored to specific issues relating to its FTA partner or issues of particular interest to the EU, such as the treatment of abnormally low tenders.

2. EU FTA APPROVAL AUTHORITY

In May 2017, the European Court of Justice (ECJ) issued a binding ruling, referred to as Opinion 2/15, that determined the EU had broad authority to approve trade agreements without ratification by its member states.[4] Its decision arose from a request by the European Commission in 2015 to resolve a dispute between the Commission and the Council of the EU, representing the member states, on the extent of the EU's competence in trade and investment matters.

---

4. European Court of Justice, Opinion 2/15 of the Court (Full Court), May 16, 2017, http://curia.europa.eu/juris/document/document.jsf?text=&docid=190727&pageIndex=0&doclang=en&mode=lst&dir=&occ=first&part=1&cid=419600.

The Court was asked to determine whether the EU had the exclusive authority to sign and ratify an FTA with Singapore or whether it had to share approval of that agreement with its member states.[5]

The ECJ confirmed that the EU had exclusive competence for trade and sustainable development matters and foreign direct investment (albeit not for investment dispute settlement and portfolio investments). While the Union's exclusive competence extended to investment market access and investment protection rules, it had to share authority for investment dispute settlement and portfolio investment. The European Commission's Director-General for Trade, Sabine Weyand, pointed out that the Court's ruling "permits the Union to include [trade and sustainable development] chapters in EU-level agreements and to ensure that these are ratified only at [the] EU level."[6] That meant EU FTAs covering market access for goods, competition, intellectual property protection, standards, trade in services, public procurement, and sustainable development (specifically, labor and environmental protections) only require the approval of the Council of the EU and ratification by the European Parliament.

However, the Court determined the EU could not conclude the Singapore FTA on its own as the member states retain authority over its provisions relating to portfolio investments and dispute settlement regimes for investments. The implementation of agreements covering those issues requires ratification by the more than 30 national and regional parliaments in the member states, as well as authorization by the Council and ratification by the European

---

5. European Commission, "The Opinion of the European Court of Justice on the EU-Singapore Trade Agreement and the Division of Competences in Trade Policy, Factsheet," September 2017, https://trade.ec.europa.eu/doclib/docs/2017/september/tradoc_156035.pdf. For an examination of the opinion, see Nikos Lavranos, "In-depth briefing: Mixed exclusivity: The Court of Justice of the EU's Opinion on the EU Singapore FTA," *Borderlex*, May 18, 2017.

6. Sabine Weyand, "Foreword," in *Law and Practice of the Common Commercial Policy. The First 10 Years after the Treaty of Lisbon*, ed. Michael J. Hahn and Guillaume Van der Loo (Leiden and Boston: Brill Nijhoff, 2020).

Parliament. A single national or regional government could block final approval.

Although the Court's decision directly applied to the EU-Singapore agreement, it had ramifications for the EU's then pending trade agreement with Vietnam. It also extended to subsequent agreements that include the areas subject to member state approval. In response to the ECJ ruling, the EU and Singapore separated their trade pact into two agreements to align with the mixed competence found in the ECJ ruling: one was an FTA, and the other was an investment protection agreement (IPA). Subsequently, the EU and Vietnam also divided their agreement into an FTA and an IPA. The FTAs and IPAs had separate ratification tracks, with the EU exclusively responsible for approving the FTA and sharing approval with the member states for the IPA ratification.[7]

3. EU'S TAILORED APPROACH TO PROCUREMENT

In contrast to the US's 'one-size-fits-all' approach to FTAs, the EU varied its approach to negotiating government procurement provisions in trade agreements. In FTAs with GPA parties, the EU insisted on enhanced coverage beyond that found in the GPA. With the neighboring states, such as Ukraine, it negotiated "deep and comprehensive trade agreements [that] envisage the progressive adoption of the EU regime for procurement."[8] In FTAs with

7. European Parliament, "EU-Singapore trade and investment deals pass major milestone," April 1, 2019, https://www.europarl.europa.eu/RegData/etudes/BRIE/2019/637940/EPRS_BRI(2019)637940_EN.pdf.

8. Stephen Woolcock, "Public Procurement in EU FTAs," in *Law and Practice of the Common Commercial Policy. The First 10 Years after the Treaty of Lisbon,* edited by Michael J. Hahn and Guillaume Van der Loo (Leiden and Boston: Brill Nijhoff, 2020), 240–46. For more information, see table 9.1 (summary of procurement provisions in FTAs negotiated by the EU) and Annex 2 (detailed comparisons of procurement provisions in selected agreements with international practice). Woolcock, "Public Procurement," table 9.1 and Annex 2.

middle-income developing economies, such as Colombia and Peru, and Central American FTAs, the EU persuaded its partners to sign up to GPA-type rules on transparency and some commitments on coverage.[9] In agreements with smaller or less-developed economies, the EU accepted only transparency rules similar to–but less comprehensive–than the GPA. One such agreement was the CARIFORUM Economic Partnership Agreement[10] with the Caribbean Community (CARICOM) countries.[11] An even narrower agreement, the EU-Southern African Development Community Economic Partnership Agreement, "simply recognize[d] the importance of transparency in public contracts."[12]

4. EU FTAS WITH GPA PARTNERS

Since 2011, the EU has implemented FTAs with five GPA parties: Canada, Japan, South Korea, Singapore, and the United Kingdom (UK). It also concluded an FTA with New Zealand in 2022. All the FTAs (except with South Korea) are 'GPA-plus,' as they cover procurement the parties do not offer under the GPA. The FTAs with Canada, Japan, and Singapore "illustrate the leverage of [the EU's] application of strict reciprocity in the GPA."[13] In exchange for access to new procurement not covered under the GPA, the EU gave those countries rights to participate in procurement it

---

9. Woolcock, "Public Procurement," 240.

10. The CARIFORUM agreement includes an open-ended rendezvous clause (Article 167(3)) on the negotiation of coverage commitments. Woolcock, "Public Procurement," 245–46.

11. The 15 member states of CARICOM are Antigua and Barbuda, the Bahamas, Barbados, Belize, Dominica, Grenada, Guyana, Haiti, Jamaica, Montserrat, Saint Kitts and Nevis, Saint Lucia, Saint Vincent and the Grenadines, Suriname, and Trinidad and Tobago.

12. Woolcock, "Public Procurement," 246.

13. Jean Heilman Grier, "GPA Reciprocal Conditions: Leverage for Bilateral Agreements," *Public Procurement Law Review* 29 (2020): 273.

withheld under GPA reciprocity clauses. In 2022, the EU was also engaged in FTA negotiations with another GPA party, Australia. The agreements are examined in the following sections in the order in which they were concluded.

4.1 EU-South Korea FTA

The EU and Korea negotiated the EU-South Korea FTA during the negotiations of the GPA 1994 revision but provisionally implemented it in July 2011, before the conclusion of the GPA 2012.[14] It was the most modest of the EU's FTAs with GPA partners. While the EU and South Korea reaffirmed their rights and obligations under the GPA 1994 in the bilateral pact, they agreed to apply the 2007 provisionally agreed GPA text (with several exceptions) to the GPA procurement, which they incorporated into the FTA. One exception modified the GPA prohibition of any requirement that a supplier must have "previously been awarded one or more contracts by a procuring entity of a given Party."[15] The FTA extended the prohibition to any requirement that a "supplier has prior work experience in the territory of that Party" (except when "essential" to meet procurement requirements).[16]

In the FTA, both GPA parties expanded their GPA-covered procurement by covering public-private partnerships (PPPs).[17] The EU opened its public works concessions,[18] and South Korea–its

---

14. EU-South Korea FTA, 2011, https://eur-lex.europa.eu/legal-content/EN/TXT/PDF/?uri=CELEX:22011A0514(01). The government procurement provisions are in the FTA's Chapter Nine and Annex 9. The FTA was formally ratified in 2015.

15. GPA, art. VIII:2.

16. EU-South Korea FTA, art. 9.1(4)(c).

17. EU-South Korea FTA, Annex 9.

18. EU public works concessions are of the same type as public works contracts, except "the consideration for the works to be carried out consists either solely in the right to exploit the work or in this right together with payment." EU-South Korea FTA, Annex 9.

build-operate-transfer (BOT) contracts.[19] They applied this coverage to projects undertaken by their GPA-covered central and subcentral government entities with a procurement value above 15 million SDRs. The FTA limited the rules applicable to BOT contracts and public works concessions to national treatment and non-discrimination obligations and several procedural requirements.[20] In addition, the FTA directed the parties to ensure the availability of an effective system for review of authorities' procurement decisions while permitting measures to encourage the participation of SMEs in BOT contracts and public works concessions.

Under the FTA, South Korea also offered all local governments located in Seoul City, Busan City, Incheon City, and Gyeonggi-do province. Subsequently, both parties incorporated their FTA coverage into the GPA 2012. South Korea extended this new coverage to all parties, whereas the EU limited it to select parties based on reciprocity.

4.2 EU-Canada Comprehensive Economic and Trade Agreement

The EU concluded its most ambitious FTA, the EU-Canada Comprehensive Economic and Trade Agreement (CETA), in October 2013.[21] Before it was implemented, the European Commission announced it would treat CETA as a "mixed" agreement and share

---

19. South Korea also covered BOT contracts in its FTA with the US.

20. The procedural requirements included the publication of a notice of the intended contract and the contract award. The notice of the intended contract must include a list and brief description of conditions for supplier participation and "the main criteria" for awarding a contract. EU-South Korea FTA, Annex 9.

21. CETA, 2017, https://www.international.gc.ca/trade-commerce/trade-agreements-accords-commerciaux/agr-acc/ceta-aecg/text-texte/toc-tdm.aspx-?lang=eng. The government procurement provisions are in CETA's Chapter 19 and Annex 19, which is comprised of Annex 19-A, Market Access Schedule of Canada, and Annex 19-B, Market Access Schedule of the EU.

its approval with its member states.[22] The Commission took this action rather than wait for the ECJ's ruling on the scope of the EU's authority to conclude trade agreements. Hence, following the approval of CETA by the Council of the EU and the European Parliament, the EU implemented it (except for its investment provisions) on a provisional basis in September 2017.[23] CETA remained a provisional agreement in 2022 as it had not yet been ratified by all the national and regional parliaments of the member states.

CETA exemplified how GPA parties to an FTA can expand procurement commitments beyond their GPA coverage.[24] While both Canada and the EU offered procurement they did not cover under the GPA, Canada significantly exceeded its GPA commitments, especially subcentral coverage. The EU had identified that coverage as one of its fundamental objectives and even a condition for negotiating any trade agreement with Canada.[25] It was successful as "Canada had been keen to negotiate for some time because of its desire to diversify from its dependence on the USA."[26]

---

22. European Commission, "European Commission proposes signature and conclusion of EU-Canada trade deal," July 5, 2016, https://ec.europa.eu/ commission/presscorner/detail/en/IP_16_2371.

23. The provisional application did not include investment protection, portfolio investment, investment dispute resolution, financial services provisions concerning portfolio investment, and resolution of investment disputes between investors and states. European Parliamentary Research Service, *CETA implementation. SMEs and regions in focus: in-depth analysis*, by Jana Titievska and Ioannis Zachariadis, November 1, 2019, https://op.europa.eu/en/ publication-detail/-/publication/5ab2969b-0f38-11ea-8c1f-01aa75ed71a1.

24. Grier, "GPA Reciprocal Conditions," 285.

25. Paul M. Lalonde, "International Procurement Law: Key Developments 2019–Part II: The Impact of Trade Agreements on Sub-national Procurement– the Example of Canada," *2019 Thomson Reuters' Government Contracts Year in Review Conference Briefs* (2020): 2–14.

26. Woolcock, "Public Procurement," 244.

Of particular significance, for the first time, Canada offered coverage of its so-called MASH sector comprised of municipalities, municipal organizations, school boards, and publicly funded academic, health, and social services entities.[27] Canada provided that coverage for all provinces and territories (except the Yukon). The EU reciprocated by giving Canada access to the procurement of all its regional or local contracting authorities and entities that included hospitals, schools, universities, as well as entities providing social services (housing, social insurance, day care). Canada also adopted the EU threshold of 200,000 SDRs for goods and services purchased by its subcentral entities in place of its higher GPA threshold of 355,000 SDRs.

Under CETA, Canada opened the procurement of 20 central government entities not covered under the GPA. The EU, in turn, gave Canada access to the central government entities of its member states withheld under the GPA.[28]

In the other entities category, Canada substantially exceeded its GPA coverage of 10 entities by opening to EU suppliers the procurement of all Crown corporations at the federal level and most Crown corporations at the provincial level, as well as corporations controlled by municipalities. It also offered mass transit procurement in all provinces (subject to certain restrictions). In purchases of mass transit vehicles, the provinces of Ontario and Quebec could require the successful bidder to provide up to 25% local content. In addition, Quebec could stipulate that the final assembly must be done in Canada.

The EU provided Canada with access to most utility sectors denied under the GPA, namely drinking water, electricity, urban transport, and transport by railways, but continued to withhold

---

27. Grier, "GPA Reciprocal Conditions," 285.

28. The EU did not extend to Canada the comprehensive coverage of its member states' central government entities it accords to certain GPA partners. Grier, "GPA Reciprocal Conditions," 285.

procurement of airports and maritime or inland ports. Extending commitments beyond its GPA coverage, the EU opened the procurement of its utilities providing gas or heat. In addition, both FTA partners opened more services to each other than under the GPA.

CETA also covered two forms of PPPs: EU works concessions contracts and a Canadian type of BOT contracts.[29] Both parties provided this coverage for contracts awarded by their central and subcentral government entities. In addition, Canada covered such contracts of its Crown corporations and other listed government enterprises. However, since the EU excluded its utilities from these commitments, Canada did not open BOT-type contracts undertaken by airports, railways, ports, water authorities, electric utilities, or gas authorities. As in the EU-South Korea FTA, Canada and the EU limited the obligations applying to these projects to non-discrimination, transparency requirements, and domestic review procedures.

CETA's procurement text adhered closely to the GPA 2012. It included provisions tailored to the bilateral arrangement as well as several elaborations. For example, as in the EU-South Korea FTA, CETA generally prohibited requiring prior work experience in the party's territory. It also simplified the process for the parties to modify their market access annexes.[30]

---

29. Canada opened construction services contracts that involve "as complete or partial consideration, any grant to the supplier of the construction service, for a specified period of time, of temporary ownership or a right to control and operate the civil or building work resulting from such contract, and demand payment for the use of such work for the duration of the contract." CETA, Annex 19-A.

30. CETA's modification process included a notice to the other party of a proposed modification and an offer of compensation (when necessary) to maintain a comparable level of coverage. The other party may object to the proposed compensation and the characterization of the modification. CETA, art. 19.18.

4.3 EU-Singapore FTA

The EU-Singapore FTA (EUSFTA) was concluded in 2014, but its implementation was delayed until the ECJ resolved the dispute between the EU and its member states over approval authority. Following the Court's ruling, the EU and Singapore separated the original agreement into an FTA and an IPA. The FTA was finally implemented on November 21, 2019.[31] The EUSFTA extended the parties' government procurement commitments beyond their GPA coverage in four areas: central government coverage, utilities and other entities, PPPs, and services.[32]

In their expansion of central government coverage, the EU followed its CETA approach and gave Singapore access to the central government entities of its member states withheld under the GPA.[33] Singapore significantly reduced the goods and services threshold for its central government entities to 50,000 SDRs (from its GPA threshold of 130,000 SDRs). Both parties built on their GPA coverage of utilities and other entities in the second area, with Singapore more than doubling its coverage of other entities from 23 entities to 57 entities. In turn, the EU reciprocated with access to the procurement of all its utilities, including the railway sector, withheld under the GPA.

The EUSFTA's procurement chapter expanded the third area, PPPs, by including a provision to cover BOT contracts.[34] The EU gave Singapore access to its works concessions under the same conditions as it did to South Korea and Canada. In expanding the

---

31. EUSFTA, 2019, accessed June 7, 2022, https://policy.trade.ec.europa.eu/eu-trade-relationships-country-and-region/countries-and-regions/singapore/eu-singapore-agreement/texts-agreements_en. The government procurement provisions are in the FTA's Chapter 9 and Annexes 9-A through 9-I.

32. Grier, "GPA Reciprocal Conditions," 287.

33. Under the GPA, the EU withheld a number of central government entities of its member states from Singapore.

34. This provision is also found in the US-Singapore FTA.

final area, the procurement of services, Singapore opened several service categories not covered under the GPA. Its expanded coverage gave it access to comparable EU services.[35]

As with other FTAs, the EUSFTA's procurement rules follow the GPA 2012 and added several provisions. They allow the parties to remove a covered entity when it is no longer under government control or influence, which the FTA defined separately for each party.[36] The text also permitted procuring entities to refer to eco-labels in the EU or green labels in Singapore in their technical specifications (subject to certain conditions). In addition, the EUSFTA replicated the prior experience prohibition found in the EU-South Korea FTA and CETA. It also allowed a procuring entity to verify whether a tender with a price that was abnormally lower than other tenders was the result of foreign subsidies and, if so, to reject it.[37]

---

35. Singapore gained access to services that included computer-related services, telecommunications services, land transport services, maintenance and repair services, sewage and refuse disposal services, and architecture and engineering services. Singapore Ministry of Trade and Industry, "European Parliament Approves EU-Singapore Free Trade Agreement and EU-Singapore Investment Procurement Agreement," February 13, 2019, https://www.mti.gov.sg/-/media/MTI/Microsites/EUSFTA/Press-Release-on-Approval-by-European-Parliament-of-EUSFTA-and-EUSIPA-final.pdf.

36. For the EU, it is when the entity performs a competitive activity and, for Singapore, when the entity has been privatized. EUSFTA, art. 9.18(2).

37. The EUSFTA provides that: "Where a procuring entity establishes that a tender is abnormally low because the supplier has obtained subsidies, it may reject the tender on that ground alone only after having consulted with the supplier and the latter is unable to prove, within a sufficient period fixed by the procuring entity, that the subsidy in question was granted in compliance with the disciplines relating to subsidies laid down in this Agreement." EUSFTA, art. 9.14.7.

4.4 EU-Japan Economic Partnership Agreement

The EU-Japan Economic Partnership Agreement (EPA) was implemented on February 1, 2019.[38] It was the third FTA in which the EU provided access to procurement withheld under the GPA in exchange for rights to participate in GPA-plus procurement.[39]

Even though Japan did not offer any new central government entities, the EU gave it the right to participate in 13 central government entities of its member states denied under the GPA. Japan significantly expanded its subcentral coverage by adding entities that were both subject to its Local Independent Administrative Agency Act and established by a subcentral entity listed in its GPA schedule. This coverage included 51 universities and colleges, 25 hospitals or medical centers, and 11 technical or industrial research centers. Japan also offered the procurement of 48 core cities, which are cities with a population of approximately 300,000 and contain roughly 15% of Japan's population, with limited obligations.[40] Japan also offered the EU access to the production, transport, and distribution of electricity by 28 prefectures and cities. This is procurement excluded under the GPA. Japan also added a designated city not covered under the GPA.

In response to Japan's coverage of its core cities, the EU reciprocated with access to its local administrative units with a population between 200,000 and 499,999. Like Japan, it limited its commitments to a non-discrimination obligation. The EU also matched

---

38. EU-Japan EPA, 2019, accessed June 7, 2022, https://policy.trade.ec.europa.eu/eu-trade-relationships-country-and region/countries-and-regions/japan/eu-japan-agreement/eu-japan-agreement-chapter-chapter_en. The government procurement provisions are in the FTA's Chapter 10 and Annex 10 (Section A for the EU and Section B for Japan).

39. Grier, "GPA Reciprocal Conditions," 286.

40. Japan limited the commitments of the core cities to national treatment in the procurement of goods and services conducted under open tendering. EU-Japan EPA, Annex 10, section B.

Japan's coverage of hospitals and universities with similar coverage of EU entities governed by public law and provided an extensive 'indicative list' of those entities.[41] Japan also covered the procurement of six other entities outside the GPA.[42]

Japan opened procurement of GPA-excluded goods and services pertaining to the operational safety of transportation to EU suppliers. It opened that procurement by subcentral entities and five railway-related entities.[43] In response, the EU allowed Japanese suppliers to participate in its GPA coverage of procurement of railway equipment and rolling stock by entities subject to its Utilities Directive and providing or operating railway networks.[44]

The EU and Japan covered more services under their EPA than the GPA. Japan added 21 service categories for its central government entities and 11 categories for its subcentral entities. Their exchange of services included telecommunications-related services and food and beverage serving services for their central government entities, and management consulting services and beverage serving services for their subcentral entities. The EU limited its food and beverage services to a national treatment regime and purchases above €750,000.

The EU-Japan EPA generally incorporated the GPA 2012 and added several rules. One new rule, directed at Japan, applied to the business evaluations (*keishin*), which suppliers must undergo

---

41. An 'indicative list' is a list of entities that are covered, but it is not a definitive list and thus can be changed.

42. The added entities included the Information Technology Promotion Agency and Pharmaceutical and Medical Devices Agency. EU-Japan EPA, Annex 10, section B.

43. The operational safety exclusion was not applied to the Hokkaido Railway Company, Japan Freight Railway Company, Japan Railway Construction Transport and Technology Agency, Shikoku Railway Company, and Tokyo Metro Co. EU-Japan EPA, Annex 10, section B.

44. The EU and Japan implemented their commitments relating to railway procurement in February 2020, one year after the EPA entered into force, EU-Japan EPA, Annex 10, section A and section B.

to tender in construction works procurement. Japan's Construction Business Act requires these evaluations. Japan committed its authorities to not discriminate against EU suppliers in the evaluations and treat the activities and qualifications "realised outside Japan" as equivalent to those performed in Japan.[45] The EPA also required the electronic publication of intended and planned procurement notices.

Similar to other EU FTAs, the EPA prohibited a requirement of prior experience within the party's territory. In addition, the EPA followed the Singapore FTA in allowing procuring entities to verify with a supplier whether an abnormally low price was the result of subsidies, but it did not provide for the rejection of such a tender. The bilateral rules also expanded on the GPA provisions relating to the administrative authorities that hear supplier challenges under domestic review mechanisms[46] and possible corrective actions to address these challenges.[47] Finally, the EPA elaborated on the process for modifying coverage.

4.5 EU-UK FTA

The EU and the UK defined their post-Brexit trade relationship in the EU-UK FTA, which was included in a larger EU-UK Trade and Cooperation Agreement.[48] The Agreement was implemented

---

45. EU-Japan EPA, art. 10.6(2).

46. The EPA stipulated that when a party has designated an administrative authority to hear supplier challenges, it must ensure, among other things, that the authority's members are independent, "secure from external influence," and at least one member has qualifications equivalent to those of judges or lawyers. EU-Japan EPA, art. 10.12(1).

47. The EPA expanded the corrective actions available in domestic reviews to include removing discriminatory technical, economic, or financial specifications, repeating the procurement procedure, setting aside the award decision, adopting a new contract award, and terminating the contract. EU-Japan EPA, art. 10.12(5).

48. EU-UK Trade and Cooperation Agreement (EU-UK FTA), April 30, 2021, https://ec.europa.eu/info/relations-united-kingdom/eu-uk-trade-and-cooperation-agreement_en. The government procurement provisions are in articles 276-94 and Annex 25.

provisionally on January 1, 2021, with full implementation on May 1, 2021, following the European Parliament's approval. In the EU-UK FTA, the parties extended their commitments beyond the GPA in two areas. First, they covered entities engaged in gas or heat activities.[49] Second, each covered privately owned entities engaged in such activities and operating on the basis of special or exclusive rights granted by an EU member state or the UK.[50]

Both partners also added several categories of services to their GPA commitments, including hotel and restaurant services, food and beverage serving services, telecommunications-related services, real estate services, other business services, and education services. Further, they limited the coverage of hotel and restaurant, food and beverage serving, and education services to a national treatment regime with the same thresholds as in the EU-Japan EPA. Despite basing their services coverage on a positive list, both parties explicitly excluded two categories of services: human health and administrative health care services and supply services of nursing and medical personnel.

While the text of the EU-UK FTA procurement chapter was based on the GPA 2012, it added several provisions. For instance, one addition required all notices relating to covered procurement, including contract awards, to be directly accessible electronically. Another prohibited the requirement of prior experience within the territory of the party conducting the procurement. A third addition, similar to EU FTAs with Japan and Singapore, allowed a procuring entity that receives a tender with an abnormally low price to verify whether the price considered the grant of subsidies. Finally, a new provision set conditions for procuring entities to take into account environmental, labor, and social considerations

---

49. These are contracting entities subject to the EU's utilities directive or the UK's utilities contract regulations. EU-UK FTA, Annex 25.

50. The EU provided Canada with similar access in CETA but limited it to contracting authorities.

throughout the procurement. Such considerations must be compatible with FTA rules and indicated in a notice or tender documentation.[51] The EU-UK FTA also elaborated on the requirements for domestic review, as did the EU-Japan EPA.

Finally, the EU-UK FTA included a national treatment obligation that extended beyond the procurement specifically covered under the agreement. It required each party to accord national treatment to locally established suppliers of the other party in any procurement. No other EU FTA included such a provision.[52]

4.6 EU-New Zealand FTA

On June 30, 2022, the EU and New Zealand concluded negotiations of the EU-New Zealand FTA. The parties are to sign the agreement after it is adopted by the Council and implement it following the European Parliament's approval and New Zealand's ratification.[53]

Under the FTA's government procurement provisions, the two partners agreed to open procurement beyond their GPA commitments on a reciprocal basis.[54] New Zealand added two central government entities to its GPA list.[55] For its part, the EU provides New Zealand with access to the approximately 200 entities it withheld under the GPA.

The EU's persistent interest in gaining access to more subcentral coverage, as reflected in its earlier FTAs, was further demonstrated

---

51. EU-UK FTA, art. 285.

52. EU-UK FTA, art. 288.

53. European Commission, "EU–New Zealand Trade Agreement: Unlocking sustainable economic growth," June 30, 2022, https://ec.europa.eu/commission/presscorner/detail/en/ip_22_4158.

54. EU-New Zealand FTA, accessed July 22, 2022, https://policy.trade.ec.europa.eu/eu-trade-relationships-country-and-region/countries-and-regions/new-zealand/eu-new-zealand-agreement/text-agreement_en. The government procurement provisions are in the FTA's Chapter 14 and appendices.

55. They are the Ministry of Housing and Urban Development and the Pike River Recovery Agency.

in this agreement. New Zealand significantly expanded its GPA list of subcentral entities from 18 to 88. However, it limited the commitments of the newly covered city, district, and regional councils to transport projects funded by the New Zealand Transport Agency. New Zealand provided similar increased coverage of its other entities, jumping from 19 under the GPA to 82 under the FTA. According to the EU, this coverage comprised all public authorities whose procurement is regulated by the New Zealand Procurement Rules. This included Crown Agents, Autonomous Crown Entities, Independent Crown Entities, Crown Entity companies, and Public Finance Act Schedule 4A Companies.[56]

The FTA also committed the parties to enter negotiations to improve coverage of subcentral and other entities if New Zealand's local authorities, state services, or state sector entities were covered under another international trade agreement or required to follow the country's Government Procurement Rules.

The EU reciprocated with coverage of the procurement of health-related goods (pharmaceuticals and medical devices) by regional government entities and the procurement of public utility providers in the fields of ports and airports. The two partners' services coverage is the same as in the GPA: New Zealand excludes the same services, and the EU maintains its positive list of covered services.

The FTA incorporated most of the GPA text and added several disciplines. They require the electronic publication of all notices and contract awards and prohibit limits on the number of suppliers invited to submit a tender "with the intention of avoiding effective competition."[57] The FTA also allows procuring entities "to take into account environmental, labour and social considerations related to

56. European Commission, "Key elements of the EU-New Zealand trade agreement," June 30, 2022, https://policy.trade.ec.europa.eu/news/key-elements-eu-new-zealand-trade-agreement-2022-06-30_en.

57. EU-New Zealand FTA, art. 14.2(1)-(3).

the object of the procurement," provided they are non-discriminatory and indicated in the notice of intended procurement or tender documentation.[58] It further permits the parties to take appropriate measures to ensure compliance with their national and international environmental, labor, and social laws, regulations, obligations, and standards provided that they are not discriminatory. In addition, as in other EU FTAs, the EU-New Zealand FTA prohibits requiring prior experience in the territory of a party and includes provisions on modifications of coverage.

5. EU FTAS WITH NON-GPA PARTNERS

5.1 EU-Vietnam FTA

The EU-Vietnam FTA,[59] implemented on August 1, 2020,[60] was the EU's "most ambitious free trade deal" with a developing country.[61] The two trading partners concluded a trade pact in December 2015, but after the 2017 ECJ ruling on EU approval authority, they split it into two agreements, as the EU had done with its Singapore agreement. On June 30, 2019, they signed both an FTA and an IPA.[62]

---

58. EU-New Zealand FTA, art. 14.2(4).

59. EU-Vietnam FTA, 2020, accessed June 7, 2022, https://ec.europa.eu/trade/policy/in-focus/eu-vietnam-agreement/. The government procurement provisions are in the FTA's Chapter 9 and Annex 9-A, EU's market access commitments, and Annex 9-B, Vietnam's market access commitments.

60. European Commission, "EU-Vietnam trade agreement enters into force," July 31, 2020, https://trade.ec.europa.eu/doclib/press/index.cfm?id=2175&title=EU-Vietnam-trade-agreement-enters-into-force.

61. European Commission, "EU-Viet Nam free trade agreement–Joint press statement by Commissioner Malmström and Minister Tran Tuan Anh," June 30, 2019, https://policy.trade.ec.europa.eu/news/eu-viet-nam-free-trade-agreement-joint-press-statement-commissioner-malmstrom-and-minister-tran-tuan-2019-06-30_en.

62. Milan Schreuer, "E.U. Signs Trade Deal with Vietnam," *New York Times*, June 30, 2019, https://www.nytimes.com/2019/06/30/business/european-union-trade-vietnam.html.

For Vietnam, the EU FTA was one of two FTAs negotiated and implemented at approximately the same time. The other was the 11-country Comprehensive and Progressive Trans-Pacific Partnership (CPTPP). A comparison of key elements of the two agreements illustrates the scope of Vietnam's commitments to open its government procurement to foreign suppliers for the first time and the special measures necessary to facilitate that market opening. Overall, Vietnam opened slightly more procurement under the EU FTA than under the CPTPP.

The FTA's procurement chapter was modeled on the GPA 2012. It permitted Vietnam to apply very high thresholds during a 15-year transition period.[63] Vietnam's transitional thresholds started at 1.5 million SDRs for goods and services purchased by central government entities, three million SDRs for such purchases by subcentral entities and other entities, and 40 million SDRs for all construction services. It was required to reduce these thresholds over the transition period. Vietnam's permanent thresholds were the same as the EU thresholds for central government entities (130,000 SDRs for goods and services and five million SDRs for construction services) but higher for the other two categories of entities: one million SDRs for goods and services (five times the EU threshold) and 15 million SDRs for construction services (triple the EU threshold).

Under the FTA, Vietnam opened the same central government entities as in the CPTPP, except for the Ministry of Public Security, which it did not cover in the EU agreement. It also applied the same limitations. The EU provided Vietnam with access to most of its GPA-covered central government entities.[64] In contrast to its exclusion of subcentral entities in the CPTPP, Vietnam opened

---

63. EU-Vietnam FTA, Annex 9-B.

64. Several member states, notably France, Bulgaria, and Poland, did not provide Vietnam with access to all their GPA-listed entities. EU-Vietnam FTA, Annex 9-A.

the procurement of Hanoi and Ho Chi Minh City to EU suppliers. The EU, in turn, provided Vietnam's suppliers with limited subcentral access. It opened cities-regions, such as the regions of Brussels and Berlin, and contracting authorities that provide health or higher education services or carry out research activities and provided indicative lists of the entities. The FTA committed the parties to "further negotiations on the coverage of additional subcentral government entities no later than 15 years" after its implementation.[65]

In its FTA with the EU, Vietnam listed 42 other entities (in contrast to 38 under the CPTPP), including the Vietnam News Agency, Vietnam Railways, Vietnam Electricity, two national universities, and more than 30 hospitals. The EU gave Vietnam access to procurement by utilities engaged in electricity and railway services and provided indicative entity lists.

Vietnam excluded certain goods from its commitments, as it did under the CPTPP.[66] The EU and Vietnam generally opened comparable services, with Vietnam offering several services that it did not cover under the CPTPP. Vietnam explicitly excluded procurement of storage or hosting of government data and related services from its commitments, even though its service coverage is based on a positive list. Both parties covered all construction services.

The EU-Vietnam FTA allowed Vietnam to apply special provisions to its purchase of pharmaceutical products, as in the CPTPP. It also permitted Vietnam to apply preferences for its SMEs, subject to more stringent conditions than in the CPTPP. Vietnam may only use preferences for SMEs with no more than 500 permanent full-time employees in procurement (excluding construction services) with an estimated value of 260,000 SDRs or less.

---

65. EU-Vietnam FTA, art. 9.22(3).

66. Those goods included rice, oils, a wide range of printed materials, automatic data processing machines, magnetic or optical readers, base stations, and transmission and radar apparatus. EU-Vietnam FTA, Annex 9-B.

Both the EU FTA and the CPTPP allowed Vietnam to request offsets in any form, including price preferences but differed in their application. The EU FTA allowed offsets for 18 years in contrast to 25 years under the CPTPP. While both agreements applied the same offset percentages—40% for the first 10 years and 30% for the remainder of the offset period—they differed in their application. The EU agreement applied the percentages to each contract's value, whereas the CPTPP applied offsets as a percent of the total value of Vietnam's covered procurement.

Like the CPTPP, the EU-Vietnam FTA exempted Vietnam from dispute settlement challenges relating to its procurement obligations for five years. But the EU FTA did not give Vietnam additional time to establish a domestic review system, as did the CPTPP. In delaying the implementation of other provisions, the EU FTA set a 10-year limit. In contrast, the CPTPP allowed implementation to be postponed until Vietnam's electronic procurement system was operational (except for a seven-year limit on a reduced tendering period). Both agreements also allowed Vietnam to delay the implementation of several other provisions.[67]

5.2 EU-Mexico Trade Agreement

When in April 2018, the EU and Mexico announced an 'agreement in principle' to modernize the trade part of a 1997 EU-Mexico Global Agreement, they had not determined the exact scope of the opening of their public procurement. In that preliminary agreement, Mexico committed to negotiating with its states on minimum coverage of their procurement before the agreement was

---

67. The delayed provisions included requirements to publish notices of intended procurement by electronic means, impose no fees for accessing electronic notices, provide specified information in notices of intended procurement, include justifications for the use of limited tendering in post-award notices, and provide 40 days for tenders. EU-Vietnam FTA, Annex 9-B.

signed.[68] Two years later, in April 2020, the EU and Mexico concluded negotiations of "the last outstanding element" of their new trade agreement.[69] Mexico pledged to open its state procurement for the first time. Overall, it agreed to provide the EU with access to more procurement than it covered under either the US-Mexico-Canada Agreement (USMCA) or the CPTPP.

Mexico committed to bring the procurement of half of its 32 states, including its federal district, under the agreement.[70] It would delay the application of the agreement to one state (Jalisco) for three years after the agreement is signed. Mexico promised to add two more states (Aguascalientes and Coahuila) within two years of signing the agreement and further extend its subcentral coverage within five years of signature. The Mexican states committed to open the procurement of government agencies and other entities such as universities, hospitals, authorities, and institutes.[71] Veracruz would be exempt from requirements to use electronic procurement for four years.

Mexico offered more central government entities under the EU agreement than the USMCA or the CPTPP but applied comparable thresholds. In addition, it covered 64 other entities under the EU

68. European Commission, "EU and Mexico reach new agreement on trade," April 21, 2018, https://ec.europa.eu/commission/presscorner/detail/en/IP_18_782; New EU-Mexico agreement: The Agreement in Principle and its texts, April 26, 2018, https://trade.ec.europa.eu/doclib/press/index.cfm?id=1833. The government procurement provisions are in the FTA's Chapter 21 and Annex 21-A, EU's market access commitments, and Annex 21-B, Mexico's market access commitments.

69. European Commission, "EU and Mexico conclude negotiations for new trade agreement," April 28, 2020, https://trade.ec.europa.eu/doclib/press/index.cfm?id=2142.

70. The states are Chihuahua, Ciudad de México, Colima, Durango, Estado de México, Guanajuato, Jalisco, Morelos, Nuevo León, Puebla, Querétaro, San Luis Potosí, Veracruz, and Zacatecas. EU-Mexico FTA, Annex 21-B.

71. Mexico excluded procurement related to its state penitentiary systems as well as specific procurement of several states. EU-Mexico FTA, Annex 21-B.

FTA in contrast to 36 other entities under the USMCA and CPTPP. The additional entities included hospitals and port administrations. Mexico specified its coverage of services under a negative list under which it covered all services except those listed as excluded. Its services coverage was the same under the EU FTA and the CPTPP, with the exception of opening the advertising services only for the EU. In addition, Mexico did not open public utility services, including telecommunications, transmission, water, energy, and transportation services, under the agreement. As in other FTAs, the EU used a positive list to specify its services coverage.

As in the USMCA and the CPTPP, Mexico was permitted to set aside a portion of its contracts from its EU FTA obligations. *Petróleos Mexicanos* and the *Comisión Federal de Electricidad* could impose a local content requirement in turnkey or major integrated projects. Under the USMCA and CPTPP, this local content provision applied to all entities.

For its part, the EU offered Mexico reciprocal access to the European procurement market, including access to its utilities operating in the electricity, water, airports, ports, and urban transport sectors. It also opened certain categories of regional contracting authorities to Mexico. Both parties undertook PPP commitments: the EU provided Mexican companies with access to work concessions awarded by its central government entities in exchange for participation in Mexico's PPPs. Unlike their exclusion in the USMCA and CPTPP, Mexico opened such contracts for its central government and other entities to EU suppliers.[72] These projects are not subject to the obligations relating to notices and domestic review procedures.

---

72. Mexico covers "projects developed under a scheme, with the purpose of providing services to the public sector, wholesalers, intermediaries or final consumers which are implemented through a long-term contractual relationship between a public authority and a private economic operator, in which infrastructure is totally or partially provided by the private economic operator." EU-Mexico FTA, Annex 21-B.

The text of the EU-Mexico agreement's procurement chapter is aligned with the GPA 2012. Like other FTAs, it added new disciplines, including an anti-corruption provision requiring each party to provide appropriate measures to prevent corruption and eliminate potential conflicts of interest in public procurement. Another permitted consideration of environmental and social elements during the procurement process provided they were non-discriminatory and linked to the procurement's subject matter. Both parties were obligated to publish all procurement notices on a single website.

For the EU, the bilateral agreement is a "mixed" agreement under the ECJ ruling, which requires approval by both the EU (the Council of the EU and the European Parliament) and the member states. In mid-2022, the EU and Mexico were engaged in consultations on "whether to divide up the agreement into a political agreement and into a strictly 'trade'-focused agreement in order to facilitate ratification (the EU's preferred choice) or to ratify it as one document, preferred by Mexico."[73]

5.3 EU-Mercosur Agreement

The EU agreed to exchange government procurement commitments with Argentina, Brazil, Paraguay, and Uruguay, the founding members of Mercosur, the South American bloc.[74] In June 2019, the

---

73. "Week in Brussels: National Board of Trade in Brussels, Chile, Mexico, Mercosur, China," *Borderlex*, May 13, 2022, https://borderlex.net/2022/05/13/week-in-brussels-national-board-of-trade-in-brussels-chile-mexico-mercosur-china/.

74. Mercosur, or the Southern Common Market, is an economic and political bloc comprised of Argentina, Brazil, Paraguay, and Uruguay. Venezuela was suspended indefinitely in 2016. "Mercosur: South America's Fractious Trade Bloc," *Council on Foreign Relations*, December 17, 2021, https://www.cfr.org/backgrounder/mercosur-south-americas-fractious-trade-bloc?utm_source=dailybrief&utm_medium=email&utm_campaign=DailyBrief2021Dec23&utm_term=DailyNewsBrief.

EU and the four countries reached an agreement in principle on a new trade arrangement,[75] which was part of a wider Association Agreement between the two regions. They published their market access annexes for government procurement two years later, in July 2021.[76]

The agreement's government procurement chapter closely followed the GPA 2012. It committed the Mercosur countries to provide broad coverage of the three branches of their central governments (executive, legislative, and judicial). Regarding subcentral coverage, Paraguay listed 17 subcentral governments, while Argentina, Brazil, and Uruguay only agreed to consult with their entities to reach "a satisfactory level of coverage."[77] Brazil and Argentina committed to concluding these consultations within two years after the agreement entered into force.

Only Uruguay covered all goods and services, with the sole exception of financial services. Argentina and Brazil excluded several categories of goods and listed the services that they would open under the agreement. Both covered works concessions. Paraguay covered several categories of services but excluded all construction services.

The agreement permits the Mercosur countries to apply transitional thresholds for 15 years (18 years for Paraguay) for the procurement of goods and services and five years for construction services. They will then apply permanent thresholds for goods and

---

75. European Commission, "EU and Mercosur reach agreement on trade," June 28, 2019, http://trade.ec.europa.eu/doclib/press/index.cfm?id=2039.

76. European Commission, "Trade part of the EU-Mercosur Association Agreement, Government Procurement" (EU-Mercosur Agreement), https://trade.ec.europa.eu/doclib/docs/2019/july/tradoc_158160.%20Government%20Procurement.pdf. The procurement provisions are in a government procurement chapter and four appendices.

77. It was defined as coverage of subcentral governments that generated at least 65% of the GDP for each country. See, for example, EU-Mercosur Agreement, Argentina, Appendix I, Annex 2.

services of 130,000 SDRs (except Paraguay will apply a 580,000 SDRs threshold). All (except Uruguay) will apply a five million SDRs threshold for construction services. Uruguay will apply a threshold of 5.6 million SDRs without any transition period.[78]

The Mercosur countries can also apply other transitional measures. Argentina may impose any type of offsets for 15 years, beginning at 40% of the value of the procurement. In addition, Argentina can apply public procurement programs aimed at favoring micro, small, and medium enterprises through price preferences and the right to improve the original tender offer. However, it must make access to such programs equally available to comparable EU enterprises registered in Argentina. Brazil's defense ministry and several other entities may apply offsets for eight years. Brazil may also apply price preferences up to 10% and set-asides up to 25% for its micro and small enterprises.

The agreement allows Paraguay to delay the application of the procurement chapter for three years after it enters into force. The EU will provide Paraguay with access to its procurement when it opens its procurement. For 18 years after it implements the trade pact, Paraguay may apply price preferences of 20% to domestic products and services[79] and may also apply offsets for 10 years under certain conditions.

The EU offered the Mercosur countries access to three EU institutions and a list of central government entities of its member states. If Argentina, Brazil, and Uruguay provide satisfactory

---

78. The Mercosur countries will start at different transitional levels for the procurement of goods and services: Argentina at 800,000 SDRs, Brazil at 330,000 SDRs, Paraguay at 1 million SDRs, and Uruguay at 212,000 SDRs. For construction services, Argentina and Brazil will transition from an initial threshold of 8 million SDRs. EU-Mercosur Agreement, Appendix I.

79. The price preferences will apply to products when Paraguayan labor, raw materials, and inputs are equal to or greater than 40%. They will apply to road works, construction, maintenance services, transportation, insurance, and consulting when the supplier's staff is more than 70% Paraguayan. EU-Mercosur Agreement, Appendix I.

coverage of their subcentral entities, the EU will open a corresponding level of subcentral coverage. The EU also committed to open services and construction services on a reciprocal basis.

The EU-Mercosur agreement has been characterized as the EU's "least ambitious agreement on public procurement in a free trade agreement in many years."[80] The agreement is more limited than other recent EU agreements because it omits utilities, government enterprises, and other entities. However, it does follow other agreements in which the EU insisted that its partners at least seek subcentral coverage.

Before the agreement is ratified, it may need to be amended to address issues relating to deforestation in the Amazon rain forest and European farmers' concerns with agricultural market access.[81] As of mid-2022, "an 'additional instrument' detailing elements related to sustainability and labour could be published in the coming months by the European Commission," which could enable the two trading partners to sign their agreement.[82]

5.4 EU-Chile Association Agreement

In November 2021, the EU and Chile reached an agreement that modernized their 2002 EU-Chile Association Agreement.[83] The Agreement included government procurement provisions, with

80. Iana Dreyer, "EU-Mercosur: Contours of a limited deal on public procurement," *Borderlex*, July 19, 2021, https://borderlex.net/2021/07/19/eu-mercosur-contours-of-a-limited-deal-on-public-procurement/?utm_source=-mailpoet&utm_medium=email&utm_campaign=the-last-newsletter-to-tal-posts-from-borderlex_2.

81. Malmström, "The EU."

82. "Week in Brussels."

83. Chile Ministry of Foreign Affairs, "Negotiations for the modernization of the Association Agreement between Chile and the European Union conclude," November 15, 2021, https://minrel.gob.cl/news/negotiations-for-the-modernization-of-the-association-agreement-between.

principles and procedures similar to the GPA and other EU FTAs.[84] In addition, as called for by the EU's negotiating objectives,[85] it prohibited national preferences.[86] While the agreement provides a minimum tendering period of 40 days, it allows the reduction to not less than 10 days under several circumstances. They include the purchase of off-the-shelf goods and services and apply when the notice of intended procurement and tender documentation are made available electronically.

The new agreement built on existing commitments, covering three categories of entities: central government entities, subcentral entities, and two utility sectors, namely maritime ports and airports. Chile covered the procurement of all services and construction services, whereas the EU listed the services and construction services opened under the agreement. In addition, they exchanged access to their public works concessions on a national treatment basis.

In May 2022, the EU's High Representative for Foreign Affairs and Security Policy Josep Borrell indicated "that signing the modernised Association Agreement with Chile before the end of the year is a distinct possibility."[87]

---

84. Agreement establishing an association between the European Community and its Member States, of the one part, and the Republic of Chile, of the other part (EU-Chile Agreement), accessed May 16, 2022, https://eur-lex.europa.eu/resource.html?uri=cellar:f83a503c-fa20-4b3a-9535-f10/4175eaf0.0004.02/DOC_2&format=PDF. The government procurement provisions are in articles 136–62 and annexes XI–XIII.

85. In its 2017 negotiating mandate, the EU indicated it was seeking "significantly enhanced mutual access to public procurement markets at all administrative levels [. . .] as well as by state-owned enterprises and undertakings with special or exclusive rights operating in the public utilities sectors." Council of the EU, "EU-Chile Modernised Association Agreement; Directives for the negotiation of a Modernised Association Agreement with Chile," 27, January 22, 2018, https://www.consilium.europa.eu//media/32405/st13553-ad-01dc01en17.pdf.

86. EU-Chile Agreement, art. 140.

87. "Week in Brussels."

6. EU FTA NEGOTIATIONS

When the EU launched trade negotiations with Australia in 2018, at the same time, it began negotiations with New Zealand.[88] It sought comprehensive coverage of procurement at all levels of government, going beyond the procurement that Australia offered under the GPA.[89] When Australia acceded to the GPA, the EU indicated the areas in which it regarded Australia's procurement as falling short of EU coverage by imposing reciprocity restrictions.[90] These restrictions could provide leverage for negotiating GPA-plus market access commitments, as in other EU FTAs.

In June 2022, the EU relaunched negotiations of a comprehensive trade agreement with a major developing country–India–with opening public procurement markets as one of its aims.[91] The EU and India had first launched negotiations for an FTA in 2007, but the talks were suspended in 2013 due to a gap in ambition. With the restart, the two trading partners hope to complete the new negotiations by the end of 2023. At the beginning of the negotiations, the EU tabled a government procurement chapter based on the GPA, with the addition of an anti-corruption

---

88. European Commission, "Commission welcomes green light to start trade negotiations with Australia and New Zealand," May 22, 2018, https://ec.europa.eu/commission/presscorner/detail/en/IP_18_3881.

89. Council of the EU, "Negotiating directives for a Free Trade Agreement with Australia," May 8, 2018, https://www.consilium.europa.eu/media/35794/st07663-ad01dc01-en18.pdf.

90. WTO, "Australia accepted as new party to government procurement pact," October 17, 2018, https://www.wto.org/english/news_e/news18_e/gpro_17oct18_e.htm.

91. European Commission, "EU and India kick-start ambitious trade agenda," June 17, 2022, https://policy.trade.ec.europa.eu/news/eu-and-india-kick-start-ambitious-trade-agenda-2022-06-17_en. The two sides also launched negotiations on an investment protection agreement and an agreement on geographical indications.

provision.[92] If the EU is successful in negotiating access to India's procurement market, it will be a major development because India has not yet opened its procurement under an international agreement.

7. EU-US NEGOTIATIONS OF THE TTIP

The EU and the US attempted to negotiate a bilateral FTA under the Obama administration. In a February 2013 report, the US-EU High Level Working Group on Jobs and Growth set out a shared goal of expanding procurement commitments between the two trading partners. It called for "substantially improved access to government procurement opportunities at all levels of government on the basis of national treatment."[93] The US and the EU entered negotiations of the Transatlantic Trade and Investment Partnership (TTIP) in July 2013. From the beginning of the negotiations, they differed on the importance of procurement. The EU assigned a high priority to obtain an expansion of US procurement commitments. It wanted to fill gaps in US coverage left over from the revision of the GPA in 2012. The US, on the other hand, had more modest ambitions similar to its goals for the Trans-Pacific Partnership, which was under negotiation at the same time. It regarded government procurement as an essential element of an agreement, as in all its FTAs, but did not accord it particular importance.

---

92. European Commission, "EU-India agreement: Documents," accessed August 6, 2022, https://policy.trade.ec.europa.eu/eu-trade-relationships-country-and-region/countries-and-regions/india/eu-india-agreement/documents_en.

93. US Trade Representative (USTR), *Final Report of the U.S.-EU High Level Working Group on Jobs and Growth*, February 11, 2013, https://ustr.gov/about-us/policy-offices/press-office/reports-and-publications/2013/final-report-us-eu-hlwg.

When the US and EU elaborated on the original shared goal with their own objectives, the disparity in their aims became apparent. The Obama administration incorporated broad objectives of its intention to launch negotiations of the TTIP in a March 2013 notice to Congress.[94] In July 2013, the European Commission published its initial position papers on issues in the TTIP negotiations, including public procurement, setting out the EU's objectives.[95] The detailed EU objectives contrasted sharply with the broad objectives of the US (see Table 11.1).[96]

TABLE 11.1. EU and US Procurement Objectives in the TTIP Negotiations

EU Objectives	US Objectives
Central government entities • Use a negative list • Cover US federal government entities not covered under GPA • Gain access to procurement subject to specific policies, such as those related to small businesses (small business set-asides)	• Expand market access opportunities for US goods, services, and suppliers to procurement markets of the EU and its member states

---

94. Letter from Acting US Trade Representative Demetrios Marantis to Speaker of the US House of Representatives John Boehner, March 20, 2013, https://ustr.gov/sites/default/files/03202013%20TTIP%20Notification%20Letter.PDF.

95. European Commission, "EU-US Transatlantic Trade and Investment Partnership: Public Procurement. Initial EU Position Paper," July 2013, https://trade.ec.europa.eu/doclib/docs/2013/july/tradoc_151623.pdf.

96. For an examination of the issues in the TTIP negotiations, see Stephen Woolcock and Jean Heilman Grier, "Public Procurement in the Transatlantic Trade and Investment Partnership Negotiations," in *Rule-Makers or Rule-Takers? Exploring the Transatlantic Trade and Investment Partnership*, eds. Daniel S. Hamilton and Jacques Pelkmans (London: Rowman & Littlefield, 2015), 297–339.

EU Objectives	US Objectives
Subcentral entities • Cover the 13 states not covered by the GPA • Remove restrictions maintained by the 37 states covered under the GPA • Cover municipalities, airports, ports, transit authorities, and railway authorities • Cover subcentral government entities "operating at the local, regional, or municipal level, as well as any other entities whose procurement policies are substantially controlled by, dependent on, or influenced by subcentral, regional or local government and which are engaged in non-commercial or non-industrial activities"	• Ensure that US suppliers are treated as favorably as domestic and other foreign goods, services, and suppliers in the EU member states • Expand opportunities to bid on government contracts (including in construction, engineering, and medical devices)
Other entities • Cover "all entities governed by public law, state-owned companies and similar operating in particular in the field of utilities," with transit/railways, urban railways, and urban transport of special interest	
Services • Cover all services with a specific interest in information technology services, particularly cloud-based services	
'Buy America' restrictions • Remove existing domestic content requirements on mass transit and highway projects • Commit to imposing no new 'Buy America' requirements on federal funds given to states or other subcentral government entities	

Source: Stephen Woolcock and Jean Heilman Grier, "Public Procurement in the Transatlantic Trade and Investment Partnership Negotiations," in *Rule-Makers or Rule-Takers? Exploring the Transatlantic Trade and Investment Partnership*, eds. Daniel S. Hamilton and Jacques Pelkmans (London: Rowman & Littlefield, 2015), table 7.

The EU's objectives were bolstered by similar requests from the European business community; for instance, BusinessEurope[97] presented its negotiation objectives.[98] It sought to remove US domestic preferences and obtain greater access to federal, state, and local procurement. At the federal level, it cited particular interest in the National Railroad Passenger Corporation (known as Amtrak), the Federal Aviation Administration, and the Government Printing Office. It also sought coverage of the 13 states not bound by the GPA and elimination of existing restrictions maintained by the 37 states subject to the GPA. The business organization also wanted coverage of the procurement of large cities.[99]

Among its highest priorities at the state and local levels, BusinessEurope sought access to procurement by public transportation agencies. It focused on state departments of transportation and a broad range of transit and rail authorities.[100] European business interest in the public transportation agencies prompted its request to remove US domestic content requirements that are conditions of federal funds given to state and local governments for highway, railway, and transit projects. European firms wanted to be able to

---

97. BusinessEurope is a major business organization in Europe, serving as "the leading advocate for growth and competitiveness" for enterprises of all sizes in 35 European countries, whose national business federations are its members. BusinessEurope, https://www.businesseurope.eu/mission-and-priorities, accessed June 11, 2022.

98. BusinessEurope, "Public Procurement in the Transatlantic Trade and Investment Partnership (TTIP)," December 11, 2013, https://www.businesseurope.eu/publications/public-procurement-transatlantic-trade-and-investment-partnership-ttip-businesseurope.

99. The cities of interest included Denver, Houston, Los Angeles, Miami, New York, San Francisco, Seattle, and Washington. BusinessEurope, "Public Procurement," 3.

100. BusinessEurope identified several transit authorities: the Chicago Transit Authority, the Los Angeles County Metropolitan Transportation Authority, and the Washington Metropolitan Area Transit Authority. Its interest in rail authorities included METRA (Chicago area), Metrolink (southern California), BART (San Francisco Bay Area), and Sound Transit Central Puget Sound (Seattle area). BusinessEurope, "Public Procurement," 8.

participate in the projects without having to meet the 'Buy American' requirements.

The TTIP negotiations differed from the US negotiations with the EU on the establishment of the GPA 1994, when the US had a specific interest in gaining access to the EU electric and telecommunications sectors. In contrast, the US was not driven by similar compelling interests in the TTIP negotiations. US businesses expressed little interest in gaining rights to participate in EU procurement subject to reciprocity conditions under the GPA.

Under the GPA, the US gave the EU the best access to its procurement that it offered to any trading partner and did not withhold any GPA-covered procurement. The EU, however, did not reciprocate with its best coverage. Instead, it denied the US legal rights to participate in a significant portion of its GPA-covered procurement. That included the procurement of services by its subcentral entities, procurement by its utilities (except in the electric and port sectors), and its comprehensive coverage of the central government entities of its member states. Notwithstanding this denial of legal access, as a practical matter, the EU generally allowed US firms to participate in such procurement.[101]

After more than three years of negotiations, the US and EU failed to finalize a TTIP agreement before the end of the Obama administration in January 2017. One of the obstacles to concluding the negotiations was the US's unwillingness to open procurement beyond its GPA obligations. The Trump administration did not revive those negotiations. In 2019, the EU member states declared their 2013 TTIP negotiating objectives "must be considered obsolete and no longer relevant."[102]

---

101. Woolcock and Grier, "Public Procurement in TTIP," 312.

102. Council of the EU, "Trade with the United States: Council authorises negotiations on elimination of tariffs for industrial goods and on conformity assessment," April 15, 2019, https://www.consilium.europa.eu/en/press/press-releases/2019/04/15/trade-with-the-united-states-council-authorises-negotiations-on-elimination-of-tariffs-for-industrial-goods-and-on-conformity-assessment/.

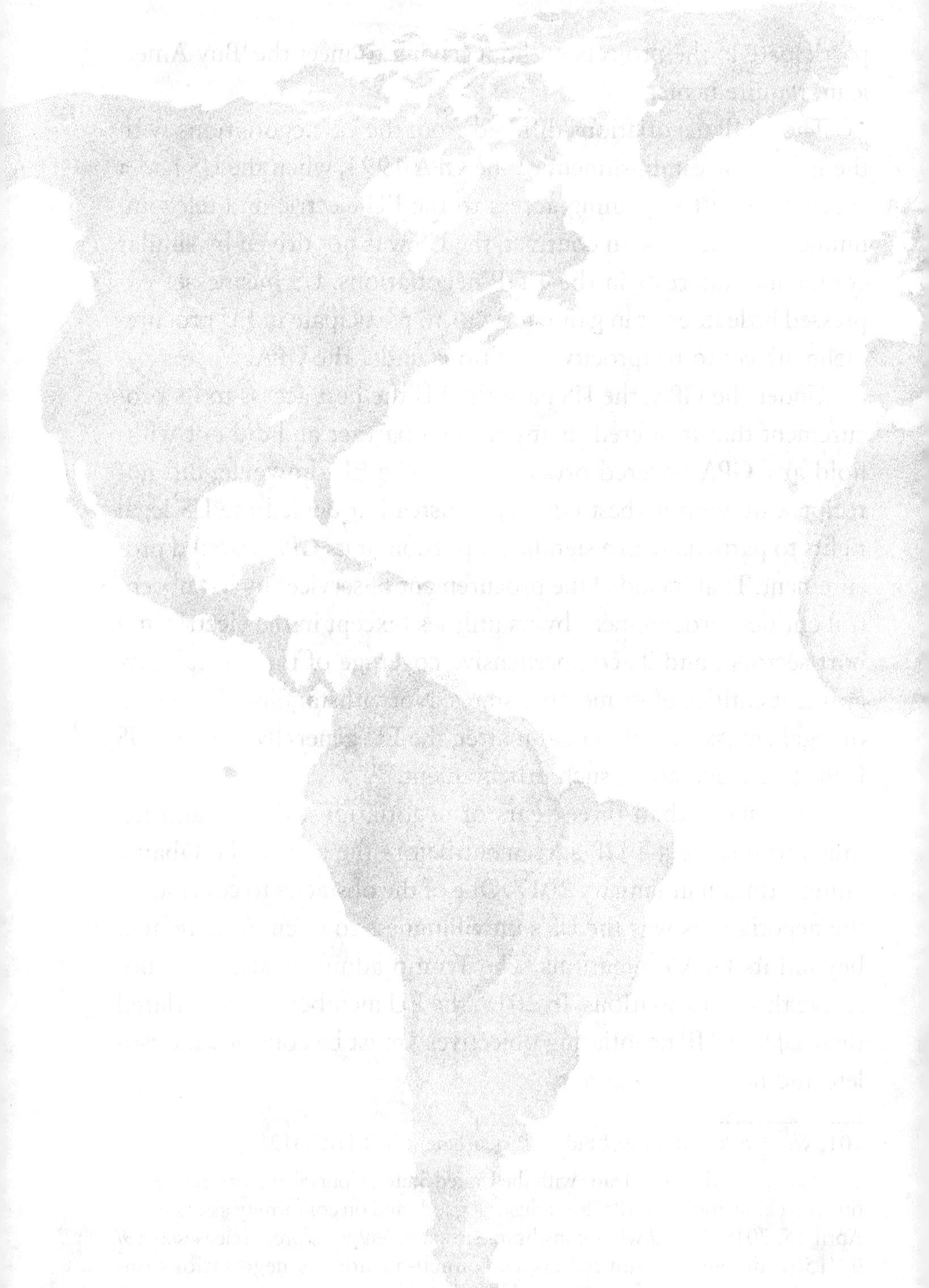

PART FOUR

PROSPECTS FOR GOVERNMENT PROCUREMENT IN THE INTERNATIONAL ARENA

INTRODUCTION

The international procurement system is sufficiently well established to allow its assessment, including its potential for growth. The year 2021 marked major anniversaries for the plurilateral agreements at the heart of that system. Forty years have passed since the implementation of the 1979 GATT Code, the first plurilateral agreement on government procurement. Twenty-five years have passed since its successor, the GPA, entered into force. Finally, ten years have passed since the parties completed the negotiations of the GPA 2012.

However, the strength of the international procurement system cannot be measured just by the longevity of its foundational agreements. The core agreement, the GPA, not only opens procurement but also serves as a moderator or a check of the actions of its members. It discourages these members from adopting unilateral measures that would be inconsistent with the agreement. It has also influenced other international procurement agreements, notably many regional and bilateral FTAs.

Any assessment must consider the ability of the GPA to address the procurement barriers of major economies by bringing them into the agreement. Currently, the best example of such an economy is that of China, which remains outside the GPA more than 20 years after it became a WTO member. Four decades after the implementation of the original plurilateral agreement, the GPA still has only 48 members, fewer than one-third of the WTO membership. If the GPA proves unable to recruit new members, it runs the risk of being perceived as an exclusive agreement mostly for developed nations and will leave much of the world's procurement beyond its disciplines.

Therefore, the state of the international procurement system can be assessed by examining key aspects of its foundational plurilateral agreement. First, what opportunities exist for expanding the membership of the GPA beyond its current roster? Specifically, what are the prospects for bringing China under GPA disciplines? Second, is the GPA maintaining its relevancy and addressing new issues? Third, how effective is it in limiting or moderating the unilateral actions of its members? The answers to these questions will point to the GPA's prospects of meeting the demands of the future and expanding beyond a small number of developed economies.

CHAPTER 12

GOVERNMENT PROCUREMENT: EXPANSION OF UNILATERALISM

1. INTRODUCTION

Forty years after the implementation of the first plurilateral procurement agreement, the 1979 GATT Code, its parties are adopting more unilateral measures. They illustrate both the strengths and weaknesses of the agreement.

In the US, President Biden has expanded the procurement policies of his predecessor. His administration tightened existing 'Buy American' requirements and vigorously implemented a far-reaching domestic preference requirement for infrastructure projects. In 2022, it was exploring other measures to further the protection of domestic procurement excluded from the US's international commitments.

The US 'Buy American' policies produced a surprising response from Canada. Frustrated by the increasingly protectionist policies of its neighbor to the south, in 2022, Canada proposed its own unilateral procurement measures. It was the first time that Canada, a country with an economy that is closely tied to that of the US, had proposed measures to match US restrictions.

Also, in 2022, the European Union (EU) adopted a pair of unilateral measures to counter aspects of the international procurement system that it viewed as unfair. The first was prompted by the failure of China and other countries (including the US) to provide reciprocal access to their procurement markets. The second was aimed at removing the adverse effects of foreign subsidies on the EU procurement market.

The measures of the three GPA parties are intended to be consistent with their obligations under the plurilateral agreement. In this context, they indicate that the GPA is functioning properly as a moderator or check on the actions of its parties.

At the same time, the measures point to the limitations of the GPA. They allow parties to adopt unilateral procurement measures that may not be consistent with the spirit of the GPA but are beyond its scope. The measures address procurement that is outside the agreement, procurement of non-GPA members, and procurement practices not addressed (or not adequately addressed) by the GPA. Furthermore, their application of such measures to countries that are not GPA parties illustrates the consequences of an international procurement system based on plurilateral, not multilateral, agreements.

2. US PROCUREMENT MEASURES: BIDEN ADMINISTRATION

At the beginning of his presidency, President Biden set the direction of his administration's government procurement policy with an executive order, "Ensuring the Future Is Made in All of America by All of America's Workers" (Order).[1] The Order's central goal was to advance the policy of maximizing the use of American goods and services by federal agencies and recipients of federal funding.

---

1. "Executive Order 14005 of January 25, 2021, Ensuring the Future Is Made in All of America by All of America's Workers," *Federal Register* 86, no. 17 (January 28, 2021): 7475, https://www.govinfo.gov/content/pkg/FR-2021-01-28/pdf/2021-02038.pdf.

It reflected promises Biden made as a presidential candidate[2] and echoed similar directives of his predecessor.[3] The Order focused on curtailing the use of waivers and strengthening 'Buy American' regulations. The Biden administration's 'Made in America' policies were "designed to increase reliance on domestic supply chains and ultimately reduce the need to spend taxpayer dollars on foreign-made goods."[4] It used 'Made in America' to describe policies that are otherwise known as 'Buy American.'

2.1 Expansion of Domestic Procurement Measures

2.1.1 Curtailing the Use of Waivers

One of the Biden administration's first actions sought to curtail the use of waivers. Federal agencies issue waivers or use exceptions (in this chapter collectively referred to as 'waivers') to the Buy American Act of 1933 (BAA) and other 'Made in American' laws[5] in three situations:

---

2. During the 2020 US presidential campaign, Joe Biden put forward a 'Buy American' plan to tighten domestic content requirements, crack down on waivers of 'Buy American' requirements, and extend such requirements to other forms of governmental assistance. It also supported 'Ship American' to ensure that American cargo was carried on US-flagged ships. Joe Biden, "The Biden Plan to Ensure the Future Is 'Made in All of America' by All of America's Workers," July 9, 2020, https://joebiden.com/made-in-america/.

3. The Biden Order also revoked two of Trump's 'Buy American' orders: a 2017 "Buy American, Hire American" Order and a 2021 order directed at the US Postal Services. "Executive Order 14005," sec. 14(a).

4. "Home page," Made in America, accessed June 17, 2022, https://www.madeinamerica.gov.

5. 'Made in America' laws are defined broadly as "all statutes, regulations, rules, and Executive Orders relating to Federal financial assistance awards or Federal procurement, including those that refer to 'Buy America' or 'Buy American,' that require, or provide a preference for, the purchase or acquisition of goods, products, or materials produced in the United States, including iron, steel, and manufactured goods offered in the United States." They include laws requiring domestic preference for maritime transport, including the Merchant Marine Act of 1920, also known as the Jones Act. "Executive Order 14005," sec. (2)(b).

- when domestic goods or services are not available

- when domestic goods or services are available, but the cost is unreasonable

- when the purchase of domestic goods or services would be inconsistent with the public interest.

In those situations, and others provided by various laws and regulations, the agency may purchase a foreign good or service.

To reduce waivers of domestic purchasing requirements, Biden established a centralized waiver review system. This policy went beyond his predecessor's approach, which merely exhorted agencies to reduce the use of waivers. He established a Made in America Office (MIAO) within the Office of Management and Budget (OMB)[6] "as the final authority in reviewing waiver requests for all projects using federal funds."[7] The MIAO's overall aim was to increase reliance on domestic supply chains and reduce the need for waivers, as well as "send clear demand signals to domestic producers by increasing the transparency of waivers."[8]

The Biden administration increased waiver transparency by establishing a central website with information on past waivers and proposed waivers.[9] It required all proposed waivers to be posted on the site prior to agencies making contract awards.[10] The MIAO

---

6. "Executive Order 14005," sec. 4.

7. US Library of Congress, Congressional Research Service, *Congress Expands Buy America Requirements in the Infrastructure Investment and Jobs Act (P.L. 117-58)*, by Christopher D. Watson, IFI1989C (2021), https://crsreports.congress.gov/product/pdf/IF/IF11989.

8. "Executive Order 14005," sec. 4.

9. "Home page," Made in America. The historical waivers made available on the site are discussed in Chapter 7.

10. OMB, Memorandum for Heads of Executive Departments and Agencies, "Increasing Opportunities for Domestic Sourcing and Reducing the Need for Waivers from Made in America Laws," June 11, 2021, 14, https://www.whitehouse.gov/wp-content/uploads/2021/06/M-21-26.pdf.

began its review of waivers with nonavailability waivers under the BAA and waivers of the Jones Act.[11]

2.1.2 Strengthening 'Made in America' Regulations

Biden's Order also proposed strengthening the enforcement of the BAA in two ways. One was to increase the US content required for a product to be considered a domestic product from 55% of the cost of all components, which was set during the Trump presidency. The other was aimed at increasing the price preferences applied to determine whether the domestic product's price is unreasonable.[12]

In response to the president's Order, the Federal Acquisition Regulatory Council (FAR Council) revised the Federal Acquisition Regulation (FAR), increasing the percentage of US-made components from 55% in three stages: to 60% in 2022, 65% in 2024, and 75% in 2029.[13] The increases in the domestic content threshold had a limited impact because they did not apply to non-Department of

---

11. OMB, "Increasing Opportunities for Domestic Sourcing," 3. In proposing waivers based on the nonavailability of domestic goods or services, agencies must include information on the impact on their mission if they were unable to acquire the item, the country of origin of the product to be purchased under the waiver, and US content (if any) of foreign products intended for purchase. OMB, "Increasing Opportunities for Domestic Sourcing," 8–9. The Jones Act is discussed in Chapter 7.

12. "Executive Order 14005," sec. 8.

13. "Federal Acquisition Regulation: Amendments to the FAR Buy American Act Requirements," *Federal Register* 87, no. 44 (March 7, 2022): 12780, https://www.govinfo.gov/content/pkg/FR-2022-03-07/pdf/2022-04173.pdf. In contrast to the typical implementation of rules 30 days after publication, implementation of the revision was delayed for more than seven months, until October 25, 2022, to allow the industry time to plan for the new domestic content thresholds and provide workforce training on the fallback threshold, described in Chapter 7. See also White House, *FACT SHEET: Biden-Harris Administration Delivers on Made in America Commitments*, March 4, 2021, https://www.whitehouse.gov/briefing-room/statements-releases/2022/03/04/fact-sheet-biden-harris-administration-delivers-on-made-in-america-commitments/.

Defense purchases of goods covered by the GPA and FTAs, which are excluded from the BAA.[14]

The FAR Council did not immediately increase price preferences, as called for by the Order. Instead, it created a framework for applying higher (or enhanced) price preferences to critical products and construction materials and critical components. It deferred establishing a definitive list of critical items and critical components and their associated enhanced price preferences to a subsequent rulemaking, anticipated later in 2022.[15] That rulemaking was expected to also address requirements for post-award reporting on the specific amount of domestic content in critical products, construction materials, and components subject to enhanced price preferences.[16] The Biden administration defended the federal government's likely payment of higher prices for critical domestic-made products and components as a result of the application of the price preferences. It contended the price preferences were essential to its supply chain resiliency strategy of creating a steady source of demand to "catalyze domestic production and bolster thin supply chains."[17]

The Biden administration was preparing–or at least exploring–additional changes in federal procurement regulations that could

---

14. "Federal Acquisition Regulation: Amendments to the FAR Buy American Act Requirements" ("FAR: Proposed Amendments"), *Federal Register* 86, no.144 (July 30, 2021): 40980.

15. The FAR Council defined "critical items" as domestic construction material or domestic end products deemed critical to US supply chain resiliency, and "critical components" as components mined, produced, or manufactured in the US and deemed critical to the US supply chain. "FAR: Amendments," 12781.

16. Such reporting is intended to help the federal government understand the extent to which entities in its supplier base are increasing their reliance on domestic sources for critical items and components. "FAR: Amendments," 12782.

17. White House, "The Biden-Harris Plan to Revitalize American Manufacturing and Secure Critical Supply Chains in 2022," February 24, 2022, https://www.whitehouse.gov/briefing-room/statements-releases/2022/02/24/the-biden-harris-plan-to-revitalize-american-manufacturing-and-secure-critical-supply-chains-in-2022/.

further promote and protect domestic sources and alter long-standing procurement policies. Some of the potential revisions were previewed by the FAR Council in its July 2021 request for public feedback on issues cited in the Biden Order. The issues included the exemption of commercial information technology (IT) from the BAA, the partial waiver for commercial off-the-shelf (COTS) items, 'Made in America' services, the use of waivers to the BAA in general, the effectiveness of current price preferences, and replacement of the component test.[18]

Component Test: In his Order, President Biden directed the FAR Council to consider replacing the BAA's component test used to determine the domestic content in a product by the value of its domestic components. His Order suggested measuring such content "by the value that is added to the product through U.S.-based production or U.S. job-supporting economic activity."[19] The FAR Council asked how domestic content might be better calculated and the strengths and shortcomings of the component test, noting that it did not seek to replace the test "at this time."[20] The Biden administration could propose a replacement test in a new rulemaking exercise.

Substantial Transformation Test: The FAR Council also scrutinized the substantial transformation test used to determine the eligibility of a good covered by the GPA or an FTA for a waiver under the Trade Agreements Act. Though the Council did not propose any revision of the test, it asked for input on its impact, including potential lost opportunities for American workers. It pointed out that under the test, a US-made product substantially transformed in the US "may have far less domestic content when compared to a domestic end product acquired under the Buy American statute."

---

18. "FAR: Proposed Amendments," 40986.
19. "Executive Order 14005," sec. 8(i).
20. "FAR: Proposed Amendments," 40982.

Such a product would be treated as US-made if it was substantially transformed in the US, even if it had 100% foreign content.[21]

Commercial IT: President Biden asked for a review of the impact of the exemption of commercial IT from the BAA and recommendations for its removal.[22] The FAR Council solicited comments on the exemption's continued relevance and whether current marketplace conditions support narrowing or lifting it.[23]

Partial Waiver for COTS Items: As of late 2022, the Biden administration was considering the continuing relevance of the waiver of COTS products.[24] In 2009, OMB waived the component test for COTS products after concluding the content requirement could limit the government's ability to purchase products already in the commercial distribution systems. In 2021, the agency indicated it was examining the waiver's relevance, whether it should be rescinded to promote 'Made in America' policies, and the impact of rescinding it.[25] In its own exercise, the FAR Council asked for comments on whether the waiver benefited domestic firms and their employees.[26]

Price Preferences on Services: The FAR Council asked how the federal government could promote the use of 'Made in America' services and whether there were critical services that should be accorded price preferences.[27] Applying price preferences to services would represent a significant change in policy as the US has never applied price preferences to services.

---

21. "FAR: Proposed Amendments," 40986.

22. "Executive Order 14005," sec. 10.

23. "FAR: Proposed Amendments," 40986.

24. The COTS items waiver is considered partial because the items are only exempt from the BAA, not the Trade Agreements Act.

25. OMB, "Increasing Opportunities for Domestic Sourcing," 14–15.

26. "FAR: Proposed Amendments," 40986.

27. "FAR: Proposed Amendments," 40986.

2.1.3 Expanding 'Buy American' Requirements for Infrastructure Projects

President Biden's 'Buy American' policies were embedded and expanded in the Infrastructure Investment and Jobs Act (Infrastructure Act or IIJA),[28] which was enacted with a broad bipartisan support in November 2021.[29] It included the most far-reaching 'Buy American' requirement that has been applied to infrastructure projects (as discussed in Chapter 7).

The Infrastructure Act prohibited the use of federal funds on any infrastructure project undertaken by a nonfederal entity[30] "unless all of the iron, steel, manufactured products, and construction materials used in the project are produced in the United States."[31] This requirement overshadowed the 'soft' domestic preference incorporated into federal funding regulations by the Trump administration.[32]

The Biden administration appeared intent on ensuring the broadest possible application of this requirement. OMB issued guidance that the preference applied to any federal financial

---

28. *IIJA*, Public Law 117-58 (2021).

29. The Senate passed the IIJA by an "overwhelmingly bipartisan" vote of 69-30 in August 2021. Emily Cochrane, "Senate Passes $1 Trillion Infrastructure Bill, Handing Biden a Bipartisan Win," *The New York Times*, August 10, 2021, https://www.nytimes.com/2021/08/10/us/politics/infrastructure-bill-passes.html. House approval followed four months later (November 5), also by a bipartisan (but smaller margin) vote of 228 to 206, marking "the final milestone for the first of two pieces in the president's sprawling economic agenda." Tony Romm, Marianna Sotomayor, and Mike DeBonis, "Congress approves $1.2 trillion infrastructure bill, sending measure to Biden for enactment," *The Washington Post*, November 6, 2021, https://www.washingtonpost.com/us-policy/2021/11/05/house-infrastructure-reconciliation-vote/.

30. The term "nonfederal entity" includes states, local governments, territories, Indian tribes, Institutions of Higher Education, and nonprofit organizations. *Code of Federal Regulations*, title 45 (2022): § 75.2.

31. *IIJA*, §§ 70901–927.

32. OMB, "Guidance for Grants and Agreements," *Federal Register* 85, no. 157 (August 13, 2020): 49506. https://www.govinfo.gov/content/pkg/FR-2020-08-13/pdf/2020-17468.pdf.

assistance program under which an award might be issued for an infrastructure project, "regardless of whether infrastructure is the primary purpose of the award."[33] It did, however, point out that when an award was made that included a project covered by the Infrastructure Act, the 'Buy American' preference would not apply to non-infrastructure spending under the award. The guidance directed agencies to ensure that their programs incorporated a 'Buy American' preference in the terms and conditions of each infrastructure project award.[34]

OMB further urged agencies to broadly interpret "infrastructure," and cited, as an example, that it included "structures, facilities, and equipment that generate, transport, and distribute energy–including electric vehicle (EV) charging."[35] As a guide to determining whether a particular construction project constitutes "infrastructure," it offered the following criteria: whether the project will serve a public function, including whether it is publicly owned and operated, privately operated on behalf of the public, or is a place of public accommodation, in contrast to a project that is privately owned and not open to the public.[36]

The Infrastructure Act applied a domestic purchasing requirement to construction materials for the first time. In initial guidance, OMB broadly defined construction materials to include nonferrous metals, plastic and polymer-based products, glass, lumber, and drywall.[37] Both the Act and OMB's definition created challenges for federal agencies in applying the preference to construction

---

33. OMB, Memorandum for Heads of Executive Departments and Agencies, "Initial Implementation Guidance on Application of Buy America Preference in Federal Financial Assistance Programs for Infrastructure," M-22-11, April 18, 2022, https://www.whitehouse.gov/wp-content/uploads/2022/04/M-22-11.pdf.

34. OMB, "Initial Implementation Guidance," 2.

35. OMB, "Initial Implementation Guidance," 4.

36. OMB, "Initial Implementation Guidance," 4.

37. OMB, "Initial Implementation Guidance," 13.

materials. The Department of Transportation (DoT) illustrated the nature of these challenges. It is the federal agency with perhaps the most experience in providing financial assistance for infrastructure projects and applying domestic content preference requirements.

Before the Act extended the domestic preference to construction materials, none of DoT's numerous programs specifically covered them. While DoT described its operating units as having long-standing experience in applying 'Buy American' preferences for iron, steel, and manufactured products, it acknowledged that "applying such policies to construction materials is a new exercise."[38] As a consequence, the Department issued a temporary (180-day) waiver of the 'Buy American' mandate for construction materials to enable it and its funding recipients to prepare for compliance with the new requirement.[39]

DoT used highway projects to illustrate the vast scope of applying the 'Buy American' requirement to construction materials. Citing the National Bridge Inventory, the Department pointed out that more than 62,000 bridges in the US include wood or timber. In addition, nearly 2,300 bridges have nonferrous metal elements, and 19,500 bridges contain polymer-based products.[40] Since all of these are subject to the new requirement, the DoT is not permitted to fund projects with such construction materials unless they are produced in the US. That means all manufacturing processes for these materials must take place in the US.

Before issuing the waiver, DoT solicited public comments on whether it should issue a temporary waiver. It received over 80 comments from a wide array of stakeholders, including state

---

38. DoT, "Temporary Waiver of Buy America Requirements for Construction Materials," *Federal Register* 87, no. 101 (May 25, 2022): 31931, https://www.govinfo.gov/content/pkg/FR-2022-05-25/pdf/2022-11195.pdf.

39. The waiver applied from May 14, 2022 to November 10, 2022. As the basis for the waiver, DoT determined that it would be inconsistent with the public interest to require the nonfederal recipients of federal funds for transportation projects to apply the new preference.

40. DoT, "Temporary Waiver," 31933.

transportation agencies, public transit agencies, airport operators, construction firms, manufacturers and suppliers, and labor organizations. The great majority supported its proposed waiver, detailing the challenges posed by the new requirement.[41]

The responses outlined measures needed for nonfederal entities to implement the new construction materials requirement. In addition to awaiting OMB's issuance of final standards for construction materials (as required by the Act), the Utah DoT cited:

> "[s]tate DOTs updating standard specifications; establishing certification processes; working with and informing industry to demonstrate their products meet the standards; working with contractors and incorporating new contract provisions prescribing Buy America requirements; and reviewing and updating stewardship and oversight agreements with [the Federal Highway Administration] to address non-compliance with Made in America standards."[42]

Other commenters, such as the Greater Orlando Aviation Authority, pointed to the need to find potential domestic sources of construction materials and build up an adequate supply base to support federally funded transportation infrastructure projects. Still, other respondents described existing supply chain challenges in the materials industry and the resulting volatility in those markets. They emphasized it was

> "extremely difficult to determine at this time whether U.S. production for these newly covered materials can support the demand the [Act's] increased funding levels will place on these markets, or whether there is sufficient or existing U.S. production at all for some of these goods."[43]

---

41. DoT, "Temporary Waiver," 31933.

42. DoT, "Temporary Waiver," 31933–34.

43. DoT, "Temporary Waiver," 31934.

Hence, DoT, one of the federal agencies with an extensive history of applying 'Buy America' requirements to infrastructure projects, has been challenged by the new requirements. It may be only 'the tip of the iceberg' as many departments and nonfederal entities do not have the reservoir of DoT's experience and must establish a 'Buy American' policy for the first time. A key question is whether the administration can implement expanded 'Buy America' requirements while delivering, in the words of DoT, "a wide range of critical infrastructure projects for States, local communities, counties, Tribal nations and farms, factories and businesses across the U.S."?[44]

One broader implication of the expansion of domestic preferences to all infrastructure projects receiving federal funds is that the US likely would not be able (assuming it was willing) to offer coverage of those projects under the GPA or other agreement in a future negotiation. If it did, it would have to exclude the preference from its commitments as it does for airport, highway, and mass transit projects under the GPA and FTAs. The US's trading partners, especially the EU and Canada, have long sought greater access to procurement by state and local governments and authorities, such as airports and water authorities, and criticized the 'Buy American' requirements. The infrastructure domestic preference will now make any potential future offer of such entities less valuable because the US would have to qualify any coverage of federally funded infrastructure projects in order to comply with the 'Buy American' requirement.[45]

---

44. DoT, "Temporary Waiver," 31931–32.

45. While the law requires the 'Buy American' requirement to be applied consistently with US trade agreements, that would not likely be interpreted to apply to new agreements or new procurement commitments.

2.2 Assessing the Impact of Trade Agreements

The Infrastructure Act directed the US Trade Representative (USTR), the Secretary of Commerce, and OMB to assess the impact of the GPA and US FTAs on the operation of 'Buy American' laws, including on the implementation of domestic preferences.[46] It further required their report, due April 2022, to be made available to the public.[47] As of late 2022, the Biden administration had not published any report.

2.3 Prospects for the Liberalization of Procurement Markets

Despite pressure to pursue new trade agreements, the Biden administration emphasized it did not intend to negotiate traditional FTAs. It resisted entreaties to re-enter the Trans-Pacific Partnership (TPP) even after China applied for admission. As an alternative, President Biden launched a major initiative called the Indo-Pacific Economic Framework (IPEF) in May 2022.[48] With the IPEF, the US aimed to deepen US economic engagement in the region.[49] The IPEF is expected to expand beyond its initial 13 participants.[50]

---

46. *IIJA*, § 70934.

47. The transparency directive contrasts with the treatment of a similar report mandated by President Trump, which was never made public (or perhaps even completed). See the discussion of the report in Chapter 8.

48. White House, *FACT SHEET: In Asia, President Biden and a Dozen Indo-Pacific Partners Launch the Indo-Pacific Economic Framework for Prosperity*, May 23, 2022, https://www.whitehouse.gov/briefing-room/statements-releases/2022/05/23/fact-sheet-in-asia-president-biden-and-a-dozen-indo-pacific-partners-launch-the-indo-pacific-economic-framework-for-prosperity/.

49. White House, *FACT SHEET: In Asia*; see also "Statement on Indo-Pacific Economic Framework for Prosperity, May 23, 2022, https://ustr.gov/about-us/policy-offices/press-office/press-releases/2022/may/statement-indo-pacific-economic-framework-prosperity.

50. In addition to the US, the participants were Australia, Brunei, Fiji, India, Indonesia, Japan, South Korea, Malaysia, New Zealand, the Philippines, Singapore, Thailand, and Vietnam.

The IPEF is a loosely defined economic framework organized around four pillars that participants would negotiate separately, and the participants could also choose the pillar(s) in which to participate. Only one pillar addresses trade. This pillar, which will be led by USTR, aims to develop high-standard rules for the digital economy, including standards on cross-border data flow and localization. It will also seek "strong labor and environment standards and corporate accountability provisions that promote a race to the top for workers through trade."[51] The IPEF differs from the TPP and other FTAs in that the US does not intend to seek tariff reductions or increased market access commitments under it, at least not initially.[52]

The other three pillars, led by the Department of Commerce, are supply chains; clean energy, decarbonization, and infrastructure; and tax and anti-corruption. Only the last pillar, which will seek commitments to enact and enforce effective tax, anti-money laundering, and anti-bribery regimes, involves government procurement.[53]

As the IPEF was being developed, there were contrasting views on its benefits and potential.[54]

---

51. White House, *FACT SHEET: In Asia*. The Commerce Department elaborated on its aims in a *Federal Register* notice in which it sought public comments on its objectives.

52. USTR, "Request for Comments on the Proposed Fair and Resilient Trade Pillar of an Indo-Pacific Economic Framework," *Federal Register* 87, no. 47 (March 10, 2022): 13789, https://www.govinfo.gov/content/pkg/FR-2022-03-10/pdf/2022-05044.pdf.

53. Department of Commerce, "Request for Comments on the Indo-Pacific Economic Framework," *Federal Register* 87, no. 48 (March 11, 2022): 13971, https://www.federalregister.gov/documents/2022/03/11/2022-05206/request-for-comments-on-the-indo-pacific-economic-framework.

54. See, for example, the views of two former USTR negotiations, Wendy Cutler and Daniel M. Price, "The Debate Papers: Is the Indo-Pacific Economic Framework Glass Half Full or Glass Half Empty?," United States Study Center, August 25, 2022, https://www.ussc.edu.au/analysis/is-the-indo-pacific-economic-framework-glass-half-full-or-glass-half-empty.

3. CANADA'S PROPOSED RECIPROCITY MEASURES

The Biden administration's 'Buy American' policies caused Canada to reconsider the openness of its federal procurement. Like many parties to the GPA, Canada maintains an essentially open procurement system, placing few restrictions on participation in its procurement.[55] However, it is now considering unilateral reciprocity measures that would allow it to close its procurement to participation by countries that do not open equivalent procurement. It is particularly targeting areas in which the US closes or restricts participation in procurement, adversely affecting Canadian suppliers.

Canada has long harbored concerns with the 'Buy American' policies that exclude Canadian suppliers from US government procurement.[56] Because its firms were not permitted to participate in US small business set-asides and were not exempt from 'Buy American' restrictions, Canada had refused to cover its provinces under the GPA.[57] In 2009, when Canadian suppliers were shut out of the $800 billion infrastructure spending in the 2009 American Recovery and Reinvestment Act (Recovery Act), it sought an exemption from the Act's 'Buy American' requirement. That led to negotiations of a 2010 bilateral procurement agreement in which

---

55. See discussion in Chapter 12.

56. Canada, House of Commons, *"Buy America" Procurement Policies: An Interim Report, Report of the Special Committee on the Economic Relationship between Canada and the United States*, June 2021, 3, accessed June 4, 2022, https://www.queensu.ca/sps/sites/spswww/files/uploaded_files/QITP%20 pdfs/2021/7%20-%20House%20of%20Commons%20Report%20on%20 Buy%20America%20Procurement%20Policies.pdf.

57. Kamala Dawar, "The Government Procurement Agreement, the Most-Favored Nation Principle, and Regional Trade Agreements," in *The Internationalization of Government Procurement Regulation*, eds. Aris C. Georgopoulos, Bernard Hoekman, and Petros C. Mavroidis (Oxford: Oxford University Press, 2017), 117.

the US excluded Canada from the Recovery Act's 'Buy American' requirement, and the two neighbors exchanged access to the procurement of their states and provinces.[58]

In the 2017-2018 renegotiations of the North American Free Trade Agreement (NAFTA), Canada strongly objected to the Trump administration's proposal to cap its (and Mexico's) access to the US procurement market at the value of the procurement they opened to the US. Ultimately, Canada, as well as Mexico, rejected that proposal. Canada was so dissatisfied with the terms offered by the US that it altogether opted out of the procurement obligations in NAFTA's replacement.

After Biden issued his 'Made in America' Order, the Canadian government grew increasingly concerned with the direction of US 'Buy American' policies. In February 2021, the Canadian House of Commons formed a special committee to study the country's economic relationship with the US. It instructed the committee to report on the "current and proposed 'Buy America' procurement rules, requirements, and policies, together with recommendations to address and safeguard Canadian interests."[59] The committee issued its report in June 2021 based on the testimony of interested stakeholders. It recommended the Canadian government seek "a full exemption" from the application of existing and future 'Buy American' policies or at least an exemption for specific Canadian sectors.[60] As justification, it cited the claim of the Canadian Manufacturers & Exporters Association that those policies undermined regional supply chains because they did not "differentiate between integrated supply chains and imported or finished goods."[61] The committee also wanted to "raise awareness" in the US of the resulting increased costs of state and

---

58. See Chapter 5 for a detailed discussion of the agreement.

59. Canada, House of Commons, *"Buy America" Procurement Policies*, 3–4.

60. Canada, House of Commons, *"Buy America" Procurement Policies*, 12–13.

61. Canada, House of Commons, *"Buy America" Procurement Policies*, 7.

municipal projects if Canada was not given an exemption from 'Buy American' policies.[62]

In its 2021 budget, the Canadian government committed to pursue unilateral procurement policies to ensure that its federal government purchased goods and services only from countries that grant Canadian businesses a similar level of market access.[63] Based on that commitment, in March 2022, Canada began a consultation process to explore the adoption of reciprocal procurement policies.[64] It outlined three potential approaches consistent with its GPA and FTAs obligations and invited stakeholders to offer other solutions.[65]

First, Canada proposed to limit access to its federal procurement (except defense purchases) "to what is strictly required by Canada's government procurement obligations."[66] Under such a strategy, Canada could provide preferential access, such as awarding "extra points in the bid evaluation process for bidders who meet prescribed content requirements," preventing certain foreign suppliers, goods, and services from competing in Canadian federal procurement, or limiting access based on the origin of the supplier, good, or service.[67] While such restrictions could be applied to the US for procurement below GPA thresholds, it is unclear to what extent procurement would be affected by them since Canada offers broad central government coverage under the GPA.

62. Canada, House of Commons, *"Buy America" Procurement Policies*, 13.

63. Government of Canada, Budget 2021, Part 2, Creating Jobs and Growth, accessed June 21, 2022, https://www.budget.gc.ca/2021/report-rapport/p2-en.html#68.

64. Government of Canada, "Consultations on reciprocal procurement policies in Canada," March 2022, https://www.international.gc.ca/trade-commerce/consultations/RP-AR/index.aspx?lang=eng. The 60-day comment period ended on May 30, 2022.

65. Government of Canada, "Consultations."

66. Government of Canada, "Consultations."

67. Government of Canada, "Consultations."

Canada's second proposal would echo the US's restrictions on infrastructure projects funded by the federal government. Canada could place conditions on its financial assistance to provinces and territories for infrastructure projects that it excluded from its international trade obligations.[68] Canada does not cover infrastructure projects undertaken by its DoT or urban rail and urban transportation projects under the GPA obligations.[69] Canada also suggested that it could impose domestic content requirements, "whereby foreign content would only be considered alongside Canadian content if that foreign content originates from a country that provides reciprocal access to infrastructure projects for Canadian suppliers, goods, and services."[70]

A third proposal would establish a set-aside program for Canadian small businesses. With such a program, it could exclude foreign suppliers (except those from the EU and the United Kingdom under their respective FTAs with Canada) from the federal procurement it sets aside for Canadian small businesses. Under the GPA, Canada has taken a broad reservation for such a program, one similar to the US reservation.[71] This reservation would provide Canada with considerable latitude in determining the value and scope of contracts subject to set-asides that would be consistent with its GPA obligations.

---

68. Government of Canada, "Consultations."

69. GPA, https://www.wto.org/english/tratop_e/gproc_e/gp_gpa_e.htm, Appendix I, Canada, Annex 6, n. 2(b) and Annex 7, n. 1(b) (excludes "urban rail and urban transportation equipment, systems, components and materials incorporated therein as well as all project related materials of iron or steel").

70. Government of Canada, "Consultations."

71. GPA, Appendix I, Canada, Annex 7, n. 2 ("This Agreement does not apply to set asides for small and minority owned businesses.")

4. EU UNILATERAL PROCUREMENT MEASURES

The EU repeatedly expressed concerns that even though it opened a large degree of its public procurement markets to third countries, its companies often encountered difficulties in gaining access to procurement opportunities in foreign markets.[72] It maintained an open procurement market because "[u]nder EU law, member states may not discriminate in favor of their own companies over those from other member states in buying goods and services."[73] Therefore, "it makes little sense [for them] to discriminate against third countries."[74] As a result, the EU struggled to gain the support of its member states for a measure that would penalize countries that denied access to EU suppliers to its procurement or refused to remove barriers to its procurement markets.

By 2022, the EU was finally able to overcome the resistance and develop a consensus on new measures. The first of these measures, the International Procurement Instrument (IPI), came into effect in August of that year. The second, the Foreign Subsidies Regulation, was expected to be implemented in 2023. While the EU intended that neither should interfere with its GPA commitments, parties could raise questions about them, depending on how they are implemented.

---

72. European Commission, "Guidance on the participation of third-country bidders and goods in the EU procurement market," July 24, 2019, https://ec.europa.eu/docsroom/documents/36601. BusinessEurope, *The EU and China: Addressing the Systemic Challenge*, January 2020, 4, https://www.businesseurope.eu/sites/buseur/files/media/reports_and_studies/2020-01-16_the_eu_and_china_-_addressing_the_systemic_challenge_-_full_paper.pdf.

73. Peter Chase, "The Missing Partnership: The United States, Europe, and China's Economic Challenge," The German Marshall Fund of the United States, 18, September 2020, https://www.gmfus.org/news/missing-partnership-united-states-europe-and-chinas-economic-challenge.

74. Chase, "The Missing Partnership," 18.

4.1 International Procurement Instrument

After a decade-long effort, in June 2022, the EU adopted a new trade regulation aimed at promoting greater reciprocity in access to international public procurement markets and improving market access opportunities for EU suppliers, goods, and services.[75] The procurement regulation, called the IPI, is intended to provide the EU with leverage to negotiate the opening of public procurement markets in third countries. It enables the EU to penalize or block tenders from countries that restrict EU participation in their home procurement markets and are not willing to negotiate an opening of their procurement.[76] The IPI entered into force on August 29, 2022.[77]

The EU adopted the IPI because of mounting concerns with the disparity between the openness of its public procurement and restrictions faced by EU suppliers in foreign procurement markets. According to the Council of the EU, "[f]ewer than half of the world's public procurement markets are currently open to European companies."[78] EU suppliers were often subject to discriminatory or restrictive practices in those markets. In proposing the measure,

---

75. Council of the EU, "International Procurement Instrument: Council gives green light to new rules promoting reciprocity," June 17, 2022, https://www.consilium.europa.eu/en/press/press-releases/2022/06/17/international-procurement-instrument-council-gives-final-go-ahead-to-new-rules-boosting-reciprocity/.

76. EU, "Regulation (EU) 2022/1031 of the European Parliament and of the Council of 23 June 2022 on the access of third-country economic operators, goods and services to the Union's public procurement and concession markets and procedures supporting negotiations on access of Union economic operators, goods and services to the public procurement and concession markets of third countries (International Procurement Instrument – IPI)," *Official Journal of the European Union* 65 (June 30, 2022): 173/1, https://eur-lex.europa.eu/legal-content/EN/TXT/PDF/?uri=CELEX:32022R1031&from=EN.

77. The Commission was required to develop guidelines within six months of the entry into force of the IPI on topics such as the origin of goods, services, and natural and legal persons. EU, Regulation (EU) 2022/1031, art. 12.

78. Council of the EU, "International Procurement Instrument."

the EU particularly focused on addressing China's procurement practices.[79]

The EU's pursuit of a means of promoting reciprocity with third countries began in 2012 when the European Commission proposed a procurement reciprocity measure that could have closed its procurement to suppliers from non-EU countries discriminating against EU suppliers in their own procurement.[80] At the time, it failed as two-thirds of the member states expressed reservations.[81]

Four years later, in 2016, the Commission tried again with a revised IPI proposal[82] that would have imposed price penalties of up to 20% on the price of tenders from countries restricting access to their home procurement and discriminating against EU suppliers.[83] That proposal drew criticism from both the business community

---

79. Chase, "The Missing Partnership," 18.

80. European Commission, "European Commission levels the playing field for European business in international procurement markets," March 21, 2012, http://trade.ec.europa.eu/doclib/press/index.cfm?id=788.

81. Council of the EU, "Amended proposal for a Regulation of the European Parliament and of the Council on the access of third-country goods and services to the Union's internal market in public procurement and procedures supporting negotiations on access of Union goods and services to the public procurement markets of third countries," 1, May 28, 2021, https://data.con-silium.europa.eu/doc/document/ST-9175-2021-INIT/en/pdf.

82. European Commission, "Amended Proposal for a Regulation of the European Parliament and of the Council on the access of third-country goods and services to the Union's internal market in public procurement and procedures supporting negotiations on access of Union goods and services to the public procurement markets of third countries," COM(2016) 34 final, January 29, 2016, http://trade.ec.europa.eu/doclib/docs/2016/january/tradoc_154187.pdf; European Commission, "European Commission Takes Action to Open Up International Procurement Markets," January 29, 2016, http://trade.ec.europa.eu/doclib/press/index.cfm?id=1448&title=European-Commission-Takes-Action-to-Open-Up-International-Procurement-Markets%20Page%202%20of.

83. The revised proposal was submitted "mainly as leverage in the [Transatlantic Trade and Investment Partnership] negotiations with the United States." Chase, "The Missing Partnership," 18.

and the European Parliament. The business community was concerned it would not effectively address issues with participation by state-owned enterprises (SOEs) in EU procurement.[84] The Parliament considered the proposal too weak and sought a reinstatement of the earlier proposed exclusions from the EU market.[85] When 14 member states maintained their reservations, the discussions were put on hold.[86]

The proposed IPI languished until 2021, when the member states adopted a mandate for negotiations with the European Parliament based on a revised IPI proposal that added the threat of market exclusion to the price adjustment mechanism.[87] In December 2021, the Parliament "backed the overall aim of the proposed [IPI] but tweaked its design, scope and member states' discretionary powers" in its application.[88] Subsequent negotiations between the EU's co-legislators (the European Parliament and the Council of the EU, representing the EU member states) resulted in the final IPI.

The IPI provides a legal basis–and leverage–for the European Commission to negotiate reciprocal access to government procurement markets in non-EU countries that have closed their procurement

---

84. BusinessEurope, *The EU and China*, 76. The business group recommended the exclusion of SOEs from a country that did not commit to opening its procurement to the EU and maintained discriminatory policies and practices against EU companies.

85. Iana Dreyer, "Procurement reciprocity: Caspary report calls for return to full market access suspension," *Borderlex*, July 12, 2017, https://borderlex.net/2017/07/12/procurement-reciprocity-caspary-report-calls-for-return-to-full-market-access-suspension/.

86. Council of the EU, "Amended proposal," 2.

87. Iana Dreyer, "IPI: Council finds compromise, paves way for trilogue," *Borderlex*, June 2, 2021, https://borderlex.net/2021/06/02/international-procurement-instrument-council-finds-compromise-paves-way-for-trilogue/.

88. European Parliament, "MEPs want the new international procurement instrument to apply more widely," December 14, 2021, https://www.europarl.europa.eu/news/hr/press-room/20211210IPR19214/meps-want-the-new-international-procurement-instrument-to-apply-more-widely.

markets to EU suppliers.[89] The Commission is authorized to investigate claims of third countries restricting the access of EU suppliers to their procurement markets. After it initiates an investigation, it must seek consultations with the third country with the aim of negotiating the removal or a remedy of its procurement restrictions.[90]

If the third country is unwilling to remove barriers, the Commission is authorized to adopt two types of IPI measures to restrict a targeted country's access to EU procurement. It may apply a penalty to the score of tenders submitted by suppliers from the targeted country or exclude such tenders entirely from the procurement. Under the "score adjustment" remedy, in procurement, where more than cost or price is considered in the evaluation of the tender, the score resulting from the tender evaluation of a targeted countries' suppliers could be reduced by as much as 50%. Where price or cost is the only contract award criterion, the level of score adjustment would be significantly higher, even up to 100%, "to ensure comparable effectiveness of the IPI measure." Once adopted, an IPI measure can remain in place for five years unless the third country withdraws or revises the offending measure or practice.[91]

The regulation applies to procurement of at least €15 million for public works and concessions and €5 million for goods and services.[92] It excludes least developed countries unless they are involved in the circumvention of an IPI measure such as transshipment.[93]

---

89. Pascal Friton, "European Procurement Developments in 2021: The EU's Persistent (and Sometimes a Little Desperate) Pursuit of a Resilient Economy," *2021 Thomson Reuters' Government Contracts Year in Review Conference Briefs,* 108 (2022).

90. EU, Regulation (EU) 2022/1031, art. 5. The Commission can self-initiate an investigation or undertake one based on a substantiated complaint from an interested party or a member state. It must complete its investigation within nine months (unless it is extended for up to five months).

91. EU, Regulation (EU) 2022/1031, art. 6.

92. EU, Regulation (EU) 2022/1031, art. 6(4).

93. EU, Regulation (EU) 2022/1031, art. 4.

The IPI aims at procurement that is not covered by the GPA or EU FTAs. However, it does not exempt GPA and FTA parties in procurement where they have not secured rights under the plurilateral agreement or an FTA. Indeed, in 2016, when the European Commission proposed a revised IPI, it emphasized that it was needed for its ongoing negotiations of the Transatlantic Trade and Investment Partnership with the US, an FTA with Japan, and China's accession to the GPA. It noted that "[t]he adoption of the IPI would send a strong signal to these and other partners and would encourage negotiators to accelerate and pursue a substantial opening of their procurement markets."[94] Hence, GPA and FTA parties could be subject to an IPI measure if the EU finds that they were discriminating against EU suppliers in procurement not covered by an agreement. USTR reported it raised concerns with the EU in 2020 and 2021 relating to the potential application of the measure to the US.[95]

4.2 Foreign Subsidies Regulation

In contrast to the decade-long development of the IPI, the EU moved expeditiously to adopt a regulation aimed at foreign subsidies that distort the EU internal market. Two years after the European Commission issued a white paper proposing a remedy for such distortions,[96] and a year after it proposed a regulation,[97] the

---

94. European Commission, "Amended Proposal," 2.

95. USTR, *2022 National Trade Estimate Report on Foreign Trade Barriers*, March 2022, 204, https://ustr.gov/sites/default/files/2022%20National%20 Trade%20Estimate%20Report%20on%20Foreign%20Trade%20Barriers.pdf.

96. European Commission, "Commission adopts White Paper on foreign subsidies in the Single Market," June 17, 2020, https://ec.europa.eu/commission/ presscorner/detail/en/ip_20_1070.

97. European Commission, "Proposal for a Regulation of the European Parliament and the Council on foreign subsidies distorting the internal market," COM/2021/223 final, May 5, 2021, https://eur-lex.europa.eu/legal-content/ EN/TXT/PDF/?uri=CELEX:52021PC0223&from=EN.

European Parliament and the Council of the EU reached a political agreement on a Foreign Subsidies Regulation (Regulation).[98] The Regulation was expected to enter into force in 2023 after its formal adoption by the Parliament and the Council.[99]

The Foreign Subsidies Regulation applies to both public procurement and concentrations (mergers and acquisitions and joint ventures). The application of the Regulation to procurement was prompted by concerns that foreign subsidies can provide foreign firms with an unfair advantage in EU public procurement by enabling bidders receiving such subsidies to win contracts with bids below market price or even below cost, to the disadvantage of European firms.[100] The Regulation gives the European Commission the power to investigate financial contributions granted by non-EU governments to companies active in the EU. Financial contributions are defined very broadly.[101]

---

98. European Parliament, "Provisional Agreement Resulting from Interinstitutional Negotiations: Regulation of the European Parliament and of the Council on foreign subsidies distorting the internal market" ("Provisional Agreement on Foreign Subsidies") July 11, 2022, art. 27, https://www.europarl.europa.eu/meetdocs/2014_2019/plmrep/COMMITTEES/INTA/DV/2022/07-13/1260231_EN.pdf.

99. EU, "Foreign Subsidies: Commission welcomes political agreement on Regulation on distortive foreign subsidies," June 30, 2022, https://ec.europa.eu/commission/presscorner/detail/e%20n/ip_22_4190. The regulation becomes directly applicable across the EU six months after its entry into force. Before the Regulation enters into force, the Commission is expected to adopt an Implementing Regulation.

100. European Commission, "Commission adopts White Paper."

101. Financial contributions that must be notified include: (i) any transfer of funds or liabilities such as capital injections, grants, loans, loan guarantees, fiscal incentives, setting off of operating losses, compensation for financial burdens imposed by public authorities, debt forgiveness, debt to equity swaps, or rescheduling; (ii) foregone public revenues otherwise due, that is tax exemptions or other tax benefits; and (iii) the provision or purchase of goods or services to public entities. European Parliament, "Provisional Agreement on Foreign Subsidies," art. 2(2)(a).

The Regulation requires notification of financial contributions received from foreign governments. The procurement notification requirement applies to companies participating in large public tenders in EU countries, where the estimated value of the procurement is at least €250 million, and the bid involves a foreign financial contribution of at least €4 million per third country. In such cases, the supplier must notify the contracting authority of all foreign financial contributions it received in the three years preceding its participation in the tender (or a declaration it had not received any).[102] In open tendering, the supplier must submit the notification (or declaration) with its tender. In procurements with multiple stages, the supplier is obligated to submit two notifications: first with the request to participate in the procurement and then as an update with the tender or final tender.[103]

The European Commission conducts a preliminary review of notifications and, if warranted, an in-depth investigation to determine whether a subsidy distorts a procurement.[104] During investigations, the procurement procedures can continue, except the contract cannot be awarded. If the Commission finds that financial

---

102. The Regulation provides detailed provisions relating to public procurement procedures. European Parliament, "Provisional Agreement on Foreign Subsidies," arts. 26-32.

103. European Parliament, "Provisional Agreement on Foreign Subsidies," art. 28.

104. The Commission's preliminary review of notifications and in-depth investigations can take up to 160 working days. Its preliminary review can take up to 20 working days from the notification with a possible extension of 10 working days, and the in-depth investigation can last up to 110 working days with a potential extension of 20 working days. European Parliament, "Provisional Agreement on Foreign Subsidies," art. 29(4). The maximum of 160 days is a significant reduction from 260 days in the Commission's initial proposal. A group of businesses from the US, Australia, India, Japan, and South Korea had raised concerns with the procedural elements of the proposed regulation, including the potential length of the Commission review. American Chamber of Commerce to the EU, *Foreign Subsidies Regulation: cross-industry perspectives*, February 15, 2022, https://www.amchameu.eu/system/files/position_papers/foreign_subsidies_regulation_views_from_key_eu_trade_and_investment_partners.pdf.

contributions constitute distortive subsidies, it can impose measures to remedy the distortion.[105]

An investigated bidder cannot be awarded the contract until cleared by the Commission. Upon a finding that a foreign subsidy distorted the internal market, the Commission can prohibit the award of a public procurement contract to the subsidized bidder unless the bidder makes "commitments that fully and effectively remove the distortion on the internal market."[106]

The Regulation was intended to close a perceived regulatory gap. While subsidies granted by EU member states were subject to a rigorous EU state aid regime, subsidies by third countries that benefit foreign operators active in the EU were unregulated. In addition, the EU's existing public procurement rules were not considered sufficient to address and remedy distortions caused by such subsidies.[107]

The European Commission acknowledged that the exclusion of bidders under the Regulation would have to be compatible with the EU's commitments under the GPA and its FTAs, especially the provision on conditions for participation.[108] That provision limits such conditions to those "essential to ensure that a supplier has the legal and financial capacities and the commercial and technical abilities to undertake the relevant procurement."[109]

The EU has included provisions related to subsidies in government procurement in FTAs with several GPA parties (Japan, Singapore, and the United Kingdom). Those FTAs allow a procuring entity to inquire about a subsidy but only the Singapore FTA allows the exclusion of a supplier in such cases.

---

105. EU, "Foreign Subsidies."

106. European Parliament, "Provisional Agreement on Foreign Subsidies," art. 30.

107. Friton, "European Procurement Developments," 102.

108. European Commission, "White Paper on leveling the playing field as regards foreign subsidies," COM(2020) 253 final, June 17, 2020, 44, https://ec.europa.eu/competition/international/overview/foreign_subsidies_white_paper.pdf.

109. GPA, art. VIII.1.

CHAPTER 13

GOVERNMENT PROCUREMENT IN CHINA AND INTERNATIONAL AGREEMENTS

1. INTRODUCTION

China poses a unique challenge to the international procurement system. Despite its growing economic prowess and stature on the world's stage, it has no international obligations to allow foreign firms to participate in its procurement on the same basis as its domestic firms. As the world's second-largest economy, its government procurement is significant, particularly when purchases by its state-controlled entities are included. As its procurement has grown over the course of the 21st century, China has developed, and continues to refine, a legal framework to govern its procurement system. It has also increasingly aligned its procurement system with international norms.

Even with the improvements to its procurement system, China maintains 'buy local' policies and practices that serve as obstacles to foreign firms that want to participate in its procurement market. Moreover, they have no legal recourse because China has yet to enter any international agreement that binds its government procurement. Although it applied to join the GPA in 2007, its negotiations have been protracted. They entered their 15th year in 2022 and have already taken as long as China's negotiations to join the WTO. While it has offered to open procurement that is commensurate in many respects with the coverage of existing GPA parties, China has not made a market access offer acceptable to the GPA parties. Moreover, with growing tensions between China and the West, especially the US, the prospects for its accession to the GPA are in question.

2. IMPORTANCE OF PROCUREMENT MARKET

China's government procurement market had quadrupled in size since 2010, when the WTO estimated its value to be roughly ¥842 billion.[1] Six years later (2016), its value had leaped to ¥3.11 trillion,[2] and it continued to climb to ¥3.3 trillion by 2019.[3] Most of this procurement has been conducted at the subcentral government level. In 2019, local government procurement comprised 91.9% of China's total procurement, with central government purchases accounting for only 8.1%.[4]

However, these government procurement figures represent only a portion of China's procurement. They do not include purchases by

1. WTO, *Trade Policy Review, Report by the Secretariat*, WT/TPR/S/300, May 27, 2014, para. 3.178.

2. WTO, *Trade Policy Review: China, Report by the Secretariat*, WT/TPR/S/375/ Rev 1, September 14, 2018, para. 3.190.

3. WTO, *Trade Policy Review, Report by the Secretariat*, WT/TPR/S/415, September 15, 2021, para. 3.210.

4. WTO, *Trade Policy Review*, 2021, para. 3.210. Of 31 provincial-level governments that reported procurement data to the central government, 10 provinces/municipalities accounted for most of China's government procurement. They were Guangdong, Shandong, Jiangsu, Henan, Zhejiang, Anhui, Sichuan, Shanghai, Guangxi, and Hebei. WTO, *Trade Policy Review*, 2021, n. 170.

China's state-owned enterprises (SOEs), which conduct most of the nation's procurement, according to a BusinessEurope report.[5] The WTO Secretariat also pointed out that a large number of infrastructure projects and public utility works are carried out by SOEs.[6] Yet, their procurement is not counted in China's government procurement figures because they are not subject to its main procurement law, the Government Procurement Law (GPL). If a purchase is not covered by this law, it is not considered government procurement and hence is not included in China's procurement figures.[7] The exclusion of SOEs likely explains why China's government procurement accounted for only 3.3% of its GDP in 2019.[8] This stands in sharp contrast to the 10% to 15% of GDP in most countries.[9]

3. LEGAL FRAMEWORK OF PROCUREMENT SYSTEM

3.1 Government Procurement Law

In less than 25 years, China has developed a broad array of laws and regulations to govern its government procurement. It adopted its first modern procurement regulation when it was in the midst of negotiations to join the WTO.[10] Then, shortly after its 2001 entry

---

5. BusinessEurope, *The EU and China: Addressing the Systemic Challenge*, January 2020, 73, https://www.businesseurope.eu/sites/buseur/files/media/reports_and_studies/2020-01-16_the_eu_and_china_-_addressing_the_systemic_challenge_-_full_paper.pdf.

6. WTO, *Trade Policy Review*, 2021, para. 3.211.

7. WTO, *Trade Policy Review: China, Report by the Secretariat*, WT/TPR/S/342, June 15, 2016, para. 3.183.

8. WTO, *Trade Policy Review*, 2021, table 3.25.

9. American Chamber of Commerce in the People's Republic of China, *2022 American Business in China White Paper*, https://www.amchamchina.org/white_paper/2022-american-business-in-china-white-paper/, 106.

10. The Interim Regulations on Government Procurement were promulgated by the MoF in 1998, based on the United Nations Model Law on Procurement of Goods, Construction and Services. WTO, Ministerial Conference, *Report of the Working Party on the Accession of China*, WT/MIN(01)/3, November 10, 2001, para. 337.

into the multilateral organization, China enacted the GPL, its most important procurement law, and implemented it at the beginning of 2003.[11] The law's implementing regulations came into effect 12 years later, in 2015.[12] The GPL, which is administered by the Ministry of Finance (MoF), governs purchasing activities conducted with fiscal funds by state organs, public institutions, and social organizations at all levels of government. It covers these entities' procurement of goods, construction projects, and services listed in a Centralized Procurement Catalogue or when the value of these items exceeds a specified threshold.[13] However, when government entities covered under the GPL use tendering in the procurement of construction works, they must follow the procedures set out in China's other major procurement law, the Tendering and Bidding Law (TBL).[14] China has adopted numerous administrative regulations and other measures to implement these and other laws.[15]

As of late 2022, the GPL did not apply to procurement by SOEs or projects covered by the TBL. It also did not apply to

---

11. The Government Procurement Law of the People's Republic of China was adopted at the 28th Session of the Ninth National People's Congress on June 29, 2002 and entered into force on January 1, 2003. It was revised in August 2014.

12. Implementing Regulations of the Government Procurement Law of the People's Republic of China, Order of the State Council No. 658, January 30, 2015.

13. The thresholds vary across the country. The State Council publishes the thresholds for procurement at the central government level, and provinces, municipalities, and autonomous regions promulgate their own thresholds. WTO, *Trade Policy Review*, 2018, n. 114.

14. WTO, *Trade Policy Review*, 2021, para. 3.192.

15. For details on the administrative measures relating to government procurement, see WTO, *Trade Policy Review: China*, 2021, table 3.26; and Alison Schonberg, *Government Procurement and Sales to State-Owned Enterprises in China: Challenges and Best Practice*, US-China Business Council (USCBC), September 2021, https://www.uschina.org/reports/government-procurement-and-sales-state-owned-enterprises-china. The USCBC report was based on interviews with 30 US companies across the information and communication technology, health care, energy, and manufacturing sectors.

procurement conducted with loans from foreign governments or international organizations, emergency procurement for natural disasters, procurement related to national security, and military procurement.[16] Neither procurement law, reportedly, applied to major procurement projects, such as the Three Gorges Dam, the Bird's Nest, and other 2008 Olympic venues in China.[17]

The GPL sets out general principles, procurement methods and procedures, and a complaint mechanism. It also defines the roles of participants in procurement activities, the supervision and monitoring duties of government bodies, and contracting rules.[18] The law requires government procurement to be conducted in a manner contributing to the state's economic and social policy goals, including environmental protection and the promotion of the development of SMEs. This emphasis on the promotion of SMEs is important as they undertake more than 70% of China's government procurement (by value), according to the WTO Secretariat.[19] China supports them through a series of procurement measures that include set-asides, implemented in January 2021.[20]

---

16. The Central Military Commission issues separate regulations concerning military procurement. WTO, *Trade Policy Review: China*, 2021, para. 3.191.

17. European Parliament, European Parliamentary Research Service, *EU international procurement instrument*, by Marcin Szczepański, March 2022, 3, https://www.europarl.europa.eu/RegData/etudes/BRIE/2020/649403/EPRS_BRI(2020)649403_EN.pdf.

18. WTO, *Trade Policy Review*, 2021, para. 3.191.

19. GPL, art. 9; WTO, *Trade Policy Review*, 2021, para 3.223.

20. The SME measures 'in principle' require contracts for goods and services below ¥2 million and construction work contracts below ¥4 million to be set aside for SMEs. In addition, at least 30% of the contracts above those thresholds (based on value) should be performed by SMEs. The measures further require that at least 60% of the contracts set aside should be awarded to small and micro businesses. In addition to set-asides, the SME goal can be met through contract splitting, consortium bidding, or subcontracting. SMEs can also be granted price preferences. Measures on Promoting the Development of Small and Medium Enterprises through Government Procurement, MoF Circular Cai Ku No. 46, 2020; WTO, *Trade Policy Review*, 2021, para. 3.223.

The GPL includes a 'Buy China' mandate that requires government entities to purchase domestic goods, construction works, and services (except when they are not available in China, cannot be acquired on reasonable commercial terms, or are for use outside China).[21] China has yet to adopt rules specifying what constitutes domestic products in its procurement regime. In 2010, the MoF, the National Development Reform Commission (NDRC), and the General Administration of Customs jointly issued draft "Administrative Measures for Government Procurement of Domestic Products" for public comment.[22] The draft measure defined a domestic product as a final product manufactured in China, for which the share of domestic production costs exceeds 50%. The US government and industry submitted comments on the draft.[23] However, as of late 2022, China had not released a final version of this regulation.[24] In 2022, the US Trade Representative (USTR) pointed out that the absence of any "specific metrics, such as a percentage of value-added within China, for foreign products to qualify for many procurements and tenders [. . .] often works to the disadvantage of foreign companies."[25]

In 2007, MoF issued Administrative Measures for Government Procurement of Imported Products.[26] These measures supplement

---

21. GPL, art. 10.

22. MoF, (For Comment Draft) Administration Measures for Government Procurement of Domestic Products, May 24, 2010. The GPL provides that the State Council will issue regulations determining what is a domestic product.

23. USTR, *2015 Report to Congress on China's WTO Compliance*, 92, December 2015. In its comments, the US expressed concerns regarding the lack of details on how the draft measure would be implemented as well as its broad application.

24. USTR, *2021 Report to Congress On China's WTO Compliance*, 44, February 2022, https://ustr.gov/sites/default/files/enforcement/WTO/2021%20USTR%20 Report%20to%20Congress%20on%20China's%20WTO%20Compliance.pdf.

25. USTR, *National Trade Estimate Report on Foreign Trade Barriers*, 99, March 31, 2022, https://ustr.gov/sites/default/files/2022%20National%20 Trade%20Estimate%20Report%20on%20Foreign%20Trade%20Barriers.pdf.

26. MoF Notice Cai Ku No. 119, 2007; WTO, *Trade Policy Review*, 2021, table 3.26.

the GPL and apply to activities in which government entities purchase imported products. They require administrative approval for entities to procure foreign products. They limit approval to products not available domestically or under reasonable commercial terms. Under the measures, "imported products" are goods produced abroad that enter the territory of China after customs declaration, inspection, and clearance.[27]

The MoF has proposed major revisions of the GPL, which would bring China's procurement system closer to conformity with the GPA. In December 2020, it invited public comments on a proposed GPL revision.[28] However, before it had implemented that proposal, the ministry solicited public comments on another revision of the GPL in July 2022.[29] This proposal could significantly expand the scope of the GPL as it appears to extend the law to SOEs engaged in procurement for public purposes. It would broaden the law's current application to state organs, institutions, and organizations to include "other procurement entities" that use fiscal funds or other state-owned assets to acquire goods, construction, and services under contracts.[30] It defined such entities as "public welfare state-owned enterprises that engage in public utilities or operate public infrastructure or public service networks for public purposes."[31] The MoF did not indicate in its 2022 proposal when it expected to finalize the GPL revision.

---

27. Schonberg, *Government Procurement*, 19.

28. MoF, "The Government Procurement Law of the People's Republic of China (Revised Draft for Solicitation of Comments), Notice to the public to solicit opinions," December 8, 2020, http://tfs.mof.gov.cn/zhengcefabu/202012/t20201204_3632547.htm. For an overview of the proposed GPL changes, see WTO, *Trade Policy Review*, 2021, para. 3.212.

29. MoF, "Government Procurement Law of the People's Republic of China (Revised Draft for Comments)," July 16, 2022, http://fgk.mof.gov.cn/ui/start/#/law_surve_portal/opinionGathering/id=1547866535346696194.

30. MoF, "GPL (Revised Draft)," art. 2.

31. MoF, "GPL (Revised Draft)," art. 12.

If China brings SOEs under the GPL, it will constitute a major change in its procurement regime. It could also contribute to a more unified procurement system. The 2022 proposal appears to establish that as a goal for the GPL.[32] Such a change would respond to concerns that the US government and the business community have raised with respect to China's two disparate procurement laws, as discussed below. It could also facilitate the coverage of SOE procurement under the GPA and other trade agreements.

The proposed revision also included a new article on International Treaties[33] that may facilitate China's entry into international agreements with procurement commitments. This article provides that China would accord most-favored-nation (MFN) treatment and national treatment to other parties in accordance with international treaties and agreements that China concluded or joined through accession.[34]

One area of concern with the new proposed revision is the establishment of a national security review regime for government procurement (first proposed in 2020). Under that regime, all government procurement activities determined to have national security implications would be subject to review. The regime has raised concerns in the foreign business community because of its potentially broad scope and uncertainty as to how it might be applied.[35]

---

32. MoF, "GPL (Revised Draft)," art. 1.

33. MoF, "GPL (Revised Draft)," art. 118.

34. This provision might provide the authority for the Chinese government to waive 'buy China' requirements in procurement covered under an agreement.

35. American Chamber, *2022 American Business*, 106.

3.2 Tendering and Bidding Law

China enacted the TBL in 1999 and implemented it in January 2000.[36] This law, which is under the NDRC's jurisdiction, provides tendering and bidding procedures for certain classes of projects. It applies to all construction and works projects below a threshold, without regard to the type of entity conducting the procurement, such as a government agency or an SOE. As the *de facto* law that applies to procurement activities by SOEs,[37] the TBL's scope extends to all tenders of these enterprises. It covers large infrastructure projects, [38] public utility projects, projects fully or partially financed by the state, and projects financed by loans and aid funds from international organizations and foreign governments, as well as large-scale, privately invested projects for public interest (mainly joint ventures).[39]

The NDRC proposed a major revision of the TBL for public comment in December 2019.[40] European and US businesses operating in China have noted potential benefits of the proposed revision as well as concerns. They have argued these revisions "could have a positive impact and lead to an increased transparency and

---

36. The Tendering and Bidding Law was adopted by the 11th Meeting of the Standing Committee of the Ninth National People's Congress on August 30, 1999, promulgated by Order No. 21 of the President of the People's Republic of China on August 30, 1999, and effective as of January 1, 2000. Implementing Regulations entered into force in 2011.

37. WTO, *Trade Policy Review*, 2018, para. 3.192. For more information, see WTO, *Trade Policy Review*, 2021, para. 3.212.

38. The large-scale infrastructure projects extend to construction, aviation, shipping, engineering, architecture, transportation, power, and water.

39. European Union Chamber of Commerce in China, *The European Business in China – Position Paper 2021/2022*, n. 41, September 23, 2021, https://www.europeanchamber.com.cn/en/publications-position-paper.

40. NDRC, "The People's Republic of China Law on Tendering and Bidding (Public Consultation Draft)," December 3, 2019, https://www.ndrc.gov.cn/hdjl/yjzq/yjfk/zbtbf/202001/t20200103_1218432.html. For an overview of the proposed changes in the TBL, see WTO, *Trade Policy Review*, 2021, para. 3.212.

improved fairness in tendering activities" and bring it closer to GPA requirements.[41]

3.3 Foreign Investment Law

China's Foreign Investment Law, implemented in January 2020, included guarantees for participation by foreign firms in its government procurement.[42] It guarantees that foreign-invested enterprises (FIEs)[43] can participate in government procurement activities through fair competition and equal treatment.[44] The law and its implementing regulations require government authorities to treat goods produced by FIEs and services provided by them in China the same as those of domestic enterprises. The authorities must neither discriminate against foreign firms in the procurement process nor restrict a supplier's participation in procurement based on its ownership, organizational form, shareholding structure, the nationality of its investors, or the brand of the product or service it offers.[45] The investment law also directed the Chinese government to establish a complaint mechanism for FIEs.[46]

---

41. EU Chamber, *The European Business*, 318; see also American Chamber, *2022 American Business*, 110.

42. Foreign Investment Law of the People's Republic of China (FIL). It was promulgated on March 15, 2019 by the National People's Congress and entered into force on January 1, 2020.

43. The FIL defined a foreign-invested enterprise as "an enterprise that is incorporated under Chinese laws within the territory of China and is wholly or partly invested by a foreign investor." FIL, art. 2.

44. FIL, art. 16.

45. Implementing Regulations of the Foreign Investment Law, implemented on January 1, 2020, art. 15. The regulations provide that government authorities must not apply differential or discriminatory treatment to FIEs in procurement activities, including the publication of procurement information, determination of conditions for suppliers, examination of supplier qualifications, and bid evaluation criteria.

46. FIL, art. 26.

4. WTO COMMITMENTS RELATING TO PROCUREMENT

During negotiations to accede to the WTO, China undertook obligations relating to government procurement and purchases by its SOEs. Its commitments were incorporated into a Working Party Report on its WTO accession.[47] Most significantly, China declared its intention to initiate negotiations for membership in the GPA by tabling a market access offer "as soon as possible" after becoming a WTO member.[48] In the interim, China promised to provide foreign suppliers with an equal opportunity to participate in its procurement under the MFN principle and conduct its procurement in a transparent manner. That promise applied to the procurement of its central and subnational government entities and public entities that were not engaged in exclusively commercial activities. China further stated that such procurement would only be subject to published laws and other measures.[49]

China also confirmed in its WTO commitments that all state-owned and state-invested enterprises would make purchases and sales based solely on commercial considerations, including price. In addition, WTO members' firms would be able to compete for purchases of these enterprises on non-discriminatory terms and conditions. Finally, it assured WTO members that the Chinese government would not influence, directly or indirectly, the commercial decisions of these enterprises, except in a manner consistent with the agreement that established the WTO. This commitment included the country of origin of goods that they purchased or sold.[50]

---

47. WTO, *Report of the WTO Working Party on the Accession of China*, WT/ACC/CHN/49, paras. 339 and 341, October 1, 2001.

48. WTO, *Report of the WTO Working Party*, para. 341.

49. WTO, *Report of the WTO Working Party*, para. 339.

50. WTO, *Report of the WTO Working Party*, para. 46.

5. GPA ACCESSION NEGOTIATIONS

5.1 Progression and Status

China became a WTO member in December 2001. Nearly five years later, after "constant pressure from its major trade partners, [China] made the first move towards fulfilling [its] commitment" to seek GPA membership.[51] In an April 2006 meeting of the US-China Joint Commission on Commerce and Trade, China pledged to table its initial offer of GPA coverage by the end of 2007.[52] As promised, it submitted its accession application and initial market access offer.[53] Over the next 12 years, it tabled six revised offers: a new offer each year from 2010 through 2014[54] and then, after a hiatus of nearly five years, a sixth revised offer in October 2019.[55]

---

51. Ping Wang, "Coverage of the WTO's Agreement on Government Procurement: Challenges of Integrating China and Other Countries with a Large State Sector into the Global Trading System," *Journal of International Economic Law* 10, no. 4 (2007): 5.

52. "The US-China Joint Commission on Commerce and Trade (JCCT) Outcomes on U.S. Requests," April 11, 2006. In addition, in its 2006 WTO Trade Policy Review, China announced it would formally initiate its accession to the GPA by tabling its Appendix I Offer no later than the end of 2007. WTO, *Trade Policy Review China*, WT/TPR/M/161, June 15, 2006, 237.

53. WTO, Committee on Government Procurement, "Application for Accession to the Agreement on Government Procurement and Initial Appendix I Offer," GPA/Acc/Chn/1, January 7, 2008. (China submitted the documents on December 28, 2007 and circulated them to the parties in January 2008.)

54. For an examination of China's negotiations to join the GPA through its 2014 revised offer, see Jean Heilman Grier, "What Are the Prospects for Concluding Work on China's GPA Accession in 2015?," *Public Procurement Law Review* 24 (2015): 221.

55. WTO, "China submits revised offer for joining government procurement pact," October 23, 2019, https://www.wto.org/english/news_e/news19_e/gpro_23oct19_e.htm; WTO, "Accession of the People's Republic of China to the Agreement on Government Procurement, Sixth Revised Offer," GPA/ACC/CHN/51, October 21, 2019.

China made several revised offers in response to commitments made in US-China trade forums. For example, in a May 2012 US-China Strategic and Economic Dialogue meeting, China committed to submit "a new comprehensive revised offer" in 2012 that responded to the requests of GPA parties.[56] Similarly, at the 24th US-China Joint Commission on Commerce and Trade meeting in December 2013, China promised to present a new revised offer in 2014 that would be "on the whole commensurate with the coverage of GPA parties."[57]

While China's initial offer was extremely modest, the revised offers gradually expanded the procurement that it was prepared to open under the GPA. A comparison of the key elements of China's 2019 offer with its initial offer and elements of earlier revised offers illustrated its efforts to align its commitments with the coverage of existing parties and advance its accession negotiations. It also highlighted the remaining issues, which are detailed in the following section.

Entities: China has offered entities in three categories: central government, subcentral government, and other entities. It expanded coverage of central government entities from an initial offer of 50 entities to 64 entities in the 2019 offer. In addition, after long contending that it would not cover defense procurement,[58] China offered nonsensitive military procurement with the listing of its Ministry of Defense and a military entity, the Logistics Support Department of the Central Military Commission.[59] Aside from the

---

56. US Department of Treasury, *U.S.-Fact Sheet – Economic Track of the Fourth Meeting of the U.S.-China Strategic and Economic Dialogue (S&ED)*, May 4, 2012, https://home.treasury.gov/news/press-releases/tg1568.

57. USTR, *24th U.S.-China Joint Commission on Commerce and Trade Fact Sheet*, December 2013, https://ustr.gov/about-us/policy-offices/press-office/fact-sheets/2013/December/JCCT-outcomes.

58. Grier, "What Are the Prospects," 225.

59. WTO, *Trade Policy Review*, 2021, para. 3.229.

issue of whether China's defense offer is comparable to that of the GPA parties, its coverage of central government entities appears generally comparable to that of the current parties.[60]

Although China did not offer any subcentral entities in its initial offer, it gradually added such entities until it offered coverage of all 22 provinces and four province-level municipalities in the 2019 offer.[61] It did not offer any minority autonomous regions at the provincial level,[62] such as Tibet, Inner Mongolia, and Xinjiang.[63]

China's 2019 offer listed 66 other entities, including 36 local colleges and universities (at least one from each province)[64]–a significant increase from the dozen regulatory commissions and entities listed in the initial offer.[65] After originally asserting that it could not cover SOEs, China included several in its 2014 offer[66] and added 16 more in 2019.[67] They included the China State Railway Group and its 18 subcentral groups, along with provincial and

---

60. In its 2014 offer, China withdrew a restriction that would have limited coverage of central government entities to those located in Beijing.

61. WTO, "Sixth Revised Offer." The province-level municipalities are Beijing, Chongqing, Shanghai, and Tianjin.

62. WTO, *Trade Policy Review*, 2021, para. 3.229.

63. In its 2019 offer, China removed two limitations in earlier offers. One had provided for the phased-in coverage of provinces over three years. The other excluded the procurement of construction services using a special fund of the central government. Grier, "What Are the Prospects," 228.

64. WTO, *Trade Policy Review*, 2021, para. 3.229; WTO, "Sixth Revised Offer."

65. Grier, "What Are the Prospects," 222. In its 2019 offer, China moved five entities listed in its Annex 3 to Annex 1. They are the Xinhua News Agency, Chinese Academy of Sciences, Chinese Academy of Social Sciences, Chinese Academy of Engineering, and Development Research Center of the State Council.

66. WTO, Committee on Government Procurement, "Accession of the People's Republic of China to the Agreement on Government Procurement, Fifth Revised Offer," GPA/ACC/CHN/45, December 23, 2014. The offer included the China Post Group, Agricultural Development Bank of China, and China Central Depository and Clearing Co., Ltd., as well as national museums, national library, several universities, and hospitals.

67. WTO, "Sixth Revised Offer;" WTO, *Trade Policy Review*, 2021, para. 3.229.

local SOEs.[68] While the 2019 offer brought its coverage of SOEs to approximately 20, it was only a fraction of its 150,000 SOEs.[69]

Thresholds: China initially proposed exceptionally high thresholds[70] for its central government entities: 500,000 SDRs for goods, four million SDRs for services, and 200 million SDRs for construction services.[71] It gradually reduced these thresholds in the revised offers until in the 2019 offer permanent thresholds were aligned with those applied by most GPA parties.[72] However, it continued to propose higher transitional thresholds for one year.[73] This represented a significant drop from the initial proposal to apply such thresholds for five years. As a measure reserved for developing countries, transitional thresholds require the approval of the current parties.

---

68. The type of provincial and other local SOEs added in China's 2019 offer (and the provinces in which they are located) are airport authorities (Beijing, Guangdong, Guizhou, Henan, Shanghai, Yunnan), highways, roads, and bridges (Hunan, Jilin, Shanxi, Sichuan), subways (Beijing, Shanghai), waterworks (Beijing, Tianjin), and a port (the Ningbo Meishan-Island International Container Terminal in Zhejiang Province). WTO, "Sixth Revised Offer."

69. World Economic Forum, *Industrial Policy and International Competition: Trade and Investment Perspectives*, 15, February 8, 2022, https://www.weforum. org/whitepapers/industrial-policy-and-international-competition-trade-and-investment-perspectives.

70. A threshold is a monetary value below which procurement is not covered under the GPA.

71. For its other entities, China proposed thresholds of 900,000 SDRs for supplies and 300 million SDRs for construction services. Grier, "What Are the Prospects," 222.

72. WTO, "China submits revised offer for joining government procurement pact," October 23, 2019. The thresholds applied by most parties are 130,000 SDRs for goods and services purchased by central government entities, 200,000 SDRs for such purchases by subcentral government entities, 400,000 SDRs for other entities, and 5 million SDRs for construction services procured by all entities.

73. In its 2019 offer, China set transitional thresholds for goods and services at 200,000 SDRs for central government entities, 500,000 SDRs for subcentral entities, and 600,000 SDRs for other entities. For construction services, it proposed a 7.5 million SDRs threshold (except for other entities, which would apply a 10 million SDRs threshold). WTO, "Sixth Revised Offer."

Goods: In the initial offer, China limited its goods coverage to three categories.[74] Its use of a positive list to specify goods coverage was contrary to the established GPA practice of covering all goods except those listed. Subsequently, China aligned its goods coverage with the GPA standard by listing its excluded goods in a goods annex. In the 2019 revision, China covered all goods "other than such products as grain, sugar and tobacco as specified in Annex 2A1" of its Protocol of Accession to the WTO.[75] It also excluded procurement by its military forces when providing foreign assistance and overseas support.[76]

Services: After China offered only two service categories in the initial offer,[77] it expanded its services coverage in the revised offers with the 2019 offer listing 35 service categories. Consistent with the approach of many GPA parties, China based its coverage of services on reciprocity, which means that it would only open a service to another party if that party reciprocated by providing China with access to the same service.[78]

Construction Services: China's 2019 offer of coverage of all construction services (except exclusions for certain entities)[79]

---

74. Its initial offer would have opened only general equipment (electrical equipment and furniture), office consumables (such as paper and floppy disks), and construction and decoration materials, including wood, cement, glass, and paint.

75. Annex 2A1 of the Protocol on China's Accession to the WTO, Products Subject to State Trading (Import) lists grain, vegetable oil, sugar, tobacco, crude oil, processed oil, chemical fertilizer, and cotton. WTO, "Accession of the People's Republic of China, Decision of 10 November 2001," WT/L/432, November 23, 2001, https://www.wto.org/english/thewto_e/acc_e/completeacc_e.htm#chn.

76. WTO, "Sixth Revised Offer."

77. The service categories were rental and leasing services for equipment and machinery and overseas training.

78. China also subjects its service coverage to the limitations and conditions in its commitments under the 1995 WTO General Agreement on Trade in Services. WTO, "Sixth Revised Offer."

79. WTO, "Sixth Revised Offer."

substantially improved its initial market access offer.[80] China also removed a dredging exclusion.

Exclusions: China incorporated several exclusions and reservations in its offers.[81] It reserved the right to impose offsets such as requirements of domestic content or transfer of technology. It also excluded procurement aimed at supporting SMEs.[82] Finally, China expressed the intention to delay its implementation of the agreement for two years after it became a GPA party.[83] That would allow it to participate in the procurement of the other parties upon accession but delay their access to its procurement for two years.

Checklist of Issues: China submitted its replies to the Checklist of Issues for Provision of Information Relating to Accession to the Agreement on Government Procurement (Checklist) in September 2008.[84] Replies to the Checklist are intended to facilitate understanding and consultations relating to an acceding country's procurement regime and its conformance to the agreement.[85]

Since tabling the 2019 offer, China updated its replies to the Checklist, described its government procurement reform efforts, and engaged with parties on its accession. Though the WTO Committee on Government Procurement expressed the hope for

---

80. The offer was limited to the construction of office and residential buildings. Grier, "What Are the Prospects," 222.

81. For example, China reserved the right to apply the GPA to particular suppliers in a given procurement for the protection of its national security interests.

82. In its initial offer, it reserved the right to deviate from the GPA's national treatment obligation in a specific procurement when it could impair national policy objectives. It subsequently removed that qualification.

83. China proposed a 15-year delay in its initial offer.

84. WTO, Committee on Government Procurement, *2008 Report of the Committee on Government Procurement*, GPA/95, para.13, December 9, 2008.

85. WTO Committee on Government Procurement, "Checklist of Issues for Provision of Information Relating to Accession to the Agreement on Government Procurement," GPA/35, June 21, 2000.

productive discussions in 2022 to move China's accession forward,[86] completion of its accession did not appear imminent.

5.2 Accession Issues

To complete China's accession to the GPA, the parties and China will need to reach an agreement on the terms and conditions for its membership in the plurilateral regime. This will require the resolution of at least four issues:

(i)   whether China's proposed coverage is satisfactory and commensurate with the coverage of the existing parties

(ii) whether China's legal framework complies with the GPA

(iii) whether to permit China to apply transitional measures for developing countries and[87]

(iv) whether to allow China to delay its GPA implementation for two years after its accession.

China's Coverage: As discussed above, China has brought its proposed coverage to a level commensurate with GPA parties in several areas. Its permanent thresholds matched those of most GPA parties, and its coverage of central and subcentral government entities (except perhaps in the defense sector) was in general accord with the parties' coverage. While the parties have recognized that China's 2019 offer was "comprehensive" and "on the whole commensurate with those of GPA Parties," they still have had concerns.[88]

For instance, in a 2022 report to Congress on China's compliance with its WTO commitments, President Biden's administration

---

86. WTO, *Report (2021) of the Committee on Government Procurement*, GPA/AR/4, paras. 3.13 and 3.14, November 12, 2021.

87. GPA, art. V.

88. WTO, *Report (2020) of the Committee on Government Procurement*, GPA/AR/3, para. 3.11, December 3, 2020.

set out its views on China's 2019 offer. Acknowledging that the offer showed progress, it concluded it "fell short of US expectations and remains far from acceptable" due to significant deficiencies in several critical areas. Those areas include thresholds, entity coverage, services coverage, and exclusions.[89]

With respect to entity coverage, the parties have insisted that China expand its coverage of SOEs that make purchases for governmental purposes, particularly in sectors that the parties open under the GPA or in which private companies operate. The European Union (EU) and several other parties with extensive coverage of utilities could be expected to seek China's coverage of SOEs engaged in comparable activities. The US and other parties could insist on coverage of entities under Chinese government control comparable to their private sector entities whose purchases are based on commercial considerations.

US and European businesses have emphasized the importance of the coverage of SOEs.[90] BusinessEurope highlighted that China should apply the GPA to state-owned contracting authorities such as China Railways, which are major customers of the European industry.[91]

The parties may also examine China's coverage of its defense sector to determine whether it is comparable to their own commitments. Unless this coverage is comparable, the GPA parties may not be willing or able to open all their defense entity coverage to China under the reciprocity principle.[92]

The American Chamber of Commerce pointed to the inadequacy of China's services offer. It identified a number of services important to the US industry that it wants China to add to its GPA

---

89. USTR, *2021 Report to Congress*, 43.

90. American Chamber, *2022 American Business*, 106.

91. BusinessEurope, *The EU and China*, 75.

92. For example, in its FTA with Oman, the US excluded coverage of the Department of Defense because Oman did not cover its defense ministry.

offer.[93] The WTO Secretariat has also noted that China did not cover some service sectors.[94]

Finally, China's proposed exclusion of procurement supporting SMEs is more extensive than comparable reservations of GPA parties, including the US, which are limited to small businesses. With China's inclusion of medium-sized enterprises, the exception could cover most of its businesses.[95] As noted above, SMEs conduct about 70% of China's procurement.

China's Legal Framework: The parties will also need to determine whether China's government procurement system complies with the GPA. This will require examination of both the GPL and the TBL because, in the view of the US, both "cover important procurements that GPA parties would consider to be government procurement eligible for coverage under the GPA."[96] The GPL is more closely aligned with GPA requirements than the TBL.[97] BusinessEurope contended that both laws include numerous *de jure* barriers that exclude European businesses from the Chinese procurement market or limit access for European bidders.[98] In addition, the existence of two parallel procurement systems

93. The services identified by the American Chamber in its 2021 White Paper were financial services, including insurance, banking, and e-payment services; express delivery services; health care services; all information and communications technology services; media and entertainment services; e-commerce services; and accounting, auditing, and bookkeeping services and services related to management consulting. American Chamber of Commerce in the People's Republic of China, 2021 *American Business in China White Paper*, 110.

94. WTO, *Trade Policy Review*, 2021, para. 3.229.

95. American Chamber, *2021 American Business*, 100.

96. USTR, *2021 Report to Congress*, 43.

97. EU Chamber, *The European Business*, 318.

98. BusinessEurope, *The EU and China*, 72; see also Peter Chase, "The Missing Partnership: The United States, Europe, and China's Economic Challenge," The German Marshall Fund of the United States, 11, September 15, 2020, https://www.gmfus.org/sites/default/files/Chinas%2520Economic%2520Challenge%2520-%252011%2520September.pdf.

that are inconsistent with one another causes confusion for foreign firms.[99]

Transitional Measures: A third issue for the parties is whether to permit China to apply transitional measures available for developing countries with the approval of the parties. China is seeking two types of transitional measures: higher temporary thresholds and offsets.

The parties may view China's need for transitional measures very differently after more than 15 years of negotiations than they would have had it acceded to the GPA shortly after it became a WTO member. They may conclude that the growth of China's economy during its protracted negotiations has removed any justification for such measures. China perhaps recognized this fact as it withdrew or reduced the scope of several transitional measures and exceptions included in the earlier market access offers. The parties' allowance of transitional measures for China would likely set a precedent for subsequent accessions. Since the parties implemented the GPA 2012 with expanded measures for developing countries, they have only approved one accession–Moldova–with a transitional measure.[100]

Delayed Implementation of the GPA: The parties will also need to address China's declared intention to delay its implementation of the GPA for two years after it accedes to the agreement.[101] The parties may allow an acceding member to delay its application of a GPA obligation for a specified period under transitional measures for developing countries.[102] However, those provisions do not provide for an acceding country to delay its entire implementation of the GPA after its accession. Moreover, in all the accessions under the GPA 2012, the Committee has required the acceding party, from

---

99. BusinessEurope, *The EU and China*, 73.

100. It allowed Moldova to apply higher thresholds for two years after its accession to the GPA.

101. This was a significant drop from the 15-year delay in its initial offer.

102. GPA, art. IV:4.

the effective date of its accession, to implement the GPA fully and provide the parties with access to its covered procurement (subject to any transitional measures).[103]

Challenges to Foreign Participation: More broadly, the parties may consider whether the terms and conditions for China's accession will address sufficiently issues that their suppliers have raised regarding participation in China's procurement. They may also address concerns that the US, the EU, and other parties have raised in the WTO regarding China's compliance with international norms.

The US government and business community, including the US-China Business Council (USCBC) and the American Chamber of Commerce in China, have long complained of the obstacles to the participation of US and other foreign firms in China's government procurement, including domestic preferences. In earlier years, the US government attempted to address concerns relating to Chinese procurement practices in a variety of forums, including the US-China Joint Commission on Commerce and Trade and the US-China Strategic and Economic Dialogue.[104]

In assessing China's compliance with its WTO obligations, President Biden's administration concluded that "China continues to implement policies favoring products, services, and technologies made or developed by Chinese-owned and Chinese-controlled companies through explicit and implicit requirements that hamper foreign companies from fairly competing in China."[105] For example, it noted that notwithstanding China's WTO commitment to equal treatment, foreign companies continued to report cases in which domestic brands and indigenous designs were required in tendering documents.

Europe, for years, "had refused to join the United States in complaints about China's trade behavior as it had not wanted to

---

103. See the discussion in Chapter 2.

104. USTR, *2021 WTO Compliance Report*, 13.

105. USTR, *2021 WTO Compliance Report*, 43–44.

be seen as ganging up on Beijing."[106] However, Europe now generally shares US's concerns. As the EU considered the adoption of measures that would allow it to penalize countries that do not offer reciprocal access to their procurement, it identified barriers to China's procurement market.[107] They included lack of transparency, 'Buy Chinese' requirements, exclusion of certain projects from procurement rules, and requirements that EU firms establish joint ventures with local companies. Major European business organizations, including BusinessEurope and the EU Chamber of Commerce in China, have detailed their complaints and concerns relating to participation by foreign firms in China's procurement markets.

In a 2020 report, BusinessEurope called on the EU to rebalance its relationship with China in order to address systemic challenges arising from the state-led economy that were leading to market distortions within China, the EU, and third-country markets.[108] The business group urged the EU to reconsider its approach to China because its efforts have often not produced the desired results, and numerous investment and trade barriers remain, including in government procurement. BusinessEurope argued that China's state domination of all aspects of the economy produces discrimination and market distortions that include a disparity in market access between Chinese and foreign firms such as a closed government procurement market. In such a market, EU firms are often prohibited from bidding, while the EU's procurement market is open to Chinese suppliers.[109]

Parties' Dilemma: The parties face a choice. If they make the terms of China's accession too arduous, China may abandon its accession negotiations. Instead of GPA membership, it could pursue access to

---

106. Chase, "*The Missing Partnership*," 11.

107. European Commission, *International Procurement Instrument, Fact Sheet*, 2019, https://trade.ec.europa.eu/doclib/docs/2019/march/tradoc_157728.pdf.

108. BusinessEurope, *The EU and China*, 6.

109. BusinessEurope, *The EU and China*, 4 and 37; Chase, "*The Missing Partnership*," 18.

other countries' government procurement through bilateral or regional FTAs. China has already applied for membership in the Comprehensive and Progressive Trans-Pacific Partnership (CPTPP). On
the other hand, if the parties allow China to join the GPA without
comprehensive coverage and the means for ensuring effective participation by foreign firms in its procurement, they may face the same
challenges that have arisen more broadly relating to China's membership in the WTO. These include the perception that existing international rules are not designed to address China's economic system.

Letting China's GPA accession continue to languish is not in the
interest of the GPA or the WTO. It sets an unfortunate precedent
for other pending accessions and will do little to encourage other
WTO members to seek GPA membership or fulfill commitments to
do so. However, China's accession should not be approved at any
price. For instance, BusinessEurope articulated a useful guide for
the negotiations. It contended that more important than China's
timely accession to the GPA is the need to ensure a maximum level
of ambition and strong enforcement provisions "should China's
accession not deliver in practice."[110]

The USCBC expressed pessimism that China's accession bid
would succeed. It suggested that China may be reluctant to make
the concessions sought by the GPA parties (such as greater access to
SOEs' procurement and equal treatment for foreign firms) because
that could disrupt its domestic priorities of using government procurement to support innovation and technological self-sufficiency.[111]

6. PROCUREMENT COMMITMENTS IN BILATERAL AND REGIONAL AGREEMENTS

In 2021, Chinese authorities indicated that they intended "to
conclude its GPA accession before liberalizing its government

---

110. BusinessEurope, *The EU and China*, 74.

111. Schonberg, *Government Procurement*, 18.

procurement market" in bilateral or regional agreements.[112] Accordingly, China has reflected that policy in its FTAs. For example, in their 2014 FTA, China and Australia agreed "to negotiate a reciprocal agreement on government procurement after the completion of China's negotiations to join the [GPA]."[113] China and New Zealand included a similar commitment in a government procurement chapter in a 2019 upgrade of the New Zealand-China FTA.[114] In addition, the Regional Comprehensive Economic Partnership, which China implemented in 2022, does not include market access commitments that would require China to liberalize its procurement market.

With the uncertainty over the conclusion of China's accession to the GPA, the question is whether it will change its policy and agree to open its government procurement in an FTA in advance of its GPA accession. In September 2021, China applied to join the 11-member CPTPP.[115] China would need to demonstrate its commitment to the agreement's objectives, as well as its ability "to meet and adhere to its high standards and ambitious market access commitments,"[116] including with respect to government procurement.

---

112. WTO, *Trade Policy Review*, 2021, para. 3.230.

113. 2014 China-Australia FTA. Australian Government Department of Foreign Affairs, *ChAFTA fact sheet: Electronic commerce, intellectual property, competition policy and government procurement*, November 20, 2014, https://www.dfat.gov.au/trade/agreements/in-force/chafta/fact-sheets/Pages/chafta-fact-sheet-electronic-commerce-ip-competition-policy-and-government-procurement.

114. New Zealand-China FTA Upgrade, *Outcomes Document*, 2019, accessed June 8, 2022, https://www.documentcloud.org/documents/6538249-NZ-China-FTA-Upgrade-Outcomes-Document-Final.html#document/p1.

115. "China applies to join Pacific trade pact in bid to boost economic clout," *Reuters*, September 17, 2021, https://www.reuters.com/world/china/china-officially-applies-join-cptpp-trade-pact-2021-09-16/.

116. CPTPP, "Joint Ministerial Statement on the occasion of the Fifth Commission Meeting," September 1, 2021, https://www.dfat.gov.au/trade/agreements/in-force/cptpp/news/cptpp-joint-ministerial-statement-occasion-fifth-commission-meeting.

CHAPTER 14

PROSPECTS FOR THE INTERNATIONAL PROCUREMENT SYSTEM AND THE GPA

1. INTRODUCTION

The future of the international procurement system is firmly tied to the future of the GPA. Not only does the GPA directly provide the framework for a substantial fraction of international procurement, but it also serves as a reference point for FTAs that include a government procurement chapter. Furthermore, it provides standards for the operation of national procurement systems. Yet there are certain indications that the GPA may be nearing the peak of its development and may not be able to advance much further. If this assessment is accurate, then the advocates of liberalization may need to look to other ways of expanding the global procurement market.

First, the GPA membership may have reached a plateau. The agreement doubled its membership during its first 25 years, but it does not appear to be able to sustain that growth. The current roster of parties suggests that the agreement only appeals to a fraction of the WTO membership. The GPA now includes all, or virtually all, developed countries. Its further expansion depends on attracting developing countries, notably the former GATT contracting parties that transitioned to the WTO. To date, only a small number of these countries have joined the GPA.

For potential members, the GPA may require too much of them while offering too few benefits in return. Many of these potential members can obtain the advantages of GPA membership without joining the agreement. Furthermore, there is evidence that the value of the agreement as a market access instrument is low, as data intimates that GPA partners make surprisingly low levels of purchases from each other.

In addition to having a stagnant membership, the GPA may also have trouble responding to new issues and changes in procurement practices. Since the 2012 revision of the GPA, its parties have not updated the agreement. Despite the mandate for new negotiations to improve it, they have taken no steps to revise the text or expand procurement commitments, nor have they completed the work programs intended to facilitate future negotiations.

If the GPA has indeed stalled, supporters may need to look at other ways to advance the international procurement system. For example, they might consider a renewed effort to bring government procurement into the mainstream of the WTO with reduced commitments. In the near term, at least, FTAs with developing countries such as those of the European Union (EU) and the Comprehensive and Progressive Trans-Pacific Partnership may be more effective vehicles for opening procurement markets. However the international procurement system advances, it will need a core agreement that establishes its fundamental principles, addresses the new challenges of procurement, and is able to attract new members.

2. GPA MEMBERSHIP CHALLENGE: PROSPECTS FOR GROWTH

The challenge for the GPA to continue to grow its membership has at least three dimensions. First is the completion of pending accession negotiations. The second is the extent to which the sources of the 25-member growth in GPA membership since 1996 are likely to contribute to similar growth in the future. The final issue is whether the parties have inadvertently undermined the benefits of joining the GPA.

2.1 Pending GPA Accession Negotiations

In 2022, six of the seven WTO members engaged in GPA accession negotiations were fulfilling commitments to seek GPA membership that they made when they became WTO members: China, Kazakhstan,[1] Kyrgyzstan,[2] North Macedonia,[3] Russia,[4] and Tajikistan.[5] Brazil, the seventh GPA accession candidate, was the most active in advancing its negotiations during 2021 and into 2022.

Brazil applied for GPA accession in 2020 and submitted both initial and revised market access offers in 2021 and an offer that it labeled as 'final' in 2022. According to the WTO Committee on Government Procurement (Committee), Brazil, as the first GPA applicant from Latin America, "was eager to prove that the benefits of

---

1. WTO, *Report of the Working Party on the Accession of the Republic of Kazakhstan*, WT/ACC/KAZ/93, para. 949, June 23, 2015.

2. WTO, *Report of the Working Party on the Accession of the Kyrgyz Republic*, T/ACC/KGZ/26, para. 120, July 31, 1998.

3. WTO, *Report of the Working Party on the Accession of the Former Yugoslav Republic of Macedonia*, WT/ACC/807/27, para. 177, September 26, 2002.

4. WTO, *Report of the Working Party on the Accession of the Russian Federation to the World Trade Organization*, WT/ACC/RUS/70, para. 1143, November 17, 2011.

5. WTO, *Report of the Working Party on the Accession of the Republic of Tajikistan*, WT/ACC/TJK/30, para. 244, November 6, 2012.

the GPA 2012 membership are accessible to all Members."[6] Brazil implemented a new Public Procurement Law on April 1, 2021,[7] intended to facilitate participation by foreign companies in public tenders by, for example, allowing them to present foreign-issued qualification documents.[8] Yet, the US Trade Representative (USTR) pointed out that Brazil's procurement law provides preferences for firms producing domestically and fulfilling certain economic stimulus requirements, even if their bids are 25% more expensive than foreign bids offering non-Brazilian products.[9] Additionally, foreign firms can only bid on technical services where there are no qualified Brazilian firms. Brazil would likely be required to remove such preferences for procurement covered under the GPA to obtain the parties' approval of its GPA accession.

In 2022, the most significant accession candidate was China, whose negotiations entered their 15th year.[10] While the negotiations are well advanced, their conclusion remains elusive. Concluding them and bringing China into the GPA could provide an impetus for accession by other WTO members in order to gain access to its huge procurement market.

The negotiations of the other GPA candidates are advancing slowly. Although Kazakhstan applied for GPA accession in 2019,

---

6. WTO, *Report (2021) of the Committee on Government Procurement*, GPA/ AR/4, para. 3.9, November 12, 2021.

7. Brazil, Public Procurement Law 14.133/2021.

8. Rafael Wallbach Schwind, "Participation of Foreign Companies in Public Tenders in Brazil and the New Brazilian Law on Public Procurement (Federal Law 14133/2021): A Big and Necessary Step Towards the WTO/GPA Accession," *aris of LAWxley*, accessed June 10, 2022, https://arisoflawxley. com/wto-gpa-brazil-accession/participation-of-foreign-companies-in-public-tenders-in-brazil-and-the-new-brazilian-law-on-public-procurement-federal-law-14133-2021-a-big-and-necessary-step-towards-the-wto-gpa-accession/.

9. USTR, *2022 National Trade Estimate Report on Foreign Trade Barriers*, March 2022, 62, https://ustr.gov/sites/default/files/2022%20National%20 Trade%20Estimate%20Report%20on%20Foreign%20Trade%20Barriers.pdf.

10. China's GPA accession negotiations are detailed in Chapter 13.

as of late 2022, it had not submitted an initial market access offer nor responded to the Checklist of Issues for Provision of Information Relating to Accession to the GPA (Checklist of Issues).

Kyrgyzstan began its accession negotiations in 1999. After a period of inactivity, it resumed active negotiations in 2016, submitting three offers in quick succession, including one labeled as 'final.' Nonetheless, in 2018, it tabled a revised final offer. In 2021, the parties reiterated their remaining concerns with both the Kyrgyz market access offer and procurement legislation, especially a proposed price preference program and transition period.[11]

North Macedonia applied for accession in 2017 and submitted an initial offer in 2018. It implemented a new public procurement law in 2019, which incorporated the principle of equal treatment of all economic operators, both domestic and foreign.[12] The Committee reported no significant progress on its accession in 2021 but urged the prompt resolution of outstanding issues on its terms of accession, noting that North Macedonia's accession "would send a strong signal to the countries in the region."[13] In September 2022, North Macedonia submitted a final offer in its accession.

In 2015, Tajikistan began its accession and submitted an initial offer. It subsequently produced a series of revised offers, including the fifth revision in 2020. The GPA parties expressed concerns, notably with a price preference program included in that offer. Tajikistan did not engage with the parties on its accession in 2021.[14]

Although Russia initiated accession in 2016, in accordance with its WTO pledge to seek membership, its accession negotiations had made little progress. With its invasion of Ukraine in 2022, Russia can no longer be considered a viable GPA accession candidate.

---

11. WTO, *Report (2021) of the Committee*, para. 3.19.

12. WTO, *Report (2021) of the Committee*, para. 3.21.

13. WTO, *Report (2021) of the Committee*, paras. 3.22 and 3.23.

14. WTO, *Report (2021) of the Committee*, paras. 3.27–3.29.

Table 14.1 summarizes the status of WTO commitments to seek GPA membership and pending accessions to the GPA.

TABLE 14.1. Status of WTO Commitments and GPA Accessions

WTO Member	WTO Accession	GPA Commitment	GPA Observer	GPA Accession Steps
Afghanistan	2016	Yes	2017	Requested observer status (2017)
Albania	2000	Yes	2001	Application for accession (2001) Replies to Checklist of Issues (2001) National implementing legislation (2002 and 2007)
Brazil	GATT party	No	2017	Application for accession (2020) Replies to Checklist of Issues (2020) Public procurement laws and regulations (2020 and 2021) Initial market access offer (2021) Revised market access offer (2021) Final offer (2022)
China	2001	Yes	2002	Application for accession (2008) Initial market access offer (2008) Replies to Checklist of Issues (2008); updated (2021) Revised offers (2010, 2011, 2012, 2014, 2015, and 2019)

WTO Member	WTO Accession	GPA Commitment	GPA Observer	GPA Accession Steps
Georgia	2000	Yes	1999	Application for accession (2002) Replies to Checklist of Issues (2002) National implementing legislation (2002) Draft informal initial offer (2003)
Jordan	2000	Yes	2000	Application for accession (2000) Replies to Checklist of Issues (2000) Entity offer (2003) Revised offer (2004) Revised entity offer (2006) Revised replies to Checklist of Issues (2008) Informal revised offer (2010)
Kazakhstan	2015	Yes	2016	Application for accession (2019)
Kyrgyzstan	1998	Yes	1999	Initial offer (1999) Replies to Checklist of Issues (2002) Updated replies to Checklist of Issues (2009) Public procurement law (2016) Revised initial offer, second revised offer, and final offer (2016) Draft amendments to procurement law (2016) Revised replies to Checklist of Issues (2017) Revised final offer (2018) Public procurement law (2019)

WTO Member	WTO Accession	GPA Commitment	GPA Observer	GPA Accession Steps
Mongolia	1997	Yes	1999	Request for observer status (1998)
North Macedonia	2003	Yes	2013	Application for accession (2017) Replies to Checklist of Issues (2017) Initial offer (2018) Final offer (2022)
Oman	2000	Yes	2001	Replies to Checklist of Issues (2001)
Panama	1997	Yes	1997	Withdrawal of application (2013)
Russia	2012	Yes	2013	Application for accession (2016) Initial offer and edited version (2017 and 2018) Replies to Checklist of Issues (2018)
Saudi Arabia	2005	Yes	2007	Request for observer status (2007)
Seychelles	2015	Yes	2015	Request for observer status (2015)
Tajikistan	2013	Yes	2014	Application for accession (2015) Initial offer (2015) Draft public procurement law (2015) Replies to Checklist of Issues (2015) Revised offer, second revised offer, and third revised offer (2016) Fourth revised offer (2017) Fifth revised offer (2020)

Source: WTO, *Committee on Government Procurement, Systematic Compilation of Documents Concerning Individual GPA Accession Processes, State-of-Play as of 10 May 2022*, GPA/S/1/Rev.4, May 10, 2022.

2.2 Potential Sources of Future Growth

In the 25 years following the implementation of the GPA, three factors accounted for its membership growth.[15] They were enlargement of the European Union (EU), accessions by former GATT contracting parties, and accessions by WTO members fulfilling pledges made when they entered the multilateral organization to join the GPA.

2.2.1 WTO Commitments to Seek GPA Accession

Fulfillment of GPA Pledges: Of the 24 WTO members that made pledges to seek GPA membership when they joined the WTO, 15 have not yet fulfilled their commitments.[16] Those members fall into three groups. First are the six members actively engaged in GPA accession negotiations in 2022. In the second category, four members with commitments applied for GPA membership in 2000 (Albania,[17] Georgia,[18] Jordan,[19]

---

15. See discussion in Chapter 2.

16. Afghanistan, Albania, China, North Macedonia, Georgia, Jordan, Kazakhstan, Kyrgyzstan, Mongolia, Oman, Panama, Russia, Saudi Arabia, Seychelles, and Tajikistan. Jean Heilman Grier, "An Assessment of WTO GPA Membership: Current Status and Future Prospects," *Public Procurement Law Review* 27 (2018): NA35. Members that have fulfilled their GPA pledges are discussed in Chapter 2.

17. WTO, *Report of the Working Party on the Accession of Albania to the World Trade Organization*, WT/ACC/ALB/51, para. 123, July 13, 2000.

18. WTO, *Report of the Working Party on the Accession of Georgia to the World Trade Organization*, WT/ACC/GEO/31, para. 117, August 31, 1999. In 2020, Georgia informed the WTO procurement committee that it was undertaking domestic work to reactivate its accession negotiations and implementing government procurement provisions in an FTA that was based primarily on the GPA with the European Free Trade Association, which is comprised of Iceland, Liechtenstein, Norway, and Switzerland. WTO, *Report (2020) of the Committee on Government Procurement*, GPA/AR/3, n. 12, December 3, 2020.

19. WTO, *Report of the Working Party on the Accession of the Hashemite Kingdom of Jordan to the World Trade Organization*, WT/ACC/JOR/33; WT/MIN(99)/9, para. 170, December 3, 1999.

and Oman[20]). But after initial activity on their accessions, the negotiations have stalled. Jordan's negotiations were the most advanced of the group, but they have been inactive for more than eight years.[21] Despite the 1996 GPA pledge,[22] Panama withdrew its application for GPA accession in 2013.[23]

In the third category, four WTO members with GPA pledges have not yet applied for accession. They are (with the year of their WTO membership): Mongolia (1999),[24] Saudi Arabia (2005),[25] Seychelles (2015),[26] and Afghanistan (2016).[27]

In 2021, Saudi Arabia indicated that it no longer considered its GPA commitment to be valid because it "pertains and was specific to a previous version of the Agreement."[28] Its only explanation was

20. WTO, *Report of the Working Party on the Accession of Oman to the World Trade Organization*, WT/ACC/OMN/26, para. 121, September 28, 2000.

21. USTR, *2022 National Trade Estimate Report*, 306. After Jordan submitted its initial offer in 2003, it tabled several revised offers in response to requests for improvements made by the US and other GPA parties and engaged in accession negotiations in the 2000s; it also participated in negotiations of the GPA 2012.

22. WTO, *Report of the Working Party on the Accession of the Republic of Panama to the World Trade Organization*, WT/ACC/PAN/19, para. 68, September 20, 1996.

23. WTO, "Application for accession to the Agreement on Government Procurement of Panama - Communication from the Republic of Panama," GPA/ACC/PAN/1, August 9, 2013.

24. WTO, *Report of the Working Party on the Accession of Mongolia*, WT/ACC/MNG/9, para. 59, June 27, 1996.

25. WTO, *Report of the Working Party on the Accession of the Kingdom of Saudi Arabia to the World Trade Organization*, WT/ACC/SAU/61, para. 231, November 1, 2005.

26. WTO, *Report of the Working Party on the Accession of the Republic of Seychelles*, WT/ACC/SYC/64, para. 322, November 5, 2014.

27. WTO, *Report of the Working Party on the Accession of the Islamic Republic of Afghanistan*, WT/ACC/AFG/36, para. 199, November 13, 2015. Afghanistan is the only LDC that committed to seek GPA membership after it became a WTO member.

28. WTO, *Trade Policy Review, The Kingdom of Saudi Arabia, Minutes of the Meeting*, WT/TPR/M/407, April 12, 2021, para. 5.21.

that it made the commitment under the GPA 1994, which suggests it considers it to be different from the amended GPA 2012, even though the revision did not alter the parties' rights or obligations. Saudi Arabia did not explain why it had not fulfilled its 2005 WTO commitment before the amended GPA was implemented in 2014. Perhaps, its reluctance to proceed with GPA accession is the result of its implementation in 2019 of a government procurement law with local content requirements that may not be compatible with the GPA.[29]

Without a reversal of the Saudi position, other WTO members may be encouraged to follow Saudi Arabia and not fulfill their commitments. The GPA parties appear to have few options–other than moral suasion–to obtain fulfillment of WTO commitments. In 2021, the parties merely expressed concern with the lack of progress in Saudi Arabia's accession and "encouraged it to take concrete steps to fulfil its accession commitment."[30] When Panama withdrew its GPA application, the parties only expressed regret, calling it "an unhelpful precedent."[31]

Future GPA Commitments in WTO Accessions: Some of the 24 developing countries engaged in WTO accession negotiations in 2022 may eventually make commitments to seek GPA membership.[32] However, most of the pending WTO accession negotiations are proceeding very slowly. Over half have been ongoing for more than

---

29. For a discussion of Saudi law, see WTO, *Trade Policy Review, Report by the Secretariat, The Kingdom of Saudi Arabia*, WT/TPR/S/407, para. 3.164–3.166, January 27, 2021.

30. WTO, *Report (2021) of the Committee*, para. 3.34.

31. WTO, *Report (2013) of the Committee on Government Procurement*, para. 3.20, GPA/121, October 24, 2013.

32. Of the 24 countries, 16 were developing countries: Algeria, Andorra, Azerbaijan, the Bahamas, Belarus, Bosnia and Herzegovina, Curaçao, Equatorial Guinea, Iran, Iraq, Lebanon, Libya, Serbia, Syria, and Uzbekistan. The other eight were LDCs: Bhutan, Comoros, Ethiopia, São Tomé and Príncipe, Somalia, South Sudan, Sudan, and Timor-Leste.

20 years, and nearly half of the candidates have not tabled market access offers.[33] In addition, more than a third of the countries negotiating WTO accession are least developed countries (LDCs) and thus are less likely to agree to seek GPA membership. Of the five LDCs that have become WTO members, only Afghanistan made a GPA pledge, and it has yet to apply for accession.[34] As a consequence, GPA membership pledges are unlikely to bring in many new GPA parties.

Countries that joined the WTO without a GPA commitment during its first 25 years did not generally indicate the reason. However, it appears several doubted their capacity to implement the GPA. For example, when Laos became a WTO member, it stated a future decision on GPA membership "would depend on the capacity of governmental agencies to manage the terms and conditions of the Agreement."[35] Other members, such as Tonga, contended the GPA was not designed for them. In its Protocol of Accession to the WTO, Tonga observed that the GPA did not take into consideration such "very small developing countries."[36] It also pointed out that few, if any, of its government contracts would be covered under GPA thresholds and its large contracts were often subject to aid organizations' procurement rules. Such reservations may resonate with other developing countries encouraged to join the GPA in the future.

---

33. Thirteen countries have been in WTO accession negotiations for more than 20 years, and some much longer (for example, Algeria applied in 1987). WTO, *Summary Table of Ongoing Accessions*, updated March 2020, https://www.wto.org/english/thewto_e/acc_e/status_e.htm.

34. The four LDCs that acceded to the WTO but did not make a GPA pledge were Cambodia, Laos, Liberia, Nepal, and Yemen.

35. WTO, *Report of the Working Party on the Accession of Lao PDR to the World Trade Organization*, WT/ACC/LAO/45, para. 162, October 1, 2012.

36. WTO, *Report of the Working Party on the Accession of Tonga to the World Trade Organization*, Ministerial Conference, WT/ACC/TON/17; WT/MIN(05)/4, para. 138, December 2, 2005.

Even developing countries that would appear to be ideal GPA candidates declined to make a GPA pledge when they joined the WTO. Vietnam is a prime example. It stated it wanted "to focus its limited resources on the implementation of the multilateral agreements [and] would consider" joining the GPA after its WTO accession.[37] It entered the WTO in 2007 and five years later became a GPA observer. However, it has not pursued membership.

Still, Vietnam has undertaken significant government procurement commitments under two major regional agreements: the Comprehensive and Progressive Trans-Pacific Partnership (CPTPP) and an FTA with the EU.[38] Between the two agreements, it has exchanged procurement commitments with 33 of the 48 GPA members.[39] Under both agreements, Vietnam negotiated extensive transitional measures. With such a high level of engagement in procurement, it should not be difficult for it to negotiate accession to the GPA. Yet, as of late 2022, it had not done so. If the GPA parties could draw Vietnam into the agreement with transitional and special measures similar to those provided under both trade pacts, it could send an important signal to other similarly situated developing countries that they can also find a place in the GPA.

2.2.2 EU Enlargement Prospects

The EU's contribution of over half the members in the GPA's first 25 years arose from circumstances that are not likely to be repeated. While the EU may add new member states and hence contribute to further expansion of the GPA, that expansion would likely

---

37. WTO, *Report of the Working Party on the Accession of Viet Nam*, WT/ACC/VNM/48, para. 347, October 27, 2006.

38. The CPTPP and EU FTA agreements are discussed in Chapters 10 and 11, respectively.

39. The tally would rise to 35 if the US and the United Kingdom (UK) were added since they participated in negotiations of Vietnam's commitments under the CPTPP's predecessor and EU FTA, respectively.

lead–at best–to very modest increases in the GPA roster and not likely for many years.

In the spring of 2022, the EU was considering several Western Balkan countries (Albania, Montenegro, North Macedonia, and Serbia) and Turkey for EU membership. Not only were the EU's enlargement plans advancing very slowly, but their viability was also in doubt. The EU's efforts to add the Western Balkan countries were effectively stalled,[40] and its accession negotiations with Turkey had come to a standstill.[41] However, Russia's invasion of Ukraine in February 2022 gave a new impetus to EU enlargement.

On June 23, 2022, the European Council approved Moldova and Ukraine as candidates for EU membership.[42] It now recognizes seven countries as candidates for accession: Albania, Moldova, Montenegro, North Macedonia, Serbia, Turkey, and Ukraine.[43] In

---

40. David M. Herszenhorn and Lili Bayer, "EU leaders back 'enlargement' for Balkans — just not anytime soon," *Politico*, October 7, 2021, https://www.politico.eu/article/eu-leaders-enlargement-balkans/.

41. The European Commission found serious deficiencies in the functioning of Turkey's institutions and judged that it was backsliding in 2021. European Commission, Commission Staff Working Document, *Turkey 2021 Report, Accompanying the document Communication from the Commission to the European Parliament, the Council, the European Economic and Social Committee and the Committee of the Regions, 2021 Communication on EU Enlargement Policy*, October 19, 2021, https://ec.europa.eu/neighbourhood-enlargement/turkey-report-2021_en; "The fiction that Turkey is a candidate to join the EU is unravelling," *The Economist*, August 26, 2021, https://www.economist.com/europe/2021/08/26/the-fiction-that-turkey-is-a-candidate-to-join-the-eu-is-unravelling.

42. European Council, "European Council conclusions on Ukraine, the membership applications of Ukraine, the Republic of Moldova and Georgia, Western Balkans and external relations, 23 June 2022," June 23, 2022, 11, https://www.consilium.europa.eu/en/press/press-releases/2022/06/23/european-council-conclusions-on-ukraine-the-membership-applications-of-ukraine-the-republic-of-moldova-and-georgia-western-balkans-and-external-relations-23-june-2022/.

43. For a discussion of the EU's enlargement prospects, see Cecilia Malmström, "A new dawn for EU enlargement?," *Peterson Institute for International Economics*, September 19, 2022, https://www.piie.com/blogs/blog/new-dawn-eu-enlargement.

addition, Bosnia and Herzegovina and Georgia have applied for EU membership.[44]

Of the seven EU candidates, three are already GPA parties: Moldova, Montenegro, and Ukraine. Two more, North Macedonia and Albania (as well as potential candidate Georgia), have applied for GPA membership to honor WTO commitments. Still, only North Macedonia's negotiations have advanced. Albania has yet to table a market access offer (even though it applied for accession in 2001).[45] Finally, neither Serbia nor Bosnia and Herzegovina are even WTO members.

2.2.3 Former GATT Contracting Parties

GPA expansion will ultimately rest on attracting former GATT contracting parties that became members of the WTO when it replaced the GATT. These countries, unlike those that have had to apply for WTO membership, did not have to go through the accession process. As a consequence, they have not been pressured to make a commitment to seek GPA membership, as have many of the countries that acceded to the WTO since 1996.

The GATT had 128 contracting parties when it transitioned into the WTO,[46] of which 24 were parties to the GATT Code. Subsequently, another 15 GATT contracting parties joined the GPA: eight through EU enlargement and seven through accession. Thus, approximately 90 former GATT contracting members have not joined the

---

44. European Council, *EU enlargement policy*, accessed July 27, 2022, https://www.consilium.europa.eu/en/policies/enlargement/.

45. Albania informed the WTO procurement committee in 2021 that since it shared the same status as North Macedonia *vis-à-vis* the EU, it "would take its further steps consequently." It also reported that its Parliament had approved a new Law on Public Procurement (Law no. 162/2020), which would further align its public procurement system with EU directives. WTO, *Report (2021) of the Committee*, para. 3.32(b).

46. Craig VanGrasstek, *The History and Future of the World Trade Organization*, WTO (2013), 87, https://www.wto.org/english/res_e/publications_e/historyandfuturewto_e.htm.

GPA.[47] They include, for example, five members of the Organisation for Economic Co-operation and Development (OECD), an organization that is comprised mostly of developed countries. OECD members that were GATT contracting parties (but have not joined the GPA) include Chile, Colombia, Costa Rica, Mexico, and Turkey.[48] As noted above, Brazil was the only former GATT contracting party engaged in GPA accession negotiations in 2022.

The challenge for the GPA parties is to attract more of the former GATT contracting parties into the GPA. In 2021, nearly half of the GPA observers (17) were former GATT contracting parties. Some had been observers for years.[49] While GPA parties can strongly encourage–or even pressure–countries that are negotiating WTO membership to make a commitment to accede to the GPA, they have no such leverage with WTO members that transitioned from the GATT.

Moreover, the GPA's geographical reach is limited. Most of its 48 members are in Europe or North America, with only seven in Asia and one in the Middle East. It has no members in Africa or Central and Latin America (which will change when Brazil completes its accession negotiations). Former GATT contracting parties in these regions should be prime candidates for GPA membership and would arguably benefit from that membership.

2.3 Weakened Incentives for GPA Accession

2.3.1 'Free Riders:' Participation in Procurement without Reciprocal Commitments

The GPA parties may be undermining an important incentive for accession by allowing 'free riders' (suppliers from non-GPA countries)

---

47. Because of changes in GATT contracting members, such as the breakup of Yugoslavia, it is difficult to determine the exact number that are now WTO members.

48. OECD, *Member countries*, accessed June 15, 2022, https://www.oecd.org/about/.

49. They are Argentina, Bahrain, Brazil, Cameroon, Chile, Colombia, Costa Rica, Côte D'Ivoire, India, Indonesia, Malaysia, Pakistan, Paraguay, the Philippines, Sri Lanka, Thailand, and Turkey.

to participate in their procurement even though their home countries do not provide reciprocal access to their procurement. Most parties effectively give the benefits of the liberalization of their procurement markets to countries that are outside the GPA, even if they block or restrict participation by suppliers from GPA parties in their own markets. The World Economic Forum has observed that this practice takes "away the incentive to bring their own procurement under international disciplines."[50]

The GPA's non-discrimination obligations only apply to the parties' goods and services. They do not extend to the goods and services of non-GPA countries. Although the GPA does not give non-parties any rights to participate in procurement opened under the agreement, it does not limit access to GPA-covered procurement. Nor does it enforce reciprocity conditions, the conditions that a GPA party imposes when another party does not open equivalent procurement. It is up to the parties to enforce their restrictions, and they often do not.

Most GPA parties do not limit participation in their GPA-covered procurement to other parties. They generally impose few, if any, restrictions on the origin of goods or services or the nationality of suppliers participating in their procurement.

Japan: The WTO Secretariat pointed out in 2020 that Japan imposed no restrictions on the place of origin of products or the nationality of suppliers in providing access to its government procurement.[51]

Canada: Canada also does not impose any statutory prohibition on the purchases of goods or services from countries with which

50. World Economic Forum, *Industrial Policy and International Competition: Trade and Investment Perspectives*, 15, February 8, 2022, https://www.weforum.org/whitepapers/industrial-policy-and-international-competition-trade-and-investment-perspectives.

51. WTO, *Trade Policy Review, Report by the Secretariat, Japan*, WT/TPR/S/397, January 22, 2020, para. 3.168.

it has not exchanged procurement commitments. It generally allows foreign suppliers, goods, and services to compete for Canadian federal procurement and does not restrict their participation in such procurement, whether or not a trade agreement applies.[52] However, Canadian courts have ruled that the benefits of a trade agreement only extend to the parties of such agreements. These benefits include access to Canada's domestic review mechanism. The courts limit access to review of federal procurement by the Canadian International Trade Tribunal (CITT). The CITT can only review the conduct of procurement covered by a trade agreement. A supplier filing a complaint must cite the government procurement provisions in an applicable trade agreement that allegedly have been breached. Nonetheless, a supplier from a third country with no procurement commitments to Canada may participate in Canadian procurement, but it would not be able to challenge the procurement.[53] The lack of legal rights to challenge a procurement may not discourage participation in a procurement.[54]

EU: The EU has generally allowed non-GPA countries to participate in its procurement without providing reciprocal access. Similarly, most EU member states allow GPA parties to participate in procurement to which they have no legal rights under the EU's

52. Government of Canada, "Consultations on Reciprocal Procurement Policies in Canada," March 2022, https://www.international.gc.ca/trade-commerce/consultations/RP-AR/index.aspx?lang=eng.

53. Keystones Supplies Company v. Department of Public Works and Government Services, PR-1998-034 (CITT), PR-1998-035 (CITT), August 19, 1999, https://decisions.citt-tcce.gc.ca/citt-tcce/p/en/item/355571/index.do?q=%22not+a+party%22; Northrop Grumman Overseas Services Corp. v. Canada (Attorney General), 2009 SCC 50, [2009] 3 S.C.R. 309, November 5, 2009, https://decisions.scc-csc.ca/scc-csc/scc-csc/en/item/7826/index.do?site_preference=normal.

54. In 2022, Canada initiated a process that could lead to more significant restrictions on access to its federal procurement by non-GPA or FTA partners, as described in Chapter 12.

application of reciprocity conditions. For example, even though US suppliers are denied rights to specific EU procurement, including the procurement of services by subcentral entities, they "often have *de facto* access to the excluded procurement."[55]

In 2019, the European Commission clarified the authority of the member states to reject bids from third countries. It advised contracting authorities they may reject bids from non-EU suppliers that do not have the right to participate in a particular procurement under the GPA or FTAs.[56] Tenders that may be excluded are those submitted by a supplier from a country without a procurement agreement with the EU, as well as, a supplier from a country with an EU agreement offering goods, services, or works in procurement not covered by the agreement.[57] The Commission's guidance "came as a little surprise to large parts of the European procurement law community since this position had never been that clearly stated by EU authorities."[58]

The Commission does not require the rejection of the tender when a bidder does not have the rights to participate in the procurement. It only acknowledges that the member states have authority to exclude them. A member state must have a national law that authorizes such an exclusion to exercise these rights

55. Stephen Woolcock and Jean Heilman Grier, "Public Procurement in the Transatlantic Trade and Investment Partnership Negotiations," in *Rule-Makers or Rule-Takers? Exploring the Transatlantic Trade and Investment Partnership*, eds. Daniel S. Hamilton and Jacques Pelkmans (London: Rowman & Littlefield, 2015), 312.

56. European Commission, "Guidance on the participation of third-country bidders and goods in the EU procurement market," July 24, 2019, 6, https://ec.europa.eu/docsroom/documents/36601.

57. European Commission, "Guidance," 6. The guidance does not apply to procurement by utilities, which are subject to a directive with its own penalties.

58. Pascal Friton, "International Procurement Law: Key Developments 2019 – Part IV: The EU's Drive for Market Foreclosure – Protectionism or Just a Means to a (Justified) End?," *2020 Thomson Reuters' Government Contracts Year in Review Conference Briefs* (2020): 2–32.

and exclude a bidder.[59] Among their differing domestic law systems, only a few member states have such authority (outside of the utilities sector).[60] Belgium and Italy forbid third-country bids unless they are subject to international commitments (the GPA or FTAs). The European Parliament's Research Service has pointed out that "Spain requires symmetric reciprocity, while Estonia, Hungary and Austria give discretion to procuring authorities" to reject bids.[61]

As an example, Hungary's public procurement law allows its procuring entities to exclude suppliers or goods from countries that do not have the right to participate in its procurement under the GPA or another international agreement.[62] The law specifically

---

59. Friton, "International Procurement Law," 2–33; see also Ioan Baciu, "The Exclusion of Third-Country Suppliers from EU Public Procurement Procedures: The Romanian Case," *European Procurement & Public Private* Partnership 16, no. 2 (2021): 154.

60. The Utilities Directive permits utilities in the water, energy, transport, and postal sectors to reject tenders with more than 50% content from a country that does not have the right to participate in EU procurement. Instead of rejecting such a tender, the utility may include it in its evaluation of tenders, provided it gives preference to equivalent tenders with less than 50% third-country content. Directive 2014/25/EU of the European Parliament and of the Council of 26 February 2014 on procurement by entities operating in the water, energy, transport, and postal services sectors (OJ L 94, 28.3.2014), art. 85. This provision does not apply to EU FTA and GPA partners that provide reciprocal access to their procurement.

61. European Parliament, European Parliamentary Research Service, *EU international procurement instrument*, by Marcin Szczepański, March 2022, 4, https://www.europarl.europa.eu/RegData/etudes/BRIE/2020/649403/EPRS_BRI(2020)649403_EN.pdf.

62. Hungarian Public Procurement Act (143/2015), art. 2 (5), https://kozbeszerzes.hu ("(5) In the course of procurement procedures, national treatment shall be given to economic operators established in the European Union as well as to goods of Community origin. As regards economic operators established outside the European Union and goods originating outside the Community, national treatment is to be given in accordance with the international obligations assumed by Hungary and the European Union in the field of public procurement").

authorizes a contracting authority to exclude tenderers who are not eligible for national treatment and tenderers who offer a product not eligible for national treatment due to its place of origin.[63]

Similarly, a Romanian law, adopted in April 2021, provides for the automatic exclusion from the award procedures of suppliers that do not reside or are established in an EU member state or one of the other listed countries.[64] The listed countries included GPA parties, provided they are covered by the EU's GPA coverage schedules, third countries in EU accession negotiations, or parties to other international agreements in which the EU provided access to its public procurement market.[65] Romanian adoption of this law was the result of an "active campaign" by the European Commission to persuade member states to take concrete measures restricting the access of suppliers (especially from China) without legal rights to participate in the EU procurement market.[66]

By contrast, Germany treats bidders equally regardless of nationality, applying the principle of non-discrimination to tenderers from third countries. It "has not made use of the possibility [described in the EU guidance] to deny third country companies access to national public procurement procedures whose home markets are not open to EU companies" (except in the utilities sector).[67] The Higher Regional Court of Düsseldorf, the German court with jurisdiction over federal public procurement matters, ruled in December 2021 that the exclusion of non-GPA companies and products (outside the Utilities Directive) from public procurement procedures would be illegal as a matter of German and EU public procurement law.[68]

---

63. Hungarian Public Procurement Act (143/2015), art. 74 (2)-(3).
64. Baciu, "The Exclusion of Third-Country Suppliers," 151.
65. Baciu, "The Exclusion of Third-Country Suppliers," 155–56.
66. Baciu, "The Exclusion of Third-Country Suppliers," 154.
67. Friton, "International Procurement Law," 2–33.
68. Decision of 1 December 2021, VII - Verg 53/20.

In issuing its 2019 third-country guidance, the Commission emphasized the existing authority of member states to reject abnormally low tenders, labeling it one of the "instruments in the EU public procurement toolbox."[69] EU procurement directives require contracting authorities to review and potentially reject abnormally low tenders.[70] Under these directives, the authorities must require bidders to explain the price or cost proposed in the tender where it appears to be abnormally low.[71] The contracting authority may reject such an offer when "it is not convinced that the bidder will be able to execute the contract at the price, or cost, offered and in accordance with the tender documents and all applicable legal obligations."[72]

In 2022, the EU made a major change in its procurement regulation when it adopted an International Procurement Instrument that allows the Commission to restrict or block participation in procurement by countries that do not provide reciprocal access to their procurement.[73] This Instrument allows EU member states to continue to implement national measures.[74] It entered into force at the end of August 2022.

---

69. European Commission, "New guidance on the participation of third country bidders in the EU procurement market," July 24, 2019, https://ec.europa.eu/growth/news/new-guidance-participation-third-country-bidders-eu-procurement-market-2019-07-24_en.

70. Directive 2014/24/EU of the European Parliament and of the Council of 26 February 2014 on public procurement, art. 69; Directive 2014/25/EU, art. 84.

71. Directive 2014/24/EU, art. 69(1) and Directive 2014/25/EU, art. 84(1).

72. European Commission, "Guidance," 16.

73. EU, "Regulation (EU) 2022/1031 of the European Parliament and of the Council of 23 June 2022 on the access of third-country economic operators, goods and services to the Union's public procurement and concession markets and procedures supporting negotiations on access of Union economic operators, goods and services to the public procurement and concession markets of third countries (International Procurement Instrument – IPI)," *Official Journal of the European Union* 65 (June 30, 2022): 173/1, https://eur-lex.europa.eu/legal-content/EN/TXT/PDF/?uri=CELEX:32022R1031&from=EN. *See* discussion of the IPI in Chapter 12.

74. EU, "Regulation (EU) 2022/1031," art. 1(3).

US Procurement Ban: The US generally prohibits participation of countries that are not GPA or FTA parties in its federal procurement, with certain exceptions such as the nonavailability of goods and services.[75] Congress enacted this ban to encourage countries to join the GPA as a means of gaining access to US procurement. This prohibition applies to the goods and services the US covers under the GPA. The procurement ban does not apply when there are no offers of US goods or services or eligible products from trade agreement countries or when such offers are not sufficient to fulfill US government requirements.[76] The ban may be waived in two circumstances.[77] Furthermore, US states are not subject to the prohibition.

Many non-GPA countries may find the 'free rider' access sufficient and have no interest in the additional rights provided by GPA membership. Hence, if the GPA parties are interested in expanding the agreement's membership, they may want to explore means of restricting the benefits of the GPA to those countries that have signed it.

2.3.2 Lack of Data on Purchases Among GPA Parties

When the GPA 2012 concluded, the parties covered procurement estimated to be worth more than $1.7 trillion annually.[78] That is a

---

75. *Trade Agreements Act of 1979*, Public Law 96-39, *U.S. Statutes at Large* 93 (1979): 144; *U.S. Code 19*, § 2512.

76. For example, in 2020, the General Services Administration (GSA) temporarily lifted the procurement ban based on the nonavailability of N95 masks and other products that the government needed in fighting the covid-19 pandemic. GSA, "Applicable to All GSA Contracting Activities, Class Determination and Findings," SPE Memo SPE-2020-11, April 3, 2020, https://www.gsa.gov/cdnstatic/SPE-2020-11_0.pdf.

77. In implementing this purchasing restriction for goods and services covered by the GPA, the Federal Acquisition Regulation (FAR) directs agencies to "acquire only U.S.-made or designated country end products or U.S. or designated country services, unless offers for such end products or services are either not received or are insufficient to fulfill the requirements." FAR 25.403(c).

78. WTO, *Agreement on Government Procurement, What is the GPA?*, accessed June 16, 2022, https://www.wto.org/english/tratop_e/gproc_e/gp_gpa_e.htm.

fivefold increase over the procurement covered under the GPA 1994. While both the overall value and the 25-year increase are impressive, they do not indicate the extent to which the GPA parties purchase from one another. The parties have recognized this data "could be an important tool in encouraging other WTO Members to accede to the Agreement."[79] Nonetheless, they do not have sufficient information to make that argument. For instance, a study by the US Government Accountability Office (GAO) concluded that "little is known about foreign sourcing in government procurement—how much governments procure from foreign-located suppliers or how much they acquire in foreign-made goods."[80] There is not even a "single internationally accepted definition of foreign sourcing."[81]

While the parties are required to report annually to the Committee on the value of the procurement they cover under the GPA, they have no obligation to provide data on the sources of the goods and services they purchase.[82] The 2012 revision of the GPA removed an obligation to report the amount they purchased from one another[83] because few, if any, parties were able to fulfill it. The challenges of providing such information include developing standards for what constitutes a foreign good or service, determining whether a good or service offered in a tender meets the standards, and ensuring accurate and uniform reporting of such information by contracting officials.

79. WTO, "Decision of the Committee on Government Procurement on a Work Programme on the Collection and Reporting of Statistical Data," March 30, 2012, https://www.wto.org/english/tratop_e/gproc_e/annexd_e.pdf.

80. GAO, *Foreign Sourcing in Government Procurement*, GAO 19-414, May 30, 2019, 2, https://www.gao.gov/products/GAO-19-414.

81. GAO, *Foreign Sourcing*, 4.

82. GPA, art. XVI:4.

83. In the negotiations of the GPA 2012, the parties did not include the GPA 1994 requirement to submit statistics on the country of origin of products and services purchased by its entities "[t]o the extent that such information is available" (art. XIX:5) because few (if any) parties were providing that information.

The GPA 2012 directed the Committee to establish a work program on the collection and dissemination of statistical data to address this deficiency in procurement data.[84] It also required the Committee to recommend how to facilitate collection of the country of origin of goods and services covered by the agreement. The Committee duly established the work program in 2014, recognizing the challenge of determining the country of origin of the goods and services procured under the agreement.[85] Eight years after establishing the work program, the Committee had not provided any indication it had addressed the deficiency in reporting on foreign sources. It only stated in its 2021 annual report it had engaged in significant work.[86]

Yet, the limited data available on foreign sourcing paints a discouraging picture. According to USTR, a report commissioned by the EU in 2011 showed that cross-border procurement, even among its member states, was very small. Reportedly, only 1.6% of total member state procurement contracts were awarded to firms operating and bidding from another member state or a non-EU country.[87]

More recently, in a 2019 report, the GAO estimated that "foreign sourcing is generally a small share of government procurement."[88] It examined purchases from foreign sources[89] by the US federal government and the central governments of Canada, the

---

84. GPA, art. XXII, 8(a)(ii).

85. WTO, "Decision of the Committee."

86. WTO, *Report (2021) of the Committee*, para. 4.5.

87. USTR, *2022 National Trade Estimate Report*, 204. That study also indicated that US firms not established in the EU received just 0.016% of total EU direct cross-border procurement awards.

88. GAO, *Foreign Sourcing*, 28; see also Jean Heilman Grier, "U.S. Government Agency Report: Limited Purchases from Foreign Sources," *Public Procurement Law Review* 28 (2019): NA252–55.

89. Foreign sourcing included procurement of goods and services from foreign-located suppliers and acquisition of foreign-made goods or foreign-supplied services. GAO, *Foreign Sourcing*, 17.

EU, Japan, South Korea, Mexico, and Norway.[90] The GAO found that foreign sourcing for these trading partners varied in value from about 2% to 19% of overall central government procurement in 2015. Canada and Norway led in shares of foreign sourcing with 11% and 19%, respectively. The EU, Mexico, and the US awarded less than 5% of their central government contracts to foreign-located firms. Japan and South Korea had the lowest shares of foreign purchases of 2% and 3%, respectively.[91]

The GAO's finding of Japan's low level of foreign purchases was supported by the WTO Trade Policy Review of Japan in 2020. The WTO Secretariat pointed out that Japan's central government entities awarded 2.4% of their contracts to foreign companies in 2018, and that was consistent with a trend over the prior five years of foreign purchases of 2% to 3%.[92] Since Japan has no restrictions on the place of origin of products or the nationality of suppliers in its government procurement, the WTO Secretariat suggested the low foreign share could be attributed partially to several factors. They include "non-regulatory barriers, the geographical distance from certain overseas markets, and a lack of knowledge of the local market."[93]

According to the GAO report, in fiscal year (FY) 2015, the US federal government awarded contracts valued at about $12 billion (about 4% of its total contracts of $291 billion) to foreign-located

---

90. All the parties (except Mexico) are signatories to the GPA. Canada, Mexico, and the US were parties to the North American Free Trade Agreement until it was replaced by the US-Mexico-Canada Agreement (USMCA) on July 1, 2020. Only the US and Mexico are parties to the USMCA.

91. GAO, *Foreign Sourcing*, 28. GAO estimated foreign sourcing for all levels of government to be between 7% and 18%.

92. WTO, *Trade Policy Review, Japan, Minutes of the Meeting Addendum*, Japan's Response to EU Question No. 14, October 7, 2020, https://docs.wto.org/dol2fe/Pages/SS/directdoc.aspx?filename=q:/WT/TPR/M397A1.pdf&Open=True.

93. WTO, *Trade Policy Review, Report by the Secretariat, Japan*, WT/TPR/S/397, para. 3.168, January 22, 2020.

firms,[94] with approximately $5 billion going to firms located in the other six parties in the study. The EU received slightly more than half of these contracts in terms of value ($2.8 billion). Most of the US's remaining contracts awarded to the other parties were divided among firms in Japan, South Korea, and Canada by contract value: $1.1 billion, $800,000, and $600,000, respectively. Firms located in Mexico and Norway obtained less than 1% of the US contracts.[95]

The GAO report relied on two approaches to foreign sourcing. One sorted the procurement based on where the firm supplying the good or service was located. The other attempted to determine where the product was made or the service provided. Nonetheless, foreign sourcing based on the country of origin of the product or service showed similar results to foreign sourcing based on the firm location.[96] According to the GAO, in FY 2015, the US awarded contracts valued at about $16.5 billion for foreign goods and services. About 43% of the overall value of that foreign-sourced procurement was for goods and services originating in the other six parties, which is the same proportion as when the firm's location was used as the "proxy measure of foreign sourcing."[97] The GAO concluded that the US "likely procured more than twice as much" from those parties as they did from the US but noted that "exact comparisons are not possible."[98]

The GAO found that the central governments of the other six parties awarded about $170.5 billion in contracts in 2015, with

---

94. A foreign-located firm could be either US-owned or foreign-owned, just as a US-located firm could be US- or foreign-owned. GAO, *Foreign Sourcing*, 15. See Chapter 9 for a discussion of Japanese procurement barriers that led to negotiations of a series of US-Japan agreements.

95. GAO, *Foreign Sourcing*, 12–14.

96. The GAO's identification of a firm as "foreign-located" does not relate to the ownership of the firm. In the study, foreign-located firms could be foreign-owned or US-owned, just as US-located firms could be foreign-owned or US-owned. GAO, *Foreign Sourcing*, 15.

97. GAO, *Foreign Sourcing*, 13–15 and table 2.

98. GAO, *Foreign Sourcing*, 12.

about $6.5 billion going to foreign sources, either foreign-located firms or imported products and services. Approximately $1.8 billion of the contracts were awarded to US-located firms or for American-made products, with Canada and Mexico accounting for almost 80% of the US-sourced contracts.[99]

The majority of the US government's foreign source procurement—whether measured by firm location or country of origin—went to countries not included in the survey. Based on contract value, the main recipients of US procurement were countries in the Middle East, including Afghanistan, the United Arab Emirates (UAE), and Saudi Arabia.[100] None had obligations to provide US firms with reciprocal access to their procurement.

The sourcing of US contracts in the Middle East was fundamentally shaped by the predominant role of the Department of Defense (DoD) in US procurement. DoD accounted for nearly 85% of the US contracts performed abroad and awarded to foreign-owned, foreign-located firms. Only four of the top 10 countries awarded DoD contracts performed outside the US were GPA parties: Germany, Japan, South Korea, and Canada. The others were Saudi Arabia, Afghanistan, the UAE, the Bahamas, Greenland, and Kuwait.[101]

Of the $11.7 billion awarded to foreign sources, DoD awarded $9.8 billion in contracts to foreign sources. It was followed distantly by the US Agency for International Development and the Department of State, with foreign sourcing of $764 million and $720 million, respectively.[102]

The GAO report reinforced the need for the GPA parties to develop common standards for the collection and reporting of data on GPA-covered procurement.[103]

---

99. GAO, *Foreign Sourcing*, 20–21 and figure 2.

100. GAO, *Foreign Sourcing*, 14.

101. GAO, *Foreign Sourcing*, 14 and 67, table 16.

102. GAO, *Foreign Sourcing*, 17–18 and 67, table 15.

103. Grier, "U.S. Government Agency Report," NA254.

Without information on the extent of foreign sourcing and data showing that the GPA parties make significant purchases from one another, it may be difficult to make a convincing argument that joining the GPA provides meaningful access to covered procurement. If the leading economies in the GPA do not make significant purchases from one another, developing countries may ask what hope there is for them to participate in those procurement markets. If the parties cannot point to significant levels of foreign sourcing among the GPA members, they will need to find stronger arguments to encourage accession.

3. NEW GPA NEGOTIATIONS

For the GPA to remain the standard for procurement commitments in bilateral and regional agreements throughout the world, it must be kept up to date. Its provisions should reflect current procurement practices and address new and emerging issues. Yet, in 2022, the Committee's work appeared to have stalled and it faced unfulfilled mandates. The Committee's work was further hampered during the second half of 2021—and continuing in 2022—by its lack of a chair because the parties could not reach a consensus on a selection.[104]

3.1 Mandate

In 2022, the GPA parties were five years past the date set in the agreement for new negotiations to update and expand the agreement. The GPA 2012, like its predecessors, contains a built-in mandate for negotiations to improve the agreement, reduce or eliminate discriminatory measures, and extend its coverage.[105] The negotiations should have begun in April 2017 (three years after the GPA 2012's implementation). The Committee acknowledged that the

---

104. WTO, *Report (2021) of the Committee*, n. 8.
105. GPA, art. XXII:7.

mandate and other directives in the GPA 2012 were overdue, stating it would "return to these items as and when appropriate."[106]

Expansion of Market Access: If new negotiations are eventually launched, a starting point could be the procurement that the parties have added to their FTAs since 2012. On this point, the EU and its FTA partners (Canada, Japan, New Zealand, Singapore, and the UK) provide excellent examples since they all added procurement not offered under the GPA. In addition, several GPA parties added procurement in the CPTPP beyond their GPA commitments. If, based on reciprocity, procurement added in FTAs was offered to all GPA parties, it could provide an incentive for additional commitments in new GPA negotiations.

Notwithstanding the GPA mandate for new negotiations, the parties would need to decide whether to launch a new round of market access negotiations. In the absence of a strong commitment from all parties to expand their covered procurement, such negotiations could be protracted and unproductive. The GPA 2012 negotiations illustrated the problems that can arise when the parties have a wide disparity in market access aims.[107]

It is questionable (even doubtful) whether the US would be prepared to expand its market access commitments given its current trend toward protectionism. It has not added new procurement to any agreement since the negotiations of the GPA 2012. The only exception was its offer of one new small federal entity in the negotiations of the Trans-Pacific Partnership, an agreement that it signed but never implemented.

Prospects for Text Negotiations: Even if the parties are not prepared to launch new market access negotiations, they could consider

---

106. WTO, *Report (2021) of the Committee*, paras. 2.16 and 2.17. Other overdue items included GPA 2012's directive to "review the operation and effectiveness of [Article V on developing countries] every five years." GPA, art. V:10.

107. This issue is discussed in Chapter 1.

negotiations to revise the text. For text-only negotiations, they have the precedent of the 1988 amendments of the GATT Code text, which were implemented in advance of the conclusion of the market access negotiations in 1994.

The GPA 2012 text is in danger of becoming stale. It has not been updated since it was revised in 2007. After that provisional text was finalized in 2007, it was set aside until the parties completed their market access negotiations at the end of 2012. That text, which is now 15 years old, needs to be revisited and revised to maintain its currency and address new and evolving issues, especially sustainability and climate change. To that end, the parties could consider negotiations that focus on improving the text of the GPA 2012.

Such a negotiation might give the GPA parties an opportunity to expand membership by making the document more appealing to other WTO members. For example, the parties could consult with key former GATT contracting parties for their views on current GPA rules, the issues that discourage membership in the GPA, and the improvements that might be made to attract them to GPA membership.

3.2 Work Programs

The GPA 2012 directed the Committee to undertake several work programs (in addition to the data program described above) to facilitate its implementation and prepare for the next round of negotiations. These programs were to address issues unresolved in the GPA 12 negotiations, such as the parties' inability to eliminate preferential programs for domestic small businesses maintained by several parties. They also were intended to tackle new issues such as sustainable procurement.[108] On March 30, 2014, the Committee initiated five work programs on SMEs, the collection and

---

108. While the GPA parties exchanged data on the contracts covered under the plurilateral agreement, they provided little, if any, information on the actual quantity of goods and services that they buy from one another. Grier, "U.S. Government Agency Report," NA254-55.

reporting of statistical data, sustainable procurement, exclusions and restrictions in parties' annexes, and safety standards in international procurement (see Table 14.2).[109]

TABLE 14.2. GPA Work Programs

Work Programs	Description
Work Program on SMEs	The aim of this work program is to seek ways to increase the participation of SMEs in government procurement.
	First, it required the parties that maintained SME provisions in their GPA commitments to provide full descriptions of their programs. Second, it directed the Committee to conduct a survey of the parties' measures and policies to promote and facilitate SME participation in government procurement and, based on the results, identify and promote best practices to advance SME participation in procurement. Finally, it directed the Committee to encourage the elimination of measures that discriminate against SMEs of other parties or the application of such measures to the SMEs of all parties.
Work Program on Sustainable Procurement	This work program directed the Committee to examine: • the objectives of sustainable procurement • how the concept of sustainable procurement is integrated into national and subnational procurement policies and • how sustainable procurement can be practiced consistently with the principle of 'best value for money' and the parties' international trade obligations.
	It also required the Committee to identify sustainable procurement measures and policies consistent with the principle of the 'best value for money' as well as the parties' international trade obligations and prepare a report on best practices.

---

109. GPA, *Work Programmes*, accessed June 16, 2022, https://www.wto.org/english/tratop_e/gproc_e/gpa_wk_prog_e.htm. For full details, see GPA, art. XXII:6-8.

Work Programs	Description
WTO Statistical Data Work Program	This work program was established to address a long-standing challenge of parties regarding collecting government procurement data and, in particular, determining the country of origin of the goods and services they procure under the GPA. It required the parties to submit information on: • their data collection methodology • whether their data includes the country of origin of the goods or services that they procure, and if so, • how they determine (or estimate) the country of origin and the technical impediments in collecting such data. Based on the submissions, it directed the Committee to make recommendations relating to the collection of the data, including ways and means to facilitate the collection of the country of origin of goods and services covered by the agreement.
Work Program on Exclusions and Restrictions in Parties' Annexes	The purpose of this work program was to address the broad range of exclusions and restrictions in parties' coverage commitments. Its overall objectives were to enhance the transparency of the scope and effect of these exclusions and restrictions and exchange information on them to facilitate future market access negotiations.
Work Program on Safety Standards in International Procurement	This work program recognized the need to balance public safety with the GPA obligation to avoid unnecessary obstacles to trade in preparing technical specifications. It directed the Committee to examine how parties' legal measures and practices address public safety concerns in relation to their implementation of the GPA and develop best practices for protecting public safety consistent with the agreement's provisions on technical specifications.

Source: WTO, *Work Programmes*, https://www.wto.org/english/tratop_e/gproc_e/gpa_wk_prog_e.htm.

In 2022, eight years after the parties had established the work programs, none of the programs had been completed. Even the work group studying sustainability issues, a major concern for the GPA parties, reportedly had made little progress.[110] Although the Committee has characterized their work as "useful in enhancing transparency on Parties' practices and as a contribution to preparations for the eventual further renegotiations of the Agreement," it has provided little public information on it.[111]

4. TRANSPARENCY IN GOVERNMENT PROCUREMENT

Given the challenges of attracting more WTO members to the GPA, its parties may want to explore other means of engaging a broader WTO membership in government procurement. One approach may be to renew the pursuit of common rules on transparency in government procurement. Such work could build on the GPA 2012's recognition of the need for an "effective multilateral framework for government procurement" and the fundamental role of integrity and predictability of government procurement systems in the functioning of the multilateral trading system.[112]

During the Doha Round of multilateral trade negotiations that began in 2001, efforts were undertaken to develop an agreement on transparency in government procurement. However, that initiative failed and was abandoned in 2003.[113] One obstacle was many

---

110. British-American Business, *A US-UK Trade & Economic Council, A New Structure for US-UK Trade Cooperation*, December 2021, https://www.babinc.org/psirteex/2021/12/A-UK-US-Trade-and-Economic-Council-Final-Copy-Web.pdf.

111. WTO, *Report (2021) of the Committee*, para. 4.11.

112. GPA, preamble ("Recognizing the need for an effective multilateral framework for government procurement, with a view to achieving greater liberalization and expansion of, and improving the framework for, the conduct of international trade").

113. For a discussion, see Chapter 1.

countries' fears that transparency commitments would lead to obligations to open their procurement markets and remove preferences for domestic suppliers.

In the ensuing 20 years, countries have developed new e-procurement tools and gained more experience with incorporating transparency into their government systems. In addition, many FTAs with transparency requirements have been negotiated across the globe. Hence, WTO members may be more receptive to an exercise confined to rules aimed at transparency in government procurement and with solid assurances that they would not lead to market access commitments.

In 2022, the World Economic Forum recommended that focusing on transparency could be a means of expanding international rules on government procurement that would attract and apply to all WTO members.[114] Common transparency requirements in procurement across countries could facilitate participation by suppliers "without the need for market access commitments."[115]

---

114. World Economic Forum, *Industrial Policy*, 16.
115. World Economic Forum, *Industrial Policy*, 16.

CONCLUSION

For over 40 years, the opposing forces of liberalization and protectionism have been shaping how government procurement has been incorporated into the global trading system. At the multilateral level, protectionism has prevailed. Government procurement was excluded from the GATT, the first multilateral trade agreement established following World War II. In the ensuing years, nothing has been able to bring it into the multilateral system. A significant segment of the multilateral participants still refuses to be bound by government procurement disciplines.

The force of liberalization has afforded access to government procurement through plurilateral and bilateral agreements. These agreements are limited in membership. They are also limited in scope, as they do not open all procurement. Rather, they allow governments to protect some of their procurement. The first of these agreements, the 1979 GATT Code, was accepted by only a subset of GATT parties and was restricted to the procurement of goods by central government entities. When the GPA replaced this agreement in 1996, it was expanded to cover procurement of subcentral and other government entities, as well as services and public works. Its membership doubled over the next 25 years. Yet it remained a plurilateral agreement that appealed only to a fraction of the WTO membership and covered only a part of all government procurement.

Despite its small footprint within the multilateral trading regime, the GPA has become the cornerstone of the international procurement system, providing the template for procurement provisions in both bilateral and regional trade agreements. Its implementation marked the beginning of the era of liberalization of procurement markets through bilateral agreements, especially FTAs. Government procurement has become an integral element of many FTAs with provisions founded on the GPA, even in FTAs between countries that are not GPA parties.

Within the GPA framework, the US demonstrated how countries could balance the political forces that promote the two extremes of liberalization and protectionism. The US not only fulfilled its obligations under the GATT Code and the GPA, but also expanded its access to foreign procurement through a series of FTAs that built on the plurilateral agreements. To enter those agreements, the US had to balance the opening of its procurement with a broad array of 'Buy American' directives mandated by Congress. It was able to waive a few domestic restrictions but had to exclude a significant part of its procurement due to restrictions such as small business set-asides.

The Trump presidency marked a sharp turn towards protectionism in the US. He issued "Buy American" orders, strengthened implementation of the Buy American Act (BAA), and threatened to withdraw the US from the GPA. His successor, President Biden, continued and expanded Trump's policies. His "Made in America" order echoed Trump's procurement policies as he called for measures to strengthen domestic purchasing requirements. His efforts were bolstered by Congress's enactment of a far-reaching domestic preference that applied to all infrastructure projects receiving federal funds. The Biden administration also indicated it did not intend to negotiate traditional FTAs or otherwise pursue new market access commitments.

As the US turns more and more to protectionist approaches, it might seek other ways of limiting its participation in the global procurement system and may indeed seek to limit the expansion of that system itself. It is plausible that a protectionist US might back away from supporting the accession of new parties to the GPA, such as China.

With the US embrace of more protectionist policies, other countries have stepped into leadership roles in the international procurement system. After President Trump pulled the US out of the Trans-Pacific Partnership (TPP), Japan led the remaining signatories to complete the agreement as the Comprehensive and Progressive Trans-Pacific Partnership, an agreement that has been attracting new members from both inside and out of the Asia-Pacific region.

The European Union (EU) leads the GPA parties in negotiating FTAs that open procurement not available through the GPA and with countries outside of the plurilateral agreement. Even with its focus on liberalization of procurement markets, it has resorted to unilateral actions to address foreign procurement practices that obstruct procurement markets. It has targeted China's denial of reciprocal access to EU suppliers in its adoption of a measure to encourage other countries to open their procurement to EU suppliers.

At present, China remains on the edge of the international procurement system as it has not undertaken disciplines under any agreement to open its procurement. That has left it free to adopt its own unilateral measures restricting access to its procurement markets. Consequently, China poses a challenge for the supporters of the international procurement system to find a way to integrate it into the system.

Contrasting China's unfettered pursuit of procurement restrictions with the unilateral measures of the US, the EU, and Canada underscores a strength of the international procurement system, specifically the GPA. Even though all seek to redress issues that the system could not solve, they are operating within the disciplines of that system and show how the GPA has served as a backstop on procurement measures that could violate the agreement. Both the EU and Canada have contended that their respective measures are consistent with the GPA. The US has respected its international obligations and developed its protectionist measures within those constraints, even as it has turned away from the liberalization of procurement markets.

Nonetheless, with the US disinclined to negotiate new FTAs and with membership in the GPA stagnant, any growth in the international procurement system will be occurring without the leadership of the US and likely outside the GPA. It will take time to determine if the US will again advocate for more liberalization of procurement markets or if regional agreements among other countries will continue to advance, leaving the US behind.

The international procurement system is strong and robust, even with its limitations. It has done much to promote open and transparent practices in government procurement within its limited membership and has set the international standard for procurement disciplines. This leads to the question of whether that system can expand to embrace a larger faction of the global economy or whether it needs to be rethought and perhaps redesigned to reach the broader international procurement community. In the end, is there a new system that would more effectively assist countries in balancing the forces of liberalization and protectionism as they expand access to government procurement?

APPENDIX 1

GATT CODE AND GPA PARTIES

WTO Member	1979 GATT Code	GPA 1994 and GPA 2012
Armenia		Yes (2011)
Australia		Yes (2019)
Canada	Yes	Yes
European Union (and the Member States)	Yes	Yes
• Austria	Yes	Yes
• Belgium	Yes	Yes
• Bulgaria		Yes (2007 EU accession)
• Croatia		Yes (2013 EU accession)
• Cyprus		Yes (2004 EU accession)
• Czech Republic		Yes (2004 EU accession)
• Denmark	Yes	Yes
• Estonia		Yes (2004 EU accession)

WTO Member	1979 GATT Code	GPA 1994 and GPA 2012
• Finland	Yes	Yes
• France	Yes	Yes
• Germany	Yes	Yes
• Greece	Yes 1981 (EU accession)	Yes
• Hungary		Yes (2004 EU accession)
• Ireland	Yes	Yes
• Italy	Yes	Yes
• Latvia		Yes (2004 EU accession)
• Lithuania		Yes (2004 EU accession)
• Luxembourg	Yes	Yes
• Malta		Yes (2004 EU accession)
• Netherlands	Yes	Yes
• Poland		Yes (2004 EU accession)
• Portugal	Yes (1986 EU accession)	Yes
• Romania		Yes (2007 EU accession)
• Slovakia		Yes (2004 EU accession)
• Slovenia		Yes (2004 EU accession)
• Spain	Yes (1986 EU accession)	Yes
• Sweden	Yes	Yes
Hong Kong, China	Yes	Yes (1997)
Iceland		Yes (2001)

WTO Member	1979 GATT Code	GPA 1994 and GPA 2012
Israel	Yes (1983)	Yes
Japan	Yes	Yes
South Korea		Yes
Liechtenstein		Yes (1997)
Moldova		Yes (2016)
Montenegro		Yes (2015)
Netherlands with respect to Aruba		Yes (1996)
New Zealand		Yes (2015)
Norway	Yes	Yes
Singapore	Yes	Yes (1997)
Switzerland	Yes	Yes
Chinese Taipei (Taiwan)		Yes (2009)
Ukraine		Yes (2016)
United Kingdom	Yes	Yes (2021, following Brexit)
United States	Yes	Yes
TOTAL	**24**	**48**

Note: The date of accession is noted in parentheses. Where "EU accession" appears after the date, it indicates that the country was brought under the GATT Code or the GPA through its accession to the EU.

Source: WTO, Government Procurement Agreement, *Parties, observers, and accessions*, accessed May 20, 2022, https://www.wto.org/english/tratop_e/gproc_e/memobs_e.htm.

APPENDIX 2

OVERVIEW OF US TRADE AGREEMENT NEGOTIATING AUTHORITY

US trade agreements, including WTO agreements and FTAs, are treated as congressional-executive agreements, not as treaties. They require approval by a majority vote of each house of Congress rather than by a two-thirds vote of the Senate, as needed for treaties. This congressional approach to international trade policy has evolved over a number of years.[1]

The US Constitution gives authority over foreign affairs to the president and authority to lay tariffs and regulate foreign commerce to Congress.[2] For 145 years, Congress exercised its authority by directly setting tariff rates. Following the passage of

---

1. US Library of Congress, Congressional Research Service, *Why Certain Trade Agreements Are Approved as Congressional-Executive Agreements Rather Than Treaties*, by Jane M. Smith, Daniel T. Shedd, and Brandon M. Murrill, 97-896 (2013): 2, https://sgp.fas.org/crs/misc/97-896.pdf.

2. US Constitution, art. I, § 8, cl. 3 (granting the legislature power "[t]o regulate Commerce with foreign Nations, and among the several States, and with the Indian Tribes.").

the highly protective Smoot-Hawley Tariff Act of 1930,[3] Congress began to delegate certain trade authority to the executive branch. First, it enacted the Reciprocal Trade Agreements Act of 1934, which allowed the president to enter into reciprocal trade agreements with foreign countries for limited periods.[4] These agreements reduced tariffs within congressionally preapproved levels and without any further congressional action. The president used this authority to enter the GATT in 1948.[5] Congress renewed this authority periodically.

When GATT parties began to negotiate agreements to eliminate non-tariff trade barriers, the US needed new legislative authority to participate in this process. Since non-tariff barrier agreements addressed a variety of regulatory matters such as government procurement, subsidies, and product standards, they required more elaborate changes in federal law than tariff agreements.[6] Hence, beginning with the Trade Act of 1974[7] and continuing through successive statutes, Congress provided the president with new authority for limited periods to negotiate and enter into tariff and non-tariff barrier agreements. This authority allowed the president to proclaim certain tariff reductions and modifications. It also required the submission of non-tariff barrier

---

3. *Tariff Act of 1930, U.S. Code* 19 (1930), §§ 1201–1641. The Tariff Act of 1930 significantly raised US tariff levels and led its trading partners to respond in kind. As a result, a rapid decline in world trade occurred, exacerbating the impact of the Great Depression. US Library of Congress, Congressional Research Service, *International Trade and Finance: Overview and Issues for the 116th Congress*, by Andres B. Schwarzenberg and Rebecca M. Nelson, R45474 (2020): 6, http://sgp.fas.org/crs/row/R45474.pdf.

4. *Reciprocal Trade Agreements Act of 1934*, Public Law 73-316, *U.S. Statutes at Large* 48 (1930): 943.

5. Congressional Research Service, *Why Certain Trade Agreements*, 2.

6. Congressional Research Service, *Why Certain Trade Agreements*, 2.

7. *Trade Act of 1974*, Public Law 93-618, *U.S. Statutes at Large* 88 (1974) 1978; *U.S. Code* 19, §§ 2101–2497b.

agreements to Congress, which would vote on their approval and legislation necessary to implement them. It preserved Congress's constitutional role to regulate foreign commerce through its consideration of implementing legislation for trade agreements that required changes in domestic law. At the same, it bolstered the negotiating credibility of the executive branch by ensuring that a trade agreement, once signed, would not be changed during the legislative process.[8]

Congress permits agreements negotiated under this authority to enter into force in the US only if both houses of Congress approve them. In this process, Congress requires any final negotiated agreement to be submitted to Congress with a draft implementing bill[9] and a Statement of Administrative Action.[10] It considers such implementing bills under so-called 'fast track' or expedited procedures. Since 2002, this 'fast-track' authority has been known as Trade Promotion Authority (TPA).[11] Congress gives the agreement an up or down vote, without amendment, provided the president fulfills the statutory obligations, which include notifications and consultations with Congress.

The Congressional Research Service has described Congress's four major goals in TPA as to:

(i)   define trade agreement policy priorities by specifying US negotiating objectives,

(ii)   ensure that the executive branch advances these objectives through various notification and consultation requirements with Congress,

---

8. Congressional Research Service, *Why Certain Trade Agreements*, 2–3.

9. The implementing bill contains any changes to existing laws that are necessary or appropriate to implement the trade agreements.

10. The Statement of Administrative Action describes how the executive branch will carry out the proposed trade agreement.

11. Congressional Research Service, *International Trade and Finance*, 6.

(iii) define the terms, conditions, and procedures under which the president may enter into trade agreements and determine which implementing bills may be approved under the expedited authority, and

(iv) reaffirm Congress's constitutional authority over trade policy by placing limitations on the use of TPA.[12]

The congressional negotiating objectives that govern FTA negotiations have expanded to include new and detailed lists of priorities. For example, the 1974 Trade Act had only one overall negotiating objective and one objective applied to sectoral negotiations. The latest TPA legislation, the Bipartisan Congressional Trade Priorities and Accountability Act of 2015, included 15 overall objectives, principal objectives, priorities, and sub-objectives.[13]

Congress first used the fast-track procedure in the Trade Act of 1974 to approve the GATT Tokyo Round Agreements, including the GATT Code, in 1979.[14] Through the Omnibus Trade and Competitiveness Act, Congress employed fast-track procedures in 1988 to grant the president authority to negotiate the Uruguay Round of multilateral trade negotiations.[15] Those negotiations led to the establishment of the WTO through the Marrakesh Agreement Establishing the World Trade Organization and its 18 ancillary agreements, one of which was the WTO

12. US Library of Congress, Congressional Research Service, *Trade Promotion Authority (TPA)*, by Ian F. Fergusson, IF10038 (2020), https://crsreports.congress.gov/product/pdf/IF/IF10038.

13. US International Trade Commission, *Economic Impact of Trade Agreements Implemented under Trade Authorities Procedures, 2021 Report*, June 2021, https://www.usitc.gov/publications/332/pub5199.pdf, 29.

14. *Trade Agreements Act of 1979*, Public Law 96-39, *U.S. Statutes at Large* 93 (1979): 144; *U.S. Code* 19, §§ 2501–2581.

15. *Omnibus Trade and Competitiveness Act*, Public Law 100-418, *U.S. Statutes at Large* 102 (1988): 1107, § 1102, *U.S. Code* 19, § 2902.

Agreement on Government Procurement.[16] To implement these agreements, Congress passed the Uruguay Round implementing legislation.

Congress has renewed or amended the 1974 Trade Act five times.[17] For the first 20 years of TPA's existence (1974-1994), it was in force continually. However, it lapsed in the periods 1994-2002 and 2007-2015.[18] It was last renewed in 2015[19] and expired again on July 1, 2021.[20]

In exercising its approval authority, Congress can require modifications of FTAs. The US International Trade Commission has noted two congressional agreements that marked important shifts in the evolution of FTA provisions. The first was the 2007 Bipartisan Trade Deal between Congress and the executive branch (also known as the May 10th Agreement), which required modifications to FTAs with Panama, Peru, Colombia, and South Korea. Among others, these changes strengthened labor and environmental

---

16. The WTO agreements, including the GPA, were implemented in US law on December 8, 1994, through the Uruguay Round Agreements Act. Scott Sheffler, "A Balancing Act: State Participation in Free Trade Agreements with 'Sub-Central' Procurement Obligations," *Public Contract Law Journal* 44, no. 4 (2015): 713–48.

17. Congressional Research Service, *International Trade and Finance*, 6.

18. *Trade Promotion Authority*, 3. See Figure 1. Congressional Requirements and Timeline Under Current TPA.

19. *Bipartisan Congressional Trade Priorities and Accountability Act of 2015*, Public Law 114-26, *U.S. Statutes at Large* 129 (2015): 320. "The 2015 battle over renewal of Trade Promotion Authority was one of the most divisive in US trade history, with most Democrats opposed to approving the legislation" that then President Barack Obama needed to finish negotiations of the Trans-Pacific Partnership. Congress voted for TPA renewal but "[m]ost Democrats in both chambers voted against the TPA bill." Doug Palmer, "Say goodbye to Trade Promotion Authority," *Politico, Weekly Trade*, June 28, 2021, https://www.politico.com/newsletters/weekly-trade/2021/06/28/say-goodbye-to-trade-promotion-authority-796173.

20. US Library of Congress, Congressional Research Service, *U.S. Trade Policy: Background and Current Issues*, by Shayerah Ilias Akhtar and Brock R. Williams, IF10156 (2022), https://crsreports.congress.gov/product/pdf/IF/IF10156.

provisions. They also aimed to improve access to medicines by cutting back on pharmaceutical intellectual property rights requirements. The second event was revisions made to the United States-Mexico-Canada Agreement in 2019, resulting from negotiations between Congress and the executive branch. Like those of the May 10th Agreement, these modifications reflected more extensive requirements in the areas of labor, environment, and enforcement while limiting pharmaceutical intellectual property rights protections.[21]

---

21. US International Trade Commission, *Economic Impact*, 14.

APPENDIX 3

US TRADE ADVISORY COMMITTEE SYSTEM

The US Congress created a private sector trade advisory system in the Trade Act of 1974 to ensure that US trade policy and trade negotiation objectives adequately reflected US commercial and economic interests.[1] It directed the president to establish sectoral or functional trade advisory committees comprised of representatives of all industry, labor, agricultural, and services' interests, including small businesses. The committees provided information and advice on the US negotiating objectives, the operation of trade agreements, and other matters relating to the development, implementation, and administration of US trade policy.[2]

Since its establishment, the trade advisory system has been broadened and reformed. Yet, it remains the central means of

---

1. *Trade Act of 1974*, Public Law 93-617, *U.S. Statutes at Large* 88 (1974) 1978; *U.S. Code* 19, § 2155.

2. Office of the US Trade Representative (USTR), *2022 Trade Policy Agenda & 2021 Annual Report of the President of the United States on the Trade Agreements Program*, 182–85.

ensuring that the Office of the US Trade Representative's (USTR) officials and negotiators receive input from a wide range of public interests. The system consists of 26 advisory committees, with a total membership of approximately 700 advisers. Advisory committee members represent comprehensive interests, which include manufacturing; agriculture; digital trade; intellectual property; services; small businesses; labor; environment, consumer, and public health organizations; and state and local governments.[3]

USTR manages the advisory committee system in collaboration with the Departments of Agriculture, Commerce, and Labor to ensure compliance with legal requirements. The advisory committees are organized into three tiers:

(i)   the President's Advisory Committee for Trade Policy and Negotiations

(ii) five policy advisory committees dealing with the environment, labor, agriculture, Africa, and state and local governments and

(iii) twenty technical advisory committees in the areas of industry and agriculture.

Membership selection is based on qualifications, geography and diversity of sectors represented, and the needs of the specific committee to maintain a balanced perspective. Committee members are required to have a security clearance in order to serve and have access to confidential trade documents. Committees meet regularly in Washington, DC, as well as via conference calls, to provide input and advice to USTR and other agencies. Members pay for their travel and related expenses.

TIER I: President's Advisory Committee on Trade Policy and Negotiations (ACTN): The ACTN is the highest level advisory

---

3. USTR, *2022 Trade Policy Agenda & 2021 Annual Report*, 182–85.

committee, with up to 45 members appointed by the president for four-year terms. This committee examines US trade policy and agreements from the wide context of the overall national interest. Its members broadly represent the key economic sectors affected by trade, including nonfederal governments, labor, industry, agriculture, small business, service industries, retailers, and consumer interests.[4]

TIER II: Policy Advisory Committees: Members of five policy advisory committees are appointed by USTR or in conjunction with other Cabinet officers.[5]

Agricultural Policy Advisory Committee: This committee is designed to represent a broad spectrum of agricultural interests, including farmers, ranchers, processors, renderers, and public advocates, reflecting the range of food and agricultural products grown and produced in the US. The Secretary of Agriculture and USTR jointly appoint a maximum of 40 members to the committee.

Labor Advisory Committee: This committee consists of up to 30 members from the US labor community, appointed jointly by USTR and the Secretary of Labor. Members represent unions from all sectors of the economy, including steel, automotive, and aerospace. They also represent farmworkers, teachers, pilots, artists, machinists, service workers, and food and commercial workers.

Intergovernmental Policy Advisory Committee on Trade: This committee, appointed by USTR, consists of a maximum of 35 members representing the states and other nonfederal governmental entities. The represented entities include the executive and legislative

---

4. A list of ACTN members is available on the USTR website. USTR, *Advisory Committees*, accessed May 18, 2022, https://ustr.gov/about-us/advisory-committees.

5. A list of the members and the interests they represent is available on the USTR website. *Advisory Committees*.

branches of the state, county, and municipal governments. Members may hold elective or appointive offices.

Trade and Environment Policy Advisory Committee: This committee consists of up to 35 members appointed by USTR. They include representatives from environmental interest groups, industry, services, academia, and nonfederal governments. The committee is designed to represent key sectors and groups of the economy with an interest in trade and environmental policy issues.

Trade Advisory Committee on Africa: This committee comprises up to 30 members appointed by USTR. It broadly represents key sectors and groups with an interest in sub-Saharan African trade and development. Members include nonprofit organizations, producers, and retailers.

TIER III: Technical and Sectoral Committees: The technical and sectoral advisory committees are organized into two areas: industry and agriculture.[6] USTR, jointly with the Secretary of Commerce, appoints members to the industry committees and with the Secretary of Agriculture–members to the agricultural committees.

There are 15 industry trade advisory committees (ITACs) (Table A3.1). The ITACs provide policy and technical advice, information, and recommendations regarding trade barriers, negotiation of trade agreements, and implementation of existing trade agreements affecting industry sectors, and perform other advisory functions relevant to US trade policy matters.[7]

---

6. USTR and the Secretaries of the Departments of Commerce or Agriculture solicit nominations to the committees. For example, the USTR and the Secretary of Commerce solicited nominations to the industry trade advisory committees for four-year terms in April 2022. USTR, "Notice of Continuation and Request for Nominations for the Industry Trade Advisory Committees," *Federal Register* 87, no. 70 (April 12, 2022): 21690, https://www.govinfo.gov/content/pkg/FR-2022-04-12/pdf/2022-07743.pdf.

7. USTR, "Notice of Continuation and Request for Nominations."

TABLE A3.1. Industry Trade Advisory Committees

ITAC	Industry Trade Sector
ITAC 1	Aerospace Equipment
ITAC 2	Automotive Equipment and Capital Goods
ITAC 3	Chemicals, Pharmaceuticals, Health/Science Products, and Services
ITAC 4	Consumer Goods
ITAC 5	Critical Minerals and Nonferrous Metals
ITAC 6	Digital Economy
ITAC 7	Energy and Energy Services
ITAC 8	Forest Products and Building Materials
ITAC 9	Small, Minority, and Women-led Business
ITAC 10	Services
ITAC 11	Steel
ITAC 12	Textiles and Clothing
ITAC 13	Customs Matters and Trade Facilitation
ITAC 14	Intellectual Property Rights
ITAC 15	Standards and Technical Trade Barriers

Each committee consists of up to 50 members representing diverse interests and perspectives, including labor unions, manufacturers, exporters, importers, service suppliers, producers, and representatives of small and large businesses.[8] The ITACs are subject to the provisions of the Federal Advisory Committee Act.[9]

---

8. A list of the committee members is available on the US Department of Commerce website. US Department of Commerce, *Industry Trade Advisory Center*, accessed May 18, 2022, https://www.trade.gov/industry-trade-advisory-center.

9. *Federal Advisory Committee Act*, Public Law 92-463, § 1, *U.S. Statutes at Large* 86 (1972): 770; *U.S. Code* 5a (1972), app II.

Six Agricultural Technical Advisory Committees focus on the following products:

- animals and animal products
- fruits and vegetables
- grains, feed, oilseeds, and planting seeds
- processed foods
- sweeteners and sweetener products
- tobacco, cotton, and peanuts

Members must represent a US entity with an interest in agricultural trade and should have expertise and knowledge of agricultural trade and commodity-specific products. Appointed members represent entities across the agricultural interests directly affected by the trade policies of concern to the committee (for example, farm producers, farm and commodity organizations, processors, traders, and consumers).[10]

---

10. A list of the members of the committees and the interests they represent is available on the US Department of Agriculture website. US Department of Agriculture, *USDA Advisory Committees*, accessed May 18, 2022, https://www.usda.gov/our-agency/staff-offices/office-executive-secretariat-oes/advisory-committees.

ACKNOWLEDGEMENTS

No book is created without a community and this book has benefited greatly from a broad community of colleagues, policymakers and policy shapers (in and out of government), researchers, blog subscribers, journalists, and friends augmented by one husband. Among the many who have contributed to this project, I am particularly grateful to Chris Yukins for encouraging me to write this book and providing insightful comments. Others who also read parts of the manuscript and offered their comments and advice include Pascal Friton, Barbara Weisel, Peter Bennett, Steve Woolcock, Peter Chase, Rob Anderson, Steve Kho, and Paul Lalonde. I also need to include my husband David who brought his extensive publication experience to this project and served as its patient editor. Every writer should have the assistance of a copy editor like Magda Wojcik whose keen eye and exacting standards made this a much more polished text. Such errors as remain in the manuscript are my responsibility.

SELECTED BIBLIOGRAPHY

The foundation for this book is the agreements, laws, regulations, and other official documents that have established or played a role in the development of the international procurement system. For this work, the most important collections of these documents are those of the World Trade Organization, the US government, and the European Union. However, the subject of international procurement is broad, and so this work has relied on the documents of many countries and organizations as well as on the growing secondary literature on international government procurement. A select list of the major sources is given below. In all cases, the notes provide a complete list of all sources as well as complete citations.

PRIMARY SOURCES

US Laws, Regulations, Notices, and Other Documents

Federal Register: https://www.federalregister.gov

US Code: https://uscode.house.gov

US Congress: https://www.congress.gov

US Laws (US Government Printing Office): https://www.govinfo.gov/app/collection/PLAW/

US Federal Regulations

US Code of Federal Regulations: https://www.archives.gov/federal-register/cfr

US Regulatory Rulemaking Process: https://www.regulations.gov

US Federal Procurement Regulations

Federal Acquisition Regulation: https://www.acquisition.gov

Defense Federal Acquisition Supplement: https://www.acquisition.gov/dfars

US Government Reports

US Government Accountability Office: https://www.gao.gov

US International Trade Commission: https://www.usitc.gov

US Library of Congress, Congressional Research Service: https://crsreports.congress.gov

US Trade Representative: https://ustr.gov

US FTAs: https://ustr.gov/trade-agreements/free-trade-agreements

US Procurement Agreements: https://ustr.gov/issue-areas/government-procurement

White House

General: https://www.whitehouse.gov

Office of Management and Budget: https://www.whitehouse.gov/omb/

European Union Agreements, Regulations, and Other Documents

Council of the European Union: https://european-union.europa.eu/institutions-law-budget/institutions-and-bodies/institutions-and-bodies-profiles/council-european-union_en

European Commission: https://ec.europa.eu/info/index_en

European Parliament: https://www.europarl.europa.eu/portal/en

European Union: https://european-union.europa.eu/index_en

EU law: https://eur-lex.europa.eu/oj/direct-access.html

EU trade websites: https://trade.ec.europa.eu

European Parliament Research Service: https://www.europarl.europa.eu/at-your-service/en/stay-informed/research-and-analysis

European Court of Justice: https://european-union.europa.eu/institutions-law-budget/institutions-and-bodies/institutions-and-bodies-profiles/court-justice-european-union-cjeu_en

WTO Documents

Documents and Resources: https://www.wto.org/english/res_e/res_e.htm

GPA: https://www.wto.org/english/tratop_e/gproc_e/gp_gpa_e.htm

Trade Policy Reviews: https://www.wto.org/english/tratop_e/tpr_e/tpr_e.htm

WTO Accessions: https://www.wto.org/english/thewto_e/acc_e/acc_e.htm

Other Documents

Countries: Documents and Laws of the Governments of Australia, Brazil, Canada, China, Germany, Hungary, Kenya, South Korea, Mexico, New Zealand, Singapore, and the United Kingdom (specific citations listed in notes)

Agreements

Comprehensive and Progressive Trans-Pacific Partnership: https://www.mfat.govt.nz/en/trade/free-trade-agreements/free-trade-agreements-in-force/cptpp/comprehensive-and-progressive-agreement-for-trans-pacific-partnership-text-and-resources/

Regional Comprehensive Economic Partnership: https://rcepsec.org/

SECONDARY SOURCES

Books and Articles

Abbott, Kenneth W., and Conrad D. Totman. "'Black Ships' and Balance Sheets: The Japanese Market and U.S.-Japan Relations." *Northwestern Journal of International Law and Business* 3, no. 1 (1981): 103–154.

Anderson, Robert D. "Renewing the WTO Agreement on Government Procurement: Progress to Date and Ongoing Negotiations." *Public Procurement Law Review* 16, no. 4 (2007): 255–73.

_____. "The UK's New Role in the WTO Agreement on Government Procurement: Understanding the Story and Seizing the Opportunity." *Public Procurement Law Review* 30, no. 3 (2021): 159–170.

Anderson, Robert D., and Christopher R. Yukins. "Withdrawing the U.S. from the WTO GPA: Assessing Potential Damage to the U.S. and Its Contracting Community." *The Government Contractor* 62, no. 6, *Thomson Reuters* (2019):1–5. https://ssrn.com/abstract=3540413.

Anderson, Robert D., Claudia Locatelli, Anna Caroline Müller, and Philippe Pelletier. "The Relationship between Services Trade and Government Procurement Commitments: Insights from Relevant WTO Agreements and Recent RTAs." *WTO Working Paper* ERSD-2014-21, November 18, 2014, 1–86. https://www.wto.org/english/res_e/reser_e/ersd201421_e.htm.

Araki, Ichiro. "Beyond Aggressive Legalism: Japan and the GATT/WTO Dispute." In *WTO and East Asia: New Perspectives*, edited by Mitsuo Matsushita and Dukgeun Ahn, 149–75. London: Cameron May, 2004.

Arrowsmith, Sue, and Robert D. Anderson, eds. *The WTO Regime on Government Procurement: Challenge and Reform*. Cambridge: Cambridge University Press, 2011.

Arrowsmith, Sue. "The Character and Role of National Challenge Procedures under the Government Procurement Agreement." *Public Procurement Law Review* 11, no. 4 (2002): 235–65.

Baciu, Ioan. "The Exclusion of Third-Country Suppliers from EU Public Procurement Procedures: The Romanian Case." *European Procurement & Public Private Partnership* 16, no. 2 (2021): 151–57.

Blank, Annet, and Gabrielle Zoe Marceau. "The History of the Government Procurement Negotiations Since 1945." *Public Procurement Law Review* 4 (1996): 77–146.

Brodsky, Robert. "TSA contracting exemption to end next month." *Government Executive*, May 27, 2008. https://www.sbc.senate.gov/public/index.cfm/articles?ID=3E05F216-E9AC-489B-B9EF-BBD5D97F6CE2.

Chaisse, Julien. "The Case for Hong Kong Joining RCEP." *East West Forum,* September 2, 2021. https://www.eastasiaforum.org/2021/09/02/the-case-for-hong-kong-joining-rcep/?utm_source=subscribe2&utm_medium=email&utm_campaign=postnotify&utm_id=379496&utm_title=The%20case%20for%20Hong%20Kong%20joining%20RCEP.

Chase, Peter. "The Missing Partnership: The United States, Europe, and China's Economic Challenge." The German Marshall Fund of the United States, 11, September 15, 2020. https://www.gmfus.org/sites/default/files/Chinas%2520Economic%2520Challenge%2520-%252011%2520September.pdf.

Cho, Eric. "Purchased in the USA: An Examination of Emerging Issues Surrounding Foreign Acquisition." *The National Contract Management Association* (2012): 28–39.

Cutler, Wendy. "America Must Return to the Trans-Pacific Partnership." *Foreign Affairs*, September 10, 2021. https://www.foreignaffairs.com/articles/2021-09-10/america-must-return-trans-pacific-partnership.

Cutler, Wendy, and Daniel M. Price. "The Debate Papers: Is the Indo-Pacific Economic Framework Glass Half Full or Glass Half Empty?." United States Study Center, August 25, 2022. https://www.ussc.edu.au/analysis/is-the-indo-pacific-economic-framework-glass-half-full-or-glass-half-empty.

Dawar, Kamala. "The Government Procurement Agreement, the Most-Favored Nation Principle, and Regional Trade Agreements." In *The Internationalization of Government Procurement Regulation*, edited by Aris Georgopoulos, Bernard Hoekman, and Petros C. Mavroidis, 111–39. Oxford: Oxford University Press, 2017.

De Graaf, Gerard, and Matthew King. "Towards a More Global Government Procurement Market: The Expansion of the GATT Government

Procurement Agreement in the Context of the Uruguay Round." *The International Lawyer* 29, no. 2 (1995): 435–52.

Friton, Pascal. "European Procurement Developments in 2021: The EU's Persistent (and Sometimes a Little Desperate) Pursuit of a Resilient Economy." *2021 Thomson Reuters' Government Contracts Year in Review Conference Briefs*, 101–11, February 2022.

———. "International Procurement Law: Key Developments 2019 – Part IV: The EU's Drive for Market Foreclosure – Protectionism or Just a Means to a (Justified) End?." *2019 Thomson Reuters Government Contracts Year in Review Conference Briefs* (2020): 2-30–2-36.

Gordon, Daniel I. "In the Beginning: The Earliest Bid Protests Filed with the US General Accounting Office." *Public Procurement Law Review* 13, no. 5 (2004): 147–64.

Górski, Jędrzej. "CPTPP and Government Procurement." *Transnational Dispute Management* 5 (2019): 1–44.

Graham, Niels. "The RCEP ratification and its implications." *Atlantic Council*, December 3, 2021. https://www.atlanticcouncil.org/blogs/econographics/the-rcep-ratification-and-its-implications/.

Grier, Jean Heilman. "An Assessment of WTO GPA Membership: Current Status and Future Prospects." *Public Procurement Law Review* 27, no. 1 (2018): NA33–48.

———. "Government Procurement in the Trans-Pacific Partnership (TPP)." *The Government Contractor* 58, no. 7, *Thomson Reuters*, February (2016): 1–6.

———. "GPA Reciprocal Conditions: Leverage for Bilateral Agreements." *Public Procurement Law Review* 29, no. 5 (2020): 272–88.

———. "Japan's Implementation of the WTO Agreement on Government Procurement." *University of Pennsylvania Journal of International Economic Law* 17 (1996): 605–57.

———. "The Role of International Trade Agreements in the Converging of Procurement Systems." Conference materials, the Government Contracts Year in Review Conference, Washington, DC, February 17, 2009.

_____. "The Use of Section 301 to Open Japanese Markets to Foreign Firms." *North Carolina Journal of International Law & Commercial Regulation* 17 (1992): 2–44.

_____. "Trade Agreements Open Foreign Procurement Markets." *Thomson Reuters Briefing Papers* 17-10 (2017): 1–11.

_____. "U.S. Government Agency Report: Limited Purchases from Foreign Sources." *Public Procurement Law Review* 28, no. 6 (2019): NA252–55.

_____. "U.S.-Japan Government Procurement Agreements." *Wisconsin International Law Journal* 14 (1995): 1–68.

_____. "What Are the Prospects for Concluding Work on China's GPA Accession in 2015?." *Public Procurement Law Review* 24, no. 6 (2015): 221–36.

"Mercosur: South America's Fractious Trade Bloc." *Council on Foreign Relations*, December 17, 2021. https://www.cfr.org/backgrounder/mercosur-south-americas-fractious-trade-bloc?utm_source=dailybrief&utm_medium=email&utm_campaign=DailyBrief2021Dec23&utm_term=DailyNewsBrief.

Hickey, David, Dustin Painter, Ken Kanzawa, and Maggie Crosswy. "Buy American Final Rule Ups the Domestic Content Ante." *Kelley Drye Client Advisory*, March 11, 2022. https://www.kelleydrye.com/News-Events/Publications/Client-Advisories/Buy-American-Final-Rule-Ups-the-Domestic-Content-A.

Hufbauer, Gary Clyde. "President Biden's elusive trade policy." *East Asia Forum*, October 31, 2021. https://www.eastasiaforum.org/2021/10/31/president-bidens-elusive-trade-policy/?utm_source=newsletter&utm_medium=email&utm_campaign=newsletter2021-10-31?utm_source=newsletter&utm_medium=email&utm_campaign=newsletter2021-10-31.

Institute of Strategic and International Studies. *National Interest Analysis of Malaysia's Participation in the Trans-Pacific Partnership.* 2015. Accessed June 22, 2022. https://fta.miti.gov.my/miti-fta/resources/ISIS_The_Grand_Finale.pdf.

Kelly, David. "The Fly America Act Controversy: An Analysis of GSA Contracts involving Foreign Carriers and Important Considerations." *Public Contract Law Journal* 47, no. 4 (2018): 509–37.

Kimura, Fukunari. "A framework for ongoing commitments to RCEP success." *East Asia Forum*, April 5, 2022. https://www.eastasiaforum.org/2022/04/05/a-framework-for-ongoing-commitments-to-rcep-success/.

Lalonde, Paul M. "International Procurement Law: Key Developments 2019–Part II: The Impact of Trade Agreements on Sub-national Procurement–the Example of Canada." *2019 Thomas Reuters Government Contracts Year in Review Conference Briefs, Thomson Reuters* (2020): 2-12–2-20.

Lilly, Meredith, Hugo Perezcano Díaz, and Christine McDaniel. "The Future of North America's Economic Relationship: From NAFTA to the New Canada-United States-Mexico Agreement and Beyond." Centre for International Governance Innovation, February 11, 2019. https://www.cigionline.org/publications/future-north-americas-economic-relationship-nafta-new-canada-united-states-mexico.

Malmström, Cecilia. "A new dawn for EU enlargement?" The Peterson Institute for International Economics, September 19, 2022. https://www.piie.com/blogs/blog/new-dawn-eu-enlargement.

———. "The EU should use its trade power strategically." The Peterson Institute for International Economics, January 4, 2022. https://www.piie.com/blogs/realtime-economic-issues-watch/eu-should-use-its-trade-power-strategically.

Nibley, Stuart B., Amy M. Conant, and Erica L. Bakies. "Real Steps Towards 'Buy American' Compliance–Part III: Understanding and Avoiding Common Areas of Noncompliance that Lead to Enforcement Actions." *The Government Contractor* 50, no.16, *Thomson Reuters* (2018):1–6.

Painter, Dustin. "U.S. Lawmakers Adopt Historic and Far Reaching Buy America Laws in Bipartisan Infrastructure Agreement." Kelley Drye Client Advisory, November 10, 2021. https://www.kelleydrye.com/News-Events/Publications/Client-Advisories/U-S-Lawmakers-Adopt-Historic-and-Far-Reaching-(1).

Pomeranz, Morton. "Toward a New International Order in Government Procurement." *Public Contract Law Journal* 12, no. 2 (1982): 129–61.

Reich, Arie. "The New GATT Agreement on Government Procurement: The Pitfalls of Plurilateralism and Strict Reciprocity." *Journal of World Trade* 31, no. 2 (1997): 125–51.

Schwind, Rafael Wallbach. "Participation of Foreign Companies in Public Tenders in Brazil and the New Brazilian Law on Public Procurement (Federal Law 14133/2021): A Big and Necessary Step Towards the WTO/GPA Accession." *aris of LAWxley*, accessed June 10, 2022. https://arisoflawxley.com/wto-gpa-brazil-accession/participation-of-foreign-companies-in-public-tenders-in-brazil-and-the-new-brazilian-law-on-public-procurement-federal-law-14133-2021-a-big-and-necessary-step-towards-the-wto-gpa-accession/.

Sheffler, Scott. "A Balancing Act: State Participation in Free Trade Agreements with 'Sub-central' Procurement Obligations." *Public Contract Law* 44, no. 4 (2015): 713–47.

Shelley, Herbert C. "The Trade Agreements Act of 1979 and Trade Reorganization." The World Trade Institute at the World Trade Center, Mar 26-28, 1980, 1–17.

Southwick, James D. "Binding the States: A Survey of State Law Conformance with the Standards of the GATT Procurement Code." *University of Pennsylvania Journal of International Law* 13 (1992): 57–99.

Sundaram, Asha. "India's RCEP exit and its regional future." *East Asia Forum,* April 13, 2022. https://www.eastasiaforum.org/2022/04/13/indias-rcep-exit-and-its-regional-future/?utm_source=subscribe2&utm_medium=email&utm_campaign=postnotify&utm_id=805493&utm_title=India%26rsquo%3Bs%20RCEP%20exit%20and%20its%20regional%20future.

VanGrasstek, Craig. "The History and Future of the World Trade Organization." World Trade Organization. Accessed June 23, 2022. https://www.wto.org/english/res_e/publications_e/historyandfuturewto_e.htm.

Wang, Ping. "Coverage of the WTO's Agreement on Government Procurement: Challenges of Integrating China and Other Countries with a Large State Sector into the Global Trading System." *Journal of International Economic Law* 10, no. 4 (2007): 887–920.

Weyand, Sabine. "Foreword." In *Law and Practice of the Common Commercial Policy. The First 10 Years after the Treaty of Lisbon,* edited by Michael J. Hahn and Guillaume Van der Loo. Leiden and Boston: Brill Nijhoff, 2020. Accessed June 22, 2022. https://brill.com/view/book/9789004393417/front-7.xml.

Woolcock, Stephen, and Jean Heilman Grier. "Public Procurement in the Transatlantic Trade and Investment Partnership Negotiations." In *Rule-Makers or Rule-Takers? Exploring the Transatlantic Trade and Investment Partnership*, edited by Daniel S. Hamilton and Jacques Pelkmans, 297–339. London: Rowman & Littlefield, 2015.

Woolcock, Stephen. "Public Procurement in EU FTAs." In *Law and Practice in the Common Commercial Policy*, edited by Michael Hahn and Guillaume Van der Loo, 235–58. Leiden: Brill Nijhoff, 2020.

World Economic Forum. *Industrial Policy and International Competition: Trade and Investment Perspectives.* February 8, 2022. https://www.weforum.org/whitepapers/industrial-policy-and-international-competition-trade-and-investment-perspectives.

Yukins, Christopher R. "International Procurement Developments in 2021–Part I: Buy American and the Biden Administration." *2021 Thomson Reuters' Government Contracts Year in Review Conference Briefs* 77 (2022).

_____. "The U.S. Federal Procurement System: An Introduction." *Upphandlingsrättslig Tidskrift* [Procurement Law Journal] 69 (2017), GWU Law School Public Law Research Paper No. 2017-75.

Yukins, Christopher R., and Allen Green. "International Trade Agreements and US Procurement Law." In *The Contractor's Guide to International Procurement*, edited by Erin Loraine Felix and Marques Peterson, 148–77. Chicago: American Bar Association, 2018.

Newspapers, Trade Journals, and Other Media

Aarup Sarah, Anne, and Ashleigh Furlong. "Russia takes first steps to withdraw from WTO, WHO." *Politico*, May 18, 2022. https://www.politico.eu/article/russia-takes-first-steps-to-withdraw-from-wto-who/.

Baschuk, Bruce. "Trump Considers Withdrawing From WTO's $1.7 Trillion Purchasing Pact." *Bloomberg News*, February 4, 2020. https://www.bloomberg.com/news/articles/2020-02-04/trump-mulls-withdrawal-from-wto-s-1-7-trillion-purchasing-pact.

"Business groups tout WTO procurement pact, warn against withdrawal." *Inside U.S. Trade*, February 19, 2020. https://insidetrade.com/trade/business-groups-tout-wto-procurement-pact-warn-against-withdrawal.

Cassella, Megan. "Trump's first-day agenda: Kill TPP, renegotiate NAFTA." *Politico*, November 9, 2016. https://www.politico.com/tipsheets/morning-trade/2016/11/trumps-first-day-agenda-kill-tpp-renegotiate-nafta-217318.

"Chamber: White House factoring in election implications of NAFTA withdrawal." *Inside U.S. Trade*, January 10, 2018. https://insidetrade.com/daily-news/chamber-white-house-factoring-election-implications-nafta-withdrawal.

"China applies to join Pacific trade pact in bid to boost economic clout." *Reuters*, September 17, 2021. https://www.reuters.com/world/china/china-officially-applies-join-cptpp-trade-pact-2021-09-16/.

Cochrane, Emily. "Senate Passes $1 Trillion Infrastructure Bill, Handing Biden a Bipartisan Win." *The New York Times*, August 10, 2021. https://www.nytimes.com/2021/08/10/us/politics/infrastructure-bill-passes.html.

Dlouhy, Jennifer A. "Trump's America-First Pipeline Plan Upsets Oil Industry." *Industry Week*, July 21, 2017. https://www.industryweek.com/supply-chain/article/22023276/trumps-americafirst-pipeline-plan-upsets-oil-industry.

"Draft NAFTA notice shows administration's intent to address core complaints, including Chapter 19." *Inside U.S. Trade*, March 29, 2017. https://insidetrade.com/daily-news/draft-nafta-notice-shows-administrations-intent-address-core-complaints-including-chapter.

Dreyer, Iana. "EU-Mercosur: Contours of a limited deal on public procurement." *Borderlex*, July 19, 2021. https://borderlex.net/2021/07/19/eu-mercosur-contours-of-a-limited-deal-on-public-procurement/?utm_source=mailpoet&utm_medium=email&utm_campaign=the-last-newsletter-total-posts-from-borderlex_2.

————. "IPI: Council finds compromise, paves way for trilogue." *Borderlex*, June 2, 2021. https://borderlex.net/2021/06/02/international-procurement-instrument-council-finds-compromise-paves-way-for-trilogue/.

————. "Procurement reciprocity: Caspary report calls for return to full market access suspension." *Borderlex*, July 12, 2017. https://borderlex.net/2017/07/12/procurement-reciprocity-caspary-report-calls-for-return-to-full-market-access-suspension/.

"EU Warns It Could Pull Back GPA Commitments Over SME Treatment." *Inside U.S. Trade*, March 2, 2007. https://insidetrade.com/inside-us-trade/eu-warns-it-could-pull-back-gpa-commitments-over-sme-treatment.

Fortnam, Brett. "Business groups form coalition to urge protection of NAFTA, oppose some U.S. proposals." *Inside U.S. Trade*, October 19, 2017.

Haider, Suhasini, and T.C.A. Sharad Raghavan. "India storms out of RCEP, says trade deal hurts Indian farmers." *The Hindu*, November 4, 2019.

https://www.thehindu.com/news/national/india-decides-against-joining-rcep-trade-deal/article29880220.ece?homepage=true.

Herszenhorn, David M., and Lili Bayer, "EU leaders back 'enlargement' for Balkans — just not anytime soon." *Politico*, October 7, 2021. https://www.politico.eu/article/eu-leaders-enlargement-balkans/.

Lavranos, Nikos. "In-depth briefing: Mixed exclusivity: The Court of Justice of the EU's Opinion on the EU Singapore FTA." *Borderlex*, May 18, 2017.

Lee, Don. "Why Trump's 'Buy American' campaign went nowhere." *Los Angeles Times*, August 31, 2020. https://www.latimes.com/politics/story/2020-08-31/trumps-buy-american-campaign-went-nowhere.

McKenna, Barrie. "Buy America ruling reversed on Colorado bridge made with Ontario steel." *The Globe and Mail*, October 7, 2014. https://www.theglobeandmail.com/report-on-business/international-business/buy-america-ruling-toppled-in-colorado-over-ontario-made-steel/article20971036/.

Miyamoto, Hidetake. "Ecuador applies for CPTPP membership to diversify trade." *Nikkei Asia*, December 29, 2021. https://asia.nikkei.com/Politics/International-relations/Ecuador-applies-for-CPTPP-membership-to-diversify-trade.

Monicken, Hannah. "U.S. withdraws push to exempt essential medicines from GPA coverage." *Inside U.S. Trade*, April 20, 2021. https://insidetrade.com/daily-news/us-withdraws-push-exempt-essential-medicines-gpa-coverage.

_____. "U.S.: Proposed GPA-exempted medicines total $393 million in procurement." *Inside U.S. Trade,* February 11, 2021. https://insidetrade.com/daily-news/us-proposed-gpa-exempted-medicines-total-393-million-procurement.

_____. "WTO members refer objections to U.S. GPA modification to arbitration." *Inside U.S. Trade*, April. 2, 2021. https://insidetrade.com/daily-news/wto-members-refer-objections-us-gpa-modification-arbitration.

"New Hampshire Joins Majority of States in Rejecting CAFTA's Restrictions on State Procurement Policy." *Public Citizen*, May 16, 2005. https://www.citizen.org/news/new-hampshire-joins-majority-of-states-in-rejecting-caftas-restrictions-on-state-procurement-policy/.

"New Zealand Ratifies TPP despite U.S. Withdrawal." *The Japan Times*, May 11, 2017. http://www.japantimes.co.jp/news/2017/05/11/business/new-zealand-ratifies-tpp-despite-u-s-withdrawal/#.WRUOa1KZO1s.

"On NAFTA, America, Canada and Mexico are miles apart." *The Economist*, October 21, 2017. https://www.economist.com/finance-and-economics/2017/10/21/on-nafta-america-canada-and-mexico-are-miles-apart.

Overly, Steven. "Japan's role in selling Biden's Indo-Pacific agenda." *Politico*, January 24, 2022. https://www.politico.com/newsletters/

weekly-trade/2022/01/24/japans-role-in-selling-bidens-indo-pacific-agenda-00001050.

Palmer, Doug. "Say goodbye to Trade Promotion Authority." *Politico*, June 28, 2021. https://www.politico.com/newsletters/weekly-trade/2021/06/28/say-goodbye-to-trade-promotion-authority-796173.

_____. "Senators urge Trump not to withdraw from Government Procurement Agreement." *Politico*, November 19, 2020. https://www.politico.com/news/2020/11/19/senators-trump-not-withdraw-government-procurement-act-438324.

Romm, Tony, Marianna Sotomayor, and Mike DeBonis. "Congress approves $1.2 trillion infrastructure bill, sending measure to Biden for enactment." *The Washington Post*, November 6, 2021. https://www.washingtonpost.com/us-policy/2021/11/05/house-infrastructure-reconciliation-vote/.

Schreuer, Milan. "E.U. Signs Trade Deal with Vietnam." *New York Times*, June 30, 2019. https://www.nytimes.com/2019/06/30/business/european-union-trade-vietnam.html.

Schuyten, Peter. "The Battle in Supercomputers: Control Data's Comeback Bid Against Cray, The Battle in Supercomputers Cray Fills Computer Gap Control Data's Corporate Pride." *New York Times*, July 22, 1980, https://www.nytimes.com/1980/07/22/archives/the-battle-in-supercomputers-control-datas-comeback-bid-against.html.

Shimizu, Kosuke. "Costa Rica wants to join CPTPP, president says." *Nikkei Asia*, July 30, 2022. https://asia.nikkei.com/Politics/International-relations/Indo-Pacific/Costa-Rica-wants-to-join-CPTPP-president-says.

Stein, Jeff. "Trump signs USMCA, revamping North American trade rules." *The Washington Post,* January 29, 2020. https://www.washingtonpost.com/business/2020/01/29/trump-usmca/.

"The European Union should not give up on enlargement." *The Economist*, October 9, 2021. https://www.economist.com/europe/2021/10/09/the-european-union-should-not-give-up-on-enlargement.

"The fiction that Turkey is a candidate to join the EU is unravelling." *The Economist*, August 28, 2021. https://www.economist.com/europe/2021/08/28/the-fiction-that-turkey-is-a-candidate-to-join-the-eu-is-unravelling?gclid=CjwKCAjw4qCKBhAVEiwAkTYsPO_mW7YJAvTVoRiJHhiBSmh9ur1_GWspM9QmYtRfZHrqeEj8G_f3EBoCU6IQAvD_BwE&gclsrc=aw.ds.

Theodore. "Lacalle Pou announces that Uruguay will request adhesion to the CPTPP." *The Postedia*, July 27, 2022. https://thepostedia.com/market/61802.html.

"Week in Brussels: National Board of Trade in Brussels, Chile, Mexico, Mercosur, China." *Borderlex*, May 13, 2022. https://borderlex.net/2022/05/13/week-in-brussels-national-board-of-trade-in-brussels-chile-mexico-mercosur-china/.

Yonhap. "S. Korea decides to join CPTPP trade agreement." *The Korea Herald*, April 15, 2022. https://www.koreaherald.com/view.php?ud=20220415000647.

Yuhas, Alan. "Congress will abandon Trans-Pacific Partnership deal, White House concedes." *The Guardian,* November 12, 2016. https://www.theguardian.com/business/2016/nov/12/tpp-trade-deal-congress-obama.

Business Reports and Publications

American Chamber of Commerce in the People's Republic of China. "2021 American Business in China White Paper." Accessed June 23, 2022. https://www.amchamchina.org/white_paper/2021-american-business-in-china-white-paper/.

American Chamber of Commerce in the People's Republic of China. "2022 American Business in China White Paper." Accessed June 23, 2022. https://www.amchamchina.org/white_paper/2022-american-business-in-china-white-paper/.

American Chamber of Commerce to the European Union. "Foreign Subsidies Regulation: key EU trade and investment partners raise concerns." June 1, 2022. http://amchameu.eu/position-papers/

foreign-subsidies-regulation-key-eu-trade-and-investment-part-ners-raise-concerns.

American Chamber of Commerce to the European Union. "Foreign Subsidies Regulation: views from key EU trade and investment partners." February 15, 2022. https://www.amchameu.eu/system/files/position_papers/foreign_subsidies_regulation_views_from_key_eu_trade_and_investment_partners.pdf.

British-American Business. *A US-UK Trade & Economic Council, A New Structure for US-UK Trade Cooperation.* December 2021. https://www.babinc.org/psirteex/2021/12/A-UK-US-Trade-and-Economic-Council-Final-Copy-Web.pdf.

BusinessEurope. "Mission and priorities." Accessed June 11, 2022. https://www.businesseurope.eu/mission-and-priorities.

BusinessEurope. "Public Procurement in the Transatlantic Trade and Investment Partnership (TTIP)." December 11, 2013. https://www.businesseurope.eu/sites/buseur/files/media/imported/2013-01314-E.pdf.

BusinessEurope. *The EU and China: Addressing the Systemic Challenge.* January 2020. https://www.businesseurope.eu/sites/buseur/files/media/reports_and_studies/2020-01-16_the_eu_and_china_-_addressing_the_systemic_challenge_-_full_paper.pdf.

Clark, Suzanne P. "The Competition for the Future." State of American Business 2022 Keynote Address, US Chamber of Commerce, January 11, 2022. https://www.uschamber.com/on-demand/economy/5-takeaways-from-suzanne-clarks-first-state-of-american-business-address?autoplay=1.

European Union Chamber of Commerce in China. *The European Business in China – Position Paper 2021/2022.* September 23, 2021. http://www.eucba.org/images/contents/files/European_Business_in_China_Position_Paper_2021_2022.pdf.

International Monetary Fund. *Fact Sheet: Special Drawing Rights.* Accessed May 17, 2022. https://www.imf.org/en/About/Factsheets/Sheets/2016/08/01/14/51/Special-Drawing-Right-SDR.

PwC. *Study on Potential Economic Impact of TPPA on the Malaysian Economy and Selected Key Economic Sectors.* December 2015.

https://fta.miti.gov.my/miti-fta/resources/TPPA_PwC_CBA_-_Final_
Report_021215_FINAL_(corrected).pdf.

Schonberg, Alison. *Government Procurement and Sales to State-Owned Enterprises in China: Challenges and Best Practice*. US-China Business Council. September 2021. https://www.uschina.org/reports/government-procurement-and-sales-state-owned-enterprises-china.

US Chamber of Commerce and Coalition of Services Industries. *Services Priorities for a Future U.S.-UK Trade Agreement*. November 7, 2019. https://www.uschamber.com/report/services-priorities-future-us-uk-trade-agreement.

US Chamber of Commerce and US-UK Business Council. *U.S.-UK Trade Negotiations: Private Sector Priorities*. May 5, 2020. https://www.uschamber.com/comment/us-united-kingdom-trade-negotiations-private-sector-priorities.

INDEX

ABOUT THE AUTHOR

Jean Heilman Grier has more than 35 years of experience in international trade, including the development of the international procurement system. In the Office of the U.S. Trade Representative (USTR), she served as the U.S. negotiator for the WTO Government Procurement Agreement and played a leading role in its 2012 revision. She also negotiated the government procurement chapters in numerous free trade agreements with countries in Asia, Central America, South America, and the Middle East. Prior to joining USTR, Ms. Grier served as Senior Counsel for Trade Agreements at the U.S. Department of Commerce where she engaged in a broad range of international trade issues. As a Fulbright Scholar at Tohoku University in Sendai, Japan, she conducted research on Japanese administrative law. She has a J.D. from the University of Minnesota and an LL.M. from the University of Washington and is a member of the District of Colombia Bar.

Currently, Ms. Grier is the Trade Principal with Djaghe, LLC., where she advises businesses, international organizations, governments, and others on international procurement and trade issues. She is the author of numerous publications on international procurement and other trade topics. Since 2013, she has written the blog, *Perspectives on Trade* (http://perspectivesontrade.com).

www.ingramcontent.com/pod-product-compliance
Lightning Source LLC
Chambersburg PA
CBHW062109020426
42335CB00013B/903